THE LITURGY IN DIALOGUE

Copyright © 2018 Holy Cross Orthodox Press
ALL RIGHTS RESERVED
Printed in the United States of America

Cover art by Vladimir Ilievski, Copyright © Holy Cross Orthodox Press

Publisher's Cataloging-In-Publication Data

Names: Calivas, Alkiviadis C. | Calivas, Alkiviadis C. Essays in theology and liturgy ; v. 5.
Title: The liturgy in dialogue : exploring & renewing the tradition / Alkiviadis C. Calivas.
Description: Brookline, Massachusetts : Holy Cross Orthodox Press, [2018] | Series: Essays in theology and liturgy ; volume 5
Identifiers: ISBN 9781935317999 | ISBN 1935317997
Subjects: LCSH: Orthodox Eastern Church--Liturgy. | Orthodox Eastern Church--Doctrines.
Classification: LCC BX350 .C352 2018 | DDC 264.019--dc23

ALKIVIADIS C. CALIVAS

THE LITURGY IN DIALOGUE
Exploring & Renewing the Tradition

ESSAYS IN THEOLOGY AND LITURGY

VOLUME FIVE

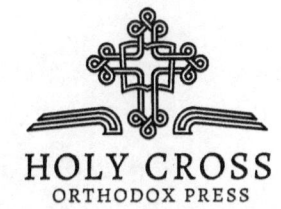

HOLY CROSS
ORTHODOX PRESS

BROOKLINE, MASSACHUSETTS
2018

CONTENTS

PREFACE xi

CHAPTER ONE 1
  EXPERIENCING THE RIGHTEOUSNESS OF GOD IN THE LITURGY 1
    A Brief Reflection on the Words *'Righteousness'* and *'Justice'* 1
    The Orthodox Liturgy 5
    God's Righteousness Permeates Every Component of the Liturgy 8
    The Liturgy Tells the Story of God's Righteousness 11
    The Liturgy and a Justice-Oriented Life 12
    When the Liturgy Ceases to Be "Dangerous" 14
    Good Liturgy Requires That We Ascend and Descend 17

CHAPTER TWO 19
  FROM THE LITURGY OF ST. BASIL TO
  THE LITURGY OF ST. JOHN CHRYSOSTOM 19
    When and Why (A Preliminary Report) 19
    The Byzantine Rite 20
      A Brief Note on Its Origins 20
    Eucharist and Church 21
    The Eucharistic Liturgies of the Byzantine Rite 24
      Three Liturgies 24
      The Structure of the Divine Liturgies of Sts. Basil and John Chrys. 26
    A New Sunday Liturgy 29
      The Brevity Argument 29
      A New Hypothesis: A Reaction to Iconoclasm 31
      A Different Hypothesis: The Effects of Holy Communion 35
      The Emergence of a New Ascetic Spirit 35
    The Fruits of Communion in the Anaphora 38
      Enumerating the Gifts of Communion 38
      The Effects of Communion in Five Early Documents 40
      Fruits of Communion in BAS and CHR 42

Similarities and Differences in BAS and CHR 43
    Communion of the Holy Spirit 43
Fruits of Communion in BAS 46
    Fruits of Communion in CHR 50
    Forgiveness of Sins in BAS and CHR 52
"Let a Man Examine Himself, and So Eat" (1 Cor. 11:28) 53
    The Need for Discernment 53
    Pre-Communion and Post-Communion Prayers 55
Holy Communion and the Saints 56
    The Saints in BAS and CHR 56
    The Categories of Saints 58
Vigilance of Soul 60
    The Meaning and Purpose of Vigilance 60
Conclusion 63

CHAPTER THREE
LITURGICAL RENEWAL IN ORTHODOX THEOLOGY AND LITURGICAL PRAXIS IN RELATION TO THE SACRAMENT OF THE DIVINE EUCHARIST 65

A Theological Reflection on the Eucharist 68
    The Church, the Eucharist, and the Eschaton 68
    The Kingdom of God Exists in the Church 71
    Baptism, Eucharist, and Church 74
    Eschatology and History 75
The Purpose and Goal of Liturgical Renewal 77
    Renewal and Reform: The Need for Reasoned Discourse 78
    Recognizing and Confronting Problems 78
    Releasing the Treasures of Tradition from Paralysis 80
    Principles and Tasks 81
    Critiquing Texts and Rituals 82
    A Rationale for Liturgical Renewal and Change 83
    The Essential Requirements for Meaningful Change 84
Some Suggestions for the Reform of the Divine Liturgy 86
    Interpreting the Divine Liturgy 87
    Textual Concerns 91
    Prayer of the Faithful or Prayer of Access? 92
    Offering or Offer? 94

    The Double Action or Movement of the Divine Liturgy 96
    Broken Rituals 98
    Hearing and Singing the Divine Liturgy 100
    Conclusion 103

CHAPTER FOUR

MARIAGE 104
    The Vision of Christian Marriage 107
        Vocation, Charism, Hope 107
        Learning to Love: Making the Vision Real 112
    Acquiring a New Identity 115
        Mutual Consent and Other Essential Conditions 118
    The Essential Characteristics of Christian Marriage 123
    The Indissolubility of Marriage: A Gift, Not a Lifeless Form 124
    Equality of the Spouses 128
    Christian Marriage Is Monogamous 130
    The Foundational Qualities and Purposes of Christian Marriage 130
        The Primacy of the Marital Union 132
    The Sacredness and Loveliness of Marital Love 133
    The Joy and Privilege of Childbearing 135
    Conclusion: Living the Vision 138

CHAPTER FIVE

RECEIVING CONVERTS INTO THE ORTHODOX CHURCH: LESSONS FROM THE CANONICAL AND LITURGICAL TRADITION 141
    Dealing with Present Realities 141
        Differing Views and Practices on Reception 141
        The SCOBA Guidelines 144
    The Prevailing Approaches to Reception 147
        The Russian Approach 147
        The Greek Approach 149
        The Conflations Approach 154
    The Baptism Controversy in the Eighteenth Century 156
        Patriarch Cyril V and St. Nikodemos 156
        The Role of the Pedalion 158
        Sociopolitical and Religious Realities 164
        The Legacy of Cyril V and the Pedalion 166

St. Nikodemos and the Principle of 'Oikonomia' 167
   Oikonomia: Canonical Stratagem or Judicious Pastoral Judgment? 167
   Is the Absolutist Position on the Boundaries of the Church Tenable? 170
Oikonomia, Church, and Sacraments in Contemporary
Theological Thought 172
   Prevailing Theories on Oikonomia 172
   Looking Beyond Past Controversies 175
Are All Heresies the Same? 177
   What Constitutes Heresy? 177
   The Canonical Tradition 179
   The Liturgical Tradition 181
   The Synod of 1484 and Its Service of Reception 184
The Rite of Reception in the Greek Orthodox Archdiocese 188
   The Priest's Handbook 188
   Rubrics: The Need for Clarity and Precision 188
Assessing the Service of Reception in the Priest's Handbook 190
   The Enarxis 190
   The Second Part of the Service 190
   What Constitutes Proper Instruction? 192
   The Profession of Faith 193
   The Anointing and the Concluding Prayers 193
Points to Ponder 193
   Respectful Suggestions 193
   On the Reception of Oriental Orthodox Christians 195
   Which Rite Should We Use? 196
A Proposed Rite of Reception 197

CHAPTER SIX

THE LORD'S DAY IN ORTHODOX LITURGICAL
PRACTICE AND SPIRITUALITY 202

The Weekly Celebration of the Paschal Mystery 202
The Components and Ethos of the Byzantine Liturgical Rite 204
The Festal Calendar, Sunday, and the Resurrection of Christ 206
The Privileged Position of Sunday, the Lord's Day 209
Sunday: The Time for Worship 211
Sunday: The Day of the Spirit 212
Church, Eucharist, Sunday, and the Eighth Day 213

Sunday: The Day of Light for the People of the Light..........216
Sunday is Everything: The Day of Sanctification,
Rest, and Godly Action..........218
The Name 'Lord's' Day..........220
Christian Identity: A Reality Check..........221
Recovering the Unique Mystical Quality of the Lord's Day..........223

CHAPTER SEVEN

THE SUNDAY LUCAN PERICOPES IN THE BYZANTINE LECTIONARY..........225
Introduction..........225
The Byzantine Lectionary System..........226
The Synaxarion Collection..........230
The Gospel of Luke in the Evangelion..........232
The Sunday Pericopes of Luke..........233
The Peculiar Features of the Sunday Lucan Pericopes..........235
The Six Mobile Lucan Sundays..........237

CHAPTER EIGHT

LITURGY AND LANGUAGE..........243
Introduction..........243
Liturgical Language in the Greek Orthodox
Archdiocese of America..........245
   Archbishop Michael's Pioneering Efforts..........246
   Archbishop Iakovos and the New Realities..........247
   A Second Authorized Translation..........250
Multiple English Translations..........251
   The Holy Cross Faculty Translation..........252
   The Translation of the SCOBA Liturgical Commission..........254
   Narthex Press Editions..........255
Archbishop Demetrios and the New Translation of the
Greek Orthodox Archdiocese..........256
   A Brief History..........256
   The New Translation: Its Purpose and Goals..........257

PREFACE

The title of the present volume, *The Liturgy in Dialogue: Exploring and Renewing the Tradition*, describes the common thread that runs through each of the eight essays that comprise it. It also describes the nature and purpose of liturgical inquiry. Liturgical scholarship is always in dialogue with the received liturgical rites when it explores their history, assesses their meanings, evaluates their effectiveness, interrogates their relevance for the modern worshipper, and recommends prayerfully adaptations for their renewal in order to uphold properly the normative principle of the inherent relationship between our Christian identity and the liturgy.

Orthodox Christians experience the Church primarily as a worshipping community. Through the sacred rites and services of the Church—the liturgy—Orthodox Christians abide in the Church, which is the eschatological community that is being continually transformed into the Body of Christ by the Holy Spirit. The liturgy draws the faithful into the mystery of God's irresistible beauty, holiness, and love allowing them to appropriate his saving grace by sharing in the reality of the Christ-event in an iconic, symbolic, and sacramental way.

The liturgy nourishes, informs, and sustains the people's faith. It brings them into a right relationship with God, with one another, with the world, and with themselves. The liturgy helps to shape their inner world and mold their outward actions. It keeps them connected to the tenets of the Orthodox faith and inspires them to conduct their lives accordingly, as persons who "have been born anew to a living hope through the resurrection of Jesus Christ from the dead and to an inheritance which is imperishable, undefiled, and unfading" (1 Peter 1:3-4).

The mystery which was once for all delivered to the saints (Jude 3) is permanently embodied in the liturgy. The liturgy is the Church's faith in motion. Through dogma and prayer, the Church invites us to continually discover, experience, and realize our true mode of being. The liturgy is the unique setting in which the Church remembers and celebrates the essential truths of the faith. It conveys, recommends, instills, and imparts to us a particular vision of faith and way of life. The liturgy builds faith and forms identity—both personal and communal—and is therefore vital to the very being of the Church and the life of her members.

Ultimately, the liturgy is functional. Its purpose is to make the union with Christ an abiding condition of life according to the capacity and desire of each person and to the grace each is given. Consequently all the faithful, clergy and laity alike, are obliged to acquire a degree of liturgical literacy, so that the deadening effects of ritual formalism, born of ignorance and superstition, may be kept at bay and the formative, restorative, and transformative powers of the liturgy may be released in the worshipping community as a whole and in the life of every individual worshipper.

The purpose and function of the liturgy is to make the Church that which she really is. In the unfolding history of the world the Church constitutes the presence of the truth, the righteousness, and the joy of God's Kingdom, which is yet to come in fullness. At the liturgy we receive our vision of the world as created, fallen, and redeemed: "You brought us into being out of nothing, and when we fell, you raised us up again. You did not cease doing everything until you led us to heaven and granted us your Kingdom to come" (Anaphora of the Divine Liturgy of St. John Chrysostom). In worship we become witnesses to the saving events of sacred history and participants in the new life that issues from God's saving activity.

The liturgy is the special place that manifests what is divine and what is human. It takes us to the threshold of another world, the divine, but it does not take us out of the world with all of its struggles, anomalies, and conflicts. Rather, it reveals through word, song, ritual, and symbol that which is truly human and explains how this humanity is the place where the Kingdom of God—its light, life, justice, peace, joy, and love—is made alive. In other words, the remembrance of the Kingdom marks both the faith and the activities of the Church and of each of her faithful members. At the liturgy we live in time by that which is beyond time, by that which has not yet come in fullness, but which is already known by faith and possessed through the holy sacraments.

Because the liturgy is so central to the actualization of the life of faith, its renewal must be a constant concern of the Church. In every generation the Church is obliged to test the depths, analyze, interpret, and evaluate the various components of the sacred rites through serious scholarly work so that the vitality of worship may be sustained appropriately, genuine piety may be formed rightly, and liturgical practice may be enriched properly. The purpose of liturgical scholarship is to help the Church discern, comprehend, and—when necessary—recover her authentic tradition, thereby facilitating the incorporation of that tradition into the contexts in which people live and worship. Authentic worship is by nature dynamic and open to legitimate renewal and reform. Put differently, the goal of liturgical renewal is to distinguish between the theological core and essential meanings of the liturgical tradition and its historical incarnations—its forms and shapes—mindful of the fact that the rule of prayer rests ultimately within the rule of faith, of which it is a significant expression.

The liturgy is constant and traditional but also living and dynamic. The core elements of the sacred rites remain constant. Its forms and expressions, however, have been shaped by the realities of history and culture. As the study of liturgy bears out, the liturgical rites—their structures, texts, and rituals—are the product of a long evolutionary process. They have developed through the centuries by way of organic development through accretion, addition, deletion, suppression, modification, and restoration. The forms are neither absolute nor immutable but subject to adaptation and change. Indeed, the historical record shows that liturgical renewal and reform have occurred throughout the centuries either deliberately or organically through spontaneous development.

The renewal of the liturgy, however, requires more than the rearrangement of material, the abbreviation of services, or the elimination of excesses and repetitions in texts and ceremonies. The first and essential task of liturgical renewal is to help the Church rediscover and restore to Orthodox worship those concepts, ideas, characteristics, and practices that will enliven and release the transformative powers of the liturgy, so that the sacred rites remain compelling, attractive, and inspirational; that they carry meaning for the contemporary worshipper. The Church is obliged in every generation to struggle against religious formalism and the decadent liturgy and piety it produces. The Church faces serious dangers when theology is unwittingly allowed to decline into uncritical, repetitive, and sterile formulations and the liturgy is unwittingly allowed to deteriorate into empty actions and words that carry little meaning and have little appeal to the heart and mind of the worshipper.

I wish to thank all those who provided suggestions and support in bringing this book to publication. I am grateful to the publisher, *Holy Cross Orthodox Press*, and especially its Director, Fr. Michael Monos, its former Director, Fr. Anton Vrame and the esteemed members of the Publications Committee for accepting my manuscript and assisting in the completion of its printed form. I am also grateful to my beloved friend and colleague, Dr. Lewis Patsavos, Professor Emeritus of Canon Law at Holy Cross Greek Orthodox School of Theology, who read and offered valuable comments on the essay, "Receiving Converts into the Orthodox Church." I wish also to thank Mr. Richard Barrett who reviewed the Greek texts. Thanks also are due to Ms. Sarah Parro, Production Manager of the Press, for her technical assistance. Ms. Rebecca Loumiotis meticulously read through the entire manuscript and greatly improved it. My debt to her is gratefully acknowledged.

The series Essays in Theology and Liturgy, as mentioned in earlier volumes, was made possible by the initial generous gift of Mr. Alexander Anagnos, a devout Orthodox Christian, philanthropist, and personal friend. It is due also to the support provided by the Holy Cross Greek Orthodox School of Theology, which I thank in the persons of its President, Rev. Fr. Christopher Metropoulos, D. Min., and its Dean, Dr. James Skedros.

Finally, I would like to express my deep gratitude to my wife, Erasmia, my children and their spouses, and my beloved grandchildren whose abiding love gave me the strength to bring this project to fruition.

I dedicate this volume with profound respect to two beloved persons: His Eminence Archbishop Demetrios Geron of America, the eminent biblical scholar, insightful theologian, gifted teacher, and wise hierarch—a cultured man of diverse gifts, astonishing intelligence, integrity and gentle strength, an exemplar of Christian virtue, an esteemed and valued colleague who has honored me with his friendship and love; and Professor Ioannis M. Fountoulis, of blessed memory, my revered teacher, mentor, and friend—a renowned liturgical scholar whose faith, research, knowledge, wisdom, and insights expressed with exceptional eloquence, clarity and detail in his lectures and writings, initiated and inspired countless people, clergy and laity alike, in the mysteries of the Orthodox liturgy.

Brookline, MA
Feast of the Meeting of our Lord
February 2, 2018

EXPERIENCING THE RIGHTEOUSNESS OF GOD IN THE LITURGY

A Brief Reflection on the Words 'Righteousness' and 'Justice'[1]

The word *righteousness*, or *justice*, appears often in the prayers of the Church. When vesting for the Divine Liturgy, for example, the priest recites these words of the Psalmist: "Let your priests be clothed with righteousness, and let your saints shout for joy" (Ps. 131/132:9). What is this righteousness with which the priest is clothed? For that matter, what is "the righteousness of God" that we must all become, according to St. Paul? "For our sake he [God] made him [Christ] to be sin who knew no sin, so that in him we might become the righteousness of God" (δικαιοσύνη Θεοῦ; 2 Cor. 5:21; cf. Rom. 6:18).

The righteousness of which the Scriptures and the liturgy speak is God's just (saving) action motivated by love. His saving action is *just* because as Creator and Covenant God, he deals with the forces of evil in the world in order to rescue his people from them. His saving action is transformative. It brings peace by making things right and just.[2]

God's righteousness is his saving deeds—his redemptive, restorative, and

---

[1] This paper was presented initially at the International Conference on Violence and Christian Spirituality, which was held at Holy Cross Greek Orthodox School of Theology in Brookline, Massachusetts. The conference was organized in 2005 by Holy Cross in cooperation with the World Council of Churches and the Boston Theological Institute. Conference papers were subsequently published in *Violence and Christian Spirituality: An Ecumenical Conversation*, ed. Emmanuel Clapsis (Geneva, 2007). The present essay is a revised version of the one printed in *Violence and Christian Spirituality*, 287–298.

[2] Christopher Marshall, *Beyond Retribution: A New Testament Vision for Justice, Crime, and Punishment* (Grand Rapids, MI, 2001), 53.

transformative works. God's righteousness is at the heart of the Gospel and consequently at the heart of the liturgy inasmuch as the liturgy constitutes a doxological expression of God's mighty works recounted in the Bible. But before I address God's righteousness in the liturgy, a word about the biblical sense of righteousness or justice is in order.

Biblical scholars tell us that the Old Testament contains multiple terms and a wide range of meanings for righteousness or justice, such as prosperity, acquittal, right order and conduct, and vindication. Of the several meanings and terms, the two most commonly used Hebrew words are *sedeq-sedaqah* and *mishpat*.[3] They are often used in combination and describe both proper order in life as willed by God and his impending just judgment (δικαιοκρισία). The two terms especially refer to divine covenant activity, to Yahweh's saving action toward Israel and toward persons in affliction, want, and distress. God's justice is a liberating action that puts things right. The Greek Old Testament renders these words with δικαιοῦν terms (δικαιοσύνη, δίκαιος, δίκη, δικαίωμα, δικαίωσις, δικαιοκρίσις). In English the two terms are rendered as *justice* (from the Latin *justus*, meaning "just" or "upright," from *jus*, "right" or "law") or as *righteousness* (from the Old English *riht*, from which come the words *right*, *righteous*, and *righteousness*).[4]

For our purposes, it is sufficient to note that the Hebrew terms and the various δικαιοῦν words, together with their related verbs and modifiers, go beyond hard, legal abstractions and refer essentially "to God's work of justice-making,"[5] which is to say, his gracious saving action to right the wrong and to give justice.

The biblical sense of righteousness is not the same as the justice of the philosophers. It is not an abstract universal principle of "right" in law and society, the means for producing happiness, fairness, and harmonious living through an arrangement of rewards and punishments. The blind and impartial justice represented by *Dike* (Δίκη), the blindfolded Greek goddess

---

[3] The *sdq* root generates such terms as *uprightness, vindication, judgment, acquittal, victory, salvation, innocence, mercy, correctness,* and *prosperity*. The *shpt* root yields such terms as *justice, rights, vindication, custom, norm,* and *deliverance*. See J. J. Scullion, "Righteousness—Old Testament," in *The Anchor Bible Dictionary*, vol. 5 (New York, 1992), 724; Marshall, *Beyond Retribution*, 46.
[4] On the Greek and English renderings of these Hebrew terms, see the article by John Reumann, "Righteousness: New Testament," in *The Anchor Bible Dictionary*, 5:746.
[5] Marshall, *Beyond Retribution*, 42.

balancing scales, is not the same as the justice of God.[6] The righteousness of God is neither blind nor totally impartial. He sees the world's iniquities and its unrighteousness. His concern is for the innocent, the poor, the helpless, and the oppressed. He will save the world from all unrighteousness, and he will vindicate the pious and the just over their oppressors.

The Creator and Covenant God, according to Fr. Theodore Stylianopoulos, acts to fulfill his promises to his people, promises of guidance, protection, and deliverance from various trials and afflictions. Context, Stylianopoulos says, is key to understanding the range of meanings of God's active righteousness. For example, he writes,

> When Christ is said to be given by God as a sin offering, God's active righteousness in this regard is the just redemption of believers from the power of sin. When God acts to punish a tyrannical oppressor, this is his just vindication of and for his people. When he makes the land fruitful, this becomes his just fruition or productivity for his people. When he rescues from sickness, danger, famine, and the like, this is his just deliverance or just salvation from these afflictions. When he acts in consistency with his covenant, this is his just covenant faithfulness.[7]

The gracious salvific activity of God, "promised beforehand through the prophets in the holy Scriptures" (Rom. 1:2), is accomplished in and through Christ, the Suffering Servant, the Righteous One, who came to declare justice that many may come to be accounted righteous (Isa. 53:11; Matt. 12:18). While the effect of what God has achieved for the world in Christ will be revealed in fullness on the last day, the eschaton has already begun. It is already a possession of the believers in hope, especially through the sacraments. Confident about things to come, we are able to discern even on this side of death, in the present age, signs of God's impending judgment—his wrath that will right the wrong—whenever the proud and the arrogant fall ignominiously to defeat.

God's judgment, while a future event, is also operative in history, as we hear in the following prayer commemorating the victory of faithful people over their oppressors:

---

[6] See John Reumann, "Righteousness: Greco-Roman World," in *The Anchor Bible Dictionary*, 5:742–745.
[7] This text is from a personal note sent to me by Fr. Theodore Stylianopoulos in response to an inquiry of mine regarding the righteousness of God.

For behold, our leaders and the entire congregation of the people, having gathered together, commemorate the wonderful and great event which Your right hand has accomplished in our days, so as to demonstrate that there is a Day of the Lord upon everyone that is insolent and arrogant, a day of falling for all who are haughty and conceited; for You have shaken the mighty with Your strength and have crushed the insolent with Your power.[8]

God's judgment or wrath, however, should not be confused with rage, hatred, jealousy, malice, and revenge—the grave sins that lead individuals, groups, and nations to commit reprehensible acts of violence. God's wrath is his absolute faithfulness to his covenantal promise to right the wrong, to defeat evil utterly on the last day. God's judgment is salvation for the righteous and self-inflicted punishment for the wicked, the unrepentant. God rescues the righteous but holds the wicked for judgment, or as St. John Chrysostom teaches, "They who blaspheme and malign [God] destroy their own salvation."[9]

God's wrath is related to his holiness, his judgments, and his righteousness. He never acts with vindictiveness and malice, even when he dispenses justice to the wicked. His justice is neither punitive nor retributive but is, rather, redemptive and restorative. His is an intervening transforming justice, his power for salvation (Rom. 1:16). Because he is the God of perfect love, he teaches us that love must reign in everything, as it did on the Cross, if evil in all its forms is to be overcome and defeated (1 John 4:7–21; cf. Luke 6:27–36).

Communion with God is life and light; willful separation from him is death and darkness (Matt. 25:31–46; John 5:24–29). God's righteousness manifested in the Christ event brings more than forgiveness of sins, healing, and reconciliation. It is also the source of freedom (2 Cor. 3:17)—freedom from our slavery "to the weak and beggarly elemental spirits" (Gal. 4:9) and to the passions that debase our humanity. Additionally, God's righteous-

---

[8] This text is from the special service commemorating the final victory of the Greek nation over the occupying fascist forces during World War II (cf. Isa. 2:12–17 and Luke 1:50–55). The service may be found in any edition of the *Ieratikon* printed by Apostolike Diakonia, the publishing house of the Church of Greece.

[9] John Chrysostom, *Homilies on the Incomprehensibility of God*, homily 3:1. Περὶ τοῦ ἀκαταλύπτου, λόγος τρίτος, α, PG 48, 719. "Τὸν μὲν γὰρ Θεὸν οὐδεὶς οὔτε ἀτιμάζων παραβλάψαι δυνάσεται, οὔτε εὐφημῶν λαμπρότερον ἀποφῆναι ... οἱ δὲ βλασφημοῦντες καὶ ἐξευτελίζοντες, τὴν οἰκείαν λυμαίνονται σωτηρίαν."

ness is the font of life (John 8:12; 1 John 5:11), mercy (Heb. 4:16), peace (Rom. 5:1), wisdom (Ps. 50/51:6; Eccles. 2:26), joy (John 17:13), and sanctification (1 Cor. 1:30).

The liturgy or worship of the Church, the privileged place that manifests both what is divine and what is human, takes faithful worshippers to the threshold of another reality (or realm), the divine. But it does not take them out of our world, with all of its struggles and conflicts. Rather, it reveals "what is fully human and shows how this full humanity is the place where the kingdom of God's justice and peace is made alive."[10]

With all this in mind, a brief response to the questions posed above would be the following: the righteousness with which the celebrants of the sacred Mysteries are clothed and which we must all become constitutes the power, holiness, mercy, loving-kindness, and goodness of God revealed in Jesus Christ. These realities remain active and are perfected when they are interiorized, when the recipients of divine grace become firmly set in what is good and holy in the unity of the Church, which stimulates and helps them to this end.

The Orthodox Liturgy

The word *liturgy*, as is commonly known, is derived from two Greek words, λαός (people) and ἔργον (work). Literally, the term means "the work of the people." It denotes the whole range of the Church's sacred rites and services, in which all the people of God—clergy and laity together—participate, each according to his or her particular role and function. Thus in this general sense, the word defines the Church's rule of prayer or worship (λατρεία) in all of its forms and manifestations. However, when the word *liturgy* is combined with the adjective *divine*, as in *Divine Liturgy* (Θεία Λειτουργία), it becomes the technical term that designates the sacred service by which the Orthodox Church celebrates the sacrament of the Eucharist.

Broadly, then, the term *liturgy* encompasses all the sacred services of the Church. These include the holy sacraments, the daily office, a large assortment of occasional services, and a considerable collection of prayers, all of

---

[10] James L. Empereur and Christopher G. Kiesling, *The Liturgy That Does Justice* (Collegeville, MN, 1990), 23.

which are codified in the Church's several liturgical books.[11] In addition to these components, the liturgy also includes a lectionary system, a calendar of feasts and fasts, various ceremonials and symbols, and highly developed and distinctive forms of the liturgical arts: architecture, iconography, hymnography, music, implements, and textiles (vesture, veils, and cloths).

The liturgical homily, or sermon, is also an integral component of the liturgy. It is itself an act of prayer, a salvific and transforming event because it brings and builds faith by proclaiming the righteousness of God and by inspiring God's people to live justly. Effective preaching leads people to believe that the faith which the liturgy proclaims and celebrates has everything to do with the activities of everyday life.[12] In similar fashion, the prayers and hymns of the divine services—superbly didactic, evocative, and inspirational—are themselves a string of tiny sermons that engage worshippers with the fundamental truths of the faith in order to set their souls aflame with divine passion, that they may learn to live righteously in accordance with the commandments.

Every component of the liturgy serves both a practical and a theological purpose. Each component, in one way or another, demonstrates and communicates the saving and transforming love that is the righteousness of God. For example, the traditional Orthodox temple (ναός), through its

---

[11] As I have noted elsewhere, all the liturgical books of the Church, each with its own complex history of development, fall into one of four major categories. The first contains the prayers and petitions used by the clergy for all the sacramental and nonsacramental rites, services, and prayers of the Church. These are the *Euchologion* (Service book, or Book of prayers) and its derivatives, the *Small Euchologion,* the *Archieratikon* (Bishop's book), the *Ieratikon* (Priest's book), and the *Diakonikon* (Deacon's book). The second category comprises the volumes that contain the fixed and variable elements of the daily office: the *Horologion* (Book of the hours), the *Octoechos* (Book of the eight tones), known also as the *Parakletike* (Book of supplications), the *Triodion* (Book of the pre-Lenten period, Lent, and Holy Week), the *Pentekostarion* (Book of the Paschaltide), and the twelve *Menaia* (one for each month, containing the services of the fixed feasts for each day of the year). The third category is composed of the books that contain the received lectionary, the assigned Scripture readings for each day, for feasts, the sacraments, and other occasional services. These are the *Evangelion* (Gospel book), the *Apostolos* (Book of Acts and the Epistles), the *Psalter* (Book of Psalms), and the *Prophetologion* (Book of the prophecies). The fourth and final category constitutes the *Typikon* and the *Diataxeis*, which are books of directives and rubrics. See Alkiviadis C. Calivas, *Aspects of Orthodox Worship* (Brookline, MA, 2003), 54–62.

[12] See, for example, Del Staigers, "Steadfast in Faith, Joyful in Hope, Untiring in Love: Preaching Everyday Mysteries," in *Liturgy and Justice: To Worship God in Spirit and Truth*, ed. Anne Y. Koester (Collegeville, MN, 2002), 169–177.

architectural style, organizational principles, and decorative program, expresses "tangibly the movement of the incarnation, of God's descent into the world, the movement of the bowed heavens,"[13] by which the advancement of all creation toward its ultimate restoration was begun. As an epiphany of the transfigured world, the church edifice has a sacramental character. It is a window onto another reality, a glimpse of the last day, when the world "will be set free from its bondage to decay and obtain the glorious liberty of the children of God" (Rom. 8:21) to share in the benefits of the redemption wrought by Christ.

The liturgy discloses and sustains the communal nature of the Church, wherein a multitude of unique persons are united to one another without confusion in a movement of self-giving love through their union with Christ. St. Maximos the Confessor underscores this fundamental truth of Christian existence in the following profoundly insightful passage:

> For numerous and of almost infinite number are the men, women, and children who are distinct from one another and vastly different by birth and appearance, by nationality and language, by customs and age, by opinions and skills, by manners and habits, by pursuit and studies, and still again by reputation, fortune, characteristics, and connections: All are born into the Church and through it are reborn and recreated in the Spirit. To all in equal measure it gives and bestows one divine form and designation, to be Christ's and to carry his name ... It is he who encloses in himself all beings by the unique, simple, and infinitely wise power of his goodness. As the center of straight lines that radiate from him he does not allow by his unique, simple, and single cause and power that the principles of beings become disjoined at the periphery but rather he circumscribes their extension in a circle and brings back to himself the distinctive elements of beings which he himself brought into existence. The purpose of this is so that the creations and products of the one God be in no way strangers and enemies to one another by having no reason or center for which they might show each other any friendly or peaceful sentiment or identity, and not run the risk of having their being separated from God to dissolve into nonbeing. Thus, as has been said, the holy Church of God is an image of God because it realizes the same union of the faithful with God ... God realizes this union among the natures of things without confusing them but in lessening and bringing together their distinction in a relationship and union with himself as cause, principle, and end.[14]

---

[13] Christos Yannaras, *The Freedom of Morality* (Crestwood, NY, 1984), 247.
[14] Maximos the Confessor, *Mystagogy I*, in *Maximus the Confessor: Selected Writings*, Clas-

As Metropolitan Kallistos Ware also observes, "In prayer we do not think only in vertical terms about the Church in glory and the communion of the saints, but we also think horizontally about our involvement with the rest of humanity."[15] That is why nothing and no one escapes the concern of the Church. ...It embraces everyone and everything, in order to bring all within the realm of salvation, within the embrace of God's justice and love.

Even a cursory reading of the received formularies (prayers, blessings, petitions, and hymns) reveals that the quality of our earthly existence is a concern of the Church. The Church is not reluctant to pray for the practical things of everyday life, with all its limitations, anxieties, pains, and fears but also all its expectations, aspirations, promises, and possibilities. The saving action of God—his righteousness—is invoked upon every area of life, spiritual as well as material, as disclosed, for example, by various petitions, some of which ask God to grant the essential gifts for a serene earthly existence and others of which request protection from the horrible devastation brought on by natural disasters and man-made calamities that severely diminish or destroy human life and test the faith of people.

The following petitions, for example, address conditions that help produce good order and good relationships free from want and strife. One prays "for favorable weather, an abundance of the fruits of the earth, and temperate seasons." Another asks "for mercy, life, peace, health, salvation, protection, forgiveness and remission of the sins of the servants of God (*NN*)." Still other petitions seek God's protection from physical, psychic, national, and natural dangers and moral harm. One example comes from the Great Litany, or *synapte*: "For our deliverance from all affliction, wrath, danger, and distress, let us pray to the Lord." Another example is from the Fervent Litany, "Again we pray for the protection of this holy church, this city, and every city and town, from wrath, famine, pestilence, earthquake, flood, fire, sword, foreign invasion, civil strife, and accidental death."

God's Righteousness Permeates Every Component of the Liturgy

Baptism, the first and essential sacrament and the absolute decisive action for a Christian, manifests the most radical change in the human con-

---

sics of Western Spirituality (New York, 1985), 187–188 (cf. Gal. 3:28; Col. 3:11).
[15] Kallistos Ware, preface to Stephano Parenti, *Praying with the Orthodox Tradition* (London, 1989), xii.

dition and in human relationships. The baptismal font is both a tomb and a womb in which the "old man" is buried and the "new man" is born (Col. 3:9–10). In the words of St. Paul, "We [are] buried with him through baptism into death, that just as Christ was raised from the dead by the glory of the Father, even so we also should walk in the newness of life" (Rom. 6:4). In baptism we partake in the death, burial, and resurrection of Christ and are incorporated into him in order to share in his deified humanity, to come under his rule, and to become like him.[16] The clearer the image of Christ is in us, the more perfect we become because perfection is nothing more than the realization of the purpose for which we have been made. And we have been made to be in Christ and to become like him by grace. In baptism we become a new creation (2 Cor. 5:17). We are born again from above by water and the Holy Spirit (John 3:3–6) and are made righteous (δίκαιοι), that we may persevere in the exercise of righteous actions, thinking and doing those things that are pleasing to God.

The new life in Christ begins with two actions. The first is the renunciation of the devil and of all his works—that is, the renunciation of the father of lies and of the false values and the illusions of this world. The second act is the acceptance of Christ with the express desire to live under the rule of God. These two actions conclude with a third, the profession of faith through the recitation of the Nicene-Constantinopolitan Creed, which is the summary of the Church's faith upon which the new life is founded. It is a faith that enlivens souls for charity, righteousness, and holiness (Col. 3:12–17).

To fructify, the grace of baptism must be continuously nurtured by the ongoing conversion of the heart—an activity encouraged and advanced by the Church's worship—so that the righteousness of God becomes the light of life and every good work the evidence and the fruit of a grace-filled life that, in the words of Fr. Emmanuel Clapsis, moves continually "from death to life, from injustice to justice, from violence to peace, from hatred to love, from vengeance to forgiveness, from selfishness to sharing, and from division to unity."[17]

---

[16] See Dumitru Staniloae, *The Sanctifying Mysteries*, vol. 5 of *The Experience of God*, trans. Ioan Ionita and Robert Barringer (Brookline, MA, 2012), 32–37.

[17] Emmanuel Clapsis, *Orthodoxy in Conversation* (Geneva, 2000), 195.

The rite of matrimony is another example.[18] It contains in concise form the entire Orthodox teaching on marriage. It highlights the characteristics, the qualities, and the purposes of Christian marriage even as it underscores, among other things, the essential equality of the spouses and the sacredness of marital intimacy. Marriage is the most sacred human relationship. Formed sacramentally, it is established as a covenant relationship between a man and a woman that they may act together to heal the wounds of their impaired masculinity and femininity. Forming by grace a right, just, and holy relationship, the spouses are called to strive daily with patience, reverence, trust, and godly fortitude in mutual love and respect to live out to the best their ability the implications of the ideal, pure marriage ordained by God.

Since the quality of marriage is conditioned by many factors—including the spiritual maturity, emotional stability, and physical health of the spouses, along with their family ties, cultural habits, and financial concerns—the rite of marriage contains requests for the practical, everyday things that contribute to the couple's growth, development, and well-being. Thus the Church prays that the couple's "goings out and comings in" (Deut. 28:6; Ps. 120/121:8)—their activities and enterprises, as well as their home relationships and quiet occupations—may be free from temptations, evils, and dangers.

Christian marriage is more than a private affair; it is an ecclesial event and an antidote against the world's proclivity for exclusion and isolation, which are manifestations of injustice. The prayers of the marriage rite stress the significance of the couple's communal responsibilities, especially toward the needy and the indigent: "Give them of the dew of heaven from above and of the abundance of the earth. Fill their home with wheat, wine, and oil, and with every good thing, so that they may share with those in need."

From these examples, it is clear that the reality of God's justice intersects and permeates every component of the liturgy.[19] However, a brief presen-

---

[18] See Theodore Stylianopoulos, "Toward a Theology of Marriage in the Orthodox Church" and Alkiviadis C. Calivas, "Marriage: The Sacrament of Love and Communion," both in *Inter-marriage: Orthodox Perspectives*, ed. Anton Vrame (Brookline, MA, 1997), 1–33 and 34–61, respectively. A revised version of the latter article appears in chapter 4 of the present volume..

[19] Roman Catholic liturgists, theologians, and sociologists have dealt with the subject and have made important contributions to the understanding of the relationship between liturgy and justice. See, for example, Empereur and Kiesling, *Liturgy That Does Justice*; Koester, *Liturgy and Justice*; Megan McKenna, *Rites of Justice: The Sacraments and Liturgy as Ethical*

tation such as this can serve only as an introduction, emphasizing the significance of the theme and inviting further investigation, since "liturgy and justice together are constitutive and expressive of the Church."[20] The paragraphs that follow provide further thoughts on how the liturgy teaches and celebrates the righteousness of God and how it can pierce the conscience of the worshippers to dare believe that they, individually and collectively, can and must become instruments of God's saving power, the energetic practitioners and agents of justice.

The Liturgy Tells the Story of God's Righteousness

The liturgy, like the Scriptures, tells the story of the Triune God, relating who he is and what he does for the life and salvation of the world.[21] The story of God is essentially related to the story of his creative and saving action, which the Scriptures call God's justice or righteousness, as St. Paul writes in his Epistle to the Romans: "For I am not ashamed of the gospel: it is the power of God for salvation to everyone who has faith, to the Jew first and also to the Greek. For in it the righteousness of God (δικαιοσύνη γὰρ Θεοῦ) is revealed through faith for faith; as it is written, 'He who through faith is righteous shall live'" (Rom. 1:16–17).

At the center of God's saving activity is our Lord and Savior Jesus Christ, the incarnate Son of God, to whom the Church Fathers have applied the title *Sun of Righteousness* contained in the prophecy of Malachi. The Sun of Righteousness is the Lord who makes right all relationships and who, at the end time, will consume the wicked like a blazing fire and will heal the just with his radiant warmth (Mal. 3:19–21, 4:1–3).[22]

Imperatives (New York, 1997). For a general discussion of the themes of peace and justice from an Orthodox perspective, see *Justice, Peace, and the Integrity of Creation: Insights from Orthodoxy*, ed. Gennadios Limouris (Geneva, 1990).

[20] Koester, *Liturgy and Justice*, ix.
[21] Calivas, *Aspects of Orthodox Worship*, 15–17.
[22] The title "Sun of Righteousness" is applied to Christ in a number of hymns. For example, the hymns of the Christmas Feast and especially the *apolytikion*, or dismissal hymn, refer to Christ in this way. The epithet also appears in a number of prayers, including the third prayer of the Orthros service: "Graciously give us the Sun of Righteousness and by the seal of your Holy Spirit preserve our life unassailed." The twelfth prayer of Orthros reads, "Illumine our hearts with the true Sun of Your Righteousness; enlighten our mind and guard all our senses, that walking, as in the day, uprightly in the way of your commandments we may attain life eternal."

The crucial events in the life of Christ constitute the decisive manifestation of God's righteousness and comprise the most radical and decisive deliverance of humankind and the world. That which humans could not do, God accomplished through the incarnation of his Son and Word, Jesus Christ. The primal wound of the original sin, which is the root cause of all strife and violence, is healed, and the absolute union with God—the most sacred, profound, and unique relationship—is achieved once for all through God's own initiative. God himself bridged the essential gulf between the created and the uncreated nature through the God-Man (Θεάνθρωπος), Christ, "who himself bore our sins in his body on the tree, that we might die to sin and live to righteousness" (1 Pet. 2:24).

The comprehensive renovation and glorification of the cosmos that was accomplished by Christ will be revealed fully in the age to come. But as St. Symeon the New Theologian says, God, in Christ, has granted us the grace to have his Kingdom already within us, so that it does not remain merely a hope.[23] The sweetness of God has already invaded our hearts. The Holy Spirit—the pledge of the future life and Kingdom—who raised Jesus from the dead draws near to dwell in us to give life to our mortal bodies (Rom. 8:11).

The Liturgy and a Justice-Oriented Life

In addition to the story of God, the liturgy also tells the story of humankind. Through word, song, symbol, ritual, and sacrament, the liturgy narrates the story of two contrasting realities, the way of death and the way of life.[24] The way of death is the story of the "old man"—the fallen and un-

---

[23] Symeon the New Theologian, *Chapters*, 3:88, in *In the Light of Christ*, by Basil Krivocheine (Crestwood, NY, 1986), 296.

[24] The concept of the two ways is derived from the Scriptures. We read, for example, the following in the book of Deuteronomy: "See, I have set before you this day life and good, death and evil ... I have set before you life and death, blessing and curse; therefore choose life" (Deut. 30:15, 19; cf. Jer. 21:8; Ps. 1:6; Prov. 4:10–27). The same concept is behind the words of our Lord regarding the two gates, the wide and the narrow: "Enter by the narrow gate; for the gate is wide and the way is easy that leads to destruction, and those who enter by it are many. For the gate is narrow and the way is hard that leads to life, and those who find it are few" (Matt. 7:13–14). The concept of the two ways is also found in ancient Christian writings, including the *Didache*, or *The Teaching of the Twelve Apostles* (1:1–6), and the *Letter of Barnabas* (chapters 18–21). The *Didache* (1:1) summarizes the essence of the concept with these words: "There are two ways, one of life and one of death; and great is the difference between the two ways."

redeemed nature that is burdened with the pervasive, seductive, deceptive, and contagious influence of sin that alienates, degrades, enslaves, corrupts, and kills. It is the story of human vulnerabilities and of human mortality, of the bestial impulses and the irrational forces within that lead us to wrong decisions and destructive choices. It is the story of our perverted liberty, our inner decadence, and our moral ambivalence, through which every form of injustice is rationalized and normalized. It is the story of our estrangement from God, from our neighbor, from our own true selves, and from the natural world that God has given us as a gift of life. It is the story of broken relationships that can be healed only through μετάνοια (repentance)—by the radical change of life, forgoing its destructive habits, ruinous addictions, and foolish illusions of self-sufficiency.

Besides the way of death, the liturgy also tells the story of the way of life. It recounts and celebrates the salvific work of Christ and of people's response to it through repentance, by which God grants forgiveness, reconciliation, redemption, liberation, sanctification, and glorification. Through the liturgy, we appropriate the saving grace of God so that we may overcome the egotistical, rebellious, and prideful spirit that consumes us, so that our feelings may be reordered, our minds may be illumined, our thoughts may be redirected, and our will may be strengthened to accomplish the works of righteousness—which is to say, in order to recover the integrity of our nature, to become what God has willed us to be, and to share in God's uncreated life and love. Thus as Philip Sherrard points out, deliverance from our perverted existence, "from evil and suffering is not a matter of escaping from the natural and inevitable limitations of creaturely existence, but of restoring or remaking its integrity."[25]

The liturgy, as noted by Walter Burghardt, has the power to fashion us into people who are able to recognize justice or injustice when we see it; it has the power to stimulate us to live justly, to denounce, diminish, and even defeat injustice.[26] The liturgy does this not by providing a detailed list of solutions for life's dilemmas, conflicts, challenges, and opportunities but by putting us "in touch with that which transcends all [our] burning concerns, our particular perplexities; [and by] freeing [us] to sort out the

---

[25] Philip Sherrard, *Christianity: Lineaments of a Sacred Tradition* (Brookline, MA, 1998), 171.
[26] Walter J. Burghardt, "Worship and Justice Reunited," in Koester, *Liturgy and Justice*, 39.

issues we have to decide, because it makes us aware of our addictions and our illusions, casts a pitiless light on myopic self-interest, detaches us from a narrow selfishness, [and] facilitates Christian discernment."[27]

When the Liturgy Ceases to Be 'Dangerous'

Now, it would be foolish to think that every Christian in every instance experiences the liturgy as a transformative event with the intensity just described. Such assumptions fail to take into account the limitations and the frailties of human nature. The liturgy presents a superb ideal that many times is inadequately realized. However, we should be less concerned with the natural alterations of dryness and inspiration, of dispiritedness and illumination to which people are subject and be more attentive to the provocative questions that one theologian asks: "Why is that in spite of hundreds of thousands of Eucharistic celebrations, Christians continue as selfish as before? Why is it that persons and people who proclaim Eucharistic love and sharing deprive the poor people of the world of food, capital, employment, and even land?"[28] Perhaps, as David Batchelder suggests, the answer lies in the fact that for many Christians the liturgy has long ceased to be *dangerous*, leaving the world and us unchanged.[29] "So much of what is offered in our churches," he says, "is worship carrying enough of the culture's toxins that it is no longer capable of disclosing the perils of the individualistic and narcissistic self."[30]

The secular spirit of the times—"our culture's toxins"—has affected parish life and has influenced the lives of people more than we care to admit. The sense of God is becoming increasingly more blurred, weak, and anemic, leaving us desensitized to his presence, unable to realize how fearful it is "to fall into the hands of the living God" (Heb. 10:31). When there is little or no faith, the liturgy is in crisis; it stops being *dangerous*. When God ceases to be relevant, the need and desire for meaningful worship diminish and slowly fade away. Faith and worship are inseparable; when one withers and dies so does the other.

---

[27] Ibid., 41.
[28] Tissa Balasuriya, *The Eucharist and Human Liberation* (Maryknoll, 1979), cited in David B. Batchelder, "Holy God, Dangerous Liturgy: Preparing the Assembly for Transforming Encounter," *Worship* 79, no. 4 (2005): 291.
[29] Batchelder, "Holy God, Dangerous Liturgy," 290.
[30] Ibid., 293.

CHAPTER ONE: EXPERIENCING THE RIGHTEOUSNESS OF GOD

There may be other reasons as well that the liturgy has become less *dangerous*—less effective in fulfilling its purpose. Perhaps we the clergy have unwittingly committed violence against the liturgy through indifference, carelessness, or neglect, robbing it of its vigor; emptying its rituals, symbols, and words of their proper meaning; making it opaque to the modern worshipper through ritual formalism; or trivializing it through irresponsible and unwise experiments. Perhaps we have robbed the liturgy of its mystical dimension by mystifying it with arcane and irrelevant explanations or by stressing the externals of worship to the detriment of its substance. Or even worse, we may be abusing components of the liturgy to control the thoughts and actions of people, riddling them with guilt instead of opening them up to the liberating power of God's saving activity, his righteousness.

It is hard to imagine how people can worship in spirit and truth (John 4:23) when clergy offer them liturgical services that are spiritless or pretentious. How can the people truly appreciate the wonder and the mystery of the liturgy when the explanations we offer them about the rites are woefully inadequate, or the language of prayer is incomprehensible, or the preaching of the Word is uninspiring, or the music is mediocre, or the liturgical actions are graceless? How can the people feel that they are an integral part of worship when we relegate them to the status of mere spectators and silent observers? And how can people experience or appreciate the transforming power of the liturgy when the community's commitment to translating its devotional acts into works of justice is lukewarm or, worse, lacking?

Authentic liturgy is an act of faith, and as such it involves personal involvement and commitment. We, clergy and laity, must want to invest ourselves in the liturgy and the purposes for which it is celebrated. This, I submit, may be the most important reason that the liturgy has ceased to be *dangerous* for many Christians. The problem is not so much with the liturgy as it is with us, with our lack of integrity. The liturgy is like a fine musical instrument. To fulfill its purpose, an instrument must be played. Now, it could be played well so as to create excellent music that moves, inspires, and elevates both the player and the listener, or it could be played amateurishly, making unpleasant, discordant noises. To gain the full effect of the liturgy, we must come to love it, learn it, and *play it well*, according the ability of each, as all good musicians do their instruments.

This metaphor, however, has another side to it. In order for a musical instrument to play well, it must be carefully and properly maintained and occasionally cleaned and tuned. Thus, if the liturgy is to remain vibrant and relevant, we are obliged to know it well by exploring its history, uncovering its meanings, and weighing its effectiveness in each generation. Ambiguous sentimentalities have no place if the liturgy is to be effective or *dangerous*. We cannot afford to perpetuate forms of worship that are heavily encrusted with cultural debris of times past and that do not allow the theological core of worship to shine forth brightly and clearly. For sure, the liturgy must be traditional, but it must also be relevant, capable of inspiring contemporary worshippers, bringing them into the realm of God's righteousness.

The liturgy is the life of Christ in us lived and celebrated. People's relationship with the Church begins with, is sustained by, and ends with the liturgy. For this reason, it must always be an enriching experience aesthetically, intellectually, and spiritually—capable of building and nourishing faith, capable of touching the heart, elevating the mind, pricking the conscience, and rousing the will to pursue righteousness. For this reason, there is an increasing urgency to provide the people with sound liturgical catechesis and "good liturgy" in every parish, which is the essential Eucharistic cell of the Church where the saving work of Christ is actively pursued, enacted, and conferred.

For the liturgy to be an educative, formative, evocative, restorative, and transformative, *dangerous* experience, God's people—clergy and laity alike—must acquire a liturgical mind. They must want to pursue and accomplish, according to the desire and capacity of each, three basic things. They must want to extract and absorb and then apply the doctrinal, ethical, and devotional riches of the liturgy to everyday life so that the truths of the faith are not barren abstractions but hymns of exulting praise and bright guideposts steering them toward the depths of divine wisdom that they may learn to live by the Spirit (Gal. 5:25), "to do justice, and to love kindness, and to walk humbly with God" (Micah 6:8).

The prayers and hymns of the Church, among other things, give expression to what we hope to achieve or what we have already accomplished in worship. Hence we must pay close attention to the contents of the prayers and hymns and take them seriously. They help to define us, our actions, intentions, and objectives. For example, the hymn "We have seen the true light" (*Εἴδομεν τὸ φῶς τὸ ἀληθινόν*), which is sung at the end of the Communion rites of the Divine Liturgy, describes what happened, what was accomplished, and what was experienced at the divine service. It refers to three specific things that the worshipping community experienced and achieved in the Divine Liturgy: "We have seen the true light; we have received the Heavenly Spirit; we have found the true faith, worshipping the undivided Trinity." The question is, did the community and its individual members really experience these three things, and to what degree were they experienced? The answer we give, collectively and individually, will, at least in part, indicate how *dangerous* the divine service was. Did the community and its members perceive the true light in the course of the service? Were they illumined by Christ, the Light of the world? Was the congregation open to the stirrings of the Holy Spirit? Was the faith of the people reinvigorated, and did they consciously give expression to it? Were they aware of God's presence in their midst, and did they worship the Holy Trinity earnestly in faith—a faith that saves (Matt. 9:22; Luke 17:19 and 18:42)? Are they ready to "depart in peace," renewed, inspired, and energized by the experience? And if so, are they moved to become "witnesses of these things" (Luke 24:48) to the world around them?

Good Liturgy Requires That We Ascend and Descend

Because the God of Christians is holy, just, merciful, and loving, Christians are called to participate in his holiness, love, mercy, and justice. In his fifth homily on the Beatitudes, St. Gregory of Nyssa relates the following about our Christian responsibilities in the affairs of everyday life in the world:

> For He says: "Blessed are the merciful for they shall obtain mercy." The obvious meaning of these words invites men to mutual charity and compassion, which are demanded by the capricious inequality of the circumstances of life. For not all live in the same conditions, neither as regards reputation, nor physical constitution, nor other assets. Life is in many ways often divided into opposites, since it may be spent as slave or master, in riches or poverty, in fame or dishonor, in bodily infirmity or in good health—in all such things there is division. Therefore the creature in need should be made equal to the

one that has a larger share, and that which is lacking should be filled by what has abundance. This is the law mercy gives men in regard to the needy... Mercy is a voluntary sorrow that joins itself to the suffering of others ... Mercy is the loving disposition to those who suffer distress. For as unkindness and cruelty have their origin in hate, so mercy springs from love, without which it could not exist ... Mercy is intensified charity. Hence a man of such dispositions of soul is truly blessed, since he has reached the summit of virtue.[31]

These words of St. Gregory are not the words of a moralist—a set of aphorisms that appear removed from and unrelated to the harsh realities of practical or "real" life. The Fathers of the Church, like the prophets before them, are neither moralists nor politicians. Their function is to teach people the truths about God, the world, and human life so that these teachings may be translated into godly action, whether in personal or public life.

On this side of death, every ascent requires a descent. The Church must not only ascend to God, but it must also descend into the depths of ordinary life, into the suffering world with settled confidence about the transformation that is to come—the promise of God's Kingdom, the Kingdom of life, light, love, joy, peace, and justice.

After sitting at Table with the Lord to hear the words of life and partake of the Bread of Life, we are always sent out again—"depart in peace." We are sent back to the world to immerse ourselves in the affairs and circumstances of everyday life, bringing the redemptive and restorative power of God to our wounded and broken world. As stewards and priests of creation, we are called to defend it against those who would exploit and pollute it. Having partaken of the Body of Christ, we must also tend to the needs of the broken human bodies and spirits that are all around us so that the rays of God's Kingdom may shine in the darkness of our fallen world, bringing healing, reconciliation, love, hope, peace, and joy to the hearts of people until the Lord comes in glory (Rev. 22:20).

---

[31] St. Gregory of Nyssa, PG 44, 1252, cited in Peter C. Phan, *Social Thought: Message of the Fathers of the Church* (Wilmington, DE, 1984), 20:128–129.

FROM THE LITURGY OF ST. BASIL TO THE LITURGY OF ST. JOHN CHRYSOSTOM
WHEN AND WHY (A PRELIMINARY REPORT)[32]

Sometime between the tenth and eleventh centuries, the Divine Liturgy of St. John Chrysostom for some unknown reason became the principal Eucharistic liturgy of Constantinople, replacing the formulary of St. Basil the Great, which until that time had been listed first in the extant manuscripts of the Greek *euchologia*, the service books of the Church.[33] This change represents a dramatic shift in the liturgical practice of the Orthodox Church. When and why did it occur? Before I attempt to address these questions, some brief general remarks on the Byzantine rite and its Eucharistic liturgies are in order so that the subject of this inquiry may be placed in a proper liturgical and historical context.

---

[32] This essay was first published in the *festschrift* honoring my respected and beloved professor Ioannis M. Fountoulis, of the Theological School of the Aristotle University of Thessaloniki. The present text is a modified version of the original, which can be found in *Γηθόσυνον Σέβασμα: Ἀντίδωρον τιμῆς καὶ μνήμης εἰς τὸν μακαριστὸν καθηγητὴν τῆς λειτουργικῆς Ἰωάννην Μ. Φουντούλην (+2007)*, ed. Panagiotis I. Skaltsis and Nikodemos A. Skrettas (Thessaloniki, 2013), 1:1015–1056.

[33] See, for example, the Barberini Codex gr. 336, the oldest extant Byzantine *euchologion* (late eighth century). A critical edition of the codex was published by Stefano Parenti and Elena Velkovska, *L'eucologio Barberini gr. 336* (Rome 1995), 1–24 (Basil) and 24–41 (Chrysostom). See also Miguel Arranz, *L'eucologio Constantinopolitano agli inizi del secolo XI: Hagiasmatarion & archieratikon* (Rome 1996), 465–497 and 537–561 (Basil), and 499–513 and 563–578 (Chrysostom); and Codex 662 of the National Library of Greece, folios 32–50 (Basil) and 50–60 (Chrysostom). Some give an eleventh-century date for Codex 662; Panagiotis Trempelas, however, gives a later date: twelfth to thirteenth century. See Trempelas, *Αἱ τρεῖς λειτουργίαι* (Athens, 1935), ζ. I thank Fr. Pavlos Koumarianos, who provided me with a photographic reproduction of Codex 662.

The Byzantine Rite

A BRIEF NOTE ON ITS ORIGINS

It is well known that the Byzantine liturgical rite (*Βυζαντινὸς λειτουργικὸς τύπος*), also known as the Constantinopolitan rite, constitutes the final unification of liturgical practice in the Orthodox Church.[34] As the primary ecclesial see of the Christian East, Constantinople, the great imperial city, became the receptacle of the liturgical traditions of the leading liturgical centers of the East: Antioch (Syria), Jerusalem (Palestine), Caesarea in Cappadocia (Pontus), and Heraclea (Thrace).[35] The Byzantine rite passed through various stages of development and is "renowned for the sumptuousness of its ceremonial and liturgical symbolism, and the heritage of the imperial splendors of Constantinople before the eighth century. [It] gradually synthesized during the ninth to the fourteenth centuries in the monasteries of the Orthodox world, beginning in the period of the struggle with Iconoclasm."[36]

The Byzantine rite spread steadily far and wide. By the thirteenth century it had become the common inheritance of all the Orthodox Churches, albeit with minor local variations, having supplanted the native rites of the other ancient patriarchates of the East. This happened not by any imposition, force, or synodical legislation but simply by practice.

For Theodore Balsamon, the noted canonist and patriarch of Antioch (d. 1214), the Byzantine, or Constantinopolitan, rite was the established liturgical practice of his day, as evidenced by his response to the question of Mark, the patriarch of Alexandria, concerning the correctness of celebrating the ancient liturgies attributed to the holy Apostles St. James the Brother of the Lord and St. Mark the Evangelist. "All the Churches of God," Balsamon wrote, "must follow the custom of the New Rome, that is Constantinople, and celebrate the liturgy according to the tradition of those great Church

---

[34] For a concise account of the formation and development of the Byzantine rite, see Robert F. Taft, *The Byzantine Rite: A Short History* (Collegeville, MN, 1992). See also Alexander Schmemann, *Introduction to Liturgical Theology* (Crestwood, NY, 1996); Panayiotis Trempelas, *Λειτουργικοί τύποι Αἰγύπτου καὶ ἀνατολῆς* (Athens, 1961), 323–369; Ioannis Fountoulis, *Λειτουργική* (Thessaloniki, 1975); Alkiviadis C. Calivas, *Aspects of Orthodox Worship* (Brookline, MA, 2003), 54–62, 63–101.

[35] See Fountoulis, *Λειτουργική*, 29–30; Trempelas, *Λειτουργικοί τύποι*, 323–324.

[36] Taft, *Byzantine Rite*, 16.

Fathers and beacons of piety, St. John Chrysostom and St. Basil."[37] For Balsamon, "in the absence of any written laws to the contrary, the customs of Rome are to be guarded and kept," as the old imperial laws would have it.[38]

Like all classical rites, the Byzantine rite is composed of several basic components and by certain characteristic theological and ritual attributes. The rite has a wide range of liturgical services, including Eucharistic liturgies, sacramental rites, and other occasional services. It also has a daily office, a lectionary system, and a calendar of feasts and fasts. In addition, it has distinctive and highly developed forms of the liturgical arts: architecture, iconography, hymnography, music, and textiles.

Eucharist and Church

The sacrament of the holy Eucharist occupies the center of the Church's life because it completes all other sacraments and recapitulates the entire economy of salvation.[39] In it we continuously encounter Christ—cru-

---

[37] Theodore Balsamon, "Ἐρωτήσεις κανονικαὶ τοῦ ἁγιωτάτου πατριάρχου Ἀλεξανδρείας κ. Μάρκου καὶ ἀποκρίσεις ἐπ' αὐτάς," in *PG* 138, 953; and in G. Rallis and M. Potlis, *Σύνταγμα τῶν θείων καὶ ἱερῶν κανόνων* (Athens 1854), 4:449. Balsamon apparently ignores canon 32 of the Penthekte Synod, which specifically mentions the Divine Liturgies of St. James (Iakovos) and St. Basil. See *Πηδάλιον*, 249–248; *Rudder*, 328. It should be noted that the ancient liturgies of James and Mark were not entirely forgotten in Jerusalem or Alexandria. In fact, in modern times, both liturgies are celebrated in many Orthodox Churches on the feast days of the two saints, October 23 and April 25, respectively. St. James is also commemorated on the Sunday after Christmas, together with St. Joseph the Betrothed and David the Prophet-King. For a brief account of the ancient Eucharistic liturgies, see Ioannis Fountoulis, *Τελετουργικὰ θέματα* (Athens, 2007), 3:140–157. See also F. E. Brightman, *Eastern Liturgies* (Oxford, 1896; reprint Piscataway, NJ, 2004). J. M. Neale, *The Liturgies of Saints Mark, James, Clement, Chrysostomos, and Basil, and the Church of Malabar* (London, 1869; reprint Piscataway, NJ, 2002).

[38] The law, as Balsamon himself indicates, is found in the *Second Book of the Basilika*, title 1: chapter 41 (Β. βιβλίον τῶν βασιλικῶν, κεφάλαιον μα' τοῦ α' τίτλου).

[39] On the historical, biblical, theological, and liturgical dimensions of the Eucharist, see the collection of articles in the two volumes *Τὸ μυστήριο τῆς Θείας Εὐχαριστίας*, Σειρὰ Ποιμαντικὴ Βιβλιοθήκη 8 (Athens, 2004); and *Ἡ Θεία Εὐχαριστία* (Drama, 2003). See also Alexander Schmemann, *The Eucharist* (Crestwood, NY, 2003); Calivas, *Aspects of Orthodox Worship*, 162–226; Hugh Wybrew, *The Orthodox Liturgy: The Development of the Eucharistic Liturgy in the Byzantine Rite* (Crestwood, NY, 1990); Paul McPartlan, *The Eucharist Makes the Church: Henri de Lubac and John Zizioulas in Dialogue* (Edinburgh, 1996); Dionysios Psarianos, *Ἡ Θεία Λειτουργία* (Athens, 1986) and its English translation, *The Divine Liturgy of St. John Chrysostom*, trans. George Dimopoulos (Margate City, NJ, 2000); Paul Evdokimov, *Ἡ Προσευχὴ τῆς ἀνατολικῆς ἐκκλησίας: Ἡ λειτουργία του Ἁγίου Ἰωάννου του Χρυσόστομου*

cified, raised from the dead, and glorified—in his personal presence. Through this meeting and communion, we become partakers of the divine nature (2 Pet. 1:4). Christ assimilates us to himself and gives us his divine and eternal life through our partaking of his Eucharistic Body and Blood.

Every Eucharist holds the possibility for transcendence, transfiguration, and holiness as participants find the Triune God in the sacred prayers, hymns, and actions of the Divine Liturgy by cultivating an awareness of the coming judgment,[40] the inspiration of repentance,[41] and the cleansing of the heart;[42] by fulfilling the commandment to love;[43] by abiding in the truth;[44] and, above all, by remembering the Kingdom, which is the eschatological fulfillment in which we will become all that we are meant to be in order to reign with God as kings and priests according to his promise.[45]

(Athens, 1980); Panagiotis Trempelas, *Από την Ορθόδοξον λατρείαν μας* (Athens, 1970). Also see the two Byzantine liturgical commentaries: Nicholas Cabasilas, *A Commentary on the Divine Liturgy*, trans. J. M. Hussey and P. A. McNulty (London, 1960); and *St. Germanus of Constantinople on the Divine Liturgy*, trans. Paul Meyendorff (Crestwood, NY, 1984).

[40] Both Divine Liturgies are replete with references to the ways by which the faithful appropriate God's saving and transforming grace. Here is one example: "For a Christian end to our lives, peaceful, without shame and suffering, and for a good account before the awesome judgment seat of Christ, let us ask the Lord" (petition of the dismissal litany). Similar examples are given in the notes that follow.

[41] "You give wisdom and understanding to the supplicant and do not overlook the sinner but have established repentance as the way of salvation ... Forgive our voluntary and involuntary transgressions, sanctify our souls and bodies, and grant that we may worship and serve You in holiness all the days of our lives" (prayer of the Trisagion Hymn).

[42] "Shine within our hearts, loving Master, the pure light of your divine knowledge and open the eyes of our minds that we may comprehend the message of your Gospel. Instill in us also reverence for Your blessed commandments, so that having conquered sinful desires, we may pursue a spiritual life, thinking and doing all those things that are pleasing to You" (prayer before the Gospel).

[43] "Let us love one another that with one mind we may confess" (prologue of the *anaphora*).

[44] "I believe in one God ..." (creed). "Fulfill now the petitions of your servants for our benefit, giving us the knowledge of your truth in this world, and granting us eternal life in the world to come" (prayer of the third antiphon).

[45] "You raised us up again. You did not cease doing everything until you led us to heaven and granted us your kingdom to come" (*anaphora* of CHR). "Make us worthy to partake of your heavenly and awesome mysteries ... for the inheritance of the kingdom of heaven" (pre-Communion prayer of CHR). "He [Christ] acquired us for himself, as his chosen people, a royal priesthood, a holy nation ... He rose on the third day, having opened a path for all flesh to the resurrection from the dead, since it was not possible that the Author of life would be dominated by corruption ... Reward them with your rich and heavenly gifts. Grant them in return for earthly things, heavenly gifts; for temporal, eternal; for corruptible, in-

CHAPTER TWO: FROM THE LITURGY OF ST. BASIL TO ST. JOHN C.

The Orthodox Church celebrates the sacrament of the Eucharist through the sacred rite called the Divine Liturgy.[46] Through the Divine Liturgy, Orthodox Christians confess their common faith, express their indissoluble unity in love, and find and take hold of another life, new, true, and eternal. In the Divine Liturgy we are not only sanctified but we are also empowered to bear fruit commensurate with the gift we receive. In the Divine Liturgy, celebrated in faith, we experience the transfiguration of our being by communicating in the Lord, becoming members of his Body, the Church. Through this transformative experience we renew each time our baptismal pledge and reaffirm our true identity, that in Christ through baptism we have become a new creation.

St. Maximos the Confessor spoke of the transforming and sanctifying power of the Eucharist in the following moving terms:

> For entrance into the church signifies not only the conversion of infidels to the true and only God but also the amendment of each one of us who believe but who yet violate the Lord's commandments under the influence of a loose and indecent life ... [W]hen someone is entangled in any kind of vice but should cease voluntarily to be held by its attention and deliberately to act according to it and changes his life for the better by preferring virtue to vice, such a person can be properly and truly considered and spoken of as entering with Christ our God and High Priest into virtue, which is the church understood figuratively ... [E]very Christian should be exhorted to frequent God's holy Church and never to abandon the holy synaxis accomplished therein because of the holy angels who remain there and who take note each time people enter and present themselves to God, and make supplication for them; likewise because of the grace of the Holy Spirit which is always invisibly present, but in a special way at the time of

---

corruptible... Receive us all into your kingdom. Declare us to be sons and daughters of the light and of the day. Grant us your peace and love, Lord our God, for you have given us all things" (*anaphora* of BAS).

[46] For more on the development of the various components and rubrics of the Divine Liturgy, see the multivolume works of Ioannis Fountoulis, *Ἀπαντήσεις εἰς Λειτουργικὰς Ἀπορίας*, vols. 1–5 (Thessaloniki, 1967, 1975, 1976, 1982, 2003); *Τελετουργικά θέματα* (Athens, 2002), 1:265–294; *Τελετουργικά θέματα* (Athens, 2007), 3:49–70; and "Ερμηνεία επτά δύσκολων σημείων του κειμένου της Θείας Λειτουργίας από τον Νικόλαον Καβάσιλα," in *Πρακτικά Θεολογικού Συνεδρίου:Νικολάου Καβάσιλα του και Χαμαετού* (Thessaloniki, 1984), 155–172. Also see Robert F. Taft, *Beyond East and West: Problems in Liturgical Understanding* (Rome, 2001), 187–232; Hanz-Joachim Schulz, *The Byzantine Liturgy* (New York, 1986).

the holy synaxis. This grace transforms and changes each person who is found there and in fact remolds him in proportion to what is more divine in him and leads him to what is revealed through the mysteries which are celebrated, even if he does not himself feel this because he is still among those who are children in Christ, unable to see either the depths of the reality or the grace operating in it, which is revealed through each of the divine symbols of salvation being accomplished, and which proceeds according to the order and progression from preliminaries to the end of everything.47

The Eucharistic Liturgies of the Byzantine Rite

THREE LITURGIES

The Byzantine rite has three Divine Liturgies:[48] the Divine Liturgy of St. Basil the Great (BAS),[49] the Divine Liturgy of St. John Chrysostom (CHR),[50] and the Divine Liturgy of the Presanctified Gifts (PRES).[51] Firmly rooted

---

[47] St. Maximos, *Mystagogy*, 9 and 24 in *Maximus Confessor: Selected Writings*, trans. George C. Berthold, Classics of Western Spirituality (New York, 1985), 198, 206–207.

[48] A critical edition of the three Divine Liturgies was published by Panagiotis Trempelas, Αἱ τρεῖς Λειτουργίαι κατὰ τοὺς ἐν Ἀθήναις Κώδικας (Athens, 1935).

[49] For the development of the Liturgy of St. Basil, see John R. K. Fenwick, *The Anaphoras of St. Basil and St. James: An Investigation into Their Common Origin*, Orientalia Christiana Analecta 240 (Rome, 1992). See also D. Richard Stuckwisch, "The Basilian *Anaphoras*," in *Essays on Early Eastern Eucharistic Prayers*, ed. Paul F. Bradshaw (Collegeville, MN, 1997), 109–130; Louis Bouyer, *Eucharist: Theology and Spirituality of the Eucharistic Prayer* (Notre Dame, 1968), 290–304.

[50] For an in-depth study of the history the Divine Liturgy of St. John Chrysostom, see Juan Mateos, *La celebration de la parole dans la liturgie byzantine*, Orientalia Christiana Analecta [OCA] 191 (Rome, 1971); and the four volumes by Robert F. Taft, *The Great Entrance: A History of the Transfer of Gifts and Other Pre-anaphoral Rites of the Liturgy of St. John Chrysostom*, OCA 200 (Rome, 1978); *A History of the Liturgy of St. John Chrysostom: The Diptychs*, OCA 238 (Rome, 1991), vol. 4; *The Precommunion Rites*, OCA 261 (Rome, 2000), vol. 5; *The Communion, Thanksgiving, and Concluding Rites*, OCA 281 (Rome 2008), vol. 6. See also Robert Taft, "St. John Chrysostom and the Byzantine *Anaphora* That Bears His Name," in Bradshaw, *Essays on Early Eastern Eucharistic Prayers*, 195–226. M. M. Solovey, *The Byzantine Divine Liturgy* (Washington, DC, 1970). Casimir Kucharek, *The Byzantine-Slav Liturgy of St. John Chrysostom* (Allendale, NJ, 1971).

[51] For a comprehensive study of PRES, see Stefanos Alexopoulos, *The Pre-Sanctified Liturgy in the Byzantine Rite: A Comparative Analysis of Its Origins, Evolution, and Structural Components* (Leuven, 2009). See also Nicholas Uspensky, *Evening Worship in the Orthodox Church* (Crestwood, NY 1985), 111–190; Ioannis Fountoulis, Λειτουργία τῶν Προηγιασμένων Δώρων, in Κείμενα Λειτουργικῆς, vol. 8 (Thessaloniki, 1971); S. Janeras, "La partie vesperal de la liturgie byzantine des presanctifies," in *Orientalia Periodica* 30 (1964): 193–222; Deme-

CHAPTER TWO: FROM THE LITURGY OF ST. BASIL TO ST. JOHN C.   25

in the Scriptures and strongly influenced by the patristic experience, these formularies take worshippers to the heart of God's boundless philanthropy and ineffable glory.

As already mentioned, BAS was until the tenth and eleventh centuries the chief Divine Liturgy of Constantinople, celebrated every Sunday and on great feast days. Now, however, it is used only ten times during the year: on the five Sundays of Great Lent; the vigils of Pascha, Christmas, and Theophany;[52] Holy Thursday; and the Feast of St. Basil on January 1. The *anaphora*, or great Eucharistic prayer, of BAS is probably the most eloquent of all Eucharistic prayers, East and West, powerful in its unity of thought, theological depth, and rich biblical imagery—a Eucharistic prayer that is decidedly creedal in nature with a grand litany of titles and attributes of the three Persons of the Trinity, their particular role and mode of being (τροπος υπαρξεως), and a stirring account of the divine economy and the blessings that flow from it.

The *anaphora* of CHR is shorter and less rhetorical than that of BAS. It is characterized by its simplicity, directness, and clarity. CHR was probably the weekday Eucharist of the Byzantine rite. By the end of the eleventh century, however, it had displaced BAS as the chief Eucharistic liturgy in Constantinople and throughout the Byzantine world.[53] Since that time, it has been continuously celebrated every Sunday and weekday in every Orthodox parish and monastery throughout the world, except on those occasions when the *typikon*, the book of rubrics and regulations, requires the celebration of BAS or PRES.

PRES is not a full Divine Liturgy because it does not contain an *anaphora*. It is composed of Vespers, the solemn transfer to the holy Table of the presanctified holy Gifts consecrated at the Divine Liturgy on the previous Sunday (or Saturday), and the order (τάξις) of distributing Holy Communion as in the other two liturgies. While in earlier times this liturgy enjoyed wider use, in current practice it is celebrated only on Wednesdays and Fri-

---

trios Moraitis, *Ἡ Λειτουργία τῶν Προηγιασμένων Δώρων* (Thessaloniki, 1955).
[52] When the feast of Christmas or Theophany falls on a Sunday or Monday, the rubrics specify that the feast has only one Divine Liturgy. There is no vesperal Divine Liturgy but only a morning liturgy celebrated on the day of the feast. In this instance, the rubrics assign the Divine Liturgy of St. Basil to the morning of the feast.
[53] Taft, *Great Entrance*, xxxii.

days of Great Lent and on the first three days of Holy Week.

THE STRUCTURE OF THE DIVINE LITURGIES OF SAINTS BASIL AND JOHN CHRYSOSTOM

Both BAS and CHR constitute complex acts of movement, sound, and sight and are characterized by a sense of harmony, beauty, dignity, and mystery. They are outwardly identical in form and are structured around two solemn entrances, the so-called Small Entrance and the Great Entrance, and around the two "lesser" processions of the Gospel and Holy Communion, which today are abbreviated forms of earlier, more elaborate ceremonies; the reading and the exposition of Holy Scripture; the exchange of the kiss of peace and the recitation of the Nicene-Constantinopolitan Creed; the great Eucharistic prayer (i.e., the *anaphora*); and the preparation for and the distribution of Holy Communion. Elaborate opening rites (ἔναρξις) and a series of dismissal rites (ἀπολύσεις) embrace the whole action.[54]

To most observers there is little, if any, difference between BAS and CHR, especially since the prayers of the priest in current practice are said in a low voice or inaudibly.[55] The more observant participant, however, will notice that while the two Divine Liturgies "sound" almost the same and share an identical structure or framework, BAS is lengthier than CHR. Even the casual observer cannot help but notice that it takes the priest longer to read some of the prayers and that the choir tends to prolong some of the hymns. To fully appreciate the differences between the two Liturgies, however, one must do more than watch the clock. One must learn to be an attentive listener and a careful reader of the texts of the two services. Then the similarities and the distinctive features of each will become evident.

---

[54] The dismissal rites originally included a recessional. Originally, the clergy and the people entered the church together in solemn procession with song to begin the Divine Liturgy. So also at the conclusion of the divine service, the clergy and the people exited the church together with song.

[55] The recitation of prayers in a low voice or inaudibly has a long and complex history. It originated in east Syria and had become prevalent throughout the Eastern Church by the end of the eighth century, in spite of imperial legislation to the contrary. Today, with varying degrees of success, many local Orthodox Churches are encouraging the clergy to recite all or some of the prayers aloud, most especially the *anaphora*. For a comprehensive treatment of the subject, see Georgios N. Filias, *Ο τρόπος αναγνώσεως των ευχών στη λατρεία της Ορθοδόξου Εκκλησίας* (Athens, 1997). For a brief account, see Calivas, *Aspects of Orthodox Worship*, 214–217.

CHAPTER TWO: FROM THE LITURGY OF ST. BASIL TO ST. JOHN C.

The received texts of both BAS and CHR contain twenty priestly prayers of varying length whose doxological endings (ἐκφωνήσεις) are the same.[56] The received texts also contain the same prescribed ritual actions and gestures, diaconal litanies, responses and hymns of the people, and rubrical information. Of the twenty priestly prayers, eleven are common to both liturgies, while nine are different.[57]

The nine different prayers in the received texts include the prayer for the dismissal of the catechumens and the two prayers for the faithful. These two prayers bridge the two parts of the Divine Liturgy, the Liturgy of the Word and the Eucharist proper.[58] The focal point of the former is the reading and the explication of the Word of God. The focal point of the latter is the transfer of the Eucharistic elements to the holy Table, their conse-

---

[56] See, for example, the text of the two Divine Liturgies in parallel columns, together with a brief but informative introduction, in Ioannis Fountoulis, Βυζαντιναί Θ. Λειτουργίαι Βασιλείου τοῦ Μεγάλου καὶ Ἰωάννου τοῦ Χρυσοστόμου (Thessaloniki, 1978). To the twenty prayers of the Divine Liturgy, we should add another, the prayer of the prothesis. While this prayer is now said at the conclusion of the Service of the *proskomide*, which is performed before the Divine Liturgy at the prothesis, or preparation table, the prayer of the prothesis is prefixed to the text of BAS in the manuscripts. Moreover, the dismissal blessings have not been counted among the twenty prayers, since they were originally part of the rites at the *skeuophylakion*, where the unconsumed consecrated Gifts were returned and consumed by the appointed persons. On the prothesis rites see Stelyios S. Muksuris, *Economia and Eschatology: Liturgical Mystagogy in the Byzantine Prothesis Rite* (Brookline, MA, 2013)..

[57] Of the eleven common prayers, one, the prayer before the Gospel, is not found in the Barberini *euchologion*. It was added around the tenth century to both formularies. The other ten have been supplied by BAS. They are the prayers of the three antiphons, the entrance, the Trisagion Hymn, the incense, the Fervent Litany, the Cherubic Hymn, before the elevation of the Amnos, and behind the *amvon*. In the early manuscript tradition—the Barberini *euchologion*, for example—CHR did not have prayers for the three antiphons, the Cherubic Hymn, or the *skeuophylakion*. They were supplied by BAS. In the Barberini *euchologion*, CHR has its own original prayers for the entrance, the Trisagion Hymn, the cathedra, and behind the amvon. In later manuscripts, these were supplanted by the prayers in BAS. In addition, in the Barberini *euchologion*, BAS and CHR both include a prayer for the cathedra (*synthronon*). However, these prayers were omitted in the printed *euchologia*, since the ascent to the *synthronon* was eventually abandoned in most Greek churches and the *synthronon* itself gradually disappeared from the apse of most sanctuaries. BAS and CHR have similar dismissal rites that are not found in the early manuscripts. These rites end with the prayer of the *skeuophylakion*. In the received text of CHR, the prayer of the *skeuophylakion* is an original creation. It was added to the text after the ninth century.

[58] In many catechetical manuals, the two parts of the Divine Liturgy are referred to as the Liturgy of the Catechumens and the Liturgy of the Faithful. This designation, however, is unfortunate and should be resisted.

cration, and their reception in Holy Communion. The other six different prayers in BAS and CHR are the prayer of the *proskomide*, the holy *anaphora*, the pre-Communion prayer (before the Lord's Prayer), the prayer of inclination, the prayer of thanksgiving after Communion, and the prayer of the *skeuophylakion* (today at the prothesis). While all these prayers are related to the *anaphora*, three in particular are especially important for our discussion: the prayer of the *proskomide*, which anticipates the *epiclesis*, the pre-Communion prayer, and the thanksgiving after Communion. The pre-Communion prayer reiterates the effects of Communion presented in the *anaphora*, while the prayer of thanksgiving expands the benefits of Communion.

From this list of prayers it is fairly easy to see that the chief differences between BAS and CHR rest chiefly in the second part of the Divine Liturgy, the Eucharist proper. These differences are both external and internal. The prayers differ not only in length but also in content, and this is especially true of the holy *anaphora*.

As Andre Jacob has shown in his comprehensive but as yet unpublished doctoral dissertation on the Divine Liturgy of St. John Chrysostom, CHR is incomplete in the early manuscripts, including the Barberini Codex.[59] According to Robert Taft, the celebrant was obliged to refer to the complete formulary of BAS for the prayers common to both Divine Liturgies.[60] By the eleventh century, however, CHR appears in a complete form in the *euchologia*, its missing prayers supplied by BAS. And equally important, CHR is now listed first, having supplanted BAS as the chief liturgy of the Byzantine rite.[61]

It is no accident that Balsamon, in his response to Patriarch Mark of Alexandria on the Divine Liturgies, mentions the name of St. John Chrysostom before that of St. Basil, even though according to the established order, the name of St. Basil was usually, if not always, commemorated first among the great hierarchs and teachers of the Church.[62] One can assume that Balsamon places St. John Chrysostom first because he was influenced by the

---

[59] Andre Jacob, "Histoire du formulaire grec de la liturgie de Saint Jean Chrysostome" (PhD diss., University of Louvain, 1968). Parenti and Velokovska, *L'eucologio Barberini*, 24–41.
[60] Taft, *Great Entrance*, xxxi–xxxii.
[61] Ibid., xxxii.
[62] Each of the three great teachers and hierarchs of the Church, Basil the Great, Gregory

fact that, by his time, CHR had become firmly established as the principal liturgy of Constantinople.

A New Sunday Liturgy: From BAS to CHR

THE BREVITY ARGUMENT

Let me now turn to the question at hand, the reasons for the shift from BAS to CHR. For centuries the debate—if one could call it that—has centered on the so-called "brevity argument," which is based on the short tract, "Homily on the Transmission of the Divine Liturgy" ("Λόγος περὶ παραδόσεως τῆς Θείας Λειτουργίας"), which is attributed to Proclus, patriarch of Constantinople (434–446). Most, if not all, Orthodox clerics and many informed laypeople are familiar with the argument. Not only was it taught in theological schools and seminaries, but it also found its way into many liturgical manuals and catechetical books. According to this thesis, the earliest apostolic Eucharistic liturgies were very long. With the passing of time, however, and as the fervor of the early Christians waned, the argument goes, successive abbreviations of the Eucharistic services were instituted by the great teachers and hierarchs of the Church in order to hold the people's interest.[63]

The brevity argument is certainly attractive, as anyone involved with liturgy knows, because the structures and content of rituals have expanded, contracted, and changed through the centuries, and the tendency toward brevity is an ever-present reality, especially in parishes. It is not difficult, therefore, to understand the appeal of the brevity argument, which Andre Jacob—at least tentatively—thought accounted for the shift from BAS to CHR.

According to the treatise of Proclus, Clement of Rome and James the Brother of the Lord wrote the most famous and the longest of the ancient apostolic formularies. The treatise then states as fact the following: "Mindful of the laxity and weakness of human beings who find the Liturgy burdensome because of its length, St. Basil gave permission to read a shorter

---

the Theologian, and John Chrysostom, is commemorated separately by the Church: on January 1, January 25, and November 13, respectively. In the eleventh century, during the reign of Constantine IX (1042–1055), Metropolitan John Mauropos of Euchaita was instrumental in introducing the Feast of the Three Hierarchs on January 30 for the joint celebration of these three great luminaries of the faith.

[63] Proclus, Λόγος περὶ παραδόσεως τῆς Θείας Λειτουργίας, PG 65: 849–852.

form of the Liturgy. Not long afterwards, our Father John of the golden tongue, wanted ... to eliminate this same satanic objection completely; therefore he removed a good deal from the Liturgy and prescribed that it be celebrated in an even briefer form."[64]

This thesis, of course, is based chiefly on external criteria, on the brevity of one text over the other. However, it does not address the dissimilarities in language, style, and theological emphases.[65] Nor does it answer the question of the shift from BAS to CHR, except indirectly. This account suggests that CHR, the shortest of the ancient formularies, was chosen over BAS in order to silence the people's protestations against lengthy services. However, the difference in length between BAS and CHR, although noticeable, is hardly so burdensome as to cause a major shift in liturgical practice, especially at a time when Sunday worship was both an act of faith and an appreciated and welcomed source of diversion from the burdens of daily life. Besides, if the treatise is truly authentic, it predates the shift by several hundred years and cannot account for it. More important, as modern scholarship has shown, the ancient formularies of BAS and CHR are not abridgements but original creations based on earlier—perhaps common—sources. Nevertheless, the thesis of Proclus became part of liturgical lore and was repeated to students of liturgy until recent times.

The brevity argument is untenable on at least on two other counts. First, using the comparative approach to liturgical history as a guideline, liturgical scholarship has established the rule that liturgical development normally, although not always, progresses from brevity to prolixity.[66] Second, some forty years ago F. J. Leroy published a study in which he argued successfully that the tract of Proclus was, in fact, a sixteenth-century forgery.[67]

---

[64] Ibid., 849, 852. See Schulz, *Byzantine Liturgy*, 5.
[65] For example, the *anaphora* of CHR emphasizes creation ex nihilo: "You brought us into being out of nothing, and when we fell, you raised us up again" (Σὺ ἐκ τοῦ μὴ ὄντος εἰς τὸ εἶναι ἡμᾶς παρήγαγες, καὶ παραπεσόντας ἀνέστησας πάλιν). This emphasis is not found in BAS or in the Divine Liturgies of James and Mark.
[66] On the sources and methods for the study of early Christian worship, see Paul F. Bradshaw, *The Search for the Origins of Christian Worship* (New York, 2002), 1–20, 118–143.
[67] F. J. Leroy, "Proclus 'De traditione divinae misse:' Un faux de C. Palaeocappa," *Orientalia Christiana Periodica* 28 (1962): 228–299. Jacob traces the forged tract of Proclus to two documents that promote the brevity argument, the tract "Questions and Responses" of Euthymios, abbot of Iveron Monastery (d. 1028); and the brief treatise of St. Mark of Ephesus

CHAPTER TWO: FROM THE LITURGY OF ST. BASIL TO ST. JOHN C.

A NEW HYPOTHESIS: A REACTION TO ICONOCLASM

Several years ago, Fr. Stefanos Alexopoulos presented a paper entitled "The Influence of Iconoclasm on Liturgy: A Case Study," in which he offered a new and more convincing hypothesis for the shift from BAS to CHR. The paper was read at the International Symposium in honor of the fortieth anniversary of St. Nersess Armenian Seminary in New Rochelle, New York. The fruits of the symposium were subsequently published in a commerative volume.[68]

After briefly commenting on the brevity argument, Fr. Alexopoulos developed his hypothesis that the shift from BAS to CHR was basically a reaction to iconoclasm—more specifically, to the Eucharistic theology of the iconoclasts, who held that the Eucharist is the image (εἰκών) and the type (τύπος) of the Body of Christ.[69]

The iconophiles, on the other hand, insisted that the Eucharist is neither an image nor a type of Christ's Body but is his actual deified Body. Once consecrated, the Eucharistic elements are changed into the very Body and Blood of Christ. The iconophiles made a clear distinction between the unconsecrated and the consecrated elements of the Eucharist. The unconsecrated elements could rightly be called antitypes (ἀντίτυπα), but the consecrated Gifts could not. The consecrated elements contain the very reality of Christ. Therefore, they are not mere figures, empty of content.

The term *antitypes* appears in the *anaphora* of BAS and designates the Eucharistic elements set forth on the holy Table for consecration and communion. The text, in part, reads as follows: "We dare to approach your holy altar, and bring forth the *antitypes* of the holy Body and Blood of your Christ. We pray to you and call upon you, O Holy of Holies, that by the favor of your goodness, your Holy Spirit may come upon us and upon these Gifts here presented, to bless, sanctify, and declare this Bread to be

---

(d. 1445) on the epiclesis. For more on this, especially as it relates to BAS and its anaphora, see Trembelas, Αἱ Τρεῖς Λειτουργίαι, n. 49, 173-179.

[68] *Worship Traditions in Armenia and the Neighboring Christian East,* ed. Roberta R. Ervine (Crestwood, NY 2006).

[69] The Eucharistic theology of the iconoclasts is contained in two sources, the *Peuseis* of the iconoclastic emperor, Constantine V, and the *Horos* of the iconoclastic Synod of Hiereia (754). Alexopoulos notes that the *Peuseis* and *Horos* are cited in Nikephoros, Antirheticus I and II, *PG* 100: 205-328. See also Stephen Gero, "The Eucharistic Doctrine of the Byzantine Iconoclasts and Its Sources," in *Byzantinische Zeitschrift,* 68 (1975).

the precious Body of our Lord and God and Savior Jesus Christ. Amen. And this Cup to be the precious Blood of our Lord and God and Savior Jesus Christ. Amen. Shed for the life and the salvation of the world. Amen. Amen. Amen."

The word *antitype* is closely related to the term *type*, which was widely used by the iconoclasts. And as Fr. Alexopoulos notes,

> the fact that the iconophiles in their apologiae return to the word ἀντίτυπα in BAS time and again suggests that the word αντιτυπα in BAS and its understanding played an important role in the disputes and was used by the iconoclasts It should be pointed out that what iconoclastic texts have survived have done so because they were preserved as quotations within the apologiae of the iconophiles. Thus we can safely assume that since the iconophiles make it a point to clarify the term ἀντίτυπα and its meaning in BAS, it was used in the iconoclastic arguments.[70]

The misunderstanding and misuse of ἀντίτυπα by the iconoclasts, Alexopoulos contends, led the Church to change its liturgical practice by shifting from BAS to CHR. In other words, the shift "took place as a reaction to the eucharistic theology of the iconoclasts and their understanding of the word ἀντίτυπα in BAS in particular."[71]

To lend support to his hypothesis, Alexopoulos cites a text that is attributed to Nikephoros, patriarch of Constantinople (806–815), but which was clearly written by someone else well after his death. It is, in fact, an after-the-fact attempt to account for the order (τάξις) of the celebration of the Divine Liturgies. The statement attributed to Nikephoros is attached to a fifteenth-century *typikon*.[72] Although the text gives no direct evidence for the shift from BAS to CHR as a reaction to iconoclasm, the causal relation can be inferred on the basis of the two interlocutors who are quoted

---

[70] Stefanos Alexopoulos, "The Influence of Iconoclasm on Liturgy: A Case Study," in *Worship Traditions in Armenia*, 131

[71] Ibid. Changes in liturgical practice for doctrinal reasons are not uncommon. Alexopoulos, for example, cites the Trinitarian doxologies of the fourth century. "[A]s a response to those who challenged the divinity of the Holy Spirit 'trinitarian doxologies' (Glory to the Father through the Son in the Holy Spirit) were leveled (Glory to the Father and the Son and the Holy Spirit) in the fourth century." St. Basil the Great addressed this issue. See his treatise, *On the Holy Spirit*, trans. David Anderson (Crestwood, NY, 1980) chapters 2–8.

[72] The text is found in Pitra, *Iuris ecclesiastici graecorum historia et monumenta* (Rome, 1869), 2:320–321; and in A. Dmitrieskij, *Opisanie liturgitseskich rukopisef* (Petrograd, 1917), 3:237–238.

in the text, Tarasios, patriarch of Constantinople (784–806), and his immediate successor, Nikephoros, both of whom were iconophiles. For the information it provides on the use of the two Divine Liturgies, it is worth citing the entire passage as it appears in Alexopoulos's paper:

> Regarding the order for the celebration of the Divine Liturgy, when it is to be celebrated. It is known that Nikephoros and Tarasios, the patriarchs of blessed memory, together with the rest of the holy synod, placed the liturgies in order, [making] the liturgy of Chrysostom the common one (to be celebrated always), and the liturgy of Basil the Great [to be celebrated] eleven times a year, that is the 14th of September, on occasion of the Exaltation of the precious and life-giving Cross, on which day every person called after our Lord fasts, the eve of Christ's birth and on the memory of the aforesaid father, that is on January 1, and also on the eve of Epiphany and on the Sundays of the Great Lent, except for Palm Sunday, and on Holy Thursday and Holy Saturday.[73] Other than these days, the liturgy of Basil the Great is not celebrated. Tarasios said the following on this matter: "It seems to me, most honorable father, that nothing obstructs us from also celebrating the liturgy of Basil the Great on the holy day of Pentecost, and on the day of the Transfiguration, and on the feast of Hypapante." Nikephoros replied to the above: "Nothing obstructs us, most honest father; it seems to me that because of the joyful [character] of the days, it is not proper [to celebrate the liturgy of Basil the Great]."[74] Regarding Presanctified Liturgy, which is of Gregory the Dialogue, our most honest father, pope of Rome,[75] we command that it be cele-

---

[73] Though in current practice, BAS is celebrated on the mornings of Holy Thursday and Holy Saturday, in fact it is an evening service celebrated with the Vespers of the holy day, as part of a vigil. The current practice, though centuries old, marks a radical departure from tradition. This is especially true for Holy Saturday. The theological and liturgical tradition of the Church precludes the celebration of a Eucharist on Holy Saturday. The Divine Liturgy of BAS on Holy Saturday, in reality, is part of the Paschal vigil. Originally, it was once the chief liturgy of Great and Holy Pascha. For more on this subject, see Alkiviadis C. Calivas, *Great Week and Pascha in the Greek Orthodox Church* (Brookline, MA, 1992), 51–62, 97–118.

[74] This comment is surprising, inasmuch as both BAS and CHR constitute joyous celebrations of the mystery of the divine economy. Hence they are not celebrated during the weekdays of Great Lent. The Eucharist is considered a feast, and as such it is incompatible with the rule of fasting. Fasting signifies anticipation, the way toward fullness. The Eucharist is the very manifestation of that fullness. The Divine Liturgy is celebrated on Saturdays and Sundays even during Great Lent because they are days of joy. Except for Holy Saturday, every other Saturday is considered a festive day, a day for the Eucharist. Perhaps, as Alexopoulos suggests, this comment is an awkward post-factum attempt to explain the limited use of BAS, which is assigned to the vigils of great feasts, which are preceded by a fast.

[75] The reference is to Pope Gregory the Great, who is called Dialogos. He is counted among the saints of the Orthodox Church.

brated three times a week during the Great Lent. This [liturgy] is one that is celebrated always amomg the Romans. "

It is also known that before the aforementioned father the above liturgies were celebrated during the whole year, that is the [liturgy] of Basil the Great [was celebrated] on every Sunday, the [liturgy] of Chrysostom the Great [was celebrated] on Saturdays, Mondays, Tuesdays, and Thursdays, and the [liturgy] of the Presanctified on Wednesdays and Fridays. However this most holy father with 170 other holy fathers[76] thus divided it up, as we said, as it was revealed by our Lord Jesus Christ. In addition the Presanctified was celebrated on September 14 in the Great Church.[77]

Fr. Alexopoulos is quick to point out that this testimony does not provide hard evidence for his thesis. He also notes that its author or redactor has confused the facts, inasmuch as the two patriarchs, as far as is known, never participated together in a synodical meeting. Nonetheless, both men were ardent iconophiles, and Nikephoros, in particular, played a leading role in the controversy with his writings against the Eucharistic theology of the iconoclasts. Significantly, the testimony attributes the shift from BAS to CHR to Nikephoros and the synod he supposedly led. Thus it attempts to place the shift—and indirectly the reason for it—in the period of the iconoclastic controversy.

The text attributed to Nikephoros, although spurious, provides additional information that sheds light on the liturgical practice of the Church following the period of the iconoclastic controversy (730–843). For example, the text affirms that BAS was once the chief Eucharistic liturgy celebrated every Sunday throughout the year, and that CHR was celebrated weekdays—specifically, on Saturdays, Mondays, Tuesdays, and Thursdays—while PRES was celebrated on Wednesdays and Fridays. Of course, there is no clear evidence that the celebration of the Eucharist occurred daily in every church. We do know, however, that Emperor Constantine IX (1042–1055) provided special subsidies for the support of a daily Eucharist in Hagia Sophia, where hitherto the Divine Liturgy had been celebrated only on Sundays, Saturdays, and feast days.[78]

---

[76] As Alexopoulos notes, there is no known synod at which 170 fathers were in attendance. Perhaps, as Pitra suggests, the number may have been read and transcribed wrongly. Instead of ρο (Greek for 170), the number could easily be read as σο (270), which could refer to the synod of 814.

[77] Alexopoulos, "Influence of Iconoclasm on Liturgy," 133.

[78] George Cedrenus, *Synopsis historiarum*, ed. I. Bekker, 2 vols. (1838–1839), 2:609; and

Significantly, the text of Nikephoros makes no mention of the brevity issue.

A DIFFERENT HYPOTHESIS: THE EFFECTS OF HOLY COMMUNION

The hypothesis of Fr. Alexopoulos caught my interest, especially since I have thought about the subject from time to time but never found the brevity argument compelling, despite the appeal of its pastoral practicality. Alexopoulos sheds new light on the matter, and if his hypothesis is correct, the shift from BAS to CHR probably occurred at an earlier date than previously thought, perhaps as early as the ninth century.

The evidence, however, keeps pointing to a tenth- or eleventh-century date. What is so significant about this period? Could there have been some force at work in the spiritual and intellectual climate of the posticonoclastic period, especially between the tenth and the eleventh century, that prompted the change from BAS to CHR? I believe there was—namely, the trend toward the individualization of worship and of Church life that began to emerge with the revival of monasticism following the iconoclastic controversy.

The shift from BAS to CHR, I submit, was not so much a response to the iconoclasts, or for that matter as a response to human weaknesses (an ever-present pastoral problem that should not be easily discounted) but a response to the individualization of piety and the sacramental life that began to permeate ecclesial life in the tenth and eleventh centuries. The *anaphora* of CHR, as I will show, was better suited to meet these new developments.

THE EMERGENCE OF A NEW ASCETIC SPIRIT

In the aftermath of the iconoclastic controversy, as Aleksandr Kazhdan notes, Byzantine culture became increasingly secular, and societal life was progressively privatized.[79] At the same time the Byzantine monas-

---

PG 121–122. Cited in J. M. Hussey, *Church and Learning in the Byzantine Empire, 867–1185* (New York, 1963), 128. By the late Middle Ages, the Eucharist was celebrated daily in many monastic communities, even though daily communion was not practiced. Most monks communed weekly. Three churches, Hagia Irene, Theotokos Chalkoprateia, and St. Theodore, all of which were in the vicinity of Hagia Sophia, were considered patriarchal churches.

[79] A. P. Kazhdan and Ann Wharton Epstein, *Change in Byzantine Culture in the Eleventh and Twelfth Centuries* (Berkeley, CA 1985), 14, 86.

tery—where communal and individual life was held together in dynamic tension—was losing its cenobitic form.[80] Monastic life was marked by a tendency toward atomization, with its concomitant emphasis on individualism. This new ascetic spirit began to pervade Church life as monasticism came to exert an ever-larger influence on ecclesial affairs.[81]

The tendency toward personal inspiration and salvation was, in some ways, a reaction against the over institutionalization of Church life at the expense of its charismatic dimension. St. Symeon the New Theologian (949–1022), whose life spanned the latter half of the tenth century and the first quarter of the eleventh, became the great exponent of a mystical theology and spirituality that was based on a living experience of God. For him and like-minded churchmen before and after him, "the whole Christian life and its perfection above all, is only a gift of grace, and cannot be lived except in and by the faith that recognizes that grace."[82] The spirituality of St. Symeon was in the tradition of the great Fathers of the Church and espoused the beliefs that the realities of worship and the sacraments are

---

[80] Balsamon, for example, bemoans that in his time few authentic cenobite monasteries survived (*PG* 138:176).

[81] In the aftermath of iconoclasm (723–843), the monasteries—as the bastions and guardians of Orthodoxy during that unsettling period—began to exert power and influence over all aspects and levels of ecclesial life. The "monasticization" of Church life and practice, beginning with the Penthekte Synod (691–692), which introduced celibacy as a requirement for the episcopal office (canon 12), was reinforced during the iconoclastic controversy. The influence of monasteries grew progressively stronger through the ensuing centuries. By the twelfth and the thirteenth centuries, the monastic office had replaced the cathedral office (ᾀσματικὴ ἀκολουθία). As Panayiotis Trempelas points out (*Λειτουργικοί τύποι*, 368), by the end of the twelfth century, monastic practices were considered ideal and worthy of imitation by parish clergy and by the more zealous Christians: "Βαθμίδων ὅμως, ἡ τῶν μοναστηρίων πρᾶξις εὗρε μιμητὰς καὶ μεταξὺ τοῦ κοσμικοῦ κλήρου καὶ μερίδες ζηλωτῶν χριστιανῶν, ἕως οὗ μετὰ τὸ τέλος τοῦ δωδεκάτου αἰῶνος τὸ καθεστὼς τῶν μόνων ἐπεβλήθη πλήρως καὶ ἐν τοῖς πόλεσιν." Some monastic luminaries, such as St. Theodore the Studite, believed and taught that monasticism realized more fully and more perfectly the essential aims of the Christian life. See John Meyendorff, *Byzantine Theology* (New York, 1979), 56. While monasticism is an integral and vital part of the Church, it does not constitute the Church. Parish and monastery are part of the same Church. Both communities are grounded on the same faith. The members of both communities are engaged in the same struggle to become "partakers of the divine nature" (2 Pet. 1:4); both are bound by the same ethical values, and both have the same eschatological anticipation. What distinguishes the two communities is the degree of their asceticism. A cloistered existence is not an indispensable precondition for the spiritual life.

[82] Louis Bouyer, "Byzantine Spirituality," in *The Spirituality of the Middle Ages*, by J. Leclerq, F. Vandenbroucke, and L. Bouyer (New York, 1968), 567.

accomplished only through a conscious experience of God, and that the institutional Church must always find and define her purpose and mission only in the Spirit, who dwells in it, sanctifying both the Church and each of its members.[83]

The tendency toward atomization that began to emerge in the posticonoclastic period affected liturgical piety, the way worship was perceived and practiced, especially within monastic circles. Devotional rules and practices and even the Eucharist were looked upon as ascetical acts, as aids and instruments in the struggle against the passions. Fr. Alexander Schmemann explains this development as follows:

> Without being noticed the receiving of Communion was subordinated to individual piety, so that piety was no longer determined by the Eucharist as in the early Church. Instead the Eucharist became an "instrument" of piety, an element of asceticism, an aid against demons ... The change here was not a reduction of the place and significance of Communion, but a change in the way it was experienced and understood. It was included within the general scheme of monasticism as an ascetical act and a form of self-edification. In this sense the view of the Eucharist as the actualization of the Church (as the people of God) and as the eschatological feast of the Kingdom was not denied or disputed. The emphasis simply shifted to the view of Communion as a beneficial ascetical act. The Eucharistic service was now seen as an opportunity to receive spiritual succor. This was in fact a change in liturgical piety.[84]

---

[83] It is essential to maintain a healthy balance between the institutional and the charismatic dimensions of Church life. Unbridled and unfocused enthusiasm is as dangerous to the Church as rigid and unresponsive institutionalism is. The former gives rise to the creation of exclusivity and elitism—of a church within a church—which openly or covertly denigrates authority and undermines the hierarchical structures of the Church. Rigid institutionalism, on the other hand, renders the structures and institutions of the Church lifeless and unresponsive to the stirrings of the Spirit.

[84] Alexander Schmemann, *Introduction to Liturgical Theology*, 141–142. The understanding of Communion as an ascetical, edifying, and instrumental act is especially reflected in the service of Holy Communion (ἀκολουθία τῆς Θείας Μεταλήψεως), various versions of which are found in the *euchologion, ieratikon*, and *horologion* of the local Churches. The service originated in monastic circles in the late Middle Ages. In the current Greek liturgical books, the service is composed of several elements: a canon whose acrostic is the Greek alphabet; three Psalms (22/23, 23/24, and 115/116), which contain Christological, soteriological, and Eucharistic themes; several hymns and didactic verses; and a series of nine prayers attributed to various authors: St. Basil the Great (2), St. John Chrysostom (3), St. John of Damascus (2), St. Symeon the Translator (1), and St. Symeon the New Theologian (1). In addition to the Service of Holy Communion, the liturgical books also contain

I believe that the *anaphora* of CHR, which casts the effects of Communion in more personal terms than does BAS, which emphasizes the ecclesial and the eschatological effects of Communion, appeared more attractive and more compatible with the new, more individualized emphases in liturgical piety.

The Fruits of Communion in the Anaphora

ENUMERATING THE GIFTS OF COMMUNION

The Divine Liturgy celebrates and communicates the mystery of salvation. The *anaphora* especially expresses both the purpose for which the Church celebrates the Divine Liturgy and the gifts the people hope to receive from it. These gifts are recounted in several prayers of the Divine Liturgy. More specifically, they are recounted in the *anaphora* following the consecration of the Eucharistic elements and before the intercessions.

The tradition of enumerating the effects, benefits, or fruits of Communion in the *anaphora*—a trait common to all ancient liturgies—is based on the New Testament references to the Eucharist. The synoptic Gospels, for example, stress the covenantal[85] and messianic nature of the Eucharist,

---

a set of prayers under the rubric "Prayers of Thanksgiving after Holy Communion." The prayer of thanksgiving attributed to St. Symeon the Translator serves as an example of seeing Communion as an aid in the spiritual struggle: "You who gladly gave me your flesh for nourishment; who are fire to consume the unworthy: burn me not, my Creator, but search out my members. Quicken my reins and my heart. Let your flame devour the thorns of all my transgressions. Purify my soul. Sanctify my thoughts. Knit firm my bones. Enlighten my senses. Pierce me with your fear. Be my continual shield. Watch over and preserve me from every word and deed that corrupts the soul. Purge me and wash me clean and adorn me. Order my ways, give me understanding, and enlighten me. Make me a temple of your Holy Spirit and no more a habitation of sin, that as from fire all evil, every passion, may flee from me who through Holy Communion am become a place for your dwelling. I bring unto you all the saints to make intercession ... Receive their prayer, O merciful Christ, and make your servant a child of light ... You only are the brightness of our souls, gracious Lord..."

[85] The covenantal nature of the Eucharist, which the synoptic gospels and St. Paul emphasize, implies forgiveness. The renewal of the covenant indicates the wondrous intervention of God in Jesus Christ by which a new bond, a new covenant, is established between God and people, a new relationship by which the law of God is interiorized and forgiveness is granted. "Behold, the days are coming says the Lord, when I will make a new covenant with the house of Israel and the house of Judah ... But this is the covenant which I will make ... I will put my law within them and I will write it upon their hearts; and I will be the their God, and they shall be my people ... for I will forgive their iniquity, and I will remember their sin no more" (Jer. 31:31–34; cf. Heb. 8:8–12).

which means that the Eucharist confers communion with God and grants a taste of future blessings. In addition to these gifts, the Gospel of Matthew adds another, "forgiveness of sins," which is assigned to the Cross and by extension to the Eucharist, through which the life-giving benefits of the "once for all" (ἐφάπαξ) sacrifice of the Cross are continuously present and communicated.[86]

In the discourse on the Bread of Life (John 6:22–59), which is replete with Eucharistic imagery, the Gospel of John maintains that the Eucharist is true food (John 6:55) and that eating the Flesh and drinking the Blood of Christ in faith results in an intimate union with him: "He who eats my flesh and drinks my blood abides in me, and I in him" (John 6:56). Communion also grants eternal life and ensures the resurrection at the eschaton: "He who eats my flesh and drinks my blood has eternal life, and I will raise him up at the last day" (John 6:54).

St. Paul, whose writing provides the earliest account of the Lord's Supper, emphasizes the eschatological character of the Eucharist: "For as often as you eat this bread and drink the cup, you proclaim the Lord's death until he comes" (1 Cor. 11:26). Moreover, he encourages the faithful to exercise discernment, fraternal love, and vigilance, and warns them against partaking of the Eucharist unworthily: "Whoever, therefore, eats the bread or drinks the cup of the Lord in an unworthy manner will be guilty of profaning the body and blood of the Lord. Let a man examine himself ... For anyone who eats and drinks without discerning the body eats and drinks judgment upon himself" (1 Cor. 11:27–29).

For St. Paul the Eucharist is also the source of ecclesial unity, which involves the union of the faithful with Christ but also of the faithful among themselves. Through the Eucharist the Church transcends all barriers. "The cup of blessing which we bless, is it not a participation in the blood of Christ? The bread which we break, is it not a participation in the body of Christ? Because there is one bread, we who are many are one body, for we all partake of the one bread" (1 Cor. 10:16–17). St. Paul also emphasizes

---

[86] See the descriptions of the Last Supper in Matt. 26:26–29; Mark 14:22–25; Luke 22:14–20. The words of institution in both BAS and CHR are not direct quotes from any of the four narratives of the Last Supper found in the synoptic gospels or in the First Letter to the Corinthians. Instead, they constitute a distinct liturgical formula based on the four texts. Both BAS and CHR attach the words "for the forgiveness of sins" to the Bread and the Cup, words that are found only in the Gospel of Matthew and then only in relation to the Cup.

the real presence of Christ in the Eucharistic elements, inasmuch as Christ identified himself with the bread and wine at the Last Supper: "the Lord Jesus on the night when he was betrayed took bread, and when he had given thanks, he broke it, and said, 'This is my body which is for you. Do this in remembrance of me.' In the same way also the cup, after supper, saying, 'This cup is the new covenant in my blood. Do this, as often as you drink it, in remembrance of me'" (1 Cor. 11:23–25). Thus at every Eucharistic celebration, Christ is present to his people.

THE EFFECTS OF COMMUNION IN FIVE EARLY DOCUMENTS

The following texts from five early liturgical documents demonstrate how the effects of Communion described in the Scriptures were eventually and systematically incorporated into liturgical texts.

The *Didache of the Twelve Apostles*, a first-century document that belongs to the genre called church orders, contains what some believe to be the oldest Eucharistic prayer.[87] It reads, in part, as follows:

> With regard to the Eucharist, give thanks in this manner: First, for the cup: We thank you, our Father, for the holy vine of David your servant, which you have revealed to us through Jesus your Child.[88] Glory be yours through all ages. Then for the bread broken: We thank you, our Father, for the life and knowledge, which you have revealed to us through Jesus your Child. Glory be yours through all ages. Just as the bread broken was first scattered on the hills, then was gathered and became one, so let your Church be gathered from the ends of the earth into your kingdom, for yours is glory and power through all ages.[89]

Another important church order, composed of material from different sources and geographical areas, while purporting to reflect the liturgical usages of the Church of Rome, is the early third-century *Apostolic Tradition* of

---

[87] Church orders are a genre of early Christian literature claiming to offer authoritative apostolic teachings and directives on matters of liturgical practice, canonical discipline, and moral conduct. For the history and contents of the genre and of the individual documents, including those cited here, see Bradshaw, *The Search for the Origins of Christian Worship*, 73–97.

[88] The original Greek uses the word παῖς, which can be interpreted to mean "child" or "servant." Most scholars prefer the word *child* when it is used for Christ.

[89] The translation of this text and those of the four that follow are from Lucien Deis, *Springtime of the Liturgy* (Collegeville, MN, 1979), 74–75. The book "presents the principal texts relating to the Christian liturgy from its beginnings to the fourth-fifth century." vii.

Hippolytus of Rome. Its *anaphora* reads, in part, as follows:

> And we pray you to send your Holy Spirit on the offering of your holy Church, to bring together in unity all those who receive it. May they be filled with the Holy Spirit who strengthens their faith in the truth. May we be able thus to praise and glorify you through your Child Jesus Christ.[90]

The *Liturgy of the Apostles Addai and Mari*, which some believe is an early third- and others a fifth-century document, contains these words:

> May your Holy Spirit come, Lord, may he rest upon this offering of your servants, may he bless and sanctify it, so that it may win for us, Lord, the forgiveness of offenses and the remission of sins, the great hope of the resurrection of the dead, and new life in the kingdom of heaven with all those who have been pleasing to you.[91]

The *Didascalia of the Twelve Apostles* is another third-century church order whose anonymous author was a bishop in northern Syria. The preamble of the treatise is of special interest. While it is not a prayer, the fruits of salvation it enumerates are mentioned in different terms in various Eucharistic prayers.

> Plantation of God, holy vineyard of his catholic Church, you the chosen who have put your confidence in the simplicity of the fear of the Lord, you who have become, through faith, heirs of his everlasting kingdom, you have who have received the power and gift of his Spirit, who have been armed by him, who have been strengthened in fear, you who share in the pure and precious blood poured out by the great God, Jesus Christ, you who have received the freedom to call the almighty God, Father, who are coheirs and friends of his beloved Son: listen to the teaching of God, all you who hope in his promises and wait (for their fulfillment).[92]

Another example comes from the *Apostolic Constitutions*, a late fourth-century church order in eight books that purports to be the work of the holy Apostles, compiled and promulgated by Clement of Rome (ca. 96). Though the document was held in esteem by many early ecclesiastical writers, it was rejected by the Penthekte Synod (691–692) as semi-Arian. The same synod, however, received the last chapter (47) of book 8 of the *Constitutions*, which contains eighty-five canons, the so-called Apostolic

---

[90] Ibid., 131.
[91] Ibid., 163.
[92] Ibid., 169.

Canons. Hence the synod noted, "on account of certain spurious passages destitute of piety ... interpolated long ago by the heterodox to the detriment of the Church ... We have suitably weeded out such ordinances in furtherance of the edification and security of the most Christian flock."[93] Book 8 of the *Constitutions* also contains the text of a Eucharistic liturgy that was never used liturgically. In spite of that, the document provides important information on liturgical matters and usages of the fourth century in Syria and Constantinople. The Eucharistic text in the *Constitutions*, as it relates to the *epiclesis* and the benefits of Communion, contains the following words:

> Send down upon this sacrifice your Holy Spirit, witness of the sufferings of the Lord Jesus, that He may make of this bread the Body of your Christ and the cup the Blood of your Christ. May those who share in it be strengthened in devotion, obtain forgiveness of sins, be delivered from the devil and his errors, be filled with the Holy Spirit, become worthy of your Christ, enter into possession of eternal life, and be reconciled with you, almighty God.[94]

The gifts, effects, benefits, or fruits of Communion recounted in these five texts highlight different emphases of the tradition. Two of the texts stress the ecclesial benefits of Communion, especially the unity of the Church and of its members. The others emphasize more personal effects, such as reconciliation, forgiveness of sins, remission of offenses, assurance of the resurrection, and new and eternal life in the Kingdom. Significantly, the invocation of the Holy Spirit or mention of his power, gift, and communion is found in four of the five documents.

THE FRUITS OF COMMUNION IN BAS AND CHR

In keeping with tradition, the *anaphora* in both BAS and CHR also specifies the fruits of Communion. The difference in the gifts listed in each of these

---

[93] See canon 2 of the Penthekte Synod: *Rudder*, 294. See also Ioannis Fountoulis, Θεία Λειτουργία τῶν Ἀποστολικῶν Διαταγῶν, Κείμενα Λειτουργικῆς 13 (Thessaloniki, 1978), 7. Fountoulis introduces the reader to the *Apostolic Constitutions* and provides the text of the Eucharistic liturgy in the original Greek, found in book 8 of the *Constitutions*. He refines the text with the necessary additions from book 2 of the *Constitutions*, as well as from the *Mystagogical Catecheses* of St. Cyril of Jerusalem and the writings of St. John Chrysostom. Saints Cyril and Chrysostom were contemporaries of the anonymous author of the *Constitutions*. On occasion, and under the supervision of Fountoulis, this liturgy was celebrated in the chapel of the Theological School of the University of Thessaloniki for instructional and devotional purposes.

[94] *Constitutions*, book 8, 12:39. Deis, *Springtime of the Liturgy*, 234–235. See also Fountoulis, Θεία Λειτουργία τῶν Ἀποστολικῶν Διαταγῶν, 50.

CHAPTER TWO: FROM THE LITURGY OF ST. BASIL TO ST. JOHN C.

liturgies, I believe, played the key role in the shift from BAS to CHR. Before proceeding to the analysis of my hypothesis, let me cite the effects of Holy Communion as they are recounted in the received text of the two liturgies.

Similarities and Differences in BAS and CHR

COMMUNION OF THE HOLY SPIRIT

BAS

And unite us all to one another who become partakers of the one Bread and the Cup, may we be united with one another in the communion of the Holy Spirit. Grant that none of us may partake of the holy Body and Blood of your Christ to judgment or condemnation; but that we may find mercy and grace with all the saints who through the ages have pleased you: forefathers, fathers, patriarchs, prophets, apostles, preachers, evangelists, martyrs, confessors, teachers, and every righteous spirit made perfect in faith; especially with our most holy, pure, most blessed, and glorious Lady, the Theotokos and ever-virgin Mary, Saint John the prophet, forerunner, and baptist, the holy glorious and most honorable Apostles, saint (N) whose memory we keep this day, and all Your saints through whose supplications visit us, O God.

ΒΑΣ

Ἡμᾶς δὲ πάντας, τοὺς ἐκ τοῦ ἑνὸς ἄρτου καὶ τοῦ ποτηρίου μετέχοντας, ἑνώσαις εἰς ἑνὸς Πνεύματος Ἁγίου κοινωνίαν, καὶ μηδένα ἡμῶν εἰς κρῖμα, ἢ εἰς κατάκριμα ποιήσαις μετασχεῖν τοῦ ἁγίου σώματος, καὶ αἵματος τοῦ Χριστοῦ σου, ἀλλ' ἵνα εὕρωμεν ἔλεον καὶ χάριν μετὰ πάντων τῶν ἁγίων, τῶν ἀπ' αἰῶνός σοι εὐαρεστησάντων, προπατόρων, πατέρων, πατριαρχῶν, προφητῶν, ἀποστόλων, κηρύκων, εὐαγγελιστῶν, μαρτύρων, ὁμολογητῶν, διδασκάλων, καὶ παντὸς πνεύματος δικαίου ἐν πίστει τετελειωμένου. Ἐξαιρέτως τῆς παναγίας, ἀχράντου, ὑπερευλογημένης, ἐνδόξου, Δεσποίνης ἡμῶν, Θεοτόκου, καὶ ἀειπαρθένου Μαρίας, τοῦ ἁγίου Ἰωάννου, προφήτου, προδρόμου καὶ βαπτιστοῦ, τῶν ἁγίων ἐνδόξων καὶ πανευφήμων Ἀποστόλων, τοῦ ἁγίου (τοῦ δεῖνος), οὗ καὶ τὴν μνήμην ἐπιτελοῦμεν, καὶ πάντων σου τῶν Ἁγίων, ὧν ταῖς ἱκεσίαις ἐπίσκεψαι ἡμᾶς, ὁ Θεός.

CHR

So that they may be to those who partake of them for vigilance of soul, forgiveness of sins, communion of Your Holy Spirit, fulfillment of the Kingdom of heaven, confidence before You, and not in judgment or condemnation. Again we offer this spiritual worship for those that repose in the faith,

ΧΡΥΣ

Ὥστε γενέσθαι τοῖς μεταλαμβάνουσιν εἰς νῆψιν ψυχῆς, εἰς ἄφεσιν ἁμαρτιῶν, εἰς κοινωνίαν τοῦ Ἁγίου σου Πνεύματος, εἰς βασιλίας οὐρανῶν πλήρωμα, εἰς παρρησίαν τὴν πρὸς σέ, μὴ εἰς κρῖμα ἢ εἰς κατάκριμα. Ἔτι προσφέρομέν σοι τὴν λογικὴν ταύτην λατρείαν ὑπὲρ τῶν ἐν πίστει ἀναπαυσαμένων

forefathers, fathers, patriarchs, prophets, apostles, preachers, evangelists, martyrs, confessors, ascetics, and for every righteous spirit made perfect in faith; especially for our most holy, pure, most blessed, and glorious Lady, the Theotokos and ever-virgin Mary, Saint John the prophet, forerunner, and baptist, the holy glorious and most honorable Apostles, Saint (N) whose memory we commemorate today, and all Your saints, through whose supplications visit us, O God.

προπατόρων, πατέρων, πατριαρχῶν, προφητῶν, ἀποστόλων, κηρύκων, εὐαγγελιστῶν, μαρτύρων, ὁμολογητῶν, ἐγκρατευτῶν, διδασκάλων, καὶ παντὸς πνεύματος δικαίου ἐν πίστει τετελειωμένου, ἐξαιρέτως τῆς παναγίας, ἀχράντου, ὑπερευλογημένης, ἐνδόξου, Δεσποίνης ἡμῶν Θεοτόκου καὶ ἀειπαρθένου Μαρίας, του Ἁγίου Ἰωάννου, προφήτου προδρόμου καὶ βαπτιστοῦ, τῶν ἁγίων, ἐνδόξων, καὶ πανευφήμων Ἀποστόλων, του ἁγίου (τοῦ δεῖνος) οὗ τὴν μνήμην ἐπιτελοῦμεν, καὶ πάντων σου τῶν ἁγίων, ὧν ταῖς ἱκεσίαις ἐπίσκεψαι ἡμᾶς, ὁ Θεός.

Even a cursory reading of these two texts reveals that the fruits, benefits, or effects of Holy Communion are different for those who receive the Gifts. The *anaphora* of BAS emphasizes the ecclesial dimensions of Holy Communion, while the *anaphora* of CHR gives greater prominence to personal benefits.

It is also clear that in both BAS and CHR, "communion of the Holy Spirit" (2 Cor. 13:14) is the fundamental gift and key to understanding the effects of Holy Communion because God's saving activity is accomplished and perfected by the Holy Spirit. By the Holy Spirit the Church remembers, experiences, receives, and transmits the entire work of salvation wrought by Christ. "In the power of the Spirit," writes Fr. Boris Bobrinsky, "this memorial of the Church is creative: it transcends space and time, makes us contemporaries [of Christ] ... contemporaries, that is, of the One who is, who was, and who is to come ... The Holy Spirit leads us into the intimacy of the trinitarian life, through Christ, toward the Father."[95] Or as St. Irenaeus taught, "Through the Spirit [we] ascend to the Son, and through the Son to the Father."[96]

The Holy Spirit sanctifies and transforms the Church—a community of sinners—into the Body of Christ, the people of God. Every Divine Liturgy is a renewal and a confirmation of the constant coming of the Holy Spirit, who is ever present in the Church, animating it and perfecting each of its members. At the Eucharist, we become Spirit bearers so that we may receive the

---

[95] Boris Bobrinsky, *The Mystery of the Trinity* (Crestwood, NY, 1999), 184, 194.
[96] St. Irenaeus, *Against Heresies*, V, 36.2.

risen and exalted Christ, the gift of the Father to the Church and the world.

The whole action of the Divine Liturgy depends on the Holy Spirit because he makes the crucified, risen, and glorified Christ present to us in the Eucharistic elements. Through his transforming and sanctifying power, the bread and wine of the Eucharist become, in a real but mysterious way, the Body and Blood of Christ—which is to say, the living Christ present in all his fullness—through which our entire being is nourished and transfigured. By partaking of the holy Gifts, we pass from sin to righteousness and from death to life. Communion in the glorified and deified human nature of Christ, made available to us in the sacramental food and drink, is both the distinct and the ultimate gift that the Father gives to his people.[97]

At the Divine Liturgy, as at every sacrament, the Holy Spirit acts to make us Christ-bearers and transparencies of God. In Christ we discover and actualize our true humanity because Christ is both perfect God and perfect Man. He is the archetype of the authentic human being. He draws us into a sacred world of infinite possibilities that we may discover our full potential and true destiny. When we partake of the divine Mysteries—the consecrated Bread and Cup—worthily and in faith, we are united to Christ and through him to one another. Day by day, as the divine image in us is perfected by grace, God's love permeates our being. We learn to love as God loves us, unconditionally. Led by grace to live a life worthy of the calling to which we have been called, with all lowliness, meekness and patience, we forbear one another in love (Eph. 4:1–3). Hearts are softened, differences are overcome, sins are forgiven, barriers fall, love prevails. By receiving Christ, we receive one another. Eucharistic *koinonia* is not just a personal communion with Christ. It is also communion with one another—members of the one Body of the risen Lord.

To fully comprehend what our union in and with Christ means, two things are required of us. We must nurture a deep personal love for Christ. This comes about through an active prayer life, both personal and communal, by reading and contemplating the Word of God in the Scriptures, by preserving the Orthodox faith in our hearts, by keeping the commandments, and by "thinking and doing all those things that are pleasing to God."[98] We must also be conscious of the presence of the Holy Spirit dwell-

---

[97] See John Meyendorff, *Byzantine Theology* (New York, 1979), 138–140, 201–206.
[98] Prayer before the Gospel in both BAS and CHR.

ing in our hearts (Rom. 8:1–27). We do this through the constant remembrance of God that leads to the ever-deepening and joyful conversion of the heart. A heart that seeks the face of the Lord (Ps. 26/27:8–9) is a heart filled with joy and gladness, with peace, with hope, and with love.

Fruits of Communion in BAS

Those who partake of the one Bread and the Cup and thereby actualize the Church in a given place and time, according to the *anaphora* of BAS, receive essentially two gifts: the communion (*koinonia*) of the one Holy Spirit, by which the unity of God's people is continually accomplished, and the realization of the eschatological hope to find mercy and grace together with the saints with whom we constitute the Church. "And unite us all to one another who become partakers of the one Bread and the Cup in the communion of the one Holy Spirit … that we may find mercy and grace with all the saints who through the ages have pleased you."

The Holy Spirit makes Christ and his salvific work present to the people at the Eucharist. The divine Bridegroom of the Church calls his people to sit together with him in the heavenly places that he may communicate to them his divine life. The Divine Liturgy is more than a sacred drama. It is the very presence of the risen and glorified Christ in the midst of his people: "Lord Jesus Christ, our God, hear us from your holy dwelling place and from the glorious throne of your kingdom. You are enthroned on high with the Father and are invisibly present among us. Come and sanctify us and let your pure Body and precious Blood be given to us by your mighty hand…"[99]

In the present age between the two comings of Christ, the Eucharist is always the messianic banquet, the meal of the Kingdom, the time and place in which the heavenly joins and mingles with the earthly. Christ's embracing love, which purifies, enlightens, perfects, and deifies, is made manifest to those who heed the call to share in the marriage supper of the Lamb (Rev. 19:9). At the Eucharist the members of the community—on either side of death—are joined to one another in love. They are initiated into the depths of the corporate life of the Church as communion in God and with God. The Divine Liturgy, from the kiss of peace to the communion of the holy Gifts, in the words of St. Maximos the Confessor, "prefigures and

---

[99] Prayer before the elevation of the Lamb.

portrays the concord, unanimity, and identity of views which we shall all have among ourselves in faith and love at the time of the revelation of the ineffable blessings to come."[100]

By sharing the Body and Blood of Christ, we are made to realize sacramentally the eschatological mystery of unity in diversity. Through the Eucharist, the divisive and destructive powers of Satan are being continuously defeated, and the life of selfless love is being revealed to God's holy people that they may learn it and be moved to abide in it. The unique and unrepeatable persons that comprise the Church are united to Christ and through him to one another by the grace of the Holy Spirit. Thus at its core, Holy Communion becomes an act of self-emptying love, through which the authenticity of all relationships is evaluated and judged, and the Holy Spirit actualizes the Church as the eschatological community in the flow of time and history.

Authentic, sacrificial, self-giving love, however, is a gift. It comes from Christ, who "emptied himself ... and became obedient unto death, even death on a cross" (Phil. 2:7–8). Empowered, nourished, and perfected by Christ's grace and mercy the community is called to become an epiphany of divine love, an image of the new humanity gathered around the risen Lord and living under his rule. Whoever desires to be in Christ must learn to love unconditionally as Christ loves. Where love is deficient, absent, or ambivalent, sin enters and abides in the hearts of men to disrupt relationships and disfigure communities. Whoever does not strive to remain true to his or her baptismal pledge—to renounce continually the false values and lies of the fallen world and to remain steadfast in the truth—risks condemnation because he or she does not properly discern or honor the Body of Christ.

In addition to the gift of unity, BAS specifies several other effects of Holy Communion. These are recounted in the pre-Communion prayer,[101] which

---

[100] St. Maximos the Confessor, *Mystagogy*, 17.
[101] The pre-Communion prayer in BAS reads as follows: "Our God, the God who saves, you teach us justly to thank you for the good things which you have done and still do for us. You are our God who has accepted these Gifts. Cleanse us from every defilement of flesh and spirit, and teach us how to live in holiness by your fear, so that receiving the portion of your holy Gifts with a clear conscience we may be united to your Christ. Having received them worthily, may we have Christ dwelling in our hearts, and may we become the temple of Your Holy Spirit. Yes, our God, let none of us be guilty before these, your awesome and heavenly mysteries, nor be infirm in body and soul by partaking them unworthily. But enable us, even

introduces the Lord's Prayer and the prayer of thanksgiving after Communion. The pre-Communion prayer first reiterates the effects of Communion mentioned in the *anaphora*. In addition to these, the prayer states that the holy Gifts constitute "a provision for eternal life" and equip those who partake of them with "an acceptable defense at the awesome judgment seat of Christ." The prayer also says that those who partake worthily "have Christ dwelling in their hearts" and become "the temple of the Holy Spirit." Furthermore, communicants are given a foretaste "of the eternal good things" the Lord has prepared for those who love him.

The prayer of thanksgiving after Communion also expands the effects of Communion in BAS. Accordingly, God grants the recipients of the holy Mysteries "sanctification and healing of souls and bodies." Additionally, God is implored that "the communion of the holy Body and Blood of Christ may become for us faith unashamed, love unfeigned, fullness of wisdom, healing of soul and body, repelling of every hostile adversary, observance of [the] commandments, and an acceptable defense at the dread judgment seat of Christ."

While the forgiveness of sins is not explicitly mentioned as a fruit of Communion in the *anaphora* of BAS, it is implied in the pre-Communion prayer: "Cleanse us from every defilement of flesh and spirit, and teach us to live in holiness by your fear, so that receiving the portion of your holy Gifts with a clear conscious we may be united with the holy Body and Blood of your Christ." Forgiveness of sins is stated explicitly in the prayer of inclination: "Make them worthy to partake without condemnation of these, your most pure and life-giving mysteries, for the forgiveness of sins and for the communion of the Holy Spirit." Forgiveness is also a theme in the prayer of the *proskomide*, which anticipates the *anaphora*. The celebrant prays, "Accept us as we draw near to your holy altar ... that we may be worthy to offer you this spiritual sacrifice without the shedding of blood, for our sins and for the transgressions of your people." Then, after enumerating the offerings

---

up to our last breath, to receive a portion of your holy Gifts worthily, as a provision for eternal life and as an acceptable defense at the awesome seat of your Christ, so that we also, together with all the saints who through the ages have pleased you, may become partakers of your eternal good things, which you, Lord, have prepared for those who love you. And make us worthy, Master, with confidence and without fear of condemnation, to dare call you, the heavenly God, Father, and to say: Our Father...."

and sacrifices of Abel, Noah, Abraham, Moses, Aaron, and Samuel,[102] the celebrant asks that God in his goodness accept the Church's offering—the Bread and the Cup—as he accepted the true worship of the holy Apostles, which is none other than the Eucharist.

The Eucharist—a sacrifice without the shedding of blood—supersedes the offerings and sacrifices of Old Testament. The Eucharist brings us before the unutterable mystery of the Father's inscrutable love and initiative: the offering of his Son in the Holy Spirit for the salvation and life of the world. The mystery of this once-for-all offering of the Father is actualized time and again at every Divine Liturgy. This does not suggest, however, that the Eucharist attempts to reclaim past events; it does not repeat what is unique and unrepeatable. Christ is not slain anew and repeatedly, for he died once for all. At each Eucharist, the Holy Spirit changes the offering of the Church into a reality that remains constant, into the Body of Christ that was sacrificed once for all and now lives. The Eucharist renders present and makes manifest the sacrifice of Christ that is being eternally celebrated upon the altar in heaven. As the great High Priest and Intercessor, Christ the God-Man continues in a state of sacrifice before the Father, making intercession on our behalf and uniting our prayers with his own (Heb. 7:24, 9:24).[103]

Finally, the prayer at the *skeuophylakion* (prothesis), which concludes the service, summarizes the meaning of the entire Eucharistic act:

> The mystery of your dispensation (οἰκονομία), O Christ our God, has been accomplished and perfected as far as it is in our power. We have had the memorial of your death. We have seen the type (τύπος) of your resurrection. We have been filled with your unending life. We have enjoyed your inexhaustible delight (τρυφή)[104] which in the world to come be well pleased to give to us all through the grace of your holy and good and life-giving Spirit, now and forever.

To increase the sense of awe in the worshipper, BAS inserts a warning in the *epiclesis*: "Grant that none of us may partake of the holy Body and

---

[102] Genesis 4:4, 8:20, 22:13; Exodus 29, 30; 1 Kings (1 Sam.) 11:15. Sacrifices in the Old Testament were offered to serve three interrelated purposes: to acknowledge God's authority through the offering of a gift, to effect union with God, and to make amends. See John J. Castelot and Aeired Cody, "Religious Institutions of Israel," in *The New Jerome Biblical Commentary* (Englewood Cliffs, NJ, 1990), 1272.

[103] See Calivas, *Aspects of Orthodox Worship*, 184–188.

[104] In some texts, the original Greek word τρυφή was inadvertently changed to τροφή, which means "food."

Blood of your Christ to judgment or condemnation." The warning, as we shall see, is fashioned after St. Paul's admonition to the Corinthians (1 Cor. 11:27–29)[105] and constitutes an implicit call to repentance and a plea for God's mercy and acceptance. Grace and mercy come to those who partake of the holy Gifts worthily, who discern the Lord's Body, who abstain from evil deeds, cleave to good works, and keep the commandments.

FRUITS OF COMMUNION IN CHR

In CHR the fruits, or effects, of Holy Communion are related to the expectation of the Kingdom and are meant to contribute to the continuous spiritual regeneration of the believers, sustaining them in a state of watchfulness and expectation and at the same time giving them a portion, a foretaste of the blessedness that is to come.

The Church is not only an eschatological community; it is also a historical community. The historical, visible community is truly the Church against which the powers of hell shall not prevail. The historical community is located within time and has not yet crossed the ultimate frontier. It is still part of the process whereby the Body reaches completion (Eph. 4:13). Hence, the members of the community need always to be vigilant, to live in expectation of the Parousia, so that they may be found worthy to receive the promises of the age to come.

The gifts of the age to come are not beyond our reach, to be bestowed and enjoyed at some point in the distant future. The Kingdom of God is at hand (Mk. 1:15). It is already in our midst, inaugurated by Christ through his incarnation, death, resurrection, and glorification. Between his two comings, Christ is present to his Church in the Holy Spirit to communicate the ineffable blessings of the Kingdom. Through the Eucharistic elements, Christ nourishes all who are in a state of readiness and watchfulness with his own glorified flesh and makes them "partakers of the divine nature" (2 Pet. 1:4). Through the Eucharist, eternity penetrates our finitude (John 6:54); the life of the Trinity flows in us. We become God-bearers (θεοφόροι) and are given the pledge of the future life and Kingdom.

Characteristically, the effects of Communion in CHR are enumerated in a clear, direct, concrete, and concise but full manner, which makes them

---

[105] St. Paul's admonition to the Corinthians is especially evident in the pre-Communion prayer of BAS: "Yes, our God, let none of us be guilty before these, your awesome and heavenly Mysteries, nor be infirm in soul and body by partaking of them unworthily."

appealing to the learned and to the unlearned, to monastics and to people in the pews. The *anaphora* of CHR lists seven effects of Communion: vigilance of soul, forgiveness of sins, communion of (in) the Holy Spirit, fulfillment of the Kingdom of heaven, filial boldness and confidence, defense against unworthiness, which brings judgment and condemnation, and rejoicing in the saints.[106] Of the seven fruits, "communion of the Holy Spirit" is primary.

In CHR, the Eucharist manifests the gifts of the future age and bestows them on the believers through the communion of the Holy Spirit. The Holy Spirit unites those who partake of the Eucharist to Christ and keeps them vigilant, alert, and sober, in expectation of the Kingdom, which is yet to come in fullness. The Holy Spirit is also the source of forgiveness (John 20:22–23), purification, and sanctification. He is the pledge and guarantee of the future life, the "fulfillment of the Kingdom of heaven" in the words of the *anaphora* of CHR. Moreover, those who partake of Holy Communion are given the courage to come before God with boldness and confidence as sons and daughters because the Holy Spirit, as St. Paul tells us, "bears witness with [their] spirit that [they] are children of God, and if children, then heirs, heirs of God and fellow heirs with Christ" (Rom 8:16–17).

The gifts mentioned in the *anaphora* of CHR are repeated in the pre-Communion prayer. The gift of "vigilance of soul," however, is omitted. In its place the prayer asks that communicants approach the "the holy and spiritual Table with a clear conscience." In addition to the remission of sins, the prayer also asks for "forgiveness of transgressions." And instead of the "fulfillment" it asks for the "inheritance of the Kingdom of heaven."

In the prayer of thanksgiving after Communion, the communicants express thanks for the gift of the "heavenly and immortal Mysteries." And so strengthened, they ask God to "direct our ways in the right path, establish us firmly in your fear, guard our lives, and make our endeavors safe."

The theme of unity, explicit in BAS, is implied in CHR. Communion of the Holy Spirit always results in our union with God and with one another because the Holy Spirit regenerates us and clothes us with Christ. If we are united to Christ, we are also most assuredly united to one another as members of the one Body, the Church.

---

[106] See Robert Taft, "The Fruits of Communion in the *Anaphora* of St. John Chrysostom," in Analecta Liturgica 15 = Studia Anselmiana 105 (Rome, 1991), 275–302; Taft, *Precommunion Rites*, 103–128.

FORGIVENESS OF SINS IN BAS AND CHR

The gift of forgiveness is mentioned in BAS, CHR, and other ancient liturgies. In fact, both BAS and CHR are replete with prayers and petitions for forgiveness of voluntary and involuntary sins and transgressions. This is made possible because the unrepeatable mystery of the Cross, by which sins are forgiven, is continuously present in the Eucharist. This, however, as Robert Taft observes, poses a problem.[107] If forgiveness is an effect of Communion, why do we also ask to receive Communion "not in judgment or condemnation?"

Forgiveness is a fruit of Communion, but not for everyone. Sin as such does not render a person unworthy of the Eucharist—"for there is no one who lives and does not sin"—but the willful, habitual attachment to sin, especially to grave or mortal sin, does. Forgiveness is a benefit of Communion for sins that do not lead to death: "All wrongdoing is sin, but there is sin which is not mortal" (1 John 5:17). Whether Communion brings forgiveness and sanctification or judgment and condemnation depends on the interior state and disposition of the recipient. Those burdened with heinous sins and addictions ought not to approach Communion because they would be "guilty of profaning the body and blood of the Lord" (1 Cor. 11:27). Grievous sins cut persons off from the Church. Restoration requires that they be subject to the discipline of penance, lest they be condemned of partaking of the Eucharist unworthily. Canonical exclusion or self-exclusion from Communion is not meant to punish but to heal and save the sinner and to uphold the dignity of the sacrament and the integrity of the community. Consider the words of St. Nicholas Cabasilas:

> Does all sin bring death to man? No indeed, but mortal sin only; that is why it is called mortal. For according to St. John [the Evangelist], there are sins which are not mortal. That is why Christians, if they have not committed such as would cut them off from Christ and bring death, are in no way prevented, when partaking of the holy mysteries, from receiving sanctification, not in name alone, but in fact, since they continue to be living members united to Christ ... The priest gives Communion to anyone who comes, but Christ only to those who are

---

[107] Taft, "Fruits of Communion," 188–190; Taft, *Precommunion Rites*, 115–117.

worthy. It is clear that there is only one who perfects and sanctifies souls through the sacrament, the Savior ... The only thing which the living who are still in the flesh have which the departed have not is this: that even those who are unworthy of Communion seem to receive sanctification since they physically receive the sacrament ... Yet the ability to receive the sacrament unworthily does not bring holiness to the living; on the contrary, it entails a dreadful punishment ... [Christ] unites us to himself and makes us each, according to our individual merit and purity, sharers through Him in those graces which are His own.[108]

The new life in Christ acquired through baptism is continually nurtured and advanced through the Eucharist. Holy Communion is a divine gift for God's holy people (τὰ ἁγία τοῖς ἁγίοις). But those whom the Divine Liturgy calls holy, as St. Nicholas Cabasilas avers, "are not only those who have attained perfection, but also those who are striving for it without having yet obtained it. That is why Christians, if they have not committed such sins as would cut them off from Christ and bring death, are in no way prevented, when partaking of the holy Mysteries, from receiving sanctification ... For no one has holiness of himself; it is not the consequence of human virtue, but comes for all from [God] and through him."[109]

"Let a Man Examine Himself, and So Eat" (1 Cor. 11:28)

THE NEED FOR DISCERNMENT

Both BAS and CHR include warnings against the unworthy reception of Communion, not only as a result "of individual guilt that comes from secret sins, [but also] of the socio-ethical demands of a life in common."[110] The warnings are meant to protect the Eucharist from undiscerning and ill-prepared communicants, who "are guilty of profaning the body and blood of the Lord" (1 Cor. 11:27). Holy Communion produces its proper

---

[108] Nicholas Cabasilas, *Commentary on the Divine Liturgy* (4:36; 5:43, 44), 89, 99, 100. Cf. St. John Chrysostom, *Homily on Matthew*, 82:5: "It is necessary to be diligent in every way, for no small punishment has been established for those who partake unworthily ... Let there be no Judas present, no one avaricious. If anyone is not a disciple, let him go away. The table does not receive such ones ... Let no inhuman person be present, no one who is cruel and merciless, no one at all who is unclean."
[109] Nicholas Cabasilas, *Commentary on the Divine Liturgy* (4:36), 88, 89.
[110] Taft, *Precommunion Rites*, p. 128.

fruits when it is received "with the fear of God, with faith, and with love," as the call to Communion declares. To the unworthy, Communion is a consuming fire, "For he who eats and drinks without discerning the body eats and drinks judgment upon himself" (1 Cor. 11:28–29).

Warnings against improper dispositions, such as impiety, immorality, irreverence, fractiousness, spiritual laziness, lack of charity, and habitual attachments,[111] have been connected to the act of Communion from the beginning, as St. Paul tells us in his First Epistle to the Corinthians (11:18–32). Such warnings were repeated by early Christian writers. After the peace of Constantine, when restored apostates and converts of convenience flooded the Church, many Church Fathers emphasized and multiplied the warnings. St. John Chrysostom, for example, urged the faithful to partake of the Eucharist frequently, but he also cautioned and exhorted them to approach the divine Mysteries with care and correct dispositions:

I observe many partaking of Christ's body lightly and incidentally, from custom and ordinance, rather than from consideration and understanding ... And how shall you stand before the judgment seat of Christ, you who dare to receive his body with polluted hands and lips? You would not presume to kiss a king with a foul-smelling mouth, but you kiss the King of Heaven with a reeking soul? That is an outrage ... That I may not, then, be the means of increasing your condemnation, *I entreat you, not to stay away, but to make yourselves worthy, both of being present and of receiving* ... It is indolence alone that renders us unworthy.[112]

As a result of such stern admonitions, new vocabulary began to be attached to the Eucharist.[113] It began to be referred to as the "dread and awesome mystery" and "a consuming fire fearful to approach." These dire warnings against unworthiness contributed to the gradual decline of frequent Communion among the general populace. It also led to the perception of Holy Communion as a reward for pious feelings and actions, as something which is earned through meritorious acts, especially strict fasting.

---

[111] When he was asked, "What is the greatest sin?," St Basil reportedly replied, "The one that enslaves you."
[112] St. John Chrysostom, *Homily on Ephesians*, 3. Emphasis mine.
[113] Taft, *Precommunion Rites*, 130n7, 179–180.

PRE-COMMUNION AND POST-COMMUNION PRAYERS

Pre-Communion and post-Communion prayers are an integral part of the three Byzantine Eucharistic liturgies and other ancient rites. The Pauline admonition gave rise to the creation of many communion prayers in addition to those of the Divine Liturgy for use by those preparing to receive Holy Communion. Beginning with the tenth century and more especially with the emergence of rubrical manuals (διατάξεις) in the twelfth and thirteenth centuries, one or more of these extraliturgical devotional prayers gradually found their way into the communion ritual of the liturgy. The Barberini Codex, for example, includes no pre- or post-Communion prayers other than those that were integral to the rite from the beginning.[114] Robert Taft has traced the origins and use of these devotional prayers in the sixth volume of his monumental study on the history of the Divine Liturgy of St. John Chrysostom.[115]

Some of these devotional prayers have survived in two collections, the first of which is the set of prayers for the communion of the clergy that has been interpolated into the text of the three Divine Liturgies.[116] The number of prayers and hymns of this collection varies both in the manuscript tradition and in the printed editions of the Divine Liturgy. The basic structure in the official Greek text was established in the fourteenth century by Philotheos Kokkinos, twice patriarch of Constantinople (1353–1355 and 1364–1376), in his Διάταξις τῆς Θείας Λειτουργίας (Manual of rubrics for the Divine Liturgy), which gained universal recognition as part of the liturgical reforms that took place in the wake of the Hesychast controversy.[117]

---

[114] See Parenti and Velkovska, *L'eucologio Barberini*, 19–22 (BAS) and 38–41 (CHR).
[115] Taft, *Communion, Thanksgiving, and Concluding Rites*, 142–203.
[116] In some parishes, it is customary for the congregation to recite some or all of these prayers together. However, it amounts to a form of ritual formalism for people not receiving Communion to engage in the reading of these prayers. Moreover, these prayers emphasize the personal over the ecclesial character of Holy Communion. One is left with the impression that Communion is a personal and not a communal act.
[117] The set of pre-Communion prayers contains two prayers, two didactic verses, and three hymns. The most famous of the prayers is the first: "I believe and confess, Lord that you are truly the Christ, the Son of the living God, who came into the world to save sinners, of whom I am the first … I also believe that this is truly your pure Body and that this is truly your precious Blood. Therefore…." This prayer was originally two separate confessional prayers, one concerning the divinity of Christ and the other the real presence. The two prayers were eventually joined to form a single devotional prayer. One of the three hymns of the set is the well-known *troparion* of Great and Holy Thursday, "Receive me today, Son of

The second collection is the anthology of private prayers found in the Office of Holy Communion (Ἀκολουθία τῆς Θείας Μεταλήψεως),[118] which represents the Athonite tradition of the fourteenth century. Medieval monastic *typika* are replete with instructions to the monks to read the prescribed devotional prayers in preparation for Holy Communion.[119] The Office of Holy Communion is also used by many devout faithful.

The communion prayers in these collections share a common characteristic. For the most part, they are penitential in nature and reflect an understanding of the reception of Holy Communion more as an act of individual piety and as an aid against the passions and much less as an act of God's people for the realization of the Church as the Body of Christ.

Holy Communion and the Saints

THE SAINTS IN BAS AND CHR

Rejoicing in the saints and vigilance of soul, two additional effects of Communion in the *anaphora* of CHR, were, I suggest, especially important and attractive to monastics. Indeed, the gift of vigilance of soul falls squarely in the area of monastic spirituality. But first, a word on the saints is in order.

Both BAS and CHR mention the saints in relation to the effects of Communion. The relationship, however, is understood and expressed differently in the two liturgies. In BAS, Holy Communion brings earthly worshippers into fellowship with the saints—the firstfruits of Christ's redemption—to share with them God's mercy and grace, both now and in the age to come. As St. Nicholas Cabasilas tells it, "It is as if one said: Give us the grace which You have already given to the saints; sanctify us as You have already sanctified so many of our race."[120]

God, as a partaker of your Mystical Supper." The cautionary Pauline language in the prayers is exemplified by one of the didactic verses, attributed to St. Symeon the Translator, which reads as follows: "Behold I draw near to Holy Communion, O Creator; burn me not as I partake thereof, for You are a fire that consumes the unworthy. Cleanse me, therefore, from every stain." The set of pre-Communion prayers appears in a variety of forms in the printed editions of the Divine Liturgy, some of which contain the entire repertoire, while others have a shorter version of it.

[118] See note 84 of this chapter.
[119] See Taft, *Communion, Thanksgiving, and Concluding Rites*, 163.
[120] Cabasilas, *Commentary on the Divine Liturgy* (4:33), 85.

In CHR, on the other hand, the holy Gifts are offered in honor of the saints, in whom the Church delights and at whose supplications the assembly awaits God's blessings and protection ("Again, we offer this spiritual worship for those who repose in the faith, forefathers, fathers, patriarchs, prophets, apostles ... through whose supplications, O God, bless us"). In CHR, the offering of the Gifts on behalf of the saints is understood as an act of love for the saints and as thanksgiving for the sanctification that God has bestowed upon them. The saints are models of Christian living beloved by all Christians, but especially by monastics, who claim the saints as the inspiration for their spiritual labors and struggles in the pursuit of holiness.

The saints teach us about the transforming power and perennial value of the Gospel. Their passion for God, their fortitude and devotion, their simplicity and meekness serve as powerful examples of Christian living. They fill us with hope. Hence, the offering of the Gifts in honor of the saints is also an act of intercession. We call upon the saints to intercede on our behalf and to ask God to pour out upon the people his favor and blessings. St. Nicholas Cabasilas explains the offering in honor of the saints this way:

These gifts belong also to the saints ... when they [the gifts] are offered to God in thanksgiving for the glory and perfection, which he has bestowed upon them. The offerings belong to God, since they are offered to him; as a divine aid, they belong also to the faithful, who have need of them; and they belong also to the saints, insofar as they are offered to God in their honor ... Just as we give alms for love of Christ, so the sacrifice is offered for love of the saints; because we love them dearly, we consider their good as our own, and congratulate them on their happiness as if we were sharers in their honor.[121]

The practice of commemorating the saints at the Divine Liturgy has a long and venerable history. It is rooted in the belief of the early Christians that even the righteous do not obtain the fullness of the Kingdom until the final general resurrection at the Parousia, when all creation will be renewed and transformed by the glory of God. Until then, the souls of the righteous are believed to dwell in a place called Paradise.[122] The first to enter Paradise,

---

[121] Ibid. (5:48), 106.
[122] Paradise, like the "bosom of Abraham," is a favorite theme in the burial rites of the Church. Both denote the place where the souls of the righteous repose, awaiting the final judgment. For example, the hymns and prayers of the burial service contain the following

according to tradition, was the repentant crucified thief: "And [Jesus] said to him, 'Truly I say to you, today you will be with me in Paradise'" (Luke 23:43).

The effect of Holy Communion in relation to the saints as expressed in BAS ("that we may find mercy and grace with all the saints") could be interpreted to mean that those who partake of the divine Mysteries share the blessedness (μακαριότητα) of Paradise with the saints in the present age so that they may also stand with them at the Parousia to gain the fullness of the promised blessings of the Kingdom. The same interpretation could be applied to CHR, insofar as the holy Gifts are offered for the saints, who, while blessed, still await the Parousia and the arrival of the fullness of the Kingdom.[123] St. Nicholas Cabasilas expresses this truth succinctly with these words: "In the [saints] the Church finds that which she seeks and obtains that for which she has prayed—the Kingdom of heaven."[124]

THE CATEGORIES OF SAINTS

In addition to the Theotokos, St. John the Baptist, the holy Apostles, and the saint or saints of the day, who are mentioned by name, both liturgies also commemorate collectively ten groups, or categories, of saints.[125] In the

---

expressions: "The choir of the saints has found the fountain of life and the door of Paradise. May I also find the way through repentance." "Give rest, O God, to your servant and place him (her) in Paradise where the choir of the saints and the righteous will shine as the stars of heaven." "Grant rest to him (her) in the bosom of Abraham and number him (her) among the righteous."

[123] The commemoration of the saints concludes with an intercession: "Through whose supplications visit us, O God." The intercessory character of the commemoration led eventually to the offering of incense immediately following the consecration of the holy Gifts, when the saints and the dead are remembered. The incense is offered at this point in the Divine Liturgy in honor of the saints and on behalf of all who repose in the faith—not in honor of the holy Gifts, as is sometimes mistakenly thought. The practice was inspired by the passage in the Book of Revelation that relates the offering of incense to the prayers of the saints: "And another angel came and stood at the altar with a golden censer; and he was given much incense to mingle with the prayers of all the saints upon the golden altar before the throne; and the smoke of the incense rose with the prayers of the saints from the hand of the angel before God" (Rev. 8:3–4; cf. 5:8, 6:9).

[124] Cabasilas, *Commentary on the Divine Liturgy* (4:33), 84.

[125] The ten categories of saints are: forefathers, fathers, patriarchs, prophets, apostles, preachers, evangelists, martyrs, confessors, and ascetics (in CHR) or teachers (in BAS). It is possible to conclude that the first four categories refer to the righteous in the Old Testament, the next three to those of the New Testament era, and the final three to faithful witnesses and holy ones who have graced the Church throughout the ages.

earliest manuscripts, however, the list contained only nine groups.[126] The category *forefathers*, now listed first in both BAS and CHR, was added in a number of later manuscripts, and from there it passed into all the printed editions of the liturgies. Of the ten categories, the last one differs in the two liturgies. BAS contains the category *teachers* (διδάσκαλοι), while CHR has the category *ascetics* (ἐγκρατευταί).

The charisma and office of teacher mentioned in BAS appears several times in the New Testament, together with other offices, such as apostle, prophet, preacher, and evangelist (Rom. 12:7; 1 Cor. 12:28; Eph. 4:11; 1 Tim. 2:7), all of which are recorded in both liturgies. These offices are identified with the early Church. They equipped it for ministry and contributed to its growth, as did the martyrs (the faithful witnesses who shed their blood for the love of Christ and his Church) and the confessors (who suffered for the faith but not to the point of death).

The ascetics in CHR represent,[127] in the first instance, all devout Christians who exercise the virtue of self-control (ἐγκράτεια), which is a fruit of the Spirit (Gal. 5:23).[128] All Christians, crucified with Christ in faith and baptism, are called to be ascetics (ἐγκρατευταί); called to mortify, to "put off the old nature with its practices [and to] put on the new nature which is being renewed in knowledge after the image of its creator" (Col. 3:9–10). Correct belief and true faith must show themselves in moral uprightness and interior excellence. And self-control is the fundamental virtue by which the impulses of the passions are defeated and the virtues of patience, love, and hope are strengthened.

From the earliest days of the Church, certain men and women felt a special calling to lead an intense interior life. Many of these people recast their relationships and their existence by giving themselves up to the ideal of voluntary chastity and poverty in an effort to realize union with Christ.

---

[126] See, for example, Parenti and Velkovska, *L'eucologio Barberini*, 36.

[127] The category ἐγκρατευταί should not be confused with the Encratites (ἐγκρατεῖς, ἐγκρατῆται, ἐγκρατῖται), who comprised the several early Christian heretical groups that espoused extreme ascetic practices and doctrines and in whose circles the apocryphal gospels and acts were produced.

[128] Cf. 2 Pet. 1:5–7, which reads, in part, "For this very reason make every effort to supplement your faith with virtue, and virtue with knowledge, and knowledge with self-control (ἐγκράτεια), and self-control with steadfastness, and steadfastness with godliness, and godliness with brotherly affection, and brotherly affection with love."

They nourished their new way of life with ceaseless prayer and lived alone or in small desert communities. In time, the appellation ἐγκρατευταί came to be identified with those Christians who voluntarily made themselves eunuchs spiritually for the sake of the Kingdom—that is, monastics, hermits, anchorites, and ascetics. Hence, most English translations of CHR use the word *ascetics* for the category ἐγκρατευταί, the ideal charismatic figures who disengaged themselves from the bonds of the flesh and the world in a type of martyrdom.

Given the ascendancy of monasticism in the posticonoclastic period, it is not difficult to imagine the attraction of CHR in monastic circles for the prominent place it accords to the ἐγκρατευταί in the *anaphora*.

Vigilance of Soul

THE MEANING AND PURPOSE OF VIGILANCE

The first effect of Communion listed in the *anaphora* of CHR is νῆψιν ψυχῆς (vigilance of soul), a fruit or benefit that is peculiar to this liturgy and to the Liturgy of St. Mark the Evangelist.[129] The Liturgy of St. Mark, as is well known, was the chief liturgy of Alexandria and Egypt at least through the twelfth and thirteenth centuries, when the liturgies of Constantinople replaced it. It is not without some interest that this liturgy also mentions vigilance of soul as an effect of Communion. Egypt, which gave birth to this Divine Liturgy, also gave birth to the great early monastic movements. The deserts of Egypt became the home of the anchorites and hermits who practiced the interior ideal of prayer absorbed in God and kept watch, maintaining guard over the heart and the intellect. According to St. Hesychios the priest (eighth or ninth century),

> Watchfulness (νῆψις) is a spiritual method which, if sedulously practiced over a long period, completely frees us with God's help from impassioned thoughts, impassioned words and evil actions. It leads, in

---

[129] See Ioannis Fountoulis, Θεία Λειτουργία τοῦ Ἀποστόλου Μάρκου, Κείμενα Λειτουργικῆς 3 (Thessaloniki, 1970), 47. See also *The Ante-Nicene Fathers*, vol. 7 (Grand Rapids, MI, 1951), 558. The effects of Communion in the *anaphora* of this liturgy are recounted as follows: "That all of us who partake thereof may tend unto faith, vigilance (νῆψιν), healing, temperance (σωφροσύνη), sanctification, the renewal of soul, body, and spirit, communion (κοινωνία) in the blessedness of eternal life and incorruptibility, the glory of your most holy Name, [and] the forgiveness of sins."

so far as this is possible, to a sure knowledge of the inapprehensible God, and helps us to penetrate the divine and hidden mysteries. It enables us to fulfill every divine commandment in the Old and New Testaments and bestows upon us every blessing of the age to come.[130]

It has been suggested that the correct reading in CHR should contain the word νίψιν (washing or purification), a homonym of νῆψιν (vigilance). Either word would fit the text,[131] especially if we were to compare the effects of Communion in the *anaphora* with those in the pre-Communion prayer, which introduces the Lord's Prayer and reiterates the effects of Communion. The pre-Communion prayer reads as follows:

> We entrust to You, loving Master, our whole life and hope, and we ask, pray, and entreat: make us worthy to partake of your heavenly and awesome Mysteries from this holy and spiritual Table *with a clear conscience*; for the remission of sins, forgiveness of transgressions, communion of the Holy Spirit, inheritance of the Kingdom of heaven, confidence before You, and not in judgment or condemnation. And make us worthy, Master, with confidence and without fear of condemnation, to dare call you, the heavenly God, Father, and to say: Our Father...

While the words *vigilance of soul* do not appear in the pre-Communion prayer, it contains the phrase "with a clear [or clean, pure] conscience" (μετὰ καθαροῦ συνειδότος). The phrase could support either νῆψις or νίψις inasmuch as a "clear or clean conscious" is the result of a vigilant, purified soul. Although vigilance of soul is closely identified with the spiritual methods and practices of monastics, it is also a desirable gift for all Christians. The pursuit of a virtuous and holy life requires all Christians to keep watch over their inward thoughts and fantasies. On the other hand, purification of soul is no less a desired outcome of Communion for every Christian, whether secular or monastic, inasmuch as the pure in heart have been promised the vision of God (Matt. 5:8).

The ancient manuscripts of CHR, the oldest Slavonic version of CHR, and the received text support the reading "vigilance of soul." However, the Barberini Codex,[132] the oldest extant manuscript of a Constantinopolitan

---

[130] St. Hesychios the Priest, "On Watchfulness and Holiness," in *The Philokalia*, trans. G. Palmer, P. Sherrard, and K. Ware (London, 1979), 1:162. For the text of the treatise in Modern Greek, see Ἁγίου Ἡσυχίου Πρεσβυτέρου, "Λόγος περί νήψεως και αρετής," in *Φιλοκαλία τῶν Ἱερῶν Νηπτικῶν*, trans. A. G. Galitis (Thessaloniki, 1984), 1:180–215.
[131] Taft, "Fruits of Communion," 287.
[132] I am grateful to Fr. Pavlos Koumarianos, who very kindly provided me with a copy of a photographic reproduction of this eighth-century manuscript.

euchologion, written in uncial, poses a problem that may or may not be significant. The Barberini Codex, at least as I read it, contains the word νίψην, which of course is an incorrect spelling of both νῆψιν and νίψιν. F. E. Brightman, in his edition of BAS and CHR from Barberini 336, transcribed the word as νῆψιν.[133] This is also true of Parenti and Velkovska: their critical edition of the Barberini Codex also transcribes the word as νῆψιν,[134] inverting the ι and the η of νίψην so that the spelling conforms to that found in the later manuscripts. They probably did so with good cause.

Misspellings in Greek manuscripts are not infrequent. It could be that the copyist simply made an error. He meant to write νῆψιν but did not; he confused and misplaced the vowels. However, one could also argue that the copyist meant to write νίψιν. Inadvertently, he turned νίψιν from a third-declension word into the first-declension word νίψην, as has happened with most, if not all, third-declension words in Modern Greek. Of course, to have weight, this argument requires that the entire manuscript be searched for similar examples. If by chance, however, νίψις is the correct reading in the Barberini Codex, then one must ask when, why, and by whom was it replaced in later manuscripts with νῆψις. In the medieval period, νῆψις was almost exclusively identified with monastic spirituality.[135]

Whether Communion imparts "vigilance of soul" or "purification of soul" is probably of little consequence for the common communicant, since either one is a most desired and wondrous gift. There is, however, a preference for the word *vigilance*, based chiefly on the manuscript tradition. It is also the preferred reading for another reason. As Taft and others indicate,[136] the word appears in the writings of St. John Chrysostom. "Chrysostom speaks often of ψυχή νήφουσα and once of νῆψις ψυχῆς and refers to the Eucharistic chalice as the pure and spiritual cup that gives νῆψιν and σωφροσύνη (vigilance and temperance)"[137]—two words, I might add, that are found in the Divine Liturgy of St. Mark.

---

[133] F. E. Brightman, *Liturgies Eastern and Western*, vol. 1, *Eastern Liturgies* (Oxford 1896, 1967), 330.
[134] Parenti and Velkovska, *L'eucologio Barberini*, 35.
[135] See, for example, Antonios Papadopoulos, Θεολογική γνωσιολογία κατά τούς νηπτικούς πατέρες (Thessaloniki, 1977), 53–56.
[136] For the references see Taft, "Fruits of Communion," 286–287.

The word νῆψις (vigilance, watchfulness, sobriety) has a long history in the spiritual tradition of the Church. Its roots are found in the New Testament.[138] It became a favorite word of the Desert Fathers and later of the Hesychasts. In fact, the great spiritual elders who practiced the virtue of vigilance, or spiritual sobriety, and instilled it in others are called neptic fathers (νηπτικοί πατέρες).

In monastic spirituality, νῆψις signifies an attitude of attentiveness that leads to the knowledge of God. Through it the soul is kept in constant wakefulness and watchfulness, in ready defense against the wiles of the devil. Vigilance of soul is obviously a highly regarded and highly desirable effect of Communion for all Christians, but most especially for those who keep perpetual vigil through the prayer of the heart. What greater aid could one ask for than to keep the soul alert, pure, and receptive to the influence of the Holy Spirit? Clearly, the gift of vigilance of soul in CHR makes its *anaphora* especially appealing to all who are engaged in the spiritual struggle, particularly to those who are immersed in the spirituality of the desert.

Conclusion

I conclude this preliminary report with two brief observations. By the time of the iconoclastic controversy, most people had ceased to participate frequently in Holy Communion. Most monastics, on the other hand, communed regularly—at least weekly, and sometimes more often. Further, as Georgios Filias has shown, the priestly prayers of the Divine Liturgy were being said by then inaudibly. It made little difference, therefore, to the congregation which Divine Liturgy was being celebrated. To the common worshipper, BAS and CHR sounded and looked the same. But the fine distinctions in the two liturgies were not lost on the clergy, especially the better educated among them and, most important, the decision makers: the influential abbots, bishops, and patriarchs.

In the posticonoclastic period, many bishops and patriarchs came out of monastic circles that practiced a vigorous spiritual life whose entire strategy involved νῆψις, the guarding of the heart. It is not difficult, therefore, to imagine that for such men, CHR was the preferred Eucharistic formulary, especially because of the clear, direct, concrete, and concise manner in which it presents the effects of Communion.

---

[138] See, for example, Matt. 26:41; 1 Cor. 15:34; 1 Thess. 5:5–6; 2 Tim. 4:5; 1 Pet. 5:8.

These effects, cast in relatively personal terms, appeared more compatible with the liturgical piety of the times, which saw worship and the sacraments as ascetical acts, as aids and instruments in the struggle against the passions. The effects of Communion in CHR also made it easier to teach the people about the meaning of Communion, relating it to the uncertainties of everyday life and to the anticipation of the Kingdom.

The reasons for the shift from BAS to CHR await further investigation and clarification. Whatever the reason for the shift, one thing is clear. Through the centuries, the Divine Liturgies of BAS and CHR have informed the mission of the Church and inspired its social consciousness. They have shaped the ecclesial identity of the people and nourished the spiritual life of countless souls who have hungered and thirsted for righteousness. Through BAS and CHR alike, Orthodox people have learned to stand humbly before God with joyous and thankful hearts to celebrate in faith and receive the gift of salvation by communing the Body and Blood of Christ "for the forgiveness of sins and life eternal."[139]

---

[139] The phrase is used at the distribution of Holy Communion.

3

LITURGICAL RENEWAL
ORTHODOX THEOLOGY AND LITURGICAL PRAXIS IN RELATION TO THE SACRAMENT OF THE DIVINE EUCHARIST

Since the Church lives, affirms, and celebrates its formative events through the liturgy,[140] liturgical renewal and reform constitute an imperative. Attempts at reforming the liturgy have been suggested and

---

[140] This essay is an expanded version of a paper for the Symposium on Liturgical Renewal, which was to take place in Athens in autumn 2007 under the auspices of the Church of Greece. The topic was given to me by the organizing committee of the Special Synodical Committee on Liturgical Renewal. The assigned title in the original Greek was "Η λειτουργική αναγέννηση στην Ορθόδοξη θεολογία και λειτουργική πράξη σε σχέση με το μυστήριο της Θείας Ευχαριστίας." The word αναγέννηση is usually translated "regeneration," "rebirth," or "revival." It is also translated "renaissance," especially when referring to the humanistic revival movement that swept through Europe between the fourteenth and seventeenth centuries. I chose to use the synonym *renewal* because it is the more frequently used term in the English-speaking world when referring to the revitalization of the Church's worship. Because of the sudden illness of His Beatitude Archbishop Christodoulos, the symposium was initially postponed and subsequently cancelled upon his death. Thanks to the initiatives of Archbishop Christodoulos, the Church of Greece has mounted an exceptional pioneering effort devoted to the study of the Orthodox liturgical tradition with an eye toward renewal through a series of symposia. The papers presented at these gatherings continue to be published and disseminated through a multivolume series bearing the title Σειρά ποιμαντική βιβλιοθήκη. Among the volumes of the series, three are of special interest to the topic at hand: *Λατρεύσωμεν εὐαρέστως τῷ Θεῷ: Τὸ Αἴτημα τῆς Λειτουργικῆς Ἀνανεώσεως στὴν Ὀρθοδόξη Ἐκκλησία* (vol. 7), which deals with various facets of liturgical renewal; *Τὸ μυστήριο τῆς Θείας Εὐχαριστίας* (vol. 8), which deals with topics related to the holy Eucharist and the Divine Liturgy; and *Ἱερουργεῖν τὸ Εὐαγγέλιον: Η Ἁγία Γραφή στὴν Ὀρθόδοξη λατρεία* (vol. 10), which deals with topics related to the lectionary. In addition, the Church of Greece publishes another series that is also dedicated to the study of various liturgical topics under the title Σειρά λογική λατρεία. Of special interest is another collection of papers on the Divine Eucharist that were read at a clergy seminar in the Metropolis of Drama, in northern Greece, *Ἡ Θεία Εὐχαριστία: Εἰσηγήσεις–πορίσματα ἱερατικοῦ συνεδρίου τῆς Ἱερᾶς Μητροπόλεως Δράμας* (Drama, 2003). For more on the nature of liturgical reform and Byzantine liturgical

tried at different times and in different places with varying degrees of success.[141]

Let me explain what I mean by *liturgical renewal and reform*. Liturgical renewal is the process by which one seeks to recover the authentic tradition of the Church's worship, while the reform, revision, modification, or adaptation of the liturgy is the means by which this tradition is incorporated into the liturgical rites and the cultures of people who worship now.[142] Through the analytical study of the liturgical tradition, the Church seeks to maintain the vitality of worship by measuring the effectiveness of the various elements that constitute the sacred rites, testing their ability to speak

---

development, see Thomas Pott, *Byzantine Liturgical Reform: A Study of Liturgical Change in the Byzantine Tradition*, trans. Paul Meyendorff (Crestwood, NY, 2010).

[141] For the seventeenth-century reforms among the Orthodox in Kiev and Moscow, see Pott, *Byzantine Liturgical Reform*, 242–260; Paul Meyendorff, *Russia, Ritual, and Reform: The Liturgical Reforms of Nikon in the 17th Century* (Crestwood, NY, 1991); and Nikolaos Ioannidis, "Προσπάθειες λειτουργικής ανανεώσεως στην Ορθόδοξη Εκκλησία της Ρωσίας," in Λατρεύσωμεν εὐαρέστως τῷ Θεῷ, 307–326. For the attempts at liturgical renewal and reform by the Church of Romania, see Konstantinos Karasaidis, "Προσπάθειες λειτουργικής ανανεώσεως στη Ορθόδοξη Εκκλησία της Ρουμανίας," in Λατρεύσωμεν εὐαρέστως τῷ Θεῷ, 327–357. A major effort at renewal and reform in the Greek Church was attempted by the Ecumenical Patriarchate in 1932 with the establishment of a special committee charged with reviewing and correcting the Church's liturgical books. See Ioannis Fountoulis, "Τὸ πρόβλημα τῆς ἀναθεωρήσεως τῶν λειτουργικῶν βιβλίων τῆς Ὀρθοδόξου Ἐκκλησίας," in Λατρεύσωμεν εὐαρέστως τῷ Θεῷ, 123–139.

[142] I use the words *liturgy* (λειτουργία) and *worship* (λατρεία) interchangeably to denote the whole range of the Church's services, and I apply the term *Divine Liturgy* (Θεία Λειτουργία) to designate the sacrament of the Eucharist. The liturgy includes all the sacred rites of the Orthodox Church that comprise her rule of prayer, which is commonly known as the Byzantine rite. The Byzantine rite includes three Eucharistic liturgies and other sacramental rites, a daily office, an assortment of occasional services including burial rites, and a considerable collection of prayers of blessing and supplication—all of which are contained the Church's several official liturgical books. The Byzantine rite also has a lectionary system, a calendar of feasts and fasts, various ceremonials and symbols, and a highly developed and distinctive form of the liturgical arts. For a concise analysis of the development of the Byzantine rite, see Robert F. Taft, *The Byzantine Rite: A Short History* (Collegeville, MN, 1992); and his essays, "The Structural Analysis of Liturgical Units: An Essay in Methodology" and "How Liturgies Grow: The Evolution of the Byzantine Divine Liturgy," in Taft, *Beyond East and West: Problems in Liturgical Understanding* (Rome, 2001), 187–232. See also Panagiotis Trembelas, Λειτουργικοὶ τύποι Αἰγύπτου καὶ ἀνατολῆς (Athens, 1961), 323–349; Theodore Koumarianos, "Βασικοί σταθμοί στην διαμόρφωση της λειτουργικής τάξεως (τυπικού) της Ορθόδοξου Εκκλησίας," in Λατρεύσωμεν εὐαρέστως τῷ Θεῷ, 85–122; Hugh Wybrew, *The Orthodox Liturgy: The Development of the Eucharistic Liturgy in the Byzantine Rite* (Crestwood, NY, 1990).

convincingly to the hearts and minds of people in their particular cultural contexts in the present historical moment.[143] In fact, the Church's witness and mission to the world suffer from ineffectiveness when its liturgical identity is not in a mode of constant regeneration.[144]

While we draw from the same sources and share a common Orthodox faith and a common liturgical tradition and praxis, our individual perspectives have been conditioned by the history and the culture of the places in which we enact our faith and worship our God, the Holy Trinity consubstantial and undivided. Each of us brings to these discussions a variety of perspectives, all of which have been fashioned and colored not only by scholarship but also by the contexts of our personal lives. My own views have been fashioned largely by my experiences as a parish priest and as a teacher of liturgics within a particular historical, cultural, and ecclesial context: the Greek Orthodox Church in the United States of America.

As Orthodox Christians, we share the fundamental belief that the Church is a living organism, a divine-human institution, the extension and fullness of the incarnation. Since the Church is "ever youthful," to use the phrase of St. Irenaeus, so is the Church's liturgy. It is dynamic and therefore open to change. As the study of liturgy bears out, our liturgical rites—their structures, texts, and rituals—are the products of a long evolutionary process. The forms of Orthodox worship have developed through the centuries by way of organic development—through accretion, addition, deletion, suppression, modification, and restoration. The forms are neither absolute nor immutable but are subject to adaptation and change. Indeed, as Evangelos Theodorou observes, "the most stable characteristic of the Orthodox liturgical tradition is not immobility but its continuous renewal."[145]

---

[143] For a critical and consciousness-raising pedagogical process that can help form a meaningful liturgical identity and disposition in the people, see Charles Gusmer, *Wholesome Worship* (Washington, DC, 1989); Gilbert Ostdiek, *Catechesis for Liturgy: A Program for Parish Involvement* (Washington, DC, 1986). Also see the three volumes by Ioannis M. Fountoulis, *Τελετουργικά θέματα* (Athens 2002, 2006, 2007).

[144] See Petros Vassiliadis, *Lex orandi: Λειτουργική θεολογία και λειτουργική αναγέννηση* (Athens, 2005), 86. This volume contains a series of important essays by Vassiliadis on liturgical renewal, the Eucharist, and the sacramental life of the Orthodox Church.

[145] Evangelos Theodorou, "Παράδοσις και ανανέωσις στην λειτουργική ζωή της Ορθόδοξου Εκκλησίας," in *Λατρευσωμεν ευαρεστως τω Θεω*, 43.

The sacred rites of the Church have expanded, contracted, and changed—sometimes deliberately by decree,[146] other times accidentally, on occasion abruptly, but almost always gradually and imperceptibly.[147] It can be argued that the invention of the printing press, more than any other factor, decelerated the legitimate development of liturgy and that the early printed editions of the sacred rites have, for the most part, determined the form and content of the prevailing rites.[148] In the paragraphs that follow, I deal with three interrelated subjects: (1) a theological reflection on the Eucharist, (2) the purpose and goal of liturgical renewal, and (3) suggestions for the reform of the Divine Liturgy.

A Theological Reflection on the Eucharist

THE CHURCH, THE EUCHARIST, AND THE ESCHATON

In recent years, the Eucharist has become the focus of theological discourse among Orthodox theologians as a result of several factors: the interest shown in the Eucharist and ecclesiology by modern biblical scholars and the members of the Faith and Order Commission of the World Council of Churches (WCC);[149] the gradual recovery of the patristic spirit and vision, with its faithfulness to biblical prophecy, by Orthodox theologians;[150] and

---

[146] A case in point is the *Typikon of the Great Church of Christ* authorized by the Ecumenical Patriarchate of Constantinople and published in 1888. For more on the development of the *typikon*, see Alkiviadis Calivas, *Aspects of Orthodox Worship* (Brookline, MA, 2003), 63–101; Alkiviadis Kalivopoulos (Calivas), Χρόνος τελέσεως τῆς Θείας Λειτουργίας (Thessaloniki, 1982), 27–48.

[147] For examples of liturgical adaptability and change, see Calivas, *Aspects of Orthodox Worship*, 138–161, 193–226.

[148] The first printed editions of the liturgical books now in use by the Greek Church, for example, were based mainly on Greek manuscripts published initially in Italy between the years 1486 and 1587. The editors of these books were usually Greeks in the employment of Italian publishing houses. The subject matter of each volume was selected and arranged in accordance with the judgment of its editors and publishers. This task, however, was accomplished without the benefit of critical research and, above all, without the approbation of the Church.

[149] For an analytical summary of the trends in modern biblical and liturgical studies on the Eucharist, see, for example, Vassiliadis, *Lex orandi*, 135–211.

[150] Fr. Georges Florovsky was the first to issue the call for a return to the Fathers not in blind or servile imitation of them but by restoring the patristic spirit, rekindling the creative fire of the Fathers, and developing their teachings. As a result, Orthodox theology is gradually divesting itself of Western scholasticism.

the work especially of Metropolitan John (Zizioulas) of Pergamon,[151] Fr. Alexander Schmemann,[152] and before them Nikolai Afanasiev,[153] who first coined the term *Eucharistic ecclesiology*. While the implications of the ideas presented by these three scholars and churchmen continue to be debated,[154] the essential principle they espoused remains unchallenged: the Eucharist and the Church are inextricably united. For this reason alone, the renewal and the reform of the Divine Liturgy, the rite by which we celebrate the Eucharist, constitute a pastoral imperative in every generation and age.

Through the works of these three scholars and those of Georges Florovsky, Dumitru Staniloae, John Romanides, John Meyendorff, Panayiotis Trembelas, and more recently Boris Bobrinskoy, Ioannis Fountoulis, Nikos Matsoukas, Petros Vassiliadis, Nenad Milosevic, and Emmanuel Clapsis, Orthodox sacramental theology has been gradually liberated from the influences of Western scholasticism that, among other things, viewed the sacraments as separate entities, independent from one another and from ecclesiology. Thanks to the insights of modern theological thought, we understand more clearly the relationship between liturgy and dogma and

---

[151] See the works of John D. Zizioulas, *Being as Communion: Studies in Personhood and the Church* (Crestwood, NY, 1985); *Eucharist, Bishop, Church: The Unity of the Church in the Divine Eucharist and the Bishop during the First Three Centuries* (Brookline, MA, 2001); *Communion and Otherness*, ed. Paul McPartlan (New York, 2006). See also Zizioulas's many articles in various academic journals, including "Θεία Εὐχαριστία καὶ Ἐκκλησία," in *Τὸ μυστήριο τῆς Θείας Εὐχαριστίας*, 25–47; Paul McPartlan, *The Eucharist Makes the Church: Henri de Lubac and John Zizioulas in Dialogue* (Edinburgh, 1996); Aristotle Papanikolaou, *Being With God: Trinity, Apophaticism, and Divine-Human Communion* (Notre Dame, IN 2006). This last study critically compares the Trinitarian theology and, by extension, the ecclesiology of Vladimir Lossky and John Zizioulas.

[152] See Alexander Schmemann, *Introduction to Liturgical Theology* (Crestwood, NY, 1996); Schmemann, *The Eucharist: Sacrament of the Kingdom* (Crestwood, NY, 1987). See also Thomas Fisch, ed., *Liturgy and Tradition: Theological Reflections of Alexander Schmemann* (Crestwood, NY, 1990).

[153] Nicholas Afanasiev, *The Church of the Holy Spirit*, translated by Vitaly Permiakov (Notre Dame, IN 2012). On the theological thought of Nikolai Afanasiev, see Aidan Nichols, *Theology in the Russian Diaspora: Church, Fathers, Eucharist in Nikolai Afanas'ev* (Cambridge, 1989). For the correctives that Zizioulas offers to the ecclesiology of Afanasiev, see McPartlan, *Eucharist Makes the Church*, 226–235.

[154] See, for example, Calinic (Kevin M.) Berger, "Does the Eucharist Make the Church? An Ecclesiological Comparison of Staniloae and Zizioulas," *St. Vladimir's Theological Quarterly* 51, no. 1 (2007): 23–70; Michael B. Aune, "Liturgy and Theology: Rethinking the Relationship," part I in *Worship* 81, no. 1 (2007): 46–68; and part II in *Worship* 81, no. 2 (2007): 141–169..

between the sacraments and the Church. As Fr. Boris Bobrinskoy reminds us, the Church "is the great sacrament and the mystery of salvation ... [She] makes us participate in the work of Christ that is communicated to us in her, in the Trinitarian economy that deeply permeates the Church in her being, her worship, her witnessing, and her structures."[155]

All these—worship, witnessing, structures—and above all the sacraments constitute the face and the voice of the Church, the very expression of its inner self, the manifestation of its essence, conscience, and mind. Worship—the Eucharist, in particular—as Metropolitan John of Pergamon says, is "an event constitutive of the being of the Church, enabling the Church to be."[156] The Eucharist is not simply one sacrament among many but the central sacrament of the Church, the source and summit of its life.[157] While every sacrament makes us partakers of the risen and glorified Christ, the Eucharist accomplishes this perfectly because, as St. Nicholas Cabasilas tells it, "in it we obtain God Himself, and God is united with us in the most perfect union ... It is not possible to go beyond it or add anything to it ... After the Eucharist there is nowhere further to go. There we must stand, and try to examine the means by which we may preserve the treasure to the end."[158]

Thanks to the pioneering work of the aforementioned theologians, it has been possible to recover and appreciate more fully the biblical and patristic notion that eschatology is inherent in both the Eucharist and the Church. The Holy Trinity works in and through the Church, most especially through the sacraments, to reveal and communicate, here and now, the powers of the Kingdom for which all of creation is destined.

The Church realizes its identity as the community of the Kingdom at the Eucharist. The worshipping community gathered in the unity of faith and love anticipates and manifests iconically the realities of the Kingdom.[159] The

---

[155] Boris Bobrinskoy, *The Mystery of the Trinity* (Crestwood, NY, 1999), 152–153.
[156] Zizioulas, *Being as Communion*, 21.
[157] For the close connection between the Eucharist, the other sacraments, and the Church, see the challenging study of Nenad Milosevic, *To Christ and the Church: The Divine Eucharist as the All-Encompassing Mystery of the Church* (Los Angeles, 2012), which first appeared in Greek under the title *Η Θεία Ευχαριστία ως κέντρον της θείας λατρείας: Η σύνδεσις των μυστηρίων μετά της Θείας Ευχαριστίας* (Thessaloniki, 2005). See also Dumitru Staniloae, *The Sanctifying Mysteries* (Brookline, MA, 2012).
[158] Cabasilas, *The Life in Christ*, 4:2.
[159] See, for example, Maximos the Confessor, *Mystagogia*, chapter 1: "Holy Church bears the imprint and image of God since it has the same activity as he does by imitation and

Eucharist imparts life, and the life it imparts is the life of God, the life of communion with God, who is himself life and communion.[160] Through the Eucharist, the Church is actualized as the Body of Christ by the Holy Spirit. At the Eucharist, the members of the Body continuously receive, nurture, and advance the gift of new life, which was bestowed at baptism, that they might become "partakers of the divine nature" (2 Pet. 1:4). Every Sunday, the first day of the week, on which Jesus rose from the dead, the Church gathers to realize her eschatological fullness through the celebration of the Eucharist, by which the unending day of the Lord, the hope and the salvation of the world, is revealed in time. The Eucharist is the presence of Christ and therefore the manifestation of his Kingdom, which is yet to come in fullness.

THE KINGDOM OF GOD EXISTS IN THE CHURCH

The Kingdom exists in the Church through the Eucharist in at least two ways. First, it constitutes the presence of the risen and glorified Christ among his people, the presence of the one "who is and who was and who is to come" (Rev. 1:4, 8). At the Eucharist, Christ comes to us from the future, from the Kingdom. In the Eucharist, we experience simultaneously two movements: one from the Kingdom, "Come, Lord Jesus" (Rev. 22:20; 1 Cor. 16:22), and the other toward the Kingdom, the Church in pilgrimage, on its way (καϑ' ὁδόν) to the Kingdom.

The Eucharist is the messianic banquet, the marriage supper of the Lamb (Rev. 19:9), at which the heavenly joins and mingles with the earthly. At the Eucharist, as St. Symeon of Thessaloniki says, we experience "the reve-

---

in figure. For God who made and brought into existence all things by his infinite power contains, gathers, and limits them and in his Providence binds both intelligible and sensible beings to himself and to one another ... It is in this way that the holy Church of God will be shown to be working for us the same effects as God, in the same way as the image reflects its archetype. For numerous and of almost infinite number are the men, women, and children who are distinct from one another and vastly different by birth and appearance, by nationality and language, by customs and age, by opinions and skills, by manners and habits, by pursuits and studies, and still again by reputation, fortune, characteristics, and connections: All are born into the Church and through it are reborn and recreated in the Spirit. To all in equal measure it gives and bestows one divine form and designation, to be Christ's and to carry his name. In accordance with faith it gives to all a single, simple, whole, and indivisible condition, which does not allow us to bring to mind the existence of the myriads of differences among them, even if they do exist, through the universal relationship and union of all things with it." *Maximus Confessor: Selected Writings* (New York, 1985), 186, 187.
[160] Zizioulas, *Being as Communion*, 81–82.

lation of eternal life: God with us, both seen and partaken" (Θεὸς μεθ' ἡμῶν ὁρώμενος τε καὶ μεταλαμβανόμενος).[161] Or as Fr. Schmemann taught, the Eucharist is not so much the repetition of Christ's advent into the world as it is the lifting up of the Church into his presence, the participation of the Church in his heavenly glory.[162]

In the Eucharistic *anamnesis* (commemoration), the Church remembers not only the historic events of Christ's life but also his glorification and second coming. The past events of salvation history are remembered and made present, but so also is the future. In Christ, the past and the future are always present realities, for "Jesus Christ is the same yesterday, today, and forever" (Heb. 13:8). At the Eucharist, we experience the fullness of Christ's presence, or as Fr. Bobrinskoy observes, "the Holy Spirit actualizes the plenary and unique presence of Christ in his multiple dimensions: the creative Logos, the Jesus of history, the Christ of glory, the Lord of the Parousia and of the judgment."[163]

The Kingdom exists in the Church in a second way. Every celebration of the Eucharist is a renewal and confirmation of the constant coming of the Holy Spirit, through whom the eschaton breaks into history. The comprehensive renovation and glorious transfiguration of the world in the age to come are already a present reality in the Eucharist through the transformation of the Eucharistic elements—the bread and wine mixed with water—by the Holy Spirit into the Body and Blood of Christ, the risen and reigning Lord. Through the Eucharist the Holy Spirit also acts to vivify the souls of believers and to actualize within them the hidden mysteries of God's Kingdom, joining them to the Triune God in a personal union. Through the Eucharist, people are given to see and experience, to the degree that their heart is pure (Matt. 5:8), the glory of God, which is the eschatological hope and destiny of humankind.

In the Eucharist, the people of God experience the continuous defeat of the divisive powers of the devil and share the eschatological gift of

---

[161] Symeon of Thessaloniki, *Dialogos*, 94 (*PG* 155: 285). The context of these words is Symeon's description of the *proskomide* which is performed at the Prothesis. They are drawn specifically from the image of the particles on the Discos. For more on the prothesis rite see Stelyios S. Muksuris, *Economia and Eschatology: Liturgical Mystagogy in the Byzantine Prothsesis Rite* (Brookline, MA, 2013).

[162] Schmemann, *Introduction to Liturgical Theology*, 72.

[163] Bobrinskoy, *Mystery of the Trinity*, 169.

reconciliation: the gift of restoration of the estranged and alienated that Christ wrought through his incarnation, death, resurrection, and glorification. The eschatological gifts are communicated by the Holy Spirit in and through the whole action of the Divine Liturgy, from the gathering of the people and the hearing and the explication of God's Word to the offering of the holy Gifts, the exchange of the kiss of peace, the profession of faith, the communion of the Eucharistic elements, and the departure in peace to attend to the affairs of everyday life. St. Maximos the Confessor describes the gift that the Divine Liturgy bestows in these words:

> Every Christian should be exhorted to frequent God's holy Church and never to abandon the holy synaxis accomplished therein ... because of the grace of the Holy Spirit which is always invisibly present ... This grace transforms and changes each person who is found there and in fact remolds him in proportion to what is more divine in him and leads him to what is revealed through the mysteries which are celebrated, even if he does not himself feel this because he is still among those who are children in Christ, unable to see either the depths of the realities or the grace operating in it.[164]

The entire action of the Divine Liturgy concludes with the communion of the Eucharistic elements—the Church's offering that the Father transforms through the action of the Spirit into the Body and Blood of Christ. Holy Communion bestows the gifts of the future age: forgiveness, purification, sanctification, *koinonia*, life eternal—all of which are communicated by our communion in the Holy Spirit.[165] Between his two comings, Christ is present to his Church in the Holy Spirit to communicate the ineffable blessings of the Kingdom. The Holy Spirit is the pledge (ἀρραβών) of the future life and Kingdom (2 Cor. 1:22, 5:5), "the guarantee of our inheritance until we acquire possession of it" (Eph. 1:14).

The Church has not yet crossed the ultimate frontier. It is still in the world gradually reaching completion in accordance with the plan of salva-

---

[164] Maximos the Confessor, *Mystagogy*, 24, in *Maximus Confessor: Selected Writings*, 206.
[165] The benefits, effects, or fruits of Holy Communion are enumerated in the *anaphora* of both Divine Liturgies, that of St. Basil the Great and that of St. John Chrysostom. See Alkiviadis Calivas, "From the Liturgy of St. Basil to the Liturgy of St. John Chrysostom: When and Why (A Preliminary Report)," in *Γηθόσυνον σέβασμα: Ἀντίδωρον τιμῆς καὶ μνήμης εἰς τὸν μακάριστον καθηγητὴν τῆς Λειτουργικῆς Ἰωάννην Μ. Φουντούλην* (Thessaloniki, 2013), 1:1015–1056. An expanded version of this essay is included in chapter 2 of the present volume.

tion. Through the Divine Liturgy, the historical community is continuously actualizing itself, really and effectively, here and now, as the Body of Christ by the power of the Holy Spirit. He dwells in the Church and in each of its members to shape their lives through his consecrating, sanctifying, and perfecting action, directing both the Church and its members toward the Kingdom from which they draw their identity, along with the power to shape their personal lives and to structure their communal mission and activities.

BAPTISM, EUCHARIST, AND CHURCH

The Church is a Eucharistic community because it is foremost a baptismal community. Baptism is the first and indispensable sacrament, the sacrament of regeneration, rebirth, and recreation.[166] Through it, "Christ and the Spirit work together to make us sons and daughters of the Father."[167] We are grafted to and clothed with Christ and are incorporated into his Body, the Church, to become a new creation. Baptism confers upon us a new life, the life in Christ, which opens us to the life of the Spirit that we may grow within the Church "to the measure of the stature of the fullness of Christ" (Eph. 4:13).

The mystery of our becoming one body with Christ ($\sigma\acute{v}\sigma\sigma\omega\mu\omicron\iota$) that begins with baptism is continuously realized and perfected in the Eucharist. What baptism inaugurates—new life—grows in us from Eucharist to Eucharist.[168] "Every Baptism tends toward the Eucharist and finds its fullness in it ... and every Eucharist finds its source in Baptism," writes Fr. Bobrinskoy.[169] "The Eucharist is in Baptism like the fruit is in the flower," notes Dom Lambert Beauduin.[170] It was no accident, therefore, that the sacraments of baptism, chrismation, and the Eucharist once formed one liturgical sequence, constituting together the sacrament of initiation. In these three sacraments the whole of the divine economy is recapitulated, and its gifts are communicated. What is accomplished in baptism and chrismation once for all—our personal Pascha and Pentecost—is continually fulfilled, advanced, and perfected in the Eucharist.

As the sacraments of initiation show, and as the Fathers have affirmed, "the true Church is christological and pneumatological, institutional and

---

[166] Rom. 6:3–11; John 3:3, 5–6; cf. 1 Pet. 1:3–23.
[167] Dumitru Staniloae, *Theology and the Church* (Crestwood, NY, 1980), 39.
[168] Bobrinskoy, *Mystery of the Trinity*, 161.
[169] Ibid., 152.
[170] Cited in Bobrinsky, 152.

spontaneous at the same time, or rather it is christological because it is pneumatological and vice-versa."[171] For this reason, I submit, Eucharistic ecclesiology should be complemented with a baptismal ecclesiology.[172]

ESCHATOLOGY AND HISTORY

The Church is both an eschatological and a historical community. The Church is first of all a historical, visible community that was founded by Christ and is vivified by the Holy Spirit. This historical community emerged and manifested itself in power on the day of Pentecost. The historical community is not simply a body of believers but the Body of Christ, the Church, the continued presence in the world of the Savior, who was once dead and now lives. This presence is made manifest through the sacraments, especially the Eucharist, as Fr. Georges Florovsky noted:

> In the Eucharist there is unveiled, invisibly but really, the fullness of the Church. Each liturgy is celebrated in union with the whole Church, and so to speak in its name, not just in the name of those who are present ... For every little Church is not only a part but the comprehensive image of the whole Church, inseparable from its unity and fullness. Therefore in each Liturgy the whole Church is present and takes part—mysteriously but really. The liturgical celebration is in a certain sense a renewed incarnation of God. In it we glimpse the God-man, Christ, as founder and head of the Church—and with Him the whole Church. In the prayer of the Eucharist the Church sees and acknowledges herself as the single and complete Body of Christ.[173]

The abiding presence of Christ in the Church through the Spirit brings about the purposes for which the incarnation took place. The Church lives not only in active expectation of the Parousia but also in ceaseless remembrance and celebration of the events that brought the Church into being and that continuously form it: "all that came to pass for our sake, the cross, the tomb, the resurrection on the third day, the ascension into heaven, the enthronement at the right hand of the Father, and the second glorious coming" (*anaphora* of St. John Chrysostom). The Spirit, whom Christ sends to the Church, abides in the Church—always present yet anticipated—in

---

[171] Staniloae, *Theology and the Church*, 40.
[172] See Maximos Aghiorgoussis, *In the Image of God* (Brookline, MA, 1999), 75–111.
[173] Georges Florovsky, "Evkharistiya i Sobornost," in *Put* 19 (1929): 7, 9, 14. Cited in Nichols, *Theology in the Russian Diaspora*, 161.

order to initiate in every liturgical event a dramatic episode of salvation for those whose hearts are aflame with the love of Christ.

The Church is the nucleus of the new creation, the place of our deification, the milieu in which we apprehend and share in the mighty, life-giving acts of Christ. Through the sacred rites, especially the Eucharist, Christ—the one "who is and who was and who is to come, the Almighty" (Rev. 1:8)—becomes our contemporary and draws us into his redemptive work. The Church is rooted in the past as well as the future. It has a history centered on Christ's past saving acts, as well as a future centered on his promises and his coming again to judge the living and the dead. The Church's present is conditioned always by its past and its future, both of which inform and shape its message and mission to the world. Past and future coincide in the present through the Church's memory, especially its Eucharistic *anamnesis*.

Through the incarnation, creation has been graced with supreme worth and value. Christ and his redemptive work stand at the center of history and fill it with ultimate meaning and purpose. Through the mysterious presence of Christ in the world through his Body, the Church, God is guiding his people from the inside and no more from the outside, to paraphrase Fr. Florovsky. Though the world is in a fallen and rebellious state, God has "not ceased doing everything until he leads us to heaven and grants us his Kingdom to come" (*anaphora* of St. John Chrysostom). As the prayers of the Divine Liturgy constantly remind us, the Triune God cares for the world through his providential love; he renews and perfects humankind and the cosmos by his transforming grace.

These brief remarks on the Eucharist cannot do justice to the theme, about which much has been written in recent times by both Orthodox and non-Orthodox theologians. Of the many things that have been said and written about the Eucharist, one stands out: "the Church constitutes the Eucharist while being constituted by it."[174] This succinct saying of Metropolitan John of Pergamon highlights the significance of the Eucharist in

---

[174] Cited in McPartlan, *The Eucharist Makes the Church*, xvii. See also John D. Zizioulas, *Being as Communion: Studies in Personhood and the Church* (Crestwood, NY, 1985), 20–21: "The celebration of the eucharist by the primitive Church was, above all, the gathering of the people of God επι το αυτο, that is, both the manifestation and the realization of the Church. Its celebration on Sunday–the day of the eschata–as well as all its liturgical content testified that during the eucharist, the Church did not live only by the memory of a historical fact–the Last Supper and the earthly life of Christ, including the cross and the res-

the life of the Church. By extension, it also underscores the importance of the Divine Liturgy, the sacred rite by which the Eucharist is celebrated.

Since the life of the local community centers chiefly on the weekly celebration of the Divine Liturgy on the Lord's Day, we must take care not to rob it of its educative, formative, evocative, restorative, and transformative powers by indifference or neglect. Robert Taft reminds us that "the purpose of the liturgy is the sanctification, the spiritual nourishment of men and women ... The prayers [and the entire action] of the liturgy do not exist for God. He knows the whole thing before we tell Him. We tell the story in the liturgy to remind us of the story ... If the story is not heard and understood by the people there is a problem."[175]

The Purpose and Goal of Liturgical Renewal

The liturgy is the essential environment, although not the exclusive one, through which we come to understand and appropriate the saving grace of God, share in the reality of the Christ event in an iconic, symbolic, and sacramental manner, and abide in the Church, which is the eschatological community that is being ceaselessly transformed into the Body of Christ by the Holy Spirit. The liturgy nourishes, enlivens, and informs our relationship with God, with his people, and with the world. It molds our inner

---

urrection–but it accomplished an *eschatological* act. It was in the eucharist that the Church would contemplate her eschatological nature, would taste the very life of the Holy Trinity; in other words she would realize man's true being as image of God's own being ... Thus the eucharist was not the act of a pre-existing Church; it was an event *constitutive* of the being of the Church, enabling the Church to *be*. The eucharist *constituted* the Church's being." Earlier, Fr. Nicholas Afanasiev (1893-1966) had coined a similar pithy statement which sums up the eucharistic nature of the Church and the ecclesial nature of the Eucharist: "*The Church makes the Eucharist, the Eucharist makes the Church*." See Michael Plekon, "Introduction: The Church of the Holy Spirit–Nicholas Afanasiev's Vision of the Euchrist and Church," in Nicholas Afanasiev, *The Church of the Holy Spirit*, trans. Vitaly Permiakov (Notre Dame, IN, 2012), xiv. A similar understanding of the Eucharist was expressed by Saturninus and Felix, two martyrs of a town in North Africa at the height of the fierce persecutions initiated by Diocletion and Maximian in AD 304. At their trial they said this about the Eucharist: "The Eucharist cannot be abandoned...As if a Christian could exist without the Eucharist or the Eucharist be celebrated without a Christian...Do you not know that a Christian is constituted by the Eucharist, and the Eucharist by a Christian? Neither avails without the other." For more on the testimony of the two martyrs see Calivas, *Aspects of Orthodox Worship*, 175-176.
[175] Robert F. Taft, *Through Their Own Eyes: Liturgy as the Byzantines Saw It* (Berkeley, CA, 2006), 160–161.

world and our outward actions. In and through the liturgy, we learn what it means to be Christians and are inspired and enabled by grace to conduct our lives accordingly.

RENEWAL AND REFORM: THE NEED FOR REASONED DISCOURSE

As Orthodox Christians we recognize that our lives are shaped and nourished in large measure by the Church's worship, through which we stand humbly before God in joyful adoration. Hence, we have a special personal attachment to the liturgy. We have particular preferences and a certain comfort level with the sacred rites as we know, experience, and celebrate them. Hence, any talk of renewal or reform of the liturgy, especially the Divine Liturgy, causes in some circles a level of anxiety and in others great apprehension, especially when renewal and reform are wrongly equated with chaos or the repudiation of tradition and the subversion of Orthodoxy.

The renewal and reform of the liturgy are sensitive and difficult issues. One must remember, however, that the liturgy is neither a private affair nor a personal refuge from the anxieties of life. Worship is an ecclesial event, enacted by all the people. Hence, the favored liturgical stimuli and preferred devotional practices of one individual or group should not be the norm for liturgical practice, just as the insights of one era should not be normative for all ages.

Solving the problems that confront the Church today will require reasoned discourse and openness of mind, free from ideology and competing interests. Renewal requires a willingness to find common ground despite differences, mindful of the fact that the Holy Spirit, who dwells in the Church, unites us all and endows us with different but complementary and mutually interdependent gifts "for building up the Body of Christ" (Eph. 4:12).

RECOGNIZING AND CONFRONTING PROBLEMS

The liturgical life of the Church is challenged today by a number of problems, such as ritual formalism, clericalism, irrelevancy, and lengthy services.

The transformative power of the liturgy is not always operative or fully realized, owing especially to the deadening effects of ritual formalism. This insidious disease arises from the undue stress people place on the externals of worship to the detriment of its substance. It is sustained by arcane, unintelligible, and irrelevant explanations that tend to mystify rather than elucidate the sacred rites.

Authentic liturgy, as an act of faith, requires personal involvement and commitment. In fact, the complex ritual splendor of the divine services points to the communal character of Orthodox worship and brings to the fore both the particularity and the interdependence of the various orders of the Church, as well as the unity of the community. The Holy Spirit empowers everyone, each according to his or her order, to exercise the priestly office. But through years of neglect we have gradually robbed the people of their rightful active role in the liturgical assembly, relegating them to the status of bystanders, of chance observers.

The liturgical tradition itself presents a challenge. Liturgical rites have a history; they originated, grew, and took shape in certain communal contexts. The many elements of the liturgy—including prayers, rituals, and rubrics—were shaped in years long past and in cultural contexts very different from our own. We know from the experiences of everyday life that the forms, expressions, and the language of one era do not always carry the same force and meaning in another. While liturgical forms and practices must be consistent with tradition, they must also be connected with the real lives of real people. Only then does the normative principle of the inherent relationship between being a Christian and the liturgy remain alive and well. How can people appreciate the transforming power of worship when the community's commitment to translate its devotional acts into good works is lukewarm or, worse, lacking?

As anyone involved with parish work knows, long, repetitive, and drawn-out services are unattractive to the modern worshipper, not for lack of faith but because of the disposition created by the demands and busyness of modern life. People are more apt to appreciate their role and to participate actively and meaningfully in the liturgy when they understand it, when it is celebrated within reasonable time limits, and when they have something to do and something to receive.

We should never take the people for granted by misjudging their patience or underestimating their abilities to contribute creatively to the process of renewal and reform. The purposes of liturgical renewal are served best when we listen to the people's concerns and respond appropriately with good liturgy, with challenging and persuasive preaching, and with convincing and edifying explanations of the Church's faith and liturgy.

While we can ill afford to rush into rash decisions that produce only inadequate solutions, neither can we afford to do nothing, to remain inactive and paralyzed for fear of alienating a certain group or of appearing to betray the past. The treasures we are in danger of losing are not the legacies of the past but the gifts of the Spirit. The Gospel and the very nature of the Church oblige us to act in the present, as the Fathers did in their time, with prophetic vision and boldness, willing and able to respond effectively to the realities and challenges that the world thrusts upon the people of God.

RELEASING THE TREASURES OF TRADITION FROM PARALYSIS

Liturgical creativity is not a departure from tradition any more than new doctrinal formulations cancel out the earlier ones. Genuine liturgical creativity seeks to release the treasures of the tradition from paralysis. Indeed, the very purpose of liturgical scholarship is to help the Church discern, comprehend, and recover its authentic tradition, thereby facilitating the incorporation of that tradition into the contexts in which people live and worship today. Authentic worship is by nature dynamic and open to legitimate progress, adaptation, change, and reform.

The renewal of the liturgy, however, requires more than the rearrangement of material, the abbreviation of services, or the elimination of excesses and repetitions in texts and ceremonies. The first and essential task of liturgical renewal is to help the Church rediscover and restore to the liturgy those concepts, ideas, characteristics, and practices that will enliven the liturgy's formative, restorative, and transformative powers, so that the sacred rites carry meaning and are compelling for the modern worshipper.

As the Church is something given historically but also constantly realized through the action of the Holy Spirit, so also is the liturgy constant and traditional but also alive and dynamic. While its core—which is remarkably rich and precious—remains constant, its forms and expressions are inescapably conditioned by the realities of history and culture. Authentic liturgy is changeless and changing, ageless but also adaptable, traditional yet relevant. The Church is always in a mode of creative continuity; as Metropolitan Savas of Pittsburgh aptly noted, it is marked by "the paradox of unchanging continuity and ceaseless creativity."

CHAPTER THREE: LITURGICAL RENEWAL

PRINCIPLES AND TASKS

The liturgy is the precious inherited treasure that binds together all Orthodox people and expresses their oneness in the faith. Because of this unifying character of our liturgical tradition and praxis, whatever we say and do as a Church about the renewal and reform of the Divine Liturgy, the Church, in the end, is obliged to accomplish two things.

First, it must establish recognizable standards of usage. This, however, should not be interpreted to mean absolute uniformity—rather, it entails only respect for the core tradition and for the Church's rule of prayer. The Church never espoused absolute uniformity in liturgical practice. Pastoral needs have often determined minor local variations. Legitimate variations are an inherent value in Orthodox worship and express the richness of tradition and the Church's respect for persons, their needs, their histories, and their cultures. Second, the Church must ensure a healthy balance among historical tradition, scholarly research, current cultural realities, and genuine liturgical piety. Such a balance would help the Church overcome the effects of ritual formalism, protect the liturgy from ephemeral societal trends, and encourage the unfettered blossoming of the liturgical arts (hymnography, music, iconography, architecture, vessels, implements, and textiles).

But before these things can happen, the Church has to articulate clearly the fundamental principles of Orthodox worship so that the rule of prayer operates properly and effectively. I believe the essential guiding principle must emerge from the Lord's words concerning the observance of the Sabbath. He said, "The Sabbath was made for man, and not man for the Sabbath" (Mark 2:27). This radical saying of Christ has the effect of subordinating Sabbath observances to human needs. Hence, we too must acknowledge and say that the liturgy is made for humankind, and not humankind for the liturgy. The liturgy exists not for itself but to attract and draw people into the mystery of salvation, into a joyful encounter and union with the Triune God. The liturgy exists in the manner of the Church, and the Church, as Petros Vassiliadis notes, "exists not for herself but for the world."[176]

In other words, worship is instrumental and not an end in itself. This fact was highlighted in the communiqué of the Conference on Orthodox Liturgical Renewal and Visible Unity, which took place in 1998 at the New

---

[176] Vassiliadis, *Lex orandi*, 85.

Skete Monastery in Cambridge, New York, in which I was honored to participate.[177] Among other things, the communiqué makes this very point: "Worship is instrumental. It cannot be an end in itself. Its primary purpose is to bring Christians into communion with the Triune God and, in God, with one another and with all creation."[178] The full communiqué is worthy of the Church's attention, inasmuch as it lists several other principles concerning the nature of worship and its implications for the present.

Liturgical renewal, to paraphrase Lambert Beauduin, seeks to change routine and monotonous acts of worship into active and intelligent participation, so that the liturgy thus practiced may arouse the slumbering faith of people and give new power, energy, and efficacy both to prayer and to works.[179] And this can be accomplished only through a process that includes a careful study of the history of every component of the sacred rites, in order to uncover their true purpose and meaning and thereby weigh their ability to quicken faith and effect change in the hearts and minds of contemporary worshippers.

CRITIQUING TEXTS AND RITUALS

As I have noted elsewhere, the critique of the received liturgical texts and time-honored rituals is both an enormous responsibility and a difficult task.[180] In fact, in the execution of this task we must be ready to encounter hesitation and even resistance. However, an unencumbered search for meanings—which is essential to authentic liturgical renewal—requires analytical studies of the components of the liturgy comparable to those carried out by biblical and patristic scholars.[181]

---

[177] For the communiqué of the conference, see Thomas FitzGerald and Peter Bouteneff, eds., *Turn to God, Rejoice in Hope: Orthodox Reflections on the Way to Harare* (Geneva, 1998), 139–146. For a Greek translation of the communiqué, see Vassiliadis, *Lex orandi*, 293–306.
[178] FitzGerald and Bouteneff, *Turn to God*, 141.
[179] Lambert Beauduin, *Liturgy the Life of the Church* (Collegeville, MN, 1926), 11. Cited in Fisch, *Liturgy and Tradition*, 2. Beauduin initiated the liturgical movement in the West during the early part of the twentieth century.
[180] Calivas, *Aspects of Orthodox Worship*, 132.
[181] For the methodologies of Orthodox biblical and patristic interpretation, see Theodore Stylianopoulos, *The New Testament: An Orthodox Perspective: Scripture, Tradition, Hermeneutics* (Brookline, MA, 1997). See also Stylianopoulos, "Comments on Chrysostom, Patristic Interpretation, and Contemporary Biblical Scholarship," *Greek Orthodox Theological Review* 54, nos. 1–4 (2009): 189–204; Stylianopoulos, *Encouraged by the Scriptures: Essays*

When critiquing liturgical texts, we are obliged to ask several questions. Here are some: Is the vision of faith embodied in a particular text conveyed fully and adequately? Is it consistent with the experiences, understandings, sensibilities, and needs of the people today? How do the text and the ritual action fare against the emerging data in biblical, patristic, and liturgical scholarship? If found wanting, could or should a particular text, rubric, or ritual action be corrected, amended, improved, modified, revised, deleted, or ended? Who would authorize these procedures, and who would make the decisions—and by what process? Questions such as these and the quest for answers are part of the liturgical renewal and reform process.

A RATIONALE FOR LITURGICAL RENEWAL AND CHANGE

At this point, I turn to two of my revered teachers, Alexander Schmemann and Ioannis Fountoulis, whose contributions to the study of the Orthodox liturgical tradition and praxis have been exceptional. Both men saw the need for liturgical renewal and reform and both were equally concerned with the difficulties and the challenges the effort presents.

Fr. Schmemann was especially cautious. He insisted that liturgical reform is intrinsically a theological enterprise and that as such, it requires a persuasive theological rationale. He was concerned, however, that those who promote reform usually have little interest in such a rationale.

> The real problem then is not that of "liturgical reform" but first of all, of the much needed "reconciliation" and mutual reintegration of liturgy, theology and piety. Here, however, I must confess my pessimism. I do not see in Orthodox theology and in general in the Orthodox Church even a recognition of that problem and it is clear to me that unless a problem is recognized its solution is either impossible or there will be a wrong solution ... Even less hope do I place

---

on Scripture, Interpretation, and Life (Brookline, MA, 2011), 19–35. In addition, see Eugen Pentiuc, *The Old Testament in Eastern Orthodox Tradition* (New York, 2014); John Breck, *Scripture in Tradition: The Bible and Its Interpretation in the Orthodox Church* (Crestwood, NY, 2001); Paul Nadim Tarazi, *The Old Testament Introduction*, vol. 1 (Crestwood, NY, 1999), vol. 2 (Crestwood, NY, 1994), vol. 3 Crestwood, NY, 1996); Tarazi, *The New Testament: Introduction*, vol. 1 (Crestwood, NY, 1999), vol.2 (Crestwood, NY, 2001), vol. 3 (Crestwood, NY, 2004), vol. 4 (Worcester, MA, 2009); Emmanuel Clapsis, *Orthodoxy in Conversation* (Brookline, MA, 2000), 11–39; Georges Florovsky, *Bible, Church, Tradition: An Eastern Orthodox View* (Belmont, MA, 1972), 9–36. Also see the essays by Orthodox scholars who address scriptural authority and interpretation in *Orthodox and Wesleyan Scriptural Understanding and Practice*, ed. S. T. Kimbrough (Crestwood, NY, 2005), 21–103.

in all kinds of liturgical "revivals" which periodically shake up the complacency of ecclesiastical "establishments" and inevitably lead to discussions about liturgical reforms. For a liturgical reform (the need for which incidentally I do not deny) must have a rationale, a consistent set of presuppositions and goals, and this rationale, as I keep repeating, can only be found in the *lex orandi* and in the organic relationship to the *lex credendi*. But I do not detect even the slightest interest in such a rationale among those—and they are many—who have liturgy in the center of their preoccupations. We find, on the one hand, a romantic and nostalgic pathos of liturgical restoration, a genuine fixation on rubrics and rules, but without any interest in the relation they may or may not have to the faith of the Church.[182]

The enactment of liturgical reforms must be determined by the Church's wisdom and vision in response to real and not imagined needs and must emanate from her theological consciousness. The essential purpose—the rationale—for pursuing liturgical reforms is to make the theological substance and intent of each sacred rite shine forth as clearly as possible, making the liturgy compelling, inspiring, and attractive. Reforms have but one purpose: to provide the Church with good liturgy. Good liturgy has the power to stir and delight the soul and to build and sustain faith. Good liturgy gives rise to authentic piety, a piety that is formed, nourished, and enriched by the objective content of the Orthodox faith.

THE ESSENTIAL REQUIREMENTS FOR MEANINGFUL CHANGE

In the paragraph that follows, extracted from an essay by Professor Ioannis Fountoulis that he presented at the Third Pan-Hellenic Liturgical Symposium sponsored by the Church of Greece in 2001, I believe one can find the necessary presuppositions or requirements for accomplishing meaningful reforms.

> What I wrote previously in another essay and what I have to say today are but simple thoughts, humble perspectives and reminders, which, nevertheless, are drawn from much study, from researching the correct liturgical order and tradition, from a love and pathos for the improvement of our liturgical affairs, from the vision for a precise order and an orderly celebration of the Divine Liturgy, the rite of "true worshippers," who worship God "in Spirit and in truth" (John 4:23–24),

---

[182] Alexander Schmemann, "Debate in the Liturgy: Liturgical Theology, Theology of Liturgy, and Liturgical Reform," *St. Vladimir's Theological Quarterly* 13, no. 4 (1969): 217–224. (Also in Fisch, *Liturgy and Tradition*, 42, 44.)

"offering to God acceptable worship, with reverence and awe" (Heb. 12:28) ... Whatever, over the course of decades [was] studied in the classroom, investigated in manuscripts and bibliographies, taught to students, and applied experimentally in liturgical laboratories, envisioning the renewal, the exactness, the tradition, the "reasonable worship," whatever it put forward prudently and carefully "in whispers" as topics of lectures and in publications ... is now "proclaimed upon the housetops" (Matt. 10:27).[183]

In these words, I discern the six essential requirements for implementing and achieving meaningful change: a passionate concern for the improvement of the Church's liturgical life, openness to the new, respect for tradition, responsible scholarship, sound methodologies, and clear achievable goals.[184]

The process of reform is serious business and requires the full commitment of the Churches. To accomplish the goals of liturgical renewal and reform, each local Church should have a special liturgical commission, much like the one that has been established by the Church of Greece.[185] In addition, I believe, all the Orthodox Churches through the good offices of the Ecumenical Patriarchate should establish a pan-Orthodox Commission on the Liturgy composed of pastors, scholars, and others skilled in the field of liturgy and related disciplines who would work in concert with the local commissions to press forward the envisioned renewal and reform. Such a pan-Orthodox commission would undertake the following basic tasks:

The commission would authorize objective historical studies of all the previous attempts at liturgical renewal and reform in order to avoid the snares of a process that is fraught with difficulties. As Paul Meyendorff notes correctly, the lessons of history must be taken seriously into account if the process is to succeed.[186]

The commission would be responsible for formulating a set of basic exegetical and hermeneutic principles and methodologies by which the multiple levels of received tradition would be examined, analyzed, interpreted, and presented.

---

[183] Fountoulis, "Τελετουργική προσέγγιση της Θείας Λειτουργίας," 154, 155–156.
[184] Evangelos Theodorou put forth twenty general principles, criteria, requirements, and goals for the renewal of liturgy in his essay "Παράδοσις και ανανέωσις," 48–57.
[185] On the establishment and the work of the Special Synodical Committee of the Church of Greece, see Metropolitan Daniel, "Ανοίκειος αναγωγή ή Απαντήσις εις αναιτιολόγητον έλεγχον υποτιθεμένων κακοδοξιών," in Εκκλησία 80, no. 3 (2003): 183–189. See also Demetrios Tzerpos, Δοκιμία λειτουργικής αγωγής κλήρου και λαού: Λειτουργική ανανέωση (Athens, 2001), 11–29.
[186] Meyendorff, *Russia, Ritual, and Reform*, 34–35.

The commission would weigh the practical worth and applicability of existing critical studies of Orthodox liturgical texts, rubrics, and rituals. Then, as the need arises, the commission would authorize individual scholars or groups of scholars to undertake specific research projects that would elucidate particular items and details of the tradition.

The commission would propose appropriate changes and the required modifications to eliminate inaccuracies, incongruities, or irrelevancies in texts, rubrics, and rituals, while taking into account local particularities and needs.

The commission would set forth the methods by which the Orthodox Churches are to receive and enact the proposals and would formulate a catechetical program to inform and educate the clergy and the laity about the proposed changes.

Some Suggestions for the Reform of the Divine Liturgy

The parish is, above all, the fundamental Eucharistic cell of the Church, where the saving work of the Church is actively pursued and carried out. The parish exists for one essential purpose: to bring salvation to the world through the preaching of the Word and the celebration of the sacraments. Everything the parish is and does springs from the weekly celebration of the Divine Liturgy. In fact, Orthodox Christian identity and life are formed largely by what people experience at the Divine Liturgy. Thus, what people know and understand about the Divine Liturgy and how they participate in it are of crucial importance.

Proposals for the renewal and the reform of the Divine Liturgy are not new. They have been discussed at different times and at various levels of intensity in academic settings and texts, in popular literature, in synodical meetings, at clergy retreats, and at parish conferences. Except for few instances, however, proposed liturgical reforms have remained on paper. On rare occasions, some reforms have been implemented but only locally and sometimes without the official approval of the Church.

In the following paragraphs, I present some suggestions for the reform of the Divine Liturgy that I believe would add to the people's deeper appreciation of its educative, formative, transformative, and sanctifying powers, make their participation in it more meaningful, uphold and strengthen the communal character of the liturgy, and stimulate a personal response of faith.

INTERPRETING THE DIVINE LITURGY

Liturgical renewal begins with effective catechesis and persuasive preaching. The Church suffers when the clergy and the people are theologically and liturgically illiterate, through no fault of their own but through the failure of the Church to educate and catechize them properly. Before all else, it is important that both the clergy and the people have a clear understanding of what the Church is doing in the Divine Liturgy. In the absence of good instruction, people are apt to invent their own meanings through private reflection or by borrowing the thoughts of others.[187] However, not all private meanings, whether personal or borrowed, are sound, valid, or edifying, especially when they are based on erroneous assumptions, false ideas, and irrational superstition. Hence the Church is responsible for helping raise the level of the people's understanding of its teachings and liturgy through a systematic and compelling program of catechesis. The Church must also educate, train, and form the clergy properly and adequately to be caring pastors, knowledgeable teachers, competent preachers, and inspired liturgists.

The Church has always explained and interpreted her liturgical rites either in the form of catechetical homilies or in the form of liturgical commentaries. In fact, the Byzantine liturgical tradition boasts a durable literary genre, the mystagogical commentaries on the Divine Liturgy[188]—starting with the *Catechetical Homilies* of Theodore of Mopsuestia[189] and continuing with the commentaries of Dionysios the Areopagite,[190] Maxi-

---

[187] On the search for meanings in texts and rituals, see Calivas, *Aspects of Orthodox Worship*, 131–137.

[188] See, for example, Ioannis Fountoulis, Τελετουργικά θέματα, 1:103–127; Theodoros Koumarianos, "Η ερμηνεία της Θείας Λειτουργίας κατα τα βυζάντινα ερμηνευτικά υπομνήματα," in Τὸ Μυστήριον τῆς Θείας Εὐχαριστίας, 179–210. For an extensive study of the Byzantine commentaries, see R. Bornert, *Les commentaires byzantins de la Divine Liturgie du VII au XV siècle* (Paris, 1966); Hanz-Joachim Schulz, *The Byzantine Liturgy: Symbolic Structure and Faith Expression*, trans. Matthew J. O'Connell (New York, 1986).

[189] See Francis Reine, *The Eucharistic Doctrine and Liturgy of the Mystagogical Catechesis of Theodore of Mopsuestia* (Washington, DC, 1942); Enrico Mazza, *Mystagogy: A Theology of Liturgy in the Patristic Age* (New York, 1989), 45–104.

[190] See *Pseudo-Dionysios: The Complete Works*, Classics of Western Spirituality (New York, 1987); Andrew Louth, *Denys the Areopagite* (Wilton, CT, 1989).

mos the Confessor,[191] and Germanos of Constantinople[192] and culminating with the commentaries of Nicholas Cabasilas, the great exponent of Byzantine liturgical theology,[193] and St. Symeon of Thessaloniki (d. 1429), the last of the classic Byzantine liturgical theologians.[194] These mystagogical works "seek to give a theological explanation not only of the sacramental fact, but of each rite making up the liturgical celebration."[195] They are integral to the Byzantine liturgical tradition and remain popular among a large segment of the population to this day.

Unfortunately, however, many clergy and catechists today do not read these treatises. They read devotional books that are poor imitations of the classic Byzantine commentaries, or they create their own explanations using excessive representational symbolism that turns the Eucharistic celebration into a drama—into a performance in which the clergy are reduced to actors and the people to an audience, a group of listeners and spectators. No wonder most congregants (ἐκκλησιαζόμενοι) today understand the Divine Liturgy more in terms of a drama—a ritual reenactment of the life of Christ through gestures and actions—than as an unfolding vision of God's reign and the fulfillment of the Church as the Body of Christ. The mystery celebrated by the Divine Liturgy cannot be adequately disclosed through contrived, arcane, and fanciful explanations or by what Fr. Taft calls "a historicizing system of dramatic narrative allegory ... that turns ritual into drama, symbol into allegory, mystery into history."[196]

The Eucharist is more than a drama, more even than words and gestures. It is an event, an encounter, and a place of mystery flooded by the presence

---

[191] See *Maximus Confessor: Selected Writings*, Classics of Western Spirituality (New York, 1985).

[192] See Paul Meyendorff, *St. Germanus of Constantinople on the Divine Liturgy* (Crestwood, NY, 1984).

[193] For Cabasilas's contribution to liturgical theology, see Nicholas Denysenko, "The *Life in Christ* by Nicholas Cabasilas: A Mystagogical Work," in *Studia Liturgica* 38, no. 2 (2008); 242–260. See also the essays in the volume Πρακτικὰ θεολογικοῦ συνεδρίου εἰς τιμὴν καὶ μνήμην τοῦ σοφωτάτου καὶ λογιωτάτου καὶ τοῖς ὅλοις ἁγιωτάτου ὁσίου πατρὸς ἡμῶν Νικολάου Καβάσιλα τοῦ καὶ Χαμαετοῦ (Thessaloniki, 1984).

[194] On the life and work of St. Symeon of Thessaloniki, see Ioannis Fountoulis, *Τὸ λειτουργικὸν ἔργον Συμεὼν Θεσσαλονίκης* (Thessaloniki, 1965); Muksuris, *Economia and Eschatology;* David Balfour, *Politico-historical works of Symeon Archbishop of Thessalonica* (Vienna, 1979); and the articles in the volume Πρακτικὰ λειτουργικοῦ συνεδρίου εἰς τιμὴν καὶ μνήμην τοῦ ἐν ἁγίοις πατρὸς ἡμῶν Συμεώνος Ἀρχιεπισκόπου Θεσσαλονίκης.

[195] Mazza, *Mystagogy*, ix.

[196] Taft, "Orthodox Liturgical Theology," 13.

of God. It is the remembrance and celebration of God's redemptive activity and the Church's appropriation of its benefits through prayers of thanksgiving and with hymns of praise for all that the Triune God has done and continues to do for the life and salvation of the world. The Eucharist is the source and summit of the Church's life. In this present age between the two comings of our Lord, the Divine Liturgy is always the messianic banquet, the meal of the Kingdom, the time and place in which the heavenly joins and mingles with the earthly. It is the lifting up of the Church into Christ's presence. It is the Church's participation in his heavenly glory.

Symbolic interpretations of the Divine Liturgy have a long and complex history. Symbols, however, differ from allegory, representation, and illustration. Symbols bear, embody, participate in, and express the reality they signify and disclose. They serve as a means of recognition and communication.[197] Primary symbols—like water, bread, wine, oil, and even the temple—are linked directly to and lead naturally to a superior reality.[198] Authentic symbols have an iconic and sacramental nature and value. They are not illustrations but manifestations.[199] Allegorical and representational interpretations, on the other hand, constitute a system of subjective meanings that are not immediately apparent because they do not belong to the intrinsic nature of a thing. They do not arise directly from the thing itself. They lead to a reality only because someone has directed us to attach a special meaning to a particular act or object.

The use of symbols is an important and effective teaching tool that helps kindle reverence and nourish faith. Reasonable, sober, and restrained symbolism acts like an icon; it leads the worshipper to a mystical experience of a particular sacred event or person. It vests liturgical acts with meanings that

---

[197] See, for example, Alexander Schmemann, "Symbols and Symbolism in the Byzantine Liturgy: Liturgical Symbols and their Theological Interpretation," in *Orthodox Theology and Diakonia: Festschrift Iakovos*, ed. Demetrios Constantelos (Brookline, MA 1981), 91-102; (Also in Fisch, *Liturgy and Tradition*, 115-128); I. Fountoulis, Τελετουργικά Θέματα, 1: 93-127; Schulz, *The Byzantine Liturgy*; Klemens Richter, *The Meaning of Sacramental Symbols* (Collegeville, MN, 1990).

[198] Fr. Schmemann was fond of saying, "The temple is that heaven on earth that realizes the assembly as the Church. It is the symbol that unites the two realities, those two dimensions of the Church—heaven and earth, one manifested in the other, one made a reality in the other." Schmemann, *Eucharist*, 45.

[199] See John of Pergamon (Zizioulas), "Συμβολισμός και ρεαλισμός στην Ορθόδοξη λατρεία," in Σύναξη 71 (1999): 6–21.

are intended to render Christ and his saving work present and active in the worshipping community.[200] Or as Robert Taft puts it, "liturgical anamnesis is not psychological recall but theophany, an active faith encounter now with the present saving activity of Christ. For what Christ was and did, He still is and does ... [T]he concrete reality of church ritual constitutes both a representation and a re-presentation—a rendering present again—of the earthly saving work of Christ."[201] More simply, symbols play a dual role: they both reveal and conceal. Hence they do not reveal fully, but neither do they conceal fully. They are a connecting bridge between and a way of understanding and explaining visible and invisible mysteries and realities.[202]

Theodore of Mopsuestia saw in the entrance of the holy Gifts Christ himself being led out and going forth to his life-giving Passion and death. His interpretation gained currency, and the Great Entrance eventually came to be seen as an iconic representation of Christ's funeral cortege. As a result, new elements were gradually introduced into the sacred rite, such as Holy Friday hymns which the clergy recite as they deposit the Gifts upon the holy Table. The Great Entrance eventually attracted the use of the *epitaphios* (the cloth icon representing Christ's burial), which deacons carried aloft in the procession, as seen in the iconic representations of the Great Entrance. This practice, however, gradually fell into disuse for a variety of reasons and finally disappeared.

Representational interpretations of the Divine Liturgy, however, are not entirely trouble free, especially when they are extravagant, exaggerated, and overemphasized. When the Divine Liturgy is explained almost exclusively in representational terms, the rite tends to be clericalized. Its true meanings are eclipsed and obscured because many of the explanations are neither suggested by nor in concert with the text of the sacred rite. An alert worshipper who is aware of these interpretations but also knows the prayers of the Divine Liturgy cannot help but notice the discrepancies between these explanations and what the Church is actually saying and doing at the Eucharistic celebration.

---

[200] See the collection of informative essays in Σύμβολα και συμβολισμοί της Ορθόδοξου Εκκλησίας: Χρονικόν, εισηγήσεις, πορίσματα Ιερατικού Συνεδρίου της Ιεράς Μητροπόλεως Δράμας (Drama, Greece, 1991).
[201] Taft, "Orthodox Liturgical Theology," 8, 9.
[202] See Σύμβολα και συμβολισμοί της Ορθόδοξου Εκκλησίας, 139–140.

The basic structures, prayers, and rituals of the Divine Liturgy were established long before the genre of the Byzantine commentaries came into being. For this reason, I believe, symbolization cannot and should not be the sole exegetical and hermeneutical method of understanding and explaining the Divine Liturgy.[203] In addition to the symbolic interpretations that have been bequeathed to us, we must also teach the history, development, and structure of the Divine Liturgy and explain the meaning of its prayers, petitions, and hymns, as well as its ritual actions and even its rubrics.[204] In other words, as with the study of the Scriptures, we must study, interpret, and explain the text of the Divine Liturgy. Put another way, we must understand and explain what we are actually saying and doing at the Eucharist, using the available data that liturgical inquiry has produced to make the sacred rite—its history, structure, language, and theology—intelligible, real, and inviting to the people, engaging them in the mystery of salvation. However, important as knowing what we do at the Divine Liturgy is, it is equally important, if not more so, that it be celebrated by the clergy and the people with unwavering faith, deep reverence, and a joyful heart. St. Nicholas Cabasilas tells us that informed and alert worshippers become

> stronger in faith and more generous in devotion and love ... [I]n beholding the unutterable freshness of the work of salvation, amazed by the abundance of God's mercy, [they will be] brought to venerate Him who had such compassion for us, who saved us at a great price: to entrust [their] souls to him, to dedicate [their] lives to him, to enkindle in [their] hearts the flame of His love.[205]

TEXTUAL CONCERNS

Interpreting and explaining the prayers and hymns of the Divine Liturgy constitute an essential and edifying exercise and methodology, but neither is it without problems. The critical investigation of the received texts has exposed certain difficulties. Let me mention some examples.

---

[203] See Pavlos Koumarianos, "Σύμβολο και πραγματικότητα στη Θεία Λειτουργία," in Σύναξη 71 (1999): 22–37.

[204] By way of example, see the works of Panagiotis Trembelas, *Από την Ορθόδοξον λατρείαν μας* (Athens, 1970); Dionysios Psarianos, *Η Θεία Λειτουργία* (Athens, 1986); Andreas Theodorou, *Τα σά εκ των σων: Ερμηνευτικό σχόλιο στην Θεία Λειτουργία* (Athens, 2000). See also Stanley S. Harakas, *Living the Liturgy* (Minneapolis, MN, 1974); Emmanuel Hatzidakis, *The Heavenly Banquet: Understanding the Divine Liturgy* (Columbia, MO, 2008).

[205] Nicholas Cabasilas, *A Commentary on the Divine Liturgy*, trans. J. M. Hussey and P. A. McNulty (London, 1960), 29.

PRAYER OF THE FAITHFUL OR PRAYER OF ACCESS?

The Divine Liturgy, as is well known, has two parts: the Liturgy of the Word (also known as the Liturgy of the Catechumens) and the Eucharist proper (also known as the Liturgy of the Faithful). The two parts are linked by a series of prayer acts that are performed after the Gospel is proclaimed and before the Great Entrance. These include the Fervent Litany and its prayer; the petitions, prayer, and dismissal of the catechumens; and the two prayers of the faithful. These components are common to the three Eucharistic liturgies of the Byzantine rite.[206] Each has its own history, and each presents its own pastoral issues. I here focus briefly on the two prayers of the faithful—more specifically, on the two in the Divine Liturgy of St. Basil the Great (BAS).

A textual analysis of these two prayers shows that they are not, in fact, prayers of the faithful but clerical *prayers of access*. Prayers of access are a basic element of the Eucharistic celebration recited by the clergy in preparation for the Eucharist proper, especially the *anaphora*.[207] Through the prayer of access, the clergy confess their unworthiness and supplicate God to enable them to offer the holy oblation.

Fr. Robert Taft argues successfully that the two prayers of the faithful in BAS are not primitive elements of BAS, at least in their present position.

---

[206] The Byzantine rite has three Divine Liturgies, one of which is attributed to St. Basil the Great and another to St. John Chrysostom. The third is the Liturgy of the Presanctified Gifts, which is attributed to St. Gregory Dialogos. For a critical historical study of the three liturgies, see Panayiotis Trembelas, *Αἱ τρεῖς λειτουργίαι* (Athens, 1935); Juan Mateos, *La celebration de la parole dans la liturgie byzantine* (Rome, 1971); Robert F. Taft, *A History of the Liturgy of St. John Chrysostom: The Great Entrance* (Rome, 1978); Taft, *The Diptychs* (Rome, 1991); Taft, *The Precommunion Rites* (Rome, 2000); Taft, *The Communion, Thanksgiving, and Concluding Rites* (Rome, 2008); John R. K. Fenwick, *The Anaphoras of St. Basil and St. James: An Investigation in Their Common Origin* (Rome, 1992); Stefanos Alexopoulos, *The Presanctified Liturgy in the Byzantine Rite: A Comparative Analysis of Its Origins, Evolution, and Structural Components* (Leuven, 2009). See also Ioannis Fountoulis, *Λειτουργια Προηγιασμενων Δωρων* (Thessaloniki, 1971); Fountoulis, *Βυζαντιναί Θ. Λειτουργίαι Βασιλείου τοῦ Μεγάλου καὶ Ἰωάννου τοῦ Χρυσοστόμου* (Thessaloniki, 1978); Louis Bouyer, *Eucharist: Theology and Spirituality of the Eucharistic Prayer* (Notre Dame, 1968), 281–304.

[207] Taft, *Great Entrance*, 277–283, 372–373. The Byzantine Eucharistic liturgies have two distinct rites in preparation for the *anaphora*: the transfer of the Gifts to the holy Table, accompanied by song, which constitutes the preparation of the people; and the preparation of the clergy through the washing of hands, the dialogue between the celebrants, the prayer of access, and the peace. These acts were once performed simultaneously by different orders of the clergy. In time, the transfer of the Gifts became the dominant feature of the pre-*anaphora* rites and overshadowed the others, some of which have been transposed.

The two were originally a single prayer, the original access prayer of BAS, which was replaced by a later addition,[208] the so-called prayer of the Cherubic Hymn ("No one is worthy" / "Οὐδεὶς ἄξιος").[209] This is itself a prayer of access found in BAS in the Barberini Codex but missing from later manuscripts. At first, as Taft notes, the "Οὐδεὶς ἄξιος" was a private, devotional addition that became popular among the clergy. By the tenth century, its place in both BAS and the Divine Liturgy of St. John Chrysostom (CHR) was well established.

When a liturgical piece is doubled, the more primitive element falls into disuse or is transposed, sometimes in an altered form. This is what happened to the original access prayer of BAS. It was transformed into the two prayers of the faithful in the received text. Juan Mateos has argued that the three prayers of the antiphons in both BAS and CHR are, in fact, the original prayers of the faithful in BAS, in the order 3, 1, 2, the last being a prayer of benediction.[210]

All this may appear to some as an inconsequential and obscure detail that is perhaps of interest to scholars but of little value to the ordinary worshipper. I would argue the opposite. It is an important detail because it points to an essential principle of authentic liturgy that needs to be upheld—namely, that worship must be logical and coherent. Even a cursory reading of the two prayers of the faithful in BAS reveals a discrepancy between the title of the prayers and their content and intent.[211]

---

[208] Ibid., 366–367.
[209] Ibid., 119–148. Here, Taft discusses the title, origins, history, and text of the prayer.
[210] Mateos, *La celebration de la parole*, 168–171. Fr. Mateos and others maintain that the Byzantine rite originally had three prayers of the faithful, the last being a prayer of inclination, or benediction. This model corresponds to the basic pattern of the sacramental rites and other sacred services in the Byzantine rite. They have two essential prayers: the accomplishing (τελεστική) prayer and the prayer of inclination. See Ioannis Fountoulis, *Τελετουργικὰ θέματα*, 1: 231.
[211] The prayer of inclination before Holy Communion in CHR is another example of incongruity. A textual analysis of the prayer and a comparison of it with parallel prayers in other liturgies (e.g., BAS, James, PRES) show that this prayer has nothing to do with the Eucharistic offering or with Holy Communion. It is a prayer of blessing and not a pre-Communion prayer. Moreover, it was probably not original to CHR, at least in this position. Taft has suggested that the present prayer of inclination in CHR may have been a final blessing over non-communicants who began to depart from the liturgy when Communion was about to be administered. See Taft, *Precommunion Rites*, 155–197.

OFFERING OR OFFER?

Another example is from the *anaphora,* the great Eucharist prayer, which comprises the heart of the Eucharistic celebration. The character and purpose of the *anaphora* is revealed through its verbs—the action words of the text.[212]

The *anamnesis* component of the *anaphora* in both BAS and CHR contains three elements: (a) the remembrance of the saving command ("Do this") and of God's acts of salvific love (the death, burial, resurrection, ascension, enthronement, and second coming of Christ); (b) the offering of the sacramental Gifts; and (c) the sacrifice of praise ("We praise You, we bless You, we give thanks to You, and we pray to You, Lord our God").[213] The entire *anamnesis* in the manuscript tradition of BAS and CHR comprised one complete sentence with only one set of active verbs, those that constitute the sacrifice of praise and express the action of the worshipping community. The sequence is as follows: Remembering [and] offering, we praise you, we bless you" (Μεμνημένοι οὖν [CHR = τοίνυν] ... Τὰ σὰ ἐκ τῶν σῶν σοὶ προσφέροντες ... Σὲ ὑμνοῦμεν, σὲ εὐλογοῦμεν, σοὶ εὐχαριστοῦμεν, Κύριε, καὶ δεόμεθά σου, ὁ Θεὸς ἡμῶν).[214] Accordingly, the object of the remembrance and the offering is the sacrifice of praise. Hence the action of the praying community is centered on the sacrifice of praise.

In a small number of late manuscripts, however, and in all the printed editions of BAS and CHR, the adverbial participle προσφέροντες (offering) was changed to a verb, προσφέρομεν (we offer). The reasons for the change are not known; nor do we know who authorized it, or whether it was done intentionally or came about accidentally. Now this modification may also appear unimportant to the ordinary worshipper, as just another detail that

---

[212] See Richard D. McCall, "The Shape of the Eucharistic Prayer: An Essay on the Unfolding of an Action," in *Worship* 75, no. 4 (2001): 321–333.

[213] See Calivas, *Aspects of Orthodox Worship*, 207–212.

[214] See Paul Meyendorff, "The Liturgical Path of Orthodoxy in America," *St. Vladimir's Theological Quarterly* 40, nos. 1–2 (1996): 56–57; Fenwick, *Anaphoras of St. Basil and St. James*, 148–160; Trembelas, *Αἱ τρεῖς λειτουργίαι*, 110; F. E. Brightman, *Eastern Liturgies* (Oxford 1896; Piscataway, NJ, 2004), 329. See also the two essays D. Richard Stuckwisch, "The Basilian *Anaphoras*," in *Essays on Early Eastern Eucharistic Prayers*, ed. Paul F. Bradshaw (Collegeville, MN, 1997), 109–130; Robert F. Taft, "St. John Chrysostom and the Byzantine *Anaphora* That Bears His Name," 195–226 in the same volume.

CHAPTER THREE: LITURGICAL RENEWAL

interests liturgists and theologians. But is it? I think not. In fact, it represents a dramatic shift in our understanding of the Church's offering.[215]

Changing the participle to a verb dramatically alters the action of the worshipping community. The oblation is now identified with the offering of the holy Gifts ("Remembering ... we offer") and not with the sacrifice of praise ("Remembering and offering, we praise"). The attention and action of the *anamnesis* have shifted to the offering of the Gifts. The change in language had another effect, as well: it led eventually to the lifting of the Discos and the Cup at the words Τὰ σὰ ἐκ τῶν σῶν, a ritual act that signifies an offering.[216]

Having lost its original significance, the sacrifice of praise has become just another hymn, sung now to cover over the voice of the priest as he recites the *epiclesis* in a low or inaudible voice. The hymn, however, is more than just another song. It is the Church's unique offering, its sacrifice of praise, which is the only possible response to the Father for the Paschal mystery that is rendered present through the sacramental Gifts. The sacrifice of praise is the climax of the Church's prayer. It leads to the *epiclesis*, to the

---

[215] See Ioannis Fountoulis, "Ερμηνεία επτά δυσκόλων σημείων του κειμένου της Θείας Λειτουργίας απο τον Νικόλαον Καβάσιλα," in *Πρακτικὰ Θεολογικοῦ Συνεδρίου–Νικολάου Καβάσιλα*, 163–164. Of equal concern is the phrase that concludes the action of the anamnesis, «κατὰ πάντα καὶ διὰ πάντα.» Is it related to the offering, «τα σὰ ἐκ τῶν σῶν σοὶ προσφέροντες» or to the sacrifice of praise that follows, «σε ὑμνοῦμεν...»? Moreover, what does the phrase mean—an important concern for translators? Various interpretations have been offered and many versions of the phrase appear in English translations of the Divine Liturgy, including but not limited to the following: "in all and for all;" "in all things and for all things;" "in behalf of all and for all;" "for all and through all;" "in all places and for all that you have done for our benefit;" "according to all and for all;" and "at all times and in all places." Four texts may help clarify the meaning of the laconic and enigmatic Greek original, Malachi 1:11; 1 Timothy 2:8; Didache 14:2; and the First Prayer of the Faithful in CHR, which reads in part, "to invoke you at every time and place—ἐπικαλεῖσθαί σε ἐν παντὶ καιρῷ καὶ τόπῳ." Based on the four texts, and the witness of Justin the Martyr (*Dialogue* 41:1) and Irenaeus (*Adv. Haer.* 4:17, 5) who identify the "pure offering" in the prophecy of Malachi (1:11) with the Eucharist, the phrase "*at all times and in all places*" appears to be the preferred rendering of the Greek original. For more see, Calivas, *Aspects of Orthodox Worship*, 218-222; and Panayiotis Trembelas, *Ἀπὸ τὴν Ὀρθόδοξον λατρείαν μᾶς* (Athens, 1970), 286-287.

[216] The lifting of the Discos and the Cup is not mentioned in any of the early manuscripts. In fact, the fourteenth-century *Diataxis* (manual of rubrics) of Patriarch Philotheos Kokkinos clearly notes that the priest and deacon only point to the Gifts at this point. See Trembelas, *Αἱ τρεῖς λειτουργίαι*, 11. The lifting of the Discos and the Cup is first mentioned in two manuscripts of the seventeenth century.

invocation of God the Father to send down his Holy Spirit upon the people and upon the holy Gifts, so that the people may be Spirit bearers and the Gifts may become the Body and Blood of Christ.

The sacrifice of praise is meant to be offered to God by the whole Church, clergy and people together, in thanksgiving for the divine economy and the benefits and gifts that spring forth from it. St. Nicholas Cabasilas said it best:

> The Church says, "We make this oblation mindful of your benefits." Surely this is thanksgiving, to honor with our holy offerings, the Benefactor for the good things He has given us. Thus expressing her thanksgiving even more clearly, she adds: "In *offering* (*προσφέροντες*) this oblation, we praise you, we bless you..." This then is the purpose of the offering of the holy gifts—to praise, to give thanks, and to supplicate, as we have said at the beginning; so the sacrifice we offer is at once eucharistic and supplicatory.[217]

The initiative for sacrifice lies not with us but with God, who continually reveals and offers himself to us in his Son, our Lord Jesus Christ. The sacrifice offered by the Church is always a response, an offering or a sacrifice in return (*ἀντιπροσφορά*). This offering in return is, above all, a sacrifice of praise and thanksgiving and an act of kenosis, of self-emptying.

My purpose in drawing attention to this specific detail in the text of the *anaphora* is to underscore another facet of liturgical inquiry. It presents various challenges that require a response. In this particular instance, textual analysis has revealed an important theological emphasis and concept that until recent years has been hidden or overlooked.[218] Is the Church ready and willing to study and evaluate the data that liturgical inquiry provides and to make the appropriate changes in the sacred rites, including the restoration—when proper and right—of language, concepts, and ideas that have been neglected, lost, or forgotten?

THE DOUBLE ACTION OR MOVEMENT OF THE DIVINE LITURGY

Oftentimes explanations of the Divine Liturgy begin with an analysis of the word *liturgy*. From the etymology of the word, we lay great emphasis on the

---

[217] Cabasilas, *Commentary on the Divine Liturgy*, 49. See also P. Trembelas, *Απο την Ορθοδοξον λατρειαν μας*, 288-289.

[218] See, for example, Fountoulis, "Ερμηνεία επτά δυσκόλων σημείων," 157–172; Panagiotis Skaltsis, "Ερμηνευτικά ζητήματα της Θείας Λειτουργίας," in *Η Θεία Ευχαριστία* (Drama, 2003), 123–154; Calivas, *Aspects of Orthodox Worship*, 193–226.

idea that worship, or the liturgy, is the work of the people. In the process, we inadvertently lose sight of God. The liturgy is not only the work of the people. First and foremost, it is an act of the Triune God. The initiative belongs to him. "We love, because he first loved us" (1 John 4:19). Our worship is an act in response. In the Divine Liturgy we meet the self-giving of God, who reveals his counsels and designs for the salvation of the world. God is at the beginning of every event, and the Divine Liturgy is something that God is doing for us but also with us.[219]

In the Eucharist, Christ is forever present and immediate to his people. Christ, our High Priest and Lord of all, is "the One who offers and is offered, the One who receives and is distributed."[220] In view of his self-giving, we have nothing more precious to offer him than our own lives through the bread and wine, in exchange for his life, which he freely gives us through the consecrated Eucharistic elements, which are truly his Body and Blood. Michael Aune describes this double movement of the Divine Liturgy using the terms *katabatic-soteriological* and *latreutic-anabatic*.[221] At the Eucharist, God is the primary subject who takes hold of the initiative and makes himself present through the sacred rites (katabatic) that he may bestow salvation and sanctification upon his people and through them upon the world (soteriological). It is he also who makes it possible for the Church to act liturgically (latreutic), to enter into communion with him through the sacred rites so that we may lift up our hearts to worship him in spirit and in truth and so glorify his holy name (anabatic).

That the Eucharistic rite is first an act of God is underscored by the dialogue with which the Divine Liturgy begins. The deacon says to the presiding bishop or presbyter, "It is time for the Lord to act" (Ps. 118/119:126). Through the setting, the actions, and the words of the Divine Liturgy, God bends the heavens to embrace us with his boundless love and mercy. And we in turn, empowered by his grace, ascend into his presence (anabatic) to "taste and see that the Lord is good" (Ps. 33/34:8).

The purpose of this brief reference to the double action or movement of the Divine Liturgy is to emphasize again the importance of textual analysis,

---

[219] Kalivopoulos, *Χρόνος τελέσεως της Θείας Λειτουργίας*, 18–19. See also Calivas, *Aspects of Orthodox Worship*, 5–6.
[220] From the prayer of the Cherubic Hymn ("Οὐδείς ἄξιος")
[221] Michael Aune, "Liturgy and Theology," 161–162.

through which we are able to uncover overlooked aspects of our worship, discern more clearly the essential purposes of the sacred rites, and discover meanings previously missed.

BROKEN RITUALS

The Divine Liturgy contains several ritual actions that have lost their original dynamic character and purpose. These are "broken" rituals, disrupted by change. With the passage of time, the original purpose of these rituals has been obscured. In their present form, broken rituals carry little meaning either for the clergy who perform them or for the people who observe them; they lend themselves to uncritical and sterile pietistic explanations. Several broken rituals come to mind: the rite of access to the cathedra in churches where there is no cathedra; censing during the reading of the Apostolos; the abandonment or suppression of the kiss of peace among the people; the lifting and the waving of the veil (ἀήρ) over the Gifts during the creed; and the several dismissals that conclude the Divine Liturgy.[222]

The Divine Liturgy, as we know, is a complex act of movement, sound, and sights characterized by a sense of harmony, beauty, dignity, and mystery. It is structured around three major processions and two lesser ones, all of which are now reduced forms of what were earlier more elaborate ceremonies.[223] Of these processions, two are the most obvious and best known: the Small Entrance and the Great Entrance. In its current truncated form, the Small Entrance is a broken ritual.[224]

---

[222] To these several broken rituals we could add practices that pertain to a hierarchical liturgy, such as the multiple blessings with the dikerotrikera (δικηροτρίκηρα—the two candle holders, one with two candles and the other with three candles), the use of two different *omophoria*, the overuse of the exclamation "Many years," and the long, excessive commemorations at the Great Entrance.

[223] The major processions include the Small and Great Entrances, which are still part of the Divine Liturgy (though in reduced forms), and the now defunct recessional, which in earlier times was the formal departure procession of the clergy and the people from the Church at the conclusion of the Divine Liturgy. The lesser entrances include the procession of the liturgical Gospel to the *amvon* and the bringing of the consecrated Gifts to the nave for the administration of Communion to the people. Of these, only the procession of the Chalice to commune the people has been retained in a reduced form. In current practice the Gospel is processed to the *amvon* only when a deacon is serving.

[224] A form of the original entrance rite has been retained at a hierarchical celebration. The hierarch enters the sanctuary for the first time, at least in theory if not in practice, at the Small Entrance.

CHAPTER THREE: LITURGICAL RENEWAL

Before the ninth century, the Divine Liturgy began with what is now called the Small Entrance. The rite consisted of the gathering and the solemn entry of the clergy and the people together into the Church with prayer and song to stand before the glory of God and to manifest their collective identity as the Church, to sing hymns of praise, to hear the proclamation of the Word of God, to offer the Eucharist, and to partake of the holy Gifts. For reasons that are not absolutely clear, the antiphons were attached to the *enarxis* (inaugural rite) of the Divine Liturgy at some point during the latter part of the seventh century and the early part of the eighth.

As a result of this change, the entrance eventually lost its original dynamic character and purpose. It was reduced gradually to its present form: a circular procession of the priest from the sanctuary into the nave and back again into the sanctuary. While the essential elements of the rite have been retained in the text of the Divine Liturgy, the people neither know them nor have a role in the entrance. In the circular procession from and to the sanctuary, the actions are performed only by the clergy. Stripped of its original purpose and significance, the entrance rite was opened to allegorical interpretation and dramatized with various symbolizations, the most favored of which is the "entrance" of Christ into his public ministry.

In the liturgy everything matters, from the use of incense to seating arrangements. Everything has a purpose and a meaning. Hence rituals that have been dislocated and disrupted by change, as a matter of principle, should be carefully modified to fulfill their real purpose or be quietly set aside. Broken rituals are usually the first to fall prey to the harmful effects of ritual formalism.

Not only the Small Entrance but also the entire first part of the Divine Liturgy requires careful analysis to evaluate what effects, positive or negative, each of its components has had on the primitive rite of entrance, the central focus of which is the entrance of the clergy and the people into the presence of the living God to glorify his name and to hear his word through the appointed lections of the holy Scriptures. Certainly, this analysis must include a significant discussion about revising the received lectionary and the importance of the preaching ministry, inasmuch as the liturgical homily is a constitutive part of the Divine Liturgy.[225]

---

[225] The Church of Greece devoted its fifth Liturgical Symposium to this theme. The papers and proceedings of the symposium have been published in Ἱερουργεῖν τὸ Εὐαγγέλιον: H

HEARING AND SINGING THE DIVINE LITURGY

The prayers of the Divine Liturgy express the faith of the Church and convey the purpose, meaning, and benefits of the Eucharistic celebration. They are intended to inspire the minds of the worshippers, enliven their faith, energize their will, warm their hearts, engender hope, and shape their actions, but also place their thoughts, motives, and actions under the judgment of God's righteousness. Every prayer, whatever it may be, is a teaching about life. Hence the prayers of the Divine Liturgy should be recited audibly.[226]

Everything that is said and done in the name of the Church should be heard and known by the whole Church.[227] As St. Paul says, unintelligible

---

Αγία Γραφή στην Ορθόδοξη Λατρεία, Σειρά ποιμαντική βιβλιοθήκη 10 (Athens, 2004). See also David Petras, "The Gospel Lectionary of the Byzantine Church," *St. Vladimir's Theological Quarterly* 41, nos. 2–3 (1997): 113–140; Ioannis Fountoulis, Τελετουργικά Θέματα, vol. 3, 161-171; Petros Vassiliades, "Το ευχαριστιακό υπόβαθρο της λειτουργικής αναγέννησης και το εξ αυτού απορρέον αίτημα της αναθεωρήσεως των περί τα βιβλικά αναγνώσματα θεμάτων της Ορθοδόξης λατρείας," in Λατρεύσωμεν ευαρέστως τώ Θεώ, 141–158. Alkiviadis C. Calivas, "The Sunday Lucan Pericopes in the Byzantine Lectionary: a Guide for Seminarians and Homilists," in *Studies in Orthodox Biblical Hermeneutics in Honor of Theodore Stylianopoulos*, ed. Eugen Pentiuc (Brookline, MA, expected publication date: summer of 2016). On the significance of the liturgical homily, see Dimitra Koukoura, Η ρητορική και η εκκλησιαστική ρητορική (Thessaloniki, 2003); Koukoura, Σπουδή στη Χριστιανική ομιλία (Thessaloniki, 2009).

[226] Except for the dialogues between the deacon and the priest, the prayer of access to the cathedra, the prayer of the Cherubic Hymn, and the private prayers of Communion, all other prayers of the liturgy are meant to be said audibly (though it could be shown that the first prayer of the faithful was also said inaudibly).

[227] It is possible to construe the inaudible recitation of prayers as a form of clericalism. One can also construe the concealment of the sanctuary by the iconostasis as a form of clericalism. In the churches of Constantinople, the sanctuary was visible to the people as late as the eleventh century. Then gradually and systematically the sanctuary was concealed from the view of the people, so that their "unsanctified glance" may not fall on the sacred mysteries, as Hugh Wybrew notes. The comments of Nicetas Stethatos on the status of the laity, cited by Wybrew, are especially revealing. Stethatos writes, "Know that the place of the laity in the assembly of the faithful during the *anaphora* is far from the divine altar. The interior of the sanctuary is reserved to the priests, deacons and sub-deacons; the area outside near the sanctuary to the monks and other ranks of our hierarchy; behind them and the platform, to the laity ... How then from such a distance can the laymen, to whom it is not allowed, contemplate the mysteries of God accomplished with trembling by his priests?" See Wybrew, *The Orthodox Liturgy*, 134. Regarding the style of the iconostasis and its relationship to the worshipper, the recommendation of the 1998 Consultation on Orthodox Liturgical Renewal and Visible Unity requires serious consideration. The consultation noted, "We must be aware of legitimate alternatives for church architecture and furnishings. For example, would not the iconostasis in a more open form serve to keep the people connected to the

sounds and mysterious babble are not a sure sign of the presence or the possession of the Spirit (1 Cor. 14:1–33; cf. Acts 8:26–40). Vague notions of what constitutes piety, mystery, and mystical contemplation should never be allowed to prevail over an intelligible experience of the sacred in the liturgy.

Amen is the people's word. Through it, they participate in, approve, and seal the prayers and actions of the clergy that are performed in their name, since the priest's prayers are offered for and on behalf of the people but also with them. In current practice, the Divine Liturgy is the only sacramental service at which most prayers are read inaudibly or in a low voice. Because the people do not hear the prayers, they cannot relate to or absorb the more substantive contents of the sacred service. They are called to prayer ("Let us pray to the Lord") but they hear only the prayer's concluding doxology, to which they add their assent ("Amen") without knowing what they are assenting to.

The manner of the recitation of prayers has been treated extensively by George Filias.[228] It is sufficient for my purposes here to note that when the practice of inaudible recitation began to take root, it was denounced as an innovation and a violation of the Church's ethos and piety. In fact, Emperor Justinian vigorously opposed the practice and in 565 issued a law forbidding it. The imperial decree is instructive because it draws attention to the reasons why reading the prayers aloud is necessary. The decree reads, in part, "Moreover we order all bishops and presbyters to say the prayers used in the Divine Oblation and in holy Baptism not inaudibly, but in a loud voice that the faithful people can hear, that the minds of those who listen may be excited to greater compunction, and may be roused to give glory to the Lord God."[229]

For the early Christians, as Fr. Robert Taft reminds us, praying aloud both in the assembly and privately at home was a normal practice. Public and private prayer and even private readings were vocalized audibly in

---

priestly function that is performed in their name?" See FitzGerald and Bouteneff, *Turn to God: Rejoice in Hope*, 142. See also Robert Arida, "Another Look at the Solid Iconstasis in the Russian Orthodox Church," in *St. Vladimir's Theological Quarterly*, vol. 52, nos. 3–4 (2008): 339–365.

[228] George N. Filias, *Ο τρόπος αναγνώσεως των ευχών στη λατρεία της Ορθόδοξου Εκκλησίας* (Athens, 1997). See also Taft, *Through Their Own Eyes*, 100–104.

[229] Justinian, *Novella* 137, in R. Schoell and G. Kroll, *Corpus juris civilis* (Berlin, 1899), 3:699.

the cultures of Judaism and Greco-Roman paganism.[230] While we cannot know for certain how clearly the prayers were heard by the people or how well they understood them, neither hearing nor understanding is an insurmountable problem for the Church today. In today's churches, with their state-of-the-art sound systems, hearing is not an issue. And most worshippers today, even those in villages, have access to liturgical texts and to a level of education that allows them to grasp, at least rudimentarily, the meanings of the prayers. Besides, liturgical preaching constitutes a form of ongoing catechetical instruction because the preacher is always conveying the faith of the Church.

Happily, in recent times some of the Churches have taken measures to reverse the practice of inaudible prayers with varying degrees of success. The Ecumenical Patriarchate, for example, has recommended and urged its clergy to read the prayers of the Divine Liturgy, especially the *anaphora*, aloud.[231] Of course, reading prayers aloud requires much of the clergy in the way of attentiveness to the text and an intelligent, intelligible, and unhurried but natural recitation. Obviously, the audible vocalization of prayers requires that they be said in their proper sequence. It also means that the length of the service will increase to some extent. This could be counterbalanced by good rhythmic chanting and by various other adjustments and modifications.

St. Paul tells us that we should glorify God with one voice and one heart (Rom. 15:6; cf. Acts 4:32) in psalms and hymns and spiritual songs, singing and making melody in [our] heart to the Lord (Eph. 5:19). Songs, as someone said, intensify speech, heighten action, and evoke memories. Liturgical renewal must also be concerned with returning to the people their ministry of prayer and song. Choirs and chanters are meant to add beauty to the services not by silencing the voice of the people but by inspiring and leading them to sing praises to the Lord. The renewal of worship should also allow for the free flowering of all the liturgical arts, including hymnography and music, and for the return of the ministry of song to the people.[232]

---

[230] Taft, *Through Their Own Eyes*, 101.
[231] *Εισήγησις της Α. Θ. Παναγιότητος, του Οικουμενικού Πατριάρχου κ.κ. Βαρθολομαίου προς τα μέλη της Ιεράς Συνάξεως της εν ενεργεία ιεραρχίας του θρόνου (1 Σεπτεμβρίου 1994)*, 3, 9.
[232] On the development of new hymnography and liturgical music, see, for example, Gregorios Stathis, "Η μουσική έκφραση των λειτουργικών ύμνων και η δυνατότητα μετάφραση

Conclusion

The fundamental aim of both renewal and reform is to help the Church maintain the vibrancy and the beauty of the liturgy, as well as its dynamic, logical, and spiritual character, so that the people of God, clergy and laity alike, may be drawn into the mystery of salvation and behold and experience the love, the righteousness, and the glory of God.

The ultimate purpose of liturgical renewal and reform, aided by effective catechesis, is to produce good, spiritual worship (λογική λατρεία—Rom. 12:1). Good liturgy glorifies God and sanctifies those who glorify him. Good liturgy, good catechesis, and good preaching make it possible for the people to be more active and more conscious participants in worship so that they are better able to extract and absorb the doctrinal, ethical, and devotional riches of the liturgy and apply them to their everyday lives and experiences.

τους στη νεοελληνική γλώσσα," in Λατρευσωμεν ευαρεστως τω Θεω, 191–212; the volume *Passion and Resurrection* published by the Monks of New Skete (Cambridge, NY, 1995); Mark Bailey, "Composing Orthodox Liturgical Music in the Contemporary World," *St. Vladimir's Theological Quarterly* 40, nos. 1–2 (1996): 65–75. See also the new compositions of the hieromonk Gerasimos Mikragianites, a large collection of which appear as an addendum in the *Great Horologion* published by *Asteros* (Athens, 1973); and the collection of new compositions in the volume *Hymns of Repentance*, published by the Monks of New Skete (Cambridge, NY, 2003). See also the contributions of the anonymous author (Christos Yannaras) Νέα εκκλησιατική ακολουθία του μυστήριου του γάμου (Athens, 1997); Νέα εκκλησιαστική ακολουθία εις κεκοιμημένους (Athens, 2008); Νεα Εκκλησιαστικη Ακολουθια του Μυστηριου του Βαπτισματος (Athens 2012); as well as Vasileios Thermos, Ασματική ακολουθία του γάμου (Athens, 2000).

4

MARRIAGE
THE SACRAMENT OF LOVE AND COMMUNION

Marriage, a particular state of life with personal, social, and ecclesial implications, is a complex and multifaceted subject.[233] According to St. Paul, marriage is a community of love, the head of which is Christ. Hence, the bond between the spouses is to be modeled on the relation of Christ to his Church. He "loved the Church and gave himself up for her, that he might sanctify her ... He nourishes and cherishes her" (Eph. 5:22–33). Christ's love for the Church is unconditional and boundless. The spouses are called to discover and acquire this sacrificial love for one another by being subject to Christ.

Marriage, as a state of life established on the Word of God and the self-giving love of the spouses for one another in imitation of God's love for the world and the Church, is a uniquely Christian ideal and constitutes the meaning and purpose of the sacrament of marriage. It is in the New Testament, as Archbishop Demetrios notes, "that we encounter a tremendous emphasis on the institution of the family. Among other examples, St. Paul speaking of the Christian marriage and family says that the bond of husband and wife is analogous to the bond of Christ and the Church, and that the mutual love of husband and wife should be like the love of Christ for his Church for which he even offered himself to death."[234]

---

[233] This essay is an expanded version of the paper presented at the conference on exogamy, or mixed marriage, sponsored by Holy Cross Greek Orthodox School of Theology, March 28–29, 1994. The paper was subsequently published in *Greek Orthodox Theological Review* 40, nos. 2–3 (1995): 247–275, and in the volume *Inter-Marriage: Orthodox Perspectives*, ed. Anton C. Vrame (Brookline, MA, 1997), 34–61. Also the paper was translated by Joseph Roelides and published in the volume *Γάμος, Αγάπη, Έρωτας*, ed. Stavros S. Fotiou (Athens, 2014): 60–104.

[234] Archbishop Demetrios, "The Orthodox Christian Family: A Dwelling of Christ and a

Several years ago, Fr. Theodore Stylianopoulos wrote an insightful essay on the sacrament of marriage titled "Toward a Theology of Marriage in the Orthodox Church."[235] The title does not suggest the absence of a theology of marriage; indeed, during the last several decades, Orthodox theologians have published important books and articles on the subject.[236] But it does

Witness of His Gospel," in the *Orthodox Observer* (July–August 2014): Clergy-Laity Congress Insert, 4.

[235] Theodore Stylianopoulos, "Toward a Theology of Marriage in the Orthodox Church," *Greek Orthodox Theological Review* 22, no. 3 (1977): 249–283; Vrame, *Inter-Marriage*, 1–33.

[236] Others who have written on the subject include the following: Dumitru Staniloae, *The Sanctifying Mysteries* (Brookline, MA, 2012), 167–191; Panayiotis Skaltsis, Γάμος και Θεία Λειτουργία: Συμβολή στην ιστορία και τη θεολογία της λατρείας (Thessaloniki, 1998); Stanley S. Harakas, *Living the Faith* (Minneapolis, MN, 1992), 225–258; William Basil Zion, *Eros and Transformation, Sexuality and Marriage: The Eastern Orthodox Perspective* (New York, 1992); John Chryssavgis, "Love and Sexuality in the Image of Divine Love," *Greek Orthodox Theological Review* 35, no. 2 (1990): 101–112; Chryssavgis, "The Sacrament of Marriage: An Orthodox Perspective," *Studia Liturgica* 19, no. 1 (1989): 17–27; Vigen Guroian, *Incarnate Love: Essays in Orthodox Ethics* (Notre Dame, 1987), 79–114; John Meyendorff, *Marriage: An Orthodox Perspective* (Crestwood, NY, 1985); Paul Evdokimov, *The Sacrament of Love* (Crestwood, NY, 1985); Christos Yannaras, *The Freedom of Morality* (Crestwood, NY, 1984), 157–172; Olivier Clement, "Life in the Body," *Ecumenical Review* 33, no. 2 (1981): 128–146; Alexandros M. Stavropoulos, "The Understanding of Marriage in the Orthodox Church," *One in Christ* 15, no. 1 (1979): 57–64; Stephanos Charalambidis, "Marriage in the Orthodox Church," *One in Christ* 15, no. 3 (1979): 204–223; Demetrios J. Constantelos, *Marriage, Sexuality, and Celibacy: A Greek Orthodox Perspective* (Minneapolis, MN, 1975); Philip Sherrard, *Christianity and Eros* (London, 1976); Sherrard, "The Sexual Relationship in Christian Thought," *Studies in Comparative Religion* 5, no. 3 (1971): 151–172; Serge Verkhovosky, "Creation of Man and the Establishment of the Family in the Light of the Book of Genesis," *St. Vladimir's Theological Quarterly* 8, no. 1 (1964): 5–30; George Khodre, "A Great Mystery: Reflections on the Meaning of Marriage," *St. Vladimir's Theological Quarterly* 8, no. 1 (1964): 31–37; Athenagoras Kokkinakis, *Parents and Priests as Servants of Redemption* (New York, 1958); Nicon Patrinacos, "The Sacramental Character of Marriage," *Greek Orthodox Theological Review* 2, no. 1 (1955): 118–132.

See also the collection of articles in Theodore Grey Dedon and Sergey Trostyanskiy, eds., *Love, Marriage, and Family in the Eastern Orthodox Tradition* (New York, 2013); Ο γάμος στη Ορθόδοξη Εκκλησία, Σειρά ποιμαντική βιβλιοθήκη 9 (Athens, 2004); Anton C. Vrame, ed., *Inter-Marriage: Orthodox Perspectives* (Brookline, MA, 1997); John Chirban, ed., *Marriage and the Family* (Brookline, MA, 1983).

See also the catechetical manuals: George Nicozisin, *Crowns of Honor and Glory: Your Marriage in the Orthodox Church* (St. Louis, MO, 1990); *Marriage: Documents of the Orthodox Church in America* (Syosset, NY, 1980); *Women and Men in the Church* (Syosset, NY, 1980); Stanley S. Harakas, *Guidelines for Marriage in the Orthodox Church* (Minneapolis, 1979); Anthony Coniaris, *Getting Ready for Marriage in the Orthodox Church* (Minneapolis, 1972).

In addition, see the studies of Efthymios Stylios, Άνθρωπος: Άρσεν και θύλη (Athens,

point to the need for a continuous systematic and comprehensive treatment of the subject, especially from the perspective of modern biblical, patristic, liturgical, ethical, canonical, and historical studies, with due consideration of the useful insights provided by the natural and social sciences on the nature of human sexuality, behavior, and personality.

The purpose of this essay is to contribute to the discussion about the meaning of marriage as it is understood, proclaimed, and celebrated by the Orthodox Church by focusing on three major themes: the vision, the essential characteristics, and the foundational qualities and purposes of sacramental marriage.

The Orthodox vision of normative marriage is lofty and may appear to the casual observer as an unrealistic ideal; it could rightly be discarded as unattainable were it not for our faith that Christians are a new creation (2 Cor. 5:17) by virtue of their baptism. Sacramental marriage cannot be viewed or understood apart from the new life in Christ. It belongs to the order of the new creation. Christians who strive to live out their lives in conformity with the Gospel walk by the Spirit, making manifest the fruits of the Spirit (Gal. 5:22) in their everyday lives, even if imperfectly. Hence the nuptial union, like the whole of the Christian life, is placed in the realm of grace, amid that power that flows from God and his Kingdom.

The Christian life, whether it is lived in a single or married state, is a *resurrectional* life. It is a life that shares in the power of Christ's resurrection, by which sin, corruption, and death have been overcome and defeated. The Christian chooses daily to break the sway of culture, habit, and life's addictions. In the midst of the snares and temptations of everyday life, Christian persons seek to live in communion with everything that is good, noble, natural, and sinless, forming themselves by God's grace in the likeness of Christ (Phil. 4:4–8).

1990); Nikos Bougatsos, *Ἡ Ὀρθόδοξη θεολογία γιὰ τὸ σκοπό τοῦ γάμου* (Athens, 1989); Philotheos Faros and Stavros Kofinas, *Γάμος* (Athens, 1989) and *Συζυγία* (Athens, 1987); Philotheos Faros, *Γονεῖς καὶ παιδιά* (Athens, 1989); Michael Kardamakis, *Ἀγάπη καὶ γάμος* (Athens, 1989); Georgios Mavromates, *Τὸ μυστήριον τῆς ἀγάπης-γάμος* (Katerini, 1988); Georgios Patronos, *Γάμος καὶ ἀγαμία* (Athens, 1985) and *Ὁ γάμος στὴ θεολογία καὶ στὴ ζωή* (Athens, 1984); Panagiotes Boumes, *Θεώρηση καὶ προβλήματα τοῦ πολιτικοῦ γάμου* (Athens, 1985); Megas L. Farantos, *Δογματικά καὶ ἠθικά* (Athens, 1983), 1:301–314; Chrestos Vantsos, *Ὁ γάμος καὶ ἡ προετοιμασία αὐτοῦ* (Athens, 1977); Georgios Vergotes, "Ἡ λειτουργικὴ διάσταση τοῦ μυστηρίου τοῦ γάμου," in *Γρηγόριος Παλαμᾶς* 70, no. 5 (1985): 136–157; Savvas Agourides, "Ἁγιογραφικὰ κείμενα περὶ γάμου," in *Ἐκκλησία* 21 and 22 (1971): 401–671.

To marry in the Lord is a vocation, a charism, and a hope. The sacrament of marriage proclaims and celebrates these things by introducing the bride and groom to the virtues of married life, inviting them to live out their lives day by day in mutual love with faith, humility, gentleness, patience, and forbearance—virtues that make life in common possible and fruitful.

The Vision of Christian Marriage

VOCATION, CHARISM, HOPE

Among the many icons depicting events in the life and ministry of our Lord Jesus Christ, there is one that portrays the wedding feast in Cana of Galilee, at which he performed the first of his signs and revealed his glory, and at which his disciples believed in him (John 2:1–11). One arrangement of this icon depicts Christ, the Theotokos, the steward of the feast, another figure, and the bridegroom and bride, who are seated at the banquet table wearing crowns.[237] Significantly, in this particular composition two figures dominate the icon: Christ, who is shown blessing the couple while looking at the Theotokos, and the bride, who is dressed resplendently in a white garment. Based chiefly on the nuptial imagery in the book of Genesis (1:26–28, 2:18–24) and in St. Paul's Letter to the Ephesians (5:22–33), this particular icon emphasizes the sacramental character of Christian marriage and highlights two of its essential elements. The first of these is that God himself is the creator of the conjugal union. Marriage is willed by God. He is both the author and the celebrant of pure marriage.[238] The icon depicts this truth through the figure of Christ shown blessing the couple.

---

[237] This depiction appears in a fourteenth-century wall painting in the Church of St. Nicholas Orfanos in Thessaloniki. A photograph of it can be found in M. Acheimastou-Potamianou, *Greek Art: Byzantine Wall Paintings* (Athens, 1994), 162–163, 248. For a brief description of the composition of this traditional icon, see Photios Kontoglou, Ἔκφρασις τῆς Ὀρθοδόξου εἰκονογραφίας, 2nd ed. (Athens, 1979), 160.

[238] This fundamental principle, based on the creation narratives in Genesis, is reflected in the prayers of the marriage rite. For example, the second prayer in the service of crowning reads, "Blessed are You, O Lord our God, the priest (ἱερουργός) of mystical and pure marriage and the law-giver of the bodily bond, guardian of incorruption, and good steward of the things of life." Similarly, the third prayer (for the joining of the hands) reads, "Holy God, you formed man out of earth and from his rib you fashioned woman and joined her to him as a fitting helper, for it seemed good to your majesty that man should not be alone on earth. Now, too, Master, stretch forth your hand from your holy dwelling place and conjoin these your servants." For more on the idea of God as the celebrant of marriage, see Patronos, *Ο γάμος στη θεολογία*, 21–29.

The second element is that marriage, as a loving relationship, is modeled after the unique reality of the loving relationship between Christ and his Church. The love and life of the couple are sustained and perfected through their active relationship with God and his love, which is a self-offering, covenant love. The icon depicts this truth by centering attention on the eternal Bridegroom, Christ, and his bride, the Church. In the icon of the wedding feast, the splendidly adorned bride represents the Church.

The icon reminds its viewers that the nuptial bond is a divine gift, a bond that God ordained in Paradise. It exists to bring two people into full communion as they achieve fullness of being in God (Gen. 2:18–21). Marriage brings us before the mysterious union of the human monad (Gen. 5:1). The human being is a conjugal being (Mark 10:7–9), or as Ladislas Orsy puts it, "Male and female together reflect the image of God. They together possess a perfection that is not given to each one individually. Man and woman, in union, reveal the image, the personality, of their Creator better than one of them alone could do it."[239]

The fall, which brought corruption and disfigurement to human nature, obscured the archetypal vision of the man–woman relationship. Sin infects the human being, and as a consequence, the quality of love and freedom in the nuptial community is compromised. The marital union is impaired, and familial relationships have become subject to temptations and distortions.

Christ, having redeemed humanity from the curse of sin and death, invites all people to appropriate for themselves the fruits of his cross and resurrection through his mystical Body, the Church. All that he did once for all for the salvation of the world has now passed over into the sacraments of the Church. The sacraments manifest the radical renewal and transfiguration of human nature and life. They allow people to become partakers of divine life and perfection. Through the sacraments, the powers of the Kingdom are made manifest, and "new life enters the human person as a real presence and gift, not as an obligation or magic."[240]

Marriage, like the whole of the Christian life, is formed sacramentally. The sacrament of marriage celebrates both the restoration of the conjugal union to its original order and its reintegration into the realm of grace. The

---

[239] Ladislas Orsy, "Married Persons: God's Chosen People," in *Christian Marriage Today*, ed. Klaus Demmer and Aldegonde Brenninkmeijer-Werhahn (Washington, DC, 1997), 41.
[240] Chryssavgis, "The Sacrament of Marriage," 17.

CHAPTER FOUR: MARRIAGE—THE SACRAMENT OF LOVE 109

sacrament reveals to the couple the dynamic dimensions of mutuality, the loveliness of human sexuality, and the nobleness of procreation. Always in union with God, the husband and wife are graced to act together to heal and overcome the impotence of impaired masculinity and femininity, and thus they rediscover and fulfill the original wholeness and communion of nuptial life.[241]

A marriage of faithful persons is anchored in the sanctifying grace that comes from the incarnation of the Son of God, by which God's immeasurable love for his creation was made manifest. Indeed, as Archbishop Demetrios affirmed in his keynote address at the forty-second Biennial Clergy–Laity Congress of the Greek Orthodox Archdiocese of America,

> The superb example for the reality of [marriage and] family as a most holy and unique institution is the Lord Jesus Christ himself. At his incarnation, he was born in a family. He was protected as a newborn baby by his family from the murderous plans of King Herod. He lived for thirty full years out of his total thirty-three years of his life on earth, in his family in Nazareth, not in the desert. He did his first miracle, recorded at the beginning of the Gospel of John, in Cana of Galilee, transforming water into wine, just in order to support and strengthen the celebration of a new marriage, of the creation of a new family.[242]

In a marriage based on faith, two unique and fragile persons, until then "strangers" to one another, are called to enter into the mystery of God's unlimited love and care in order to deepen in the knowledge of one another, such that each becomes for the other an instrument of salvation and deification. Sacramental marriage derives its essential character from baptism and the Eucharist. Thus it is intimately related to the faith community and receives its identity from its orientation toward the Kingdom of God. The primary context of Christian marriage is ecclesial. The couple becomes one flesh in a mystery of unity that has no fuller expression than that of the Church and the sacrament of the Eucharist.[243]

---

[241] Charalambidis, "Marriage in the Orthodox Church," 206. For more on the origins and manifestations of impaired masculinity and femininity, see Vasilios Thermos, *Οδύνη Σώματος Χριστού: Κεφάλαια εκκλησιαστικής αυτογνωσίας* (Athens, 2009), 115–140.
[242] Archbishop Demetrios, "The Orthodox Christian Family," 4.
[243] See Meyendorff, *Marriage: An Orthodox Perspective*, 22–26; Kardamakis, *Αγάπη και γάμος*, 97–104; M. Francis Mannion, "The Four Elements of Love," in *Liturgy* 4, no. 2 (1984): 20.

Hence, it is not without significance that the Eucharist, at least through the ninth century, was the locus of the marriage rites of the Church.[244] In the early Church, the marriage of Christians was accomplished in accordance with the rites and customs of their local societies.[245] As I have noted elsewhere, studies have shown that marriage ceremonies in the ancient Greco-Roman world involved three special actions over which the father of the bride presided: the *engyesis* (ἐγγύησις: pledge, or betrothal), the *ekdosis* (ἐκδόσις: giving in marriage), and the *stephanoma* (στεφάνωμα: crowning, or garlanding).[246] The traditional role of the father in these family rituals, which eventually constituted key elements of the marriage rites of the Church, devolved upon the bishop or presbyter, the shepherd and father of the local faith community. In the early Church, marriages were transformed into a sacrament of the Kingdom when the couple received Holy Communion with the blessing of the bishop in the presence of the entire community at the Eucharistic assembly. The nucleus of the rites of matrimony that we know today was already shaped by the fourth century.[247]

A Christian marriage that is celebrated and lived in faith becomes more than a biological fact and more than a social custom or a legal institution. The sacrament consecrates the union of two people into a single substance, making them into a living icon of God and a prophetic image of his Kingdom. United in the love of God, the nuptial community is called to become a little kingdom, a house of God, a domestic Church.[248]

---

[244] For the connection of marriage to the Eucharist, see Panayiotis Skaltsis, Γάμος καὶ Θεία Λειτουργία. Also see Philip Zymaris, "Marriage and the Eucharist: From Unity to Schizophrenia; The Positive Theology of Marriage and Its Distortion from an Eastern Orthodox Point of View," in *Love, Marriage, and Family in the Eastern Orthodox Tradition*, 134–151. For the connection of all the sacraments to the Eucharist, see Nenad Milosevic, *To Christ and the Church: The Divine Eucharist as the All-Encompassing Mystery of the Church* (Los Angeles, 2012).

[245] For a brief description of marriage in the Greco-Roman world, see German Martinez, *Wedding to Marriage* (Washington, DC, 1993), 53–60.

[246] See the essay, "The Challenges of Intra-Christian Marriages: A Case Study," in Alkiviadis C. Calivas, *Challenges and Opportunities: The Church in Her Mission to the World* (Brookline, MA, 2001), 103.

[247] For the development of the marriage rites, see Ioannis M. Fountoulis, Τελετουργικά Θέματα (Athens 2007), 3:89–107; Panayiotis Trembelas, Μικρὸν εὐχολόγιον (Athens, 1950), 1:9–96; A. Stavrinou, Ἡ Ἱερολογία τοῦ γάμου (Constantinople, 1923).

[248] See, for example, Evdokimov, *Sacrament of Love*, 118; Patronos, Ο γάμος στη θεολογία, 39–49.

These positive foundational affirmations about Christian marriage may seem an inapplicable utopian ideal, far from empirical reality. Yet as I have already noted, Christian marriage can be seen, understood, and lived only from the perspective of new life in Christ. The Church's sacrament embodies the ideal vision of marriage and graces the couple with the potential to realize it. As the seed gives forth according to the ground in which it was planted, so the full effectiveness of sacramental nuptial life is made manifest to a greater or lesser degree by the faith commitment of the couple. Living faith is more than knowledge, just as genuine love is more than feelings. Both faith and love require commitment and action. The Church's nuptial service, through its prayers and ritual actions, reveals the mystery of perfect love and communion in all its hidden dimensions and possibilities and calls the couple to accept this gift and to nurture it prayerfully with watchful attention.

The rite of matrimony contains in precise and concise form the entire Orthodox teaching on marriage.[249] The service currently in use by the Church consists of two separate, independent, and self-contained rites that have been linked together for many centuries. These rites reflect the basic two-stage process of the nuptial union, betrothal and marriage, which symbolically summarize the entire married life.[250] The first is called the service of betrothal or engagement (ἀκολουθία ἐπὶ ἀρραβῶνος καὶ μνήστρα). The second, the rite of marriage proper, is usually referred to as the service of crowning, named for the characteristic ritual crowning of the groom and bride (ἀκολουθία τοῦ στεφανώματος).[251]

---

[249] Chryssavgis, "Sacrament of Marriage," 24. For a concise analysis of the rite of matrimony, see Stylianopoulos, "Toward a Theology of Marriage," 250–267; Evdokimov, *Sacrament of Love*, 148–159. See also Patrick Viscuso, "The Formation of Marriage in Late Byzantium," *St. Vladimir's Theological Quarterly* 35, no. 4 (1991): 309–325; Meyendorff, *Marriage: An Orthodox Perspective*, 32–48; Meyendorff, "Christian Marriage in Byzantium: The Canonical and Liturgical Tradition," in *Dumbarton Oaks Papers* 44 (1990): 99–107; Alvian N. Smirensky, "The Evolution of the Present Rite of Matrimony and Parallel Canonical Developments," *St. Vladimir's Theological Quarterly* 6, no. 1 (1964): 38–47.

[250] Evdokimov, *Sacrament of Love*, 70. For more on the rites of matrimony, see Kenneth Stevenson, *Nuptial Blessing: A Study of Christian Marriage Rites* (New York, 1983), 9–26, 97–104; Mark Searle and Kenneth W. Stevenson, *Documents of the Marriage Liturgy* (Collegeville, MN, 1992).

[251] In recent years, Christos Yannaras published anonymously a *New Ecclesiastical Service of the Sacrament of Marriage / Νέα εκκλησιατική ακολουθία του μυστηρίου του γάμου* (Athens,

LEARNING TO LOVE: MAKING THE VISION REAL

In many respects, a Christian marriage is similar to other marriages in its external form and structure. It is experienced, however, in a radically different way. Relationships, authority, and personal identity are experienced on a wholly other plane in the context and spirit of new life in Christ. In loving and being loved, Christian spouses must be willing to enter daily into the life of Christ, through whom they discover that "perfect love is love crucified,"[252] or as St. Paul teaches, that "love is patient and kind ... it does not insist on its own way ... love bears all things, believes all things, endures all things. Love never ends" (1 Cor. 13:4–8).

Sacrificial love requires of individuals the will to die daily to the dreadful condition of fallen human nature: to pride, envy, deceit, wrath, insensitivity, selfishness, and every kind of sinful desire and self-delusion that distorts and, ultimately, destroys the human person. In marriage, according to Olivier Clement, Christian couples are called "to thrust aside the masks which are incorporated into our face, the neurotic personages which are bound to our person, to tear away the dead skins, and in confidence and humility, in obedience to faith, to let the very life of the risen Christ emerge in us."[253]

Perfect love is not obvious. We can learn it only from God. God, "in his Trinitarian openness, constitutes the secret source of love."[254] God himself

---

1997). His proposed service takes place immediately after the Divine Liturgy. The structure of the service and its rubrics are similar to those of the traditional service, but he replaces the familiar prayers with new ones of his own creation, adds an elaborate public affirmation of consent, includes new hymnographic material, and substitutes the traditional Gospel lesson (John 2:1–11) with another reading (John 17:10–26). Fr. Vasilios Thermos has also proposed a new service, *Sung Service of Marriage / Ασματική ακολουθία του γάμου* (Athens, 2000). His rite contains two unique features: an entire Orthros service, composed by him, and the insertion of the traditional wedding service within the Divine Liturgy. The betrothal service is conducted after the *apolysis* of Orthros and before the Divine Liturgy. The prayers of the three antiphons of the Divine Liturgy are replaced with the first three prayers of the received rite. The fourth prayer of the received rite is recited after the Gospel and the Fervent Litany. The bride and groom receive Holy Communion at the appointed time. The remaining parts of the traditional service are added after the prayer behind the *amvon*. The original prayers of Yannaras and the lovely poetic compositions of Thermos deserve further study. Some editions of the *Archieratikon* (Bishop's book) published by Apostoliki Diakonia of the Church of Greece also contain a marriage rite within the Divine Liturgy as described by Fr. Thermos.

[252] Evdokimov, *Sacrament of Love*, 155.
[253] Olivier Clement, "Life in the Body," 138. See also Kardarnakis, *Αγάπη και γάμος*, 91–96.
[254] Clement, "Life in the Body," 144.

CHAPTER FOUR: MARRIAGE—THE SACRAMENT OF LOVE

is love (1 John 4:8, 16) and his love disclosed to us precedes, establishes, renews, and perfects our love.[255] As John Chryssavgis tells it, "When two human persons love and are united in marriage, they reflect God himself—and this love can never be exhausted psychologically, sociologically, medically, economically, or legally."[256] The sacrament of marriage seals the love of two persons with the abiding, loving, and sanctifying presence of Christ. With Christ at its beginning and end, "the dimension of love in human life contains the various elements of *eros* (ascending, ecstatic love), *charitas* (compassionate love or sympathy), and *agape* (love as grace and self-sacrifice to the end)."[257]

By loving Christ, and through him each other, the spouses come to know one another's distinct identity, complete one another in a dynamic way, and discover in each other God's image. Drawn to each other, and together to him who is the source of all love, their eros is constantly transfigured to unfailing love—into agape. Persons who marry in the Lord come to appreciate God's commandment "to love your neighbor as yourself" (Matt. 19:19) on the deepest possible levels of existence. A husband and wife become intimate lovers because they are, first of all, neighbor and friend to each other in the most unique and conclusive way.

The couple's gift of self to each other is to come to love in a divine way, and this way of loving is unconditional. Such love invests the couple's whole being with the redeeming presence of Christ, who is himself love incarnate. This graceful presence integrates and enriches the personal and sexual love of a husband and wife and enables them to reach ever-new and ever-deeper levels of communion, friendship, maturity, openness, honesty, and holiness.

A marriage in the Lord is sustained by the Holy Spirit, who grants to the spouses such gifts as are necessary for them to live a godly life in peace, truth, harmony, and love.[258] This is not to say, however, that a Church marriage is free of problems, temptations, tensions, pain, and suffering. Rather, it means that in the obedience of faith, spouses are open to the influence of the power of the Holy Spirit. He allows the life of the risen Christ to

---

[255] Ibid.
[256] Chryssavgis, "Sacrament of Marriage," 17. See also Patronos, Ὁ γάμος στὴ θεολογία, 91–101.
[257] Chryssavgis, "Sacrament of Marriage," 17.
[258] See, for example, the last prayer of the betrothal service, the first prayer of the service of crowning, and the prayer after the Gospel in the same service.

grow in them so that they may come to transcend ordinary life, with its temptations, contradictions, and uncertainties and so that they may come to appreciate more deeply its wonders, joys, and potentialities.

Learning to live together requires patience, courage, humility, the willingness to forgive, and the ability to give up resentments. Couples have to learn to come to terms with their limitations and to negotiate and adjust the environments and structures in which they move and act.[259] Love is more than warm feelings. It is an attitude and a disposition of illumined self-giving. It is the way of enduring faithfulness and commitment to the mystery of perfect love, by which a husband and wife are led to renewed freedom, love, hope, and joy through their many estrangements and returns.[260] Indeed, as Philip Mamalakis points out, "At the heart of the marital union are the hundreds of small bids for connection between couples ... The daily communicating in marriage, as bids for connection, are not just about sharing information, but about nurturing connection and intimacy ... The nature of sharing and listening is that it is a 'turning toward,' and as such, expresses care and love."[261]

The quality of marital and family life is conditioned by many factors, including the spiritual maturity, emotional stability, and physical health of the spouses. Family relationships, cultural traditions and habits, and financial worries also affect the marriage. These and other distressful situations and uncertainties both in the home and at work can become disruptive and burdensome. When left unattended, such conditions can lead to serious problems and deficiencies in marital and family life. We must not forget, as Archbishop Demetrios points out, that the Bible itself shows that the family can be a place of joy but "also the arena of terrible tragedies and crimes." In the book of Genesis, he continues, "the first homicide on earth is reported, and this terrible crime happens within the first family with the two sons of Adam and Eve, when Cain kills his brother Abel (Gen. 4:1–16). We do not need to report the deceitful conspiracy of Jacob and his mother Rebec-

---

[259] Engaged and recently married couples would benefit greatly by reading the book of Charles Joanides, *Attending to Your Marriage: A Resource for Christian Couples* (Minneapolis, MN, 2006).
[260] See Clement, "Life in the Body," 145.
[261] Philip Mamalakis, "Turning Toward as a Pastoral Theology of Marriage," in *Servant of the Gospel: Studies in Honor of His All-Holiness Ecumenical Patriarch Bartholomew*, ed. Thomas FitzGerald (Brookline, MA, 2011), 129–130.

ca against his brother Esau. Or, Joseph being sold into slavery by his own brothers (Gen. 37:1–36)."[262]

To avoid difficulties and heart-rending tragedies, spouses are obliged to be humble and patient with each other and to work hard at resolving their differences through the exercise of mutual trust, forgiveness, tenderness, and kindliness. This task, however, requires more than the goodwill of the spouses. Human capacities and capabilities are easily depleted. Spouses therefore must learn to nurture their interior life through prayer, the sacraments of the Church, spiritual guidance and care, and works of genuine piety and charity. These things not only energize the person but also lend themselves to the continuous renewal of the marital bond.

For these reasons, the Church has incorporated into the rite of matrimony requests and petitions for the practical, everyday things that contribute to the growth, development, and well-being of the nuptial union and community. Thus the Church prays that the couple's "goings out and comings in" (Deut. 28:6; Ps. 121:8)—their activities and enterprises, as well as their home relationships and quiet occupations—may be free of temptations, evils, and dangers. The Church prays for the peaceful life, the prosperity, the compatibility, and the longevity of the couple, along with a stable family life and the enjoyment of good children.[263]

Acquiring a New Identity

Personhood exists ultimately only in God, who freely shares this mode of existence with humankind. Christ—who is the model and archetype of the true human being (1 John 3:2; Col. 3:10)—reveals to each man and woman the unfathomable depths of their personhood. He is their alpha

---

[262] Archbishop Demetrios, "The Orthodox Christian Family," 3.
[263] Petitions and prayers for the spiritual, emotional, and physical well-being of the couple abound in the received betrothal and crowning services. By way of example, I cite a portion of the first prayer of the Crowning service: "Most holy Master ... bless this marriage and give to your servants (N) and (N) a peaceful life, length of days, self-control (sobriety), love for another in the bond of peace, long-lived offspring, grace upon their children, and an unfading crown of glory. Count them worthy to see their children's children, preserve their bed undefiled; and give them of the dew of heaven from above, and of the fatness of the earth. Fill their houses with wheat, wine, and oil, and every good thing, that they may give in turn to them that are in need, bestowing also to those here present with them all petitions which are for salvation."

and omega, their beginning and end, their purpose and destiny (Rev. 21:6). The inner man or woman is not ours by nature: it is a gift, bestowed by God upon everyone who comes into the world (John 1:9). Therefore the ultimate truth about a human being, both as nature and as person, is to be found in his or her vocation to become a conscious personal existence—that is, to exist as God himself exists: relationally.[264] While sin brings decay and the disintegration of the human being, participation in the life of Christ restores and renews the inward man or woman day by day.

Two baptized and communicating Christians who marry in the Lord become one flesh. Their souls and bodies commingle without confusion or change. Without ceasing to be male and female, they become one being, a single substance. They acquire a new identity in their personal relationship of co-inherence. They fulfill and complete each other in a way that was previously unknown to them while each was under parental authority (Matt. 19:4–5).[265] Consciousness of self at previously unknown and unexperienced levels is now discovered and understood by each primarily through the mediation of the other. Their physical, spiritual, and personal unity becomes a dynamic and transforming event. Their personhood, in all its potentialities, is realized day by day in their nuptial consubstantiality and in their union with God.

Thus Christian marriage is more than a social and religious sanction of a biological fact. As Christos Yannaras notes, "Through a reciprocal relinquishment of the individual will and acceptance of the other's will, the unity of man and wife comes to be built not on the natural premise of the individual sexual impulse but on the premise of ecclesial communion, which is self-transcendence and self-offering." And he adds, "Marriage draws its identity not from the natural relationship, but from the relationship in the realm of the Kingdom."[266]

---

[264] See, for example, John D. Zizioulas, *Being as Communion* (Crestwood, NY, 1985), 15–65.

[265] See Agourides, "Ἁγιογραφικὰ κείμενα περὶ γάμου," 515. The Christological, ecclesiological, and eschatological dimensions, extensions, and perspectives of marriage are founded on the creation narratives in the Book of Genesis. Other important Scripture texts on marriage include the Song of Songs; the Book of Tobit; Isaiah 54:1–8; Jeremiah 3:6–13; Ezekiel 16:23; Malachi 2:10–16; Hosea 1–2; Proverbs 31; Mark 10:1–12; Luke 16:18; 1 Corinthians 7:1–17, 11:7–12; Ephesians 5:21–33; Colossians 3:18–21; 1 Timothy 2:14–15.

[266] Yannaras, *Freedom of Morality*, 162.

Accordingly, Christian marriage can never be considered merely a private affair or an individual matter. It is an ecclesial event. It is the entrance of the couple into the gathered Church to share its life and values, forming all personal and familial life in the direction of the Kingdom of God. Thus the prayers of the marriage rite place the couple within the acts of God in history. The spouses are called to enter into the mystery of salvation history to become servants of redemption and faithful witnesses to the work of God.[267] As Alexandros Stavropoulos writes,

> The couple enters into the whole history of married couples from the creation of the first pair. They are identified to some degree with the patriarchal couples, and they share in the Lord's first miracle at Cana. They stand alongside all the married couples of Church history and they are called to live out their own married history as a means of transfiguring their union into a new creation worthy to enter the Kingdom.[268]

The anamnetic character of the priestly prayers of the marriage rite, with their recurring reference to Cana and to Old Testament couples and mat-

---

[267] The role of marriage at creation and throughout salvation history is mentioned in the prayers of the marriage rite. The last prayer in the betrothal service, for example, reads in part, "In the beginning you did make them male and female and by you the woman is joined unto the man as a fitting helper for the procreation of the human race. Therefore, Lord our God who has sent forth your truth upon your inheritance, and your covenant unto your servants, our fathers, your elect from generation to generation, look upon your servants ... establish and make firm their betrothal." In addition to the patriarchs, the prayers in the betrothal service also refer to other Old Testament personalities, including Joseph, Daniel, Tamar, and Moses.

In the service of crowning, we read the following in the first prayer of the rite: "O God most pure, maker of every creature, who did transform the rib of our forefather Adam into a woman because of your love toward humankind, and did bless them and say to them, be fruitful and multiply, and fill the earth and subdue it; who did make of the two one flesh: Therefore a man leaves his father and mother and cleaves to his wife, and the two shall become one flesh, and what God has joined together, let no man put asunder." The prayer makes further reference to the rich blessings of marriage by mentioning the Old Testament patriarchal couples, whose offspring played a role in salvation history. It also mentions the parents of St. John the Baptist and the forefathers of Mary the Theotokos. The second prayer also refers to Old and New Testament couples who were the recipients of God's special blessings, including the patriarchal couples, as well as Moses and Zipporah, Zechariah and Elizabeth, and Joachim and Anna. Also mentioned are other Old Testament personalities: Noah, Enoch, Shem, Elijah, Jonah, and the three youths. The prayer also makes reference to St. Helen, who found the precious Cross of Christ, and to the forty martyrs of Sevastia, who received the crowns of martyrdom.

[268] Stavropoulos, "The Understanding of Marriage," 58.

rimonial events, is of particular interest and significance.[269] The *anamnesis*, or remembrance, of the mighty acts of God in history as revealed in the Scriptures and as they relate to a specific act of the Church constitutes a key element in all the sacramental rites of the Church.[270] In the sacrament of matrimony, as Fr. Theodore Stylianopoulos notes,

> God is asked to bless the marriage of every couple as he did that of Abraham and Sarah, Isaac and Rebecca, Jacob and Rachel, and many others down to Zachariah and Elizabeth who gave birth to the Forerunner. Every marriage of persons who are in communion with God, even in the Old Testament, is sacramental in the essential sense of being a locus and vehicle of the holy presence of the living God.[271]

In other words, every devout couple anchored and living in Christ is sealed with the presence of Christ, and their family is given the possibility to witness to the transforming power of God in human affairs. Archbishop Demetrios explains this reality as follows: "We see the Christian Orthodox family as a dwelling of Christ and a witness of his Gospel ... It is a home for Christ, his permanent residence ... It is so by its strong faith in him, a faith that is transmitted from generation to generation in the genealogical history of each family."[272]

MUTUAL CONSENT AND OTHER ESSENTIAL CONDITIONS

From the perspective of the Orthodox Church, what is truly new in Christian marriage is the possibility that the unity of husband and wife can be expanded and transfigured into a new reality—into the Kingdom itself—

---

[269] In addition to the names of Old and New Testament persons, the Lord's presence at the wedding feast in Cana of Galilee is a favorite subject: "O God, our God, who did come to Cana of Galilee, and did bless there the marriage feast, bless also these your servants." The Gospel lesson assigned to the rite is John 2:1–11, which recounts the first of Jesus's signs, performed at the Cana wedding feast.

[270] The remembrance, or *anamnesis*, of persons or events related to the conferral of a particular blessing is a constitutive part of every consecratory prayer. This is true of the marriage rite, as well. Of the several prayers in the received rite of crowning, two are essential—namely, the third and the fourth in the series. Succinct and to the point, they encompass the essence of sacramental marriage. The first of these prayers reads thus: "Holy God, you formed man out of the earth, then fashioned woman out of his rib and joined her to him as a fitting helpmate and partner. For it seemed good to your majesty." The other prayer reads, "Lord, God, as part of your divine plan of salvation, you saw fit by your presence at Cana in Galilee to declare marriage honorable."

[271] Stylianopoulos, "Toward a Theology of Marriage," 270.

[272] Archbishop Demetrios, "The Orthodox Christian Family," 4.

through a kenotic (self-emptying) experience. Marriage in the Lord cannot be reduced to some form of utilitarianism or legalism. It is more than a contract serving utilitarian needs and ends, and it is more than a mutual attraction based on natural eroticism. Christian marriage is something unique not because of any abstract law or moral ban but because in its very essence it is a mystery, a sacrament of the Kingdom, by which two unique and unrepeatable persons are united to one another and together to Christ, who shares his Body with them through the Eucharist.

The strength of the nuptial bond, therefore, is not autonomous and self-evident or self-explanatory. Its efficacy as an institution of Christian witness is possible only in the context of the faith community. Through the marriage rite, the bride and groom affirm their faith as well as their willingness to integrate themselves into the life of the Church, no longer as autonomous individuals but as equal partners, as a community of two interdependent persons who find fulfillment and completion in one another through Christ in the Church that is his Body. This is why sacramental marriage ideally presupposes a common faith. Unity in faith makes marriage complete inasmuch as the partners can share the sacraments.[273]

For an Orthodox Christian who wishes to marry, a Church marriage is not an option but a fundamental condition, not because a Church wedding sanctions sexual and other relationships but because it preserves, celebrates, and communicates a particular vision and understanding of marital and familial life. Through the rite of matrimony, the bride and groom are gifted with and empowered by divine grace to begin their nuptial vocation and mission as servants of redemption—as two people who are energized by the Holy Spirit to realize in themselves the image of Christ through a progressive share in his risen and exalted life, witnessing thereby to the transforming power of God's redemptive activity, which touches, vivifies, and sanctifies everyone who believes in him.[274]

---

[273] See Lewis J. Patsavos, *Spiritual Dimensions of the Canons* (Brookline, MA, 2003), 52.

[274] By virtue of their baptism, all Christians are called to be servants of redemption. Perhaps in no other expression of the Christian life is this calling realized more completely or more practically than in Christian parenthood and priesthood. This concept is developed by Bishop Athenagoras Kokkinakis in his study on marriage and the priesthood, *Parents and Priests as Servants of Redemption: An Interpretation of the Doctrines of the Eastern Orthodox Church on the Sacraments of Matrimony and the Priesthood* (New York, 1958).

The free-will consent of the partners is a constitutive element of the sacrament of matrimony. The decision to marry in the Lord is a highly personal one. It is to be arrived at prayerfully, in the counsel of one's heart. The freedom to choose one's own partner is restricted only by those canonical, legal, or moral impediments that would distort the purpose of Christian marriage. While personal choice and mutual consent are essential elements of the sacrament, the privilege is not absolute. The freedom to choose one's partner is conditioned both by civil law and by moral imperatives and canonical regulations.[275]

It is conceivable that through the exercise of free choice, one may compromise his or her relationship with the Church and even forfeit communion. An interreligious marriage (a marriage between an Orthodox Christian and a non-Christian), for example, is disallowed by the canons. It generates great personal, familial, and communal difficulties. Yet as much as the Church and Orthodox Christian families try to prevent such marriages, the problem is that they happen in multireligious, multiethnic, and multicultural secular societies, such as our own in the United States of America. In America, people of various backgrounds live, study, play, and work side by side daily. Relationships are formed, some of which may lead to a marriage that the Church will not bless sacramentally, thus placing the Orthodox partner in a serious dilemma.

Differences in faith can create degrees of disharmony and disunity between the spouses and within their families and can lead to the weakening of religious identity, to confessional relativism, or to religious indifference. Even intra-Christian marriages could affect the orderly life of the nuptial community. Hence as Fr. Stanley Harakas correctly observes, "Shared faith and traditions spare couples and their children, as well as their extended families, many serious problems, and help strengthen the bonds between them." He continues, "Even so, the Orthodox Church will bless marriages between Orthodox and non-Orthodox partners provided that the non-Orthodox partner is a Christian who has been baptized, in water, in the Name

---

[275] On the canonical impediments to marriage and the theological principles behind them, see Lewis J. Patsavos, "Impediments of Relationship in the Sacrament of Marriage," in FitzGerald, *Servant of the Gospel*, 139–157. For guidelines pertaining to marriage in the Church, see Stanley S. Harakas, "Pastoral Guidelines, Weddings," in *Yearbook of the Greek Orthodox Archdiocese of America*, which is published annually by the Greek Orthodox Archdiocese of America. In the 2015 edition, these guidelines are found on pages 271–272.

of the Father and the Son and the Holy Spirit and the couple should be willing to baptize their children in the Orthodox Church and raise and nurture them in accordance with the Orthodox faith."[276]

Given the increasing number of intra-Christian marriages, the Church has an obligation to embrace with love and concern the ecumenical couples, the "mixed marriages" that have been blessed sacramentally by the Church. On one hand, every effort should be made to strengthen the faith commitment of the Orthodox spouse, and on the other, no effort should be spared to welcome, to the degree possible, the non-Orthodox partner as a peripheral member of the Church. The non-Orthodox partner should be treated with care, sensitivity, respect, and dignity as the spouse and parent of fellow members of the faith community. Nurturing family unity must be among the most serious pastoral concerns of the Church. Clergy are obliged to offer counsel and to help couples deal with and overcome the concerns and conflicts that may arise from confessional differences.[277]

Though smaller in number than intra-Christian marriages, interreligious marriages also occur and are a cause for concern, since the Orthodox partner in such marriages is prevented from receiving the sacraments. Could not the Church study this issue in a creative and compassionate way by consulting the Scriptures and tradition so as to avoid the permanent exclusion of the Orthodox partner from the sacramental life of the Church, especially when such an individual, in every other way, remains true to the tenets of the Orthodox faith? Could not the Church under certain conditions and through some form of penance allow for the reconciliation of a son or daughter who has married outside the Church?

Following this brief parenthesis on mixed marriages, I now return to the idea of mutual consent. Despite the fact that the consent of both bride and groom is essential, consent itself does not make the sacrament. For this reason, the marriage rite of the Orthodox Church does not envision, require, or contain the exchange of vows and promises or any ring-giving formulas. These practices are based essentially on the principle that the partners themselves are the ministers of their own marriage. In the Orthodox under-

---

[276] Harakas, "Pastoral Guidelines, Weddings," 271.
[277] See the two volumes by Charles Joanides, *Ministering to Intermarried Couples: A Resource for Clergy and Lay Workers* (New York, 2004); Joanides, *When You Intermarry: A Resource for Inter-Christian, Intercultural Couples, Parents, and Families* (New York, 2002).

standing, God is the essential minister of marriage. He works through the couple and is the celebrant of the mystery through the bishop or presbyter performing the sacrament and through the participating faith community.

For the Church, the full significance of mutual consent is ultimately grounded on two principles, the first of which is the couple's willingness to submit their decision and life to Christ and to the spiritual care of his Church (Eph. 5:21). The second is the couple's willingness to abide freely in the vision of marriage that draws its strength and identity from God and his Kingdom, not only from their mutual vows, promises, and aspirations—well-intentioned as those may be.

According to current Greek practice, except for the presence of the couple, there is no other formal public declaration of consent in the marriage rite. In practice, however, mutual consent to wed is given by the bride and groom privately before the parish priest when the petition to marry, addressed to the local bishop, is prepared. By signing the petition, the couple affirms their will to marry and that there are no impediments to their marriage. The Russian and other Orthodox Churches, on the other hand, use a public declaration of consent at the start of the marriage rite.[278]

The liturgical tradition of the Church provides ample evidence of various forms of public affirmations that the bride and groom are required to make. It would be good to reintroduce the use of such affirmations, where they do not exist, in order to highlight the significance of the consent and the commitment of the couple to the purposes of Christian marriage. The public declaration of consent should contain three fundamental statements: that the groom and bride enter the marriage of their own free will; that there are no canonical, legal, or moral impediments to their marriage; and that they pledge, by God's grace, to uphold the purposes and the sanctity of the nuptial bond.[279]

---

[278] For the use of declarations of consent in the manuscript tradition, see Trembelas, *Μικρόν Εὐχολόγιον*, 20, 22, 28–30, 42. The declaration of the Slavonic text reads as follows: "Do you, (N), have a good, free, and unconstrained will and firm intention to take as your wife this woman, (N), whom you see before you? —I have, reverend father. Have you promised yourself to any other bride? —I have not promised myself, reverend father." The same questions are put to the bride (with the appropriate changes).

[279] The following brief formula may be considered as an appropriate public declaration of consent: "Do you, (N), freely accept to take as your wife this woman, (N), whom you see

The Essential Characteristics of Christian Marriage

Marriage is established and constituted with the appropriate prayers and signs of the Church, since it is God himself who is both its creator and celebrant. Through canonically ordained bishops or presbyters, the Church, as the redeemed community, calls upon God to unite and sanctify the spouses and to help them prosper in life and in faith. The explicit liturgical act celebrated by the Church, as Bruce Beck notes, is essential,

> because marriage, like human kind, is fallen, and not simply able to be sanctioned and blessed. Like the sacrament of Baptism, the marriage rite renews and restores human love into the image or icon of Christ and His Bride, the Church ... This restoration of nuptial love through the sacrament of marriage is a new creation; just as a catechumen, after having emerged from the font and having been chrismated, is a new creation, so too is the newly married couple a new entity in the Kingdom of God.[280]

The conjugal union thus established is founded upon and formed by three essential characteristics: the indissolubility of the nuptial bond, the equality of the spouses, and their monogamous relationship.

These three factors point to the original and essential unity of the human being as ordained by God. This unity, however, has been fragmented and obscured by the fall—the act of disobedience of Adam and Eve, the progenitors of the race—whereby primal innocence was lost, and the image of God in the human being became disfigured. As a result, sinful desires and passions have thrown the original order and harmony of human relations into disarray.

Marriage in the Lord moves beyond conventional societal norms. It challenges the spouses consecrated to God to discover daily and to make real in their fragile and delicate union the original beauty and oneness of creation by introducing them to the potentialities of sacrificial love and the power of fidelity, by which they may attain the harmony of body and soul.

---

before you? Do you declare also that there are no impediments to your marriage, and do you affirm your commitment to advance with her, by God's grace, in life and faith? —I do, reverend father." The same formula (with the appropriate changes) would be addressed to the bride.

[280] Bruce Beck, "The Sacrament of Marriage and Union with God," in Dedon and Trostyanskiy, *Love, Marriage and Family*, 58..

Drawn to each other by love or, as it sometimes happens, through match-making, the spouses bring to their marriage the gift of self, with all its wonders and talents, as well as their inadequacies, limitations, and weaknesses, which they must learn to forgive in their spouse and overcome in themselves time and again. Through an ever-deepening process of interpersonal involvement and co-inherence that heightens the awareness of their distinctiveness as well as their mutuality and oneness, the spouses render themselves open to the transforming and sanctifying power of unconditional, sacrificial love. In and by this love, they come to know and realize for themselves the three fundamental characteristics of Christian marriage.

The Indissolubility of Marriage: A Gift, Not a Lifeless Form

Marital bonds are indissoluble. Christian marriage is understood to be a lifelong event, a dynamic, unfolding, loving relationship that unites two unrepeatable people into one flesh, into a single body (Gen. 2:24; Matt. 19:5). Marital bonds are established as a covenant relationship between two persons who willingly accept both the challenge and the opportunity to be "subject to one another out of reverence for Christ" (Eph. 5:21).

The indissolubility of the marital bond is grounded essentially in the Christological and Trinitarian archetypes that constitute the basis of our understanding of the human being and of the conjugal union. According to the Christological archetype, we are called to achieve the unity of the one and indivisible human nature. According to the Trinitarian archetype, we are reminded of the personal and relational character of human nature and of the vocation of male and female in union with each other and with God to achieve wholeness and perfection.[281] Thus indissolubility becomes a mark of unfailing love and commitment to the original purpose of creation.

Moreover, the indissolubility of the marital bond viewed in its Christological dimension reflects the unity of Christ and his Church, the model of the conjugal union. For this reason, Christian spouses conscientiously seek to transform their home into a domestic Church—that is, into a community that bears the essential marks and characteristics of the Church: oneness, holiness, catholicity, and apostolicity.[282]

---

[281] See Stylios, Ἄνθρωπος: Ἄρσεν καί Θῦλη, 54–70.
[282] Stavropoulos, "Understanding of Marriage," 59–60.

CHAPTER FOUR: MARRIAGE—THE SACRAMENT OF LOVE

Succinctly put, this means that the nuptial community in its pilgrimage to the Kingdom celebrates the mystery of unity in diversity. It experiences the sanctifying presence of God in its very being and in all its activities. It is rooted firmly in the truths of the faith. It experiences "the *pleroma* (fullness), the all, of the common life lived always, everywhere and by all married couples who have consecrated themselves to the living God."[283] The nuptial community accomplishes its life and task in a conciliar mode and strives to realize its vocation to bear witness to the Gospel in all areas of human life and endeavors.[284]

The permanence of the nuptial bond, however, does not come automatically. Matrimonial permanence is a gift, not a lifeless legal prescription or form. Marriages can and do fail. In this fallen and sinful world, matrimonial relationships are often severely tested. Human brokenness, together with its many dilemmas and, as someone once said, its "distorted habits, feelings and attitudes about possessions, status, work, security, guilt, sex, love, family, and friends," is an always present threat to conjugal and familial unity. The upbuilding of marriage as a community of love entails hard work and above all faithfulness to God, who graces the couple with the will and the spiritual fortitude to sustain the dynamism of all familial relationships and to advance understanding, unity, affection, and holiness among the members of the nuptial community.

On the authority of Christ, the Church upholds with all seriousness the absolute permanence of the marital bond. Yet at the same time, it has cautiously introduced qualifications and admitted exceptions to the indissolubility of marriage.[285] These qualifications are mentioned in the Scrip-

---

[283] Ibid., 61.
[284] The manner by which the Church conducts its affairs is both hierarchical and synodal (conciliar) in nature. Both modes of operation are essential to the Church and are exercised on all levels of ecclesial life. The synodal system is simultaneously hierarchical in that the ministry of leadership is recognized and esteemed. The synodal system protects the Church from the dangers and limitations of autocratic rule and constitutes a unity in which the parts condition and complement each other in a continuous process of sharing. It permits gifts to surface and bloom and allows (hierarchical) authority to be exercised creatively within the bounds of mutual respect, love, and accountability. These systems are applicable to the nuptial community.
[285] For a discussion of the qualifications and exemptions to the indissolubility of marriage see, John H. Erickson, *The Challenge of Our Past* (Crestwood, NY, 1991), 39–51; Theodore Stylianopoulos, "The Indissolubility of Marriage in the New Testament: Principle and

tures and revolve generally around the fact of physical and spiritual death.²⁸⁶ Gradually, the Church came to admit other exceptions as well that, according to Fr. John Erickson, assimilate death and adultery. He writes this:

> The Byzantine ideal of symphony between *imperium* and *sacerdotium* assumed the concordance of civil law and church law ... In divorce matters the valid reasons enumerated by the civil law were reduced to two types: those which could be assimilated to death (disappearance with presumption of death, permanent insanity, monastic habit, episcopal consecration) ... and those which could be assimilated to adultery, which thus could be interpreted in the light of the Matthean exceptive clause (endangering the life of the spouse, secret abortion, forcing the spouse to prostitution ...)—in other words, serious assault on the moral and spiritual foundations of marriage.²⁸⁷

The liturgical tradition of the Church also reflects the ideal of the permanence of the marital bond. Though the Church joins in matrimony both widowed and divorced persons, it does so through a different rite, the service of second marriage (ἀκολουθία εἰς δίγαμον), which is characterized by a distinct penitential tone.²⁸⁸

The choice between right and wrong marriages must be seen in the context of a lifelong union and pilgrimage toward the Kingdom of God. Psychological and other factors may affect the ability of the spouses to relate authentically to each other as husband and wife. When such conditions are left unattended or cannot be overcome, the nuptial bond is exposed to painful and distressful conditions that can lead to separation and divorce. Divorce produces as much anguish as death does because it is the withering away of a living relationship into emotional and spiritual deadness, often after very cruel and humiliating experiences. As Fr. Michael Plekon observes, "There are real incompatibilities only discovered in time. There are people who are mis-loved as well as not-loved, abused, betrayed, and abandoned

---

Practice," *Greek Orthodox Theological Review* 34, no. 4 (1989): 335–345; Peter L'Huillier, "The Indissolubility of Marriage in Orthodox Law and Practice," *St. Vladimir's Theological Quarterly* 32, no. 3 (1988): 199–221. Patronos, Ὁ γάμος στὴ θεολογία καὶ στὴ ζωή, 119–131.
²⁸⁶ See, for example, Stylianopoulos, "The Indissolubility of Marriage," 340–343.
²⁸⁷ Erickson, *Challenge of Our Past*, 46. The Church has reserved the right to recognize that a marriage has dissolved for other reasons also, such as apostasy, serious illness and abandonment, and serious spiritual failures that cause profound incompatibilities, resulting in the complete withering of love.
²⁸⁸ The Church allows a second marriage, tolerates a third, and forbids a fourth.

CHAPTER FOUR: MARRIAGE—THE SACRAMENT OF LOVE

without leaving the premises ... Indissolubility cannot have primacy over the good of the spouses, over love."[289]

The Church admits divorce and remarriage as a concession to human frailty and imperfection. These concessions reflect the Church's pastoral concern for wounded souls, as well as its refusal to abandon divorced persons in their pain, weakness, failure, guilt, or sin. The ultimate aim of the Church in allowing divorce is twofold: to uphold the dignity and the holiness of marriage as a sacrament of communion and love, in essence and not in name only; and to bring healing, relief, and hope to those who bear the terrible burden and the pain of a dissolved marital bond, spouses as well as innocent children.[290]

Long ago, Fr. John Meyendorff proposed a radical new approach to the problem of ecclesial divorce that deserves attention and serious consideration. He wrote,

> Practically, and in conformity with Scripture and Church tradition, I would suggest that our Church authorities stop "giving divorces" (since the latter are secured anyway through civil courts) and rather, on the basis of a recognition, based upon the civil divorce, that marriage does not in fact exist, issue "permissions to remarry." Of course, in each particular case pastoral counseling and investigation should make sure that reconciliation is impossible; and the "permission to remarry" should entail at least some form of penance (in conformity with each individual case) and give the right to a Church blessing according to the rite of second marriage.[291]

The Church permits the remarriage of widows, widowers, and divorced persons. It is less known that the Church also grants annulments (ἀκυρώσις γάμου), a rarely used procedure by which the Church acknowledges that the marital union was violated in some significant way prior to the rite of matrimony. In other words, in granting an annulment, the Church recognizes

---

[289] Michael Plekon, "The Sacrament of Love: Paul Evdokimov's Vision of Marriage, Love, and Vocation," in Dedon and Trostyanskiy, *Love, Marriage, and Family*, 37.

[290] For a helpful resource on the theme of marriage, divorce, and remarriage, see Charles Joanides, *Challenges in Pastoral Care: Divorce and Remarriage* (New York, 2013). The book is a valuable guide for pastoral caregivers and for parishioners on a wide range of issues related to marital conflict, failed marriages, myths and truths about divorce, flawed financial strategies, infidelity, domestic violence, spousal, drug, and alcohol abuse, sexual addictions and compulsions, remarriage, and stepfamily challenges.

[291] Meyendorff, *Marriage: An Orthodox Perspective*, 65.

that though a marriage has taken place, the essential presuppositions for marriage were absent from the start.²⁹²

In an insightful passage, Fr. Theodore Stylianopoulos describes the tension between the vigorous ethical demands of the Gospel and the ambiguities of the present age as they apply to the radicalness of Christ's teaching and the permanence of the marital bond:

> The mystery of the eschatological kingdom revealed in Christ both as a present and future reality involves an unavoidable tension between the newness of the Kingdom and the conditions of the old age which continues until the fullness of the Kingdom arrives. Those who in faith receive the blessings of the Kingdom are also called to live by its radical demands. Yet again not even the most devoted follower of Christ can claim to have fulfilled the total ethic of the Sermon on the Mount. The higher principle of the Kingdom can therefore be neither law, which condemns even sincere believers unable to live by its demands, nor cheap grace which trivializes Christ's teaching ... The specific challenge is to accept the full force of Christ's radical teachings and to seek to interpret and apply them with discernment and compassion in the given circumstances and conditions which confront us, while patiently enduring the ambiguities and tensions which inevitably rise.²⁹³

Equality of the Spouses

The nuptial community is understood to be patterned after the divine life of the Holy Trinity. According to traditional Orthodox belief, the Godhead is a Trinity of consubstantial, co-equal, and co-eternal hypostases or persons in perfect unity. The same Orthodox faith confesses that humanity, by virtue of its creation according to the image of divinity, is a community of co-equal and co-essential persons united in exactly the same nature.²⁹⁴ Hence with this model in mind, we recognize and uphold the absolute equality of the spouses in the matrimonial union.

Though the divine Persons of the Trinity are consubstantial, their modes of being and action are different. Though they co-inhere in each other, they

---

²⁹² On the indissolubility of marriage, divorce, and annulments, see Calivas, *Challenges and Opportunities*, 108–115.
²⁹³ Stylianopoulos, "The Indissolubility of Marriage," 338.
²⁹⁴ See Thomas Hopko, "On the Male Character of Christian Priesthood," in *Women and the Priesthood*, ed. Thomas Hopko (Crestwood, NY, 1983), 98–99.

CHAPTER FOUR: MARRIAGE—THE SACRAMENT OF LOVE

are neither the same nor interchangeable in their eternal common divinity. In similar fashion, according to Fr. Thomas Hopko, "the mode of being and action of the male in creation is different from the mode of being and action of the female within the same nature of created being ... so the male and female are not the same and are not interchangeable in the unique forms of their common humanity."[295]

As co-essential and co-equal, men and women share all the attributes and virtues of their common humanity; only the manner by which these are realized is different.[296] Thus in dealing with the sexual differentiation of the spouses in marriage, one cannot speak in terms of the superiority of one and the inferiority of the other. On the contrary, the Scriptures, as noted earlier, are clear in stating that both men and women have been created according to the image of God. They share one and the same essence—as well as one and the same destiny, to acquire the likeness of God. The singular ἄνθρωπος (human being) contains the plurality of male and female: "So God created man in his own image, in the image of God he created him; male and female he created them" (Gen. 1:27; cf. Gen. 5:1).

Nevertheless, though equal, the spouses relate to each other according to an order established by God, with the man as the head and the woman as the helpmate (fitting helper) and suitable partner (βοηθὸν κατ' αὐτόν) who corresponds to him (Gen. 2:18; cf. Tobit 8:6). She is of the same nature and completes his being (Gen 2:18). The husband and wife complement each other, and in their complementarity, they are able to recognize and experience both their distinctiveness and their inherent equality.

This basic relational order between the spouses is enriched further by the model based on the relationship of God and his chosen people, Israel (Hosea 2:19–20; cf. Isa. 54:5–6),[297] especially on the relationship of Christ and his Church (Eph. 5:21–33; Col. 3:18–19). Indeed, as Fr. Hopko observes, "If men and women wish to realize the ideal of their perfect manner of being within the human community, they must seek to perfect in their mu-

---

[295] Ibid., 107.
[296] Ibid.
[297] Among the prophets, Hosea especially presents God's unfailing love for Israel through the image of marriage. At the center of this relationship are God's just dispositions and faithful love for his chosen people: "And I will betroth you to me forever; I will betroth you to me in righteousness and in justice, in steadfast love, and in mercy. I will betroth you to me in faithfulness; and you shall know the Lord" (Hosea 2:19–20).

tual relations the relationship between Christ and the Church. They must seek to do so within the actual conditions and possibilities of life which are uniquely theirs."[298]

According to these models, the husband is called to love his wife unselfishly and unconditionally, stamp her image upon his heart, take joy in her dignity and gifts, comfort her and long for her well-being, and protect, honor, and nourish their bond through his unfailing fidelity. Recognizing that authority is for the sake of loving service, the wife in turn is called to respect the headship of her husband in their mutual submission to Christ. Her vocation is to honor the nuptial relationship with her own unfailing love and faithfulness, as well as her unselfish devotion and wise counsel, modesty and graciousness, courage and strength, and abiding faith and piety. As wife and mother, she mirrors life and fills it with self-giving love through her gift of "the hidden person of the heart" (1 Pet. 3:4).

Christian Marriage Is Monogamous

From all that has been said thus far, it is clear that a Christian marriage presupposes a monogamous relationship. Monogamy, which is consistent with the Christian ideal of agape, is implied in the creation narratives in the book of Genesis. It is upheld by the prophets, confirmed by Christ, and sustained by the Church.

A monogamous relationship based on God's covenantal love allows the spouses to develop trust and deepen affections. The monogamous relationship sustains the unity of the nuptial community and guards its members from the destructive influences of envy, conceit, lust, arrogance, deception, manipulation, and dominance. Monogamy preserves the personal dignity and equality of the spouses and ensures the stability and purity of their marital relations. Monogamy fosters and promotes the purposes of Christian marriage; polygamy distorts and negates them.

The Foundational Qualities and Purposes of Christian Marriage

The ultimate purpose of sacramental marriage is to create those conditions and presuppositions that will allow the spouses to grow in holiness

---

[298] Hopko, "On the Male Character," 109.

CHAPTER FOUR: MARRIAGE—THE SACRAMENT OF LOVE

and develop together in the likeness of God. In this process of becoming, the spouses are called to reveal to one another the face of Christ in accordance with the measure of their faith and the purity of their hearts. To fulfill this ultimate nuptial vocation, the spouses must first learn to recognize, accept as their own, and make use of the foundational qualities and purposes of sacramental marriage.

The fundamental teachings on marriage are contained in the creation narratives of the book of Genesis. These key principles have been further advanced and enriched by the teachings of the prophets and the apostles. Basically, the Scriptures and holy Tradition affirm three qualities and purposes of marriage: the primacy of the marital union among all other human relationships, the sacredness of marital love, and the joy and privilege of childbearing.

These qualities and purposes of Christian marriage are encapsulated in the two foundational prayers of the rite around which the service gradually developed. The first of these, which is now the third prayer of the service of crowning, was the original consecratory prayer of the rite. The second, now the fourth prayer of the same service, originally served as the prayer of bowing in the Barberini Codex, the earliest extant *euchologion* of the Byzantine rite.[299] The two prayers read as follows:

> Holy God, you formed man out of earth, then fashioned woman out of his rib and joined her to him as a fitting helper, for it seemed good to your majesty that man should not be alone upon the earth. Do you yourself now, Master, stretch forth your hand from your holy dwelling-place and join in marriage (ἁρμόσον) this your servant (N) and this your servant (N), for by you is the woman married (ἁρμόζεται) to the man.[300] Unite them in oneness of mind, crown them into one flesh. Grant them fruit of the womb, the enjoyment of good children. For yours is the dominion, and yours the kingdom and the power and the glory of the Father and of the Son and of the Holy Spirit, now and forever....
>
> Lord our God, in your divine plan of salvation you saw fit by your presence at Cana in Galilee to declare marriage honorable. Do you, the

---

[299] See *L'eucologio Barberini gr. 336*, ed. Stefano Parenti and Elena Velkovska (Rome, 1995), 207–208.

[300] The verb ἁρμόζω, which is used here twice, means "to fit together" or "to join together." In reference to marriage, the verb is used to mean "to marry," "to give in marriage," or "to be married to."

same Lord, now also keep in peace and concord your servants (*N*) and (*N*), whom you have been pleased to unite in marriage. Declare their marriage honorable. Keep their bed undefiled. Let their life together remain blameless, so that they may attain to a ripe old age, walking in your commandments with a pure heart. For you are our God, the God who shows mercy and saves, to you we give glory, together with your eternal Father and your all-holy and good and life-giving Spirit, now and forever and to the ages of ages.

THE PRIMACY OF THE MARITAL UNION

Long ago, I read somewhere that the creation narratives in the book of Genesis leave readers with a lovely and essential image: a solitary couple, pulling away from parental bonds so that they can stand together as a new community before the Lord. This portrait highlights the most significant feature and the primary aim of Christian marriage. It is the union of two people, male and female, joined in a communion of unconditional love for their mutual companionship and their personal fulfillment, completion, and perfection in Christ.

The task of growing together in Christ is grounded on the mutual trust and love of the couple and in their ability to develop together spiritually and emotionally. These things, in turn, are nurtured by honesty and commitment, by fidelity and tenderness, and especially by the constant movement of the spouses to deeper and higher levels of consciousness and loving activity through mutual co-inherence and prayer. Oneness in mind and heart is fostered by a common vision and purpose, particularly by a common faith and a value system that grows from that faith. The nuptial community, in both its inner and outer relationships and its behavioral patterns, is conditioned by these and other determinants. They provide its focus and its incentives for life.

The mutual companionship and personal fulfillment of the spouses rest upon their developing view of the world and of their place in it. With the passage of time, a couple's view of the world and of their life can lose its vitality; it can become limiting, rigid, static, and stifling. Or it can—through attention, care, and effort—be dynamic, vibrant, productive, and fulfilling. The direction a couple's life takes depends, in large measure, on their mutual affection and respect, their capacity to forgive and sustain one another through the complexities, uncertainties, challenges, and vicissitudes of daily life, and on their ability to create quiet, meaningful opportunities that can refresh, strengthen, and deepen their marital bond. In short, to make the vision of sacramental marriage real in their lives, the spouses must struggle patiently and wisely to overcome the deadly temptations of the fallen world—lust, greed, covetousness, selfish ambitions, dissensions, pride, and the like (Gal. 5:19–21)—by being open and responsive to God's grace and thereby acquiring the mind of Christ, his wisdom, and his kenotic love.

A grace-filled life is vital to the well-being of the nuptial community, a point that has been emphasized by M. Scott Peck, a Christian psychiatrist, who said this:

> People's capacity to love, and hence their will to grow, is nurtured not only by the love of their parents during childhood but also throughout their lives by grace, or God's love. This is a powerful force eternal to their consciousness which operates through the agency of their own unconscious as well as through the agency of loving persons other than their parents and through additional ways which we do not understand. It is because of grace that it is possible for people to transcend the traumas of loveless parenting and become themselves loving individuals who have risen far above their parents on the scale of human evolution ... I believe that grace is available to everyone, that we are cloaked in the love of God, no one less nobly than the other ... To be aware of grace, to personally experience its constant presence, to know one's nearness to God, is to know and continually experience an inner tranquility and peace that few possess. On the other hand, this knowledge and awareness brings with it enormous responsibility. To experience one's closeness to God is also to experience the obligation to be the agent of his power and love. The call to grace is a call to a life of effortful caring, to a life of service and whatever sacrifice seems required.[301]

The Sacredness and Loveliness of Marital Love

The task of living and growing together in love and holiness is aided by sexual fulfillment, for sexuality implicates the person whose substance is imprinted on his or her body. Thus according to Olivier Clement, "human sexuality and intercourse must be understood as a dimension of the person, a language of the relation between persons. This unity of the flesh denotes

---

[301] M. Scott Peck. *The Road Less Traveled: A New Psychology of Love, Traditional Values, and Spiritual Growth* (New York, 1978), 300, 302.

not only the union of bodies but the interwovenness of two lives."³⁰² Human sexuality is a gift from God and therefore good. It exists to further the growth of mutual companionship in marriage by drawing the husband and wife into a loving, caring, and intimate communion of body and soul. Through their bodily union, the husband and wife experience, express, and develop their sexual distinctiveness. The sexual life of a couple, however, is more than physical activity. Because a human being is an incarnate spirit, the experience of sexual intercourse involves the whole person. The human body not only hides but also discloses the inner world of each of the spouses. In their embrace, the spouses communicate to each other their innermost feelings, affections, and hopes—their very person.

For this reason sexuality cannot be reduced simply to desire, function, or procreation. It is not just a biological function, like hunger and sleep. Nor is it concupiscence, a defective desire which is legitimized only by procreation. It is in itself lovely, holy, and good. "It is bound by God to the deepest and most creative aspects of human nature," as John Chryssavgis notes.³⁰³ In fact, the Scriptures refer to sexual intimacy as an act of knowing. To know means to reveal, to share, and to hold.

Oftentimes, people are plagued by wrong ideas about human sexuality. These ideas are rooted usually in various dualistic notions about the human being and can range from fear and disdain of sex to uncontrolled promiscuity and overt immorality.³⁰⁴ Like all unhallowed things of the fallen world, human sexuality can remain graceless. It can be trivialized into a mere diversion determined by sensual appetite. It can deteriorate into narcissistic, abusive, and predatory behavior. Or it can sink into depravity and perversion and become a reprehensible addiction. In the end, graceless, trivial, or abusive sex is cruel and destructive. It devalues the human body and dehumanizes the person given to wantonness.

Marital fidelity, together with marital modesty, decency, self-control, purity of heart, and prudence, brings human sexuality into the realm of grace. Sexual intimacy based on fidelity and creative love develops into a means of self-transcendence and a window through which God's love and

---

³⁰² Clement, "Life in the Body," 141.
³⁰³ Chryssavgis, "Love and Sex in the Image of Divine Love," 102.
³⁰⁴ See Peter Brown, *The Body and Society: Men, Women, and Sexual Renunciation in Early Christianity* (New York, 1988).

life shine into marital love and life. The human body becomes for the spouses a body of communion. Their physical relationship is transformed into a union of persons, opening them to opportunities for personal growth and transparency. "Through the natural relationship of marriage," writes Christos Yannaras, "the two are united into one flesh, and through the eucharistic relationship of the mystery of marriage, this one flesh, the shared life of two persons, is made incorruptible and immortal."[305]

As affirmed by the Book of Proverbs, marital intimacy and faithfulness form a wellspring of joy and fulfillment: "Drink water from your own cistern, flowing water from your own well ... Let your fountain be blessed, and rejoice in the wife of your youth, a lovely hind, a graceful doe. Let her affection fill you at all times with delight, be infatuated with her love" (Prov. 5:15, 18–19). Both the Old and New Testaments uphold the value of human sexual love as intrinsically good. In fact, the mutuality and fidelity between husband and wife and the sensuousness of their relationship form the content of the Song of Songs, a canonical book of the Old Testament. The sages of Israel saw in the language of the Song of Songs, also known as the Song of Solomon or as the Canticles, an expression of divine love, of the Lord's love as husband of his people (Hosea 2:16–19). In the Christian tradition, the Song of Songs has been interpreted symbolically to express several levels of meaning, including the self-giving love of Christ for his Church and the love of the individual soul for God.

Interestingly, in popular language, Greek people refer both to the marriage service and to the marital union with the word χαρά (joy) because people know intuitively that marital life in all its splendor is a source of joy. Jesus performed the first of his wondrous signs at a joyous wedding feast in Cana of Galilee, and he used the image of a wedding banquet in his parables to speak about the mysteries of God's Kingdom (Matt. 22:1–14; Luke 14:15–24), which is a Kingdom of joy, life, light, truth, and love.

The Joy and Privilege of Childbearing

Sexual intimacy, while related in the first instance to the upbuilding of companionship and co-inherence, also allows the spouses to become co-creators with God.

---

[305] Yannaras, *Freedom of Morality*, 163. See also Patronos, Ὁ γάμος στὴ θεολογία καὶ στὴ ζωή, 71–90.

Creation of new life from fleshly love is a special privilege, joy, and blessing. Children are the very crown of the marital union and an indication of the mysterious presence of God's creative love in the lives of two people. Children are the sign and expression of the oneness of the spouses. A childless marriage owing to biological infertility, however, is no less complete than a marriage with children since the essential purpose of marriage is the unity of the spouses, not the reproduction of the species. What is at stake in marriage is the desire and the ability of the spouses to make their home, whether with or without children, a locus of love, a place where the values of the Gospel are kept, the faith of the Church is alive, and the agape of Christ embraces all.[306]

St. John Chrysostom addresses the issue and explains it in remarkably vivid and beautiful imagery:

> How do they become one flesh? As if she were gold receiving the purest of gold, the woman receives the man's seed with rich pleasure, and within her it is nourished, cherished and refined. It is mingled with her own substance and she returns it as child! The child is a bridge connecting the mother to the father, so that three become one flesh, as when two cities divided by a river are joined by a bridge. And here that bridge is formed by the substance of each ... But suppose there is no child; do they remain two or one? No: their intercourse effects the joining of their bodies, and they are made one, just as when perfume is mixed with ointment.[307]

Giving birth to children is a profound privilege. The privilege, however, carries with it immense responsibilities. Spouses must not only share in the creative power of God; they must also imitate his self-giving love and providential concern for creation through the continuous nurturance and affectionate care of their children. Children are worthy of great love but also of careful upbringing (Eph. 6:4).

Parenting is a complex, multidimensional role. It requires of parents more than meeting the physical needs of their child—food, shelter, clothing, and the like. Parents must also provide their children with a caring home, a decent life, a good education, and proper medical care. However,

---

[306] See John A. McGuckin, "The Mystery of Marriage: An Orthodox Christian Reflection," in Dedon and Trostyanskiy, *Love, Marriage, and Family*, 20–21.

[307] St. John Chrysostom, *On Marriage and Family Life*, trans. C. Roth and D. Anderson (Crestwood, NY, 1986), 76. (The passage is from homily 12 on Col. 4:18).

the role of Christian parents entails much more. They are obliged to lead their children by example, by their own rich interior life. They are called to bring up their children in the training and admonition of the Lord (Eph. 6:4), to nurture them in the faith, to give them spiritual guidance, to protect them against sin, and to create for them a loving environment in which they may develop into mature and wholesome human beings and faithful disciples of Jesus Christ.

The late theologian and educator John Boojamra reminded us that a Christian family is the center from which all values arise. It is the matrix of trust, personhood, and intimacy. It is the educator of first resort where the ability to faith is born and nurtured in a community of love, and it is the place where a child grows trustingly into the world outside and learns to appreciate it as wonder-filled object of service.[308]

Bringing children into the world requires serious, prayerful, honest, and sincere reflection, and the decision to regulate the size of one's family is the personal responsibility of the spouses. This decision, however, should not be based on hedonistic, selfish, or prideful reasons. A serious commitment to the Gospel and to the purposes of Christian marriage precludes the deliberate avoidance of bearing children. The calculated and intentional decision by the spouses not to bear children frustrates one of the basic purposes of marriage and thereby undermines its sacramental character. Furthermore, the use of abortion as a means of birth control is clearly immoral. From the earliest times, the Church has consistently opposed abortion, as recorded in the ancient church order *The Didache of the Twelve Apostles*, "You shall not kill an unborn child or murder a newborn infant" (chapter 2). And as the eminent ethicist Fr. Stanley Harakas notes, "Little flexibility exists in principle, the main exception in ethical teaching being the saving of the threatened life of the mother"[309] And, I would add, other grievous circumstances that would likely produce great harm and irreparable damage such as incest and rape.

---

[308] John Boojamra, "Theological and Pedagogical Perspectives on the Family as Educator," in *Greek Orthodox Theological Review*, vol. 29, no. 1 (1984): 16–32.

[309] See Stanley S. Harakas, *Health and Medicine in the Eastern Orthodox Tradition* (New York, 1990), 156–157. Also see John Breck, *The Sacred Gift of Life: Orthodox Christianity and Bioethics* (Crestwood, NY, 1998), 146–175, 259–263. In the same volume, Breck deals with other related matters such as procreation and the beginning of life, assisted reproductive technologies, and genetic engineering.

While married love includes procreation, it does not define it. Sexual intimacy serves first to promote and enhance the mutuality and closeness of the spouses. It is not a biological function limited exclusively to procreation. Thus the suspension of fertility through appropriate means of contraception is not wrong or immoral. The responsible use of birth control for the purpose of spacing children or limiting their number can be addressed only by the couple. Regarding this matter, Metropolitan Chrysostomos Zapheres notes, "While the Orthodox Church fully acknowledges the role of procreation in the marital sexual act, she does not share the deterministic understanding of the act ... which ignores love as a dimension of great value in sexual intercourse between husband and wife."[310]

Conclusion: Living the Vision

Among the many pastoral concerns of the Church today, perhaps none is more vital than that of marriage and the family. There is good reason for Christians to be concerned about the status of these two God-given institutions in our society. Clearly, they are undergoing extraordinary stress, as demonstrated by the increase in divorce rates and in the number of dysfunctional families. This breakdown of family life strikes at the very heart of ecclesial life.

The issues at stake are not so much sociological and political as they are theological and ecclesiological. Vigen Guroian framed the problem correctly when he wrote that "the real Orthodox critique of marriage and family does not come from these institutions' failure within the culture as

---

[310] Chrysostomos Zapheres, "An Orthodox Opinion: The Morality of Contraception," *Orthodox Observer* (September 1974): 5. Some Orthodox theologians have a different view and consider the use of contraceptives immoral. Some local Church authorities have issued statements condemning birth control. However, neither the New Testament nor the Greek Fathers claim that childbirth justifies marriage. Further, there are no Church canons addressing this issue. The union of a man and woman in marriage is a holy end in itself. Indeed, as Michael Plekon notes "In the Eastern Church, there is no absolute prohibition to [contraception]. Rather it is a matter of freedom—that of the spouses and their spiritual father, their circumstances, their abilities." See Plekon, "The Sacrament of Love," 36. For more on the subject of contraception and birth control, see, among others, Harakas, *Living the Faith: the Praxis of Eastern Orthodox Ethics* (Minneapolis, MN, 1992), 130–138; Evdokimov, *The Sacrament of Love*, 174–180; Meyendorff, *Marriage: An Orthodox Perspective*, 65–73; Constantelos, *Marriage, Sexuality, and Celibacy*, 62–69; Farantos, *Δογματικά και Ηθικά*, 337–344; Patronos, *Ὁ γάμος στή θεολογία καί στή ζωή*, 103–118.

described by the social scientists. Rather, the critique rests in their failure to be what they are called to be by the Church. The warrant for arguing in this way is that Orthodox theology regards marriage as fundamentally an ecclesiological reality."[311]

The real concern of the Church regarding the situation in which we find ourselves today is not just recovering stable family life for the sake of society, as noble as this goal may be, but grounding family life in the realities of God's Kingdom, from which it draws its identity.[312] The radical transforming power that flows from the Kingdom allows and enables the nuptial community to sustain the norms, values, and virtues of the Christian life, by which all marital and familial relationships are enriched.

It is not enough to speak about marriage and its many rich blessings. It is as important for the Church through an energetic pastoral ministry and a vibrant catechesis to help people continually discover and realize for themselves and their families the values of the Gospel and the vision of marriage and family life as it is understood, proclaimed, and celebrated by the Church. Marriage is a great spiritual event of life. It is the task of the Church to help people build strong solid marriages and, when necessary, to reach out to, help strengthen, and lend support to those marriages that are weak and struggling.[313]

The well-being of the "home church" (κατ' οἶκον ἐκκλησία) has always been a matter of deep concern for the Church. This concern is embodied even in the great Eucharistic prayer, the *anaphora*. We read, for example, the following eloquent words of prayer in the *anaphora* of the Divine Liturgy of St. Basil:

> Remember, Lord, the people here present and them that are absent with good cause. Have mercy on them and on us according to the multitude of your mercy; fill their store-houses with every good thing; maintain their marriage-bonds in peace and concord; nurture the infants; instruct the young; strengthen the aged, encourage the faint-hearted, gather together again them that are scattered ... You know the name and age of each, even from their mother's womb. For you, Lord, are the helper of the helpless, the hope of the hopeless, the savior of them that are storm-tossed, the haven of those in peril, the

---

[311] Guroian, *Incarnate Love*, 81.
[312] Ibid., 81.
[313] Stylianopoulos, "Toward a Theology of Marriage," 281.

physician of them that are sick ... Be all things to all, you who knows each person, his request, his household, and his need."[314]

The Church, as Fr. Stylianopoulos notes, has a tremendous spiritual investment in marriage. For "Christian persons make Christian couples. Christian couples make Christian marriages. Christian marriages make Christian homes. Christian homes make Christian families. Christian families make up the Church."[315]

The nuptial bond is a divine gift. Marital bonds must be strengthened, renewed, and nourished continually. It is the task of the Church to promulgate its unique vision of marriage and to help Christian people live by it.

---

[314] *The Divine Liturgy of Our Father among the Saints Basil the Great* (Brookline, MA, 1988).
[315] Stylianopoulos, "Toward a Theology of Marriage," 281.

5

RECEIVING CONVERTS INTO THE ORTHODOX CHURCH
LESSONS FROM THE CANONICAL AND LITURGICAL TRADITION

Dealing with Present Realities[316]

DIFFERING VIEWS AND PRACTICES ON RECEPTION

The way by which converts are received into the Church is or should be a matter of concern for the Orthodox Churches in America, chiefly for two reasons, one theoretical the other practical.[317] First, as with other canonical and liturgical matters, the absence of a consistent policy and a uniform practice is an unnecessary irritant and a source of scandal. It creates confusion and, more important, it raises questions about the sound-

---

[316] This essay was written in response to the request of His Eminence Metropolitan Methodios of Boston, chairman of the Liturgical Committee of the Holy Eparchial Synod of the Greek Orthodox Archdiocese of America, that I examine the several liturgical services for the reception of converts currently in use by the jurisdictions that comprise the Assembly of Canonical Orthodox Bishops of the United States of America, paying special attention to the practice of the Greek Archdiocese of America. The examination of these rites, however, could not be done in a vacuum—that is, without reference to their historical, canonical, and liturgical antecedents and to the underlying ecclesiology and sacramental theology that helped shape them.

An earlier version of this essay appeared in *Greek Orthodox Theological Review* 54, nos. 1–4 (2009): 1–76.

[317] In America, especially, we have become accustomed to speaking of several Orthodox Churches. The fact, however, is that there is only one Orthodox Church, which sees itself as the center of operation of the Holy Spirit and as the "pillar and bulwark of the truth" (1 Tim. 3:15).

ness of the theology behind each practice. Is each one equally true? Adding to the confusion are the several interpretations of ecclesiastical economy, or oikonomia (οἰκονομία), which is used to support and justify a particular practice of reception.318 Does each interpretation of oikonomia, as Lewis Patsavos observes, reflect the true sense of the principle of ecclesiastical economy?319

Undoubtedly, to justify present-day conditions, some will point to the time of the ancient Church, when diversity in liturgical practice was a fact. However, the historical record also shows that variety of practice did not exist within a local Church. How then can the Orthodox Churches in America—which, though not yet united administratively, nevertheless constitute a local Church in principle—justify divergent practices, especially when these differences bear directly upon principles of ecclesiology and sacramental theology?

Although there were divergent practices in the ancient Church, it is important to note that their theological underpinnings did not go unchallenged. For example, the ecclesiology espoused by St. Cyprian—with its narrow sense of the limits of the Church, categorical rejection of all sacraments performed outside the canonical Church, and insistence on the rebaptism of all heterodox converts, schismatics and heretics alike— never enjoyed broad application in the East or the West.[320] In fact, as we shall see, in the canonical and liturgical tradition of the East, heterodox baptism was neither rejected nor accepted outright. Its validity was determined essen-

---

[318] The term *ecclesiastical economy* is used by a number of Orthodox theologians to differentiate it from *divine economy*—from what the Greek Fathers call God's household plan or management (*oikonomia*) of his creation, his providential plan for the salvation of the world, expressed chiefly in the Christ event.

[319] See Lewis J. Patsavos, "Response to John Erickson's 'Divergences in Pastoral Practice in the Reception of Converts,'" in *Orthodox Perspectives on Pastoral Praxis*, ed. Theodore Stylianopoulos (Brookline, MA, 1988), 179–180. I am grateful to Dr. Patsavos for reading parts of this essay and sharing with me his perceptive insights on the canonical tradition of the Church.

[320] See Georges Florovsky, "The Limits of the Church," *Church Quarterly Review* 117 (1933): 117–131. This article was reprinted with minor editorial changes in *Sourozh* 26 (1986): 13–24. Because it is easier access, all references to the article refer to the *Sourozh* edition. The article was also translated into Greek under the title "Τα όρια της Εκκλησίας" and incorporated into a small volume of other important articles by Fr. Florovsky, *Το σώμα του ζώντος Χριστού: Μία Ορθόδοξη ερμηνεία της Εκκλησίας*, Θεολογικά Δοκίμια 3 (Thessaloniki, 1972), 129–148.

tially by the proximity of the group's theology to the Orthodox faith and the group's ability to manifest love as a true measure of authentic discipleship (John 13:34–35).

The second reason for uneasiness about the lack of uniformity in receiving converts is of a more practical nature, a pastoral concern. Individual clergy within the several jurisdictions have been influenced by the writings of modern-day proponents of Cyprianic ecclesiology. One such study, for example, is the book *I Confess One Baptism* by Fr. George D. Metallinos, a professor at the University of Athens, which was published in 1983 and circulated in English translation in 1994. As indicated by the book's subtitle, *Interpretation and Application of Canon 7 of the Second Ecumenical Council by the Kollyvades and Constantine Oikonomos*, the author presents a synthesis of the arguments of the eighteenth- and nineteenth-century supporters of the controversial decision of Patriarch Cyril V of Constantinople that required the rebaptism of Roman Catholic and all other converts.[321]

With a narrow understanding of heresy and a legalistic, excessively strict approach to the canons, there are clergymen among us who, contrary to the prevailing official position of the Church, insist on rebaptizing all heterodox converts, including Roman Catholic and mainline Protestant Christians. Such subjective behavior, however, places one above the Church and leads to arbitrary actions that undermine ecclesial authority and invite chaos.

The need to rebaptize all heretics and schismatics rests on the belief that they were never truly baptized. The term *rebaptism*, although convenient, is misleading and problematic. Such baptism cannot be construed as a second baptism, for that would contradict the Church's faith as expressed in the Nicene-Constantinopolitan Creed, "I acknowledge one baptism for the forgiveness of sins." The insistence on rebaptizing all heterodox converts, regardless of confessional origin, is, in fact, an unapologetic belief in the complete absence of grace outside the canonical borders of the Church. But the canonical and liturgical tradition of the Church does not mirror such an absolutist position, which is based essentially on Cyprianic ecclesiology.

---

[321] George D. Metallinos, Ομολογώ εν βάπτισμα (Athens 1983). The book was translated into English by the hieromonk Seraphim Dedes of the Monastery of St. Paul and published under the title *I Confess One Baptism* (Mt. Athos, 1994). Despite the available historical evidence to the contrary, the author is intent on showing that the rebaptism of all converts represents the normative practice of the Church.

In recent years, the diverse modes of reception and their attending complex issues have been brought forward and discussed by a number of theologians, including three canonists, Archbishop Peter L'Huillier,[322] Professor John Erickson,[323] and Professor Theodoros Yiagkos;[324] a liturgist, Professor John Klentos;[325] a patrologist, Fr. George Dragas;[326] and two dogmaticians, Metropolitan Chrysostomos Constantinides[327] and Professor Ioannis Karmiris.[328] Their scholarship and insights are invaluable and invite further study so that the Orthodox Churches in America may arrive at a more sustainable theological position and adopt a coherent and consistent policy, as well as a uniform practice of reception.

THE SCOBA GUIDELINES

In 1966, the Standing Conference of Canonical Orthodox Bishops in America (SCOBA), the precursor of today's Assembly of Canonical Orthodox Bishops of the United States of America, addressed the issue of receiving converts within the broader context of the Church's involvement in ecumenical relations by issuing a set of directives.[329] These directives were

---

[322] Peter L'Huillier, "The Reception of Roman Catholics into Orthodoxy: Historical Variations and Norms," *St. Vladimir's Theological Quarterly* 24, no. 2 (1980): 75–82.

[323] John Erickson, "The Reception of Non-Orthodox into the Orthodox Church: Contemporary Practice," *St. Vladimir's Theological Quarterly* 41, no.1 (1997): 1–17; and Erickson, "Divergencies in Pastoral Practice in the Reception of Converts," in *Orthodox Perspectives on Pastoral Praxis*, ed. Theodore Stylianopoulos (Brookline, MA, 1988), 150–177.

[324] Theodoros Yiagkos, "Το άγιον βάπτισμα και ο τρόπος αποδοχής των αιρετικών και σχιματικών," in *Το Άγιον Βάπτισμα*, Σειρά ποιμαντική βιβλιοθήκη 6 (Athens, 2003), 153–183; also see his collection of articles *Κανόνες και λατρεία* (Thessaloniki, 2006), 404–441.

[325] John Klentos, "Rebaptizing Converts into the Orthodox Church: Old Perspectives on a New Problem,"
Studia Liturgical 29, no. 2 (1999): 216–234.

[326] George D. Dragas, "The Manner of Reception of Roman Catholic Converts into the Orthodox Church with Special Reference to the Decisions of the Synods of 1484 (Constantinople), 1755 (Constantinople) and 1667 (Moscow)," *Greek Orthodox Theological Review* 44, nos. 1–4 (1999): 235–271.

[327] Chrysostomos Constantinides, *Η αναγνώριση των μυστηρίων των ετεροδόξων στις διαχρονικές σχέσεις Ορθοδοξίας και Ρωμαιοκαθολικισμού* (Thessaloniki, 1995).

[328] Ioannis Karmiris, "Ways of Accepting Non-Orthodox Christians into the Orthodox Church," *Greek Orthodox Theological Review* 1, no. 1 (1954): 38–47.

[329] The 1966 *Guidelines* published by the Standing Conference of the Canonical Orthodox Bishops in the Americas (SCOBA) were written by the Rev. Leonidas Contos, at the time director of the Interchurch Office of the Greek Orthodox Archdiocese of North and South America. The directives concerning the reception of converts are contained in one para-

incorporated into SCOBA's *Guidelines for Orthodox Christians in Ecumenical Relations*.[330] An expanded version of the *Guidelines* was published in 1973 that remains in force, although it is not considered an official ecclesiastical document.

The directives regarding the reception of converts in both the 1966 and the 1973 version are brief, general, imprecise, and in some ways ambiguous. As a result, they were unable to forge a common policy and practice. In the section "Sacraments and Other Liturgical Services," the *Guidelines* state the following:

> When receiving into the Orthodox Church a person who comes voluntarily from another confession, the Orthodox priest will accept the candidate by means of whichever of the three modes described by the Sixth Ecumenical Council is appropriate (Canon 95): a) Baptism by triune immersion; b) Chrismation; c) Confession of faith. Proof of the fact of baptism must be established by an authentic document or by testimony of a qualified witness. The priest must undertake to instruct the applicant in matters of the Faith and practice that govern the inner life and outward behavior of the Orthodox Christian. If the applicant has not been baptized in the Name of the Holy Trinity in a Christian church whose baptism could be accepted in the Orthodox Church by the principle of *oikonomia*, he or she must be baptized as prescribed in the Service books. In case of doubt, reference to the Bishop is mandatory.[331]

This broad directive has several weaknesses. First, the text of canon 95 of the Penthekte or Trullo Synod, upon which the directive is based, is not quoted even partially. More important, its application to present-day realities is not spelled out. There is no attempt to interpret and reconcile the canon to today's needs and circumstances. Of the heretical and schismatic groups mentioned in the canon, for example, only the Nestorians and non-Chalcedonians exist today,[332] and they, according to canon 95, are to

---

graph in the section "Sacraments and Sacramentals" (page 26). In 1973 the *Guidelines* were revised and augmented as a result of "the evolving nature of the ecumenical movement and the rise of new agencies." The new and expanded *Guidelines* were written by the Rev. Robert G. Stephanopoulos, at the time general secretary of SCOBA. All further references to the *Guidelines* cite the 1973 edition.

[330] Robert G. Stephanopoulos, *Guidelines for Orthodox Christians in Ecumenical Relations* (New York 1973), 18–19.

[331] Ibid.

[332] For the text of the canon, see *Πηδάλιον* (Athens, 1957), 304; and the English translation, *Rudder* (Chicago, 1957), 400–401. See also Erickson, "Reception of Non-Orthodox," 2.

be received through a certificate called a *libellus* (λίβελλος)—a formal written confession of faith that includes a renunciation of errors and an acceptance of Orthodox teaching.

Another weakness in the directive is its imprecision. It does not name the Christian churches "whose baptism could be accepted in the Orthodox Church by the principle of *oikonomia*." This is an opportunity, once and for all, to list all of the churches and denominations whose baptism could be accepted and those whose baptism could not. For all other denominations and unknown sects, an exhortation should be issued to the clergy requiring episcopal sanction before receiving the convert into the Orthodox Church. The directive is imprecise on two other counts, as well. The determining factor is based on the principle of ecclesiastical economy. But there is no single commonly accepted definition of *oikonomia*.[333] Different understandings of *oikonomia* may lead to different practices. More important, what, if any, ecclesiological implications does the "acceptance" of another community's baptism have, even through economy?

The ambiguity in the directives is magnified further by two additional instructions:

1. Chrismation is normally administered immediately after the Rite of Baptism as contained in the Service books.

2. An applicant from another Christian community who has been baptized already in the Name of the Holy Trinity may be received into the Orthodox Church according to the order prescribed by the Bishop.[334]

What does the first entry mean? How is the priest receiving a convert to interpret it? What service is he to use? When, where, and how is he to perform it? More important, what is the nature and the intended purpose of the service of chrismation he is to use? Is it the entire postbaptismal rite in the current service books, or another type of service? Should all converts received by chrismation be treated alike regardless of their confessional origin?

The second entry, noting that "an applicant ... may be received ... according to the order prescribed by the bishop," is just as ambiguous and opens the door to diverse practices. Could a bishop determine the process of reception in his diocese on his own initiative, apart from his synod? And what if this

---

[333] See Ieronymos Kotsonis, *Προβλήματα τῆς "ἐκκλησιαστικῆς οἰκονομίας"* (Athens, 1957), 14–16.

[334] Stephanopoulos, *Guidelines*, 19.

CHAPTER FIVE: RECEIVING CONVERTS INTO CHURCH 147

"order" happens to differ from the time-honored practices of the Church? Such actions lead to a bishop's placing himself above his synod, a canonical anomaly of great magnitude with dire consequences for the Church.

In the absence of a comprehensive set of directives and a commonly accepted authorized rite or rites of reception, even in outline form, the clergy continue to receive converts in accordance with the customs and traditions of their respective jurisdictions. The SCOBA *Guidelines* have not been able to create a viable uniform practice of reception, which is another sign of our disunity and of the many perils it harbors.

The Prevailing Approaches to Reception

Several reception procedures of the jurisdictions have been studied by John Erickson. He was able to distinguish among them three major lines, or approaches, which, for purposes of convenience, he calls the Russian approach, the Greek approach, and conflations of the two.[335] More important, he discerned that each of these approaches reveals "not only diversity of practice but also divergent approaches to ecclesiology and sacramental theology."[336]

THE RUSSIAN APPROACH

The Russian approach, according to Fr. Erickson, was pioneered by Peter Moghila, the Metropolitan of Kiev, in the seventeenth century.[337] According to this approach, mainline Trinitarian Protestants, as well as unconfirmed Roman (or Latin) Catholics, are to be received by chrismation following the full postbaptismal rite of the Orthodox Church. While the baptism of Trinitarian Protestants is considered valid, it is nevertheless incomplete, for two reasons. Protestants lack apostolic succession, which is deemed essential for the Church. As a result, they do not have a valid sacrament of chrismation.

Unconfirmed Catholics (usually rare) are received by chrismation simply because they never partook of the sacrament of chrismation (i.e., confirmation). Baptized and confirmed Latin Catholics, Nestorians, and non-Chalcedonians, on the other hand, are to be received by a profession of

---

[335] Erickson, "Reception of Non-Orthodox," 4–13.
[336] Ibid., 4.
[337] Ibid., 4–6.

faith, since these churches have valid orders and therefore valid sacraments of baptism and chrismation. As I demonstrate below, the reception of Latin converts solely by a profession of faith differs from the Greek approach.

As Fr. Erickson observes, the Russian approach "offers a clear and coherent modern application of Trullo canon 95"[338] (about which more in a moment). Moreover, as he notes, "Moghila and his heirs relate the completion of Christian initiation to the presence of apostolic ministry,"[339] a line of reasoning used as early as the fourth century.[340]

A series of reception rites reflecting the Russian approach have been incorporated into the *Great Book of Needs*,[341] compiled and translated from the *Velikii Trebnik*, the Slavonic version of the Greek *euchologion*. The same rites are also found in the *Service Book of the Holy Orthodox-Catholic Apostolic Church*, compiled, translated, and arranged by Isabel Florence Hapgood, which was commissioned by Bishop Nicholas of the Russian North American Mission and first published in 1906 by his successor, Archbishop Tikhon. The Hapgood service book was subsequently published by the Antiochian Orthodox Christian Archdiocese of North America in several editions, the seventh of which was released in 1996.[342]

---

[338] Ibid., 6.
[339] Ibid.
[340] On this point, Erickson cites Didymos the Blind of Alexandria, who explained that those coming from heretical groups that practice Trinitarian baptism "are to be anointed because they do not have holy chrism, for only a bishop by means of heavenly grace consecrates chrism" (*On the Trinity*, PG 39: 720–22).
[341] *Great Book of Needs*, vol. 1, translated from church Slavonic (South Canaan, PA, 2000), 61–119. The book contains several reception rites for various occasions. The rites include offices for the reception of persons who were raised in heresy but who received a "valid" Trinitarian baptism, for those from the Armenian confession and other non-Chalcedonians (Coptic, Jacobite, Ethiopian, and Indian), for Nestorians, for Roman Catholics/Latins, for Lutherans, and for Reformed. At different points in the service, this rite contains, as required, appropriate words for the groups for which a given rite is intended. The next rite is for a person who must also be chrismated in addition to signing a *libellus*. Another rite is for the reception of Jewish converts and for those coming from Islam and paganism. A rite for seriously ill heterodox who wish to be admitted to the Church follows. The final rite is the "Rule of Methodios, Patriarch of Constantinople, Concerning the Return from Apostasy of Various Persons to the True Orthodox Faith."
[342] Isabel Florence Hapgood, *Service Book of the Holy Orthodox-Catholic Apostolic Church*, 7th ed. (Englewood, NJ, 1996), 454–469. "The Office for receiving into the Orthodox Faith such persons as have not previously been Orthodox," according to the rubrics, is meant for Roman Catholics/Latins, Armenians, Lutherans, and Reformed Christians. The service contains a series of specific recantations and professions of faith for each of the groups men-

A condensed conversion rite based entirely on the services in the *Great Book of Needs* and in the Hapgood service book was published in 1995 by Fr. Spencer Kezios, a priest of the Greek Orthodox Archdiocese of America, in the Narthex Press series.[343] The service of reception in *Sacraments and Services, Book 1* in the Narthex Press series contains few rubrics and begins with a slightly altered version of the Prayer of Inscription, or the Prayer for the Making of a Catechumen, from the received rite of baptism. Originally, this prayer was used for the formal enrollment of a non-Christian in the catechumenate and as such is hardly appropriate for a convert from another Christian confession. Next, the candidate affirms his or her intention to be united to the Orthodox Church and repudiates all heresies, ancient and modern. Through a series of six questions posed by the celebrant, the candidate affirms his or her belief in some basic tenets of the Orthodox faith, by responding, "I do."[344] The candidate then recites the Nicene-Constantinopolitan Creed. A litany of several petitions follows, after which the celebrant anoints the candidate with holy chrism using the standard formula, "The Seal of the Gift of the Holy Spirit." Two improvised prayers, composed of phrases from the postbaptismal prayers of the received rite of baptism, conclude the service. The weaknesses of a conversion service such as this will be discussed later.

THE GREEK APPROACH

The Greek approach, Erickson notes, "is less well known ... and is more difficult to interpret, since it has not ... had a smooth, continuous history."[345] He is correct in this assessment. The Greek approach, rooted in ancient synodical decisions, has in the last several centuries undergone changes prompted both by historical events and theological argumentation.

In broad terms, the modes of reception in the Greek East were determined by the relevant canons of the local and ecumenical synods. Although

---

tioned. Like the *Great Book of Needs*, Hapgood's book also includes a service of reception for "Jews, Mohammedans (Saracens), and Heathens," 467–469.

[343] "The Reception of Converts by Chrismation," in *Sacraments and Services, Book 1*, ed. Spencer T. Kezios (North Ridge, CA), 148–156. The English translation of the services in the series is by Fr. Leonidas Contos.

[344] The six questions pertain to the holy canons, the interpretation of the holy Scriptures, the seven sacraments, the Eucharist, the veneration of the saints, and the power of the Church to bind and to loose.

[345] Erickson, "Reception of Non-Orthodox," 6–7.

in some ecclesial circles the baptism of heretics and schismatics was categorically rejected, rebaptism of all heterodox never became the normative practice of the Church because not all who are outside the canonical borders of the Church are considered heretics in the strict sense.[346]

St. Basil the Great, for example, used a threefold distinction to identify those outside the Church, designating them according to the content of their faith and their relationship to the Church as heretics, schismatics, or dissidents.[347] Canons of local and ecumenical synods made similar distinctions. In the fourth century, and again in the seventh, the process of reception was clearly defined by the Second Ecumenical Synod of 381 (canon 7) and the Penthekte Ecumenical Synod of 691–692 (canon 95). These two canons constitute the authoritative standard—the norm or exactness (ἀκρίβεια)—for procedures of reception, a fact that escapes the rigorists.

Each of these synods, through the receptive canon, names the heresies it had to deal with, and each synod places each heterodox community in a particular category. The canon of the Penthekte repeats the canon of the Second Synod almost verbatim, adding to its list of heretics three new groups, as well as a new mode of reception. Canon 7 of the Second Synod lists two categories of heretics. Those in the first group are to be received by a certificate, a *libellus*, in which they recant heretical beliefs and profess the Orthodox faith, and by an anointing with holy myron, or chrism. Those in the second category—heretics in the strict sense—are to be received by baptism, as having never been baptized.[348] On the other hand, canon 95 of the Penthekte Synod places heterodox converts into one of three categories, providing for each a different mode of reception. The canon repeats the two methods of reception (by baptism or chrismation) sanctioned by the Second Ecumenical Synod and adds a third mode: by a *libellus* and an oral profession of faith only.

---

[346] As Erickson points out, "In the East, just as in the West, churchmen from at least the third century onward faced the problem of how to receive convert schismatics and heretics ... Broadly speaking, in antiquity and continuing well into the Middle Ages, developments in the East and West proceeded analogously; similar problems produced similar solutions and explanations" ("Divergencies," 156).

[347] St. Basil's "Letter to Amphilochios on the Canons," in Ἕλληνες πατέρες τῆς ἐκκλησίας (Thessaloniki, 1972), 1:184–185. Also in the Loeb Classical Library's *Saint Basil: The Letters* (Cambridge, MA, 1962), 3:7–10.

[348] For the full text of the canon, see *Πηδάλιον*, 163; *Rudder*, 217.

The three modes of reception were also introduced into the Church's *euchologia*, or service books. The earliest extant *euchologion* of the Byzantine or Constantinopolitan rite, the Barberini Codex (gr. 336, dating to the late eighth century), for example, contains rubrics and an order of services based on the provisions of canon 95 of the Penthekte Synod, which it quotes almost verbatim.[349] These three modes of reception became the standard practice and the established norm of the Church, although at different times and places the third mode was set aside in favor of the second for reasons unrelated to matters of faith. Sometimes what was meant to be a temporary measure became the prevailing practice.

Following the schism of 1054, the East faced a new problem, something not foreseen by previous conciliar decisions: how to receive Latin Christians. Initially, Latins were admitted to communion directly,[350] but by the end of twelfth century, as Theodore Balsamon (d. after 1195) indicates, their reception had become more formalized, accomplished by catechism and a *libellus*.[351]

This mode of reception was to change again as the schism deepened. A host of sociopolitical and religious factors contributed to changing attitudes toward the Latins, including the Crusades and the establishment of a series of Latin states and bishoprics in former territories of the East. Papal religious propaganda and political manipulation further intensified

---

[349] Stefano Parenti and Elena Velkovska, *L'eucologio Barberini gr. 336* (Rome, 1995), 152–158. Similar distinctions are employed in the eleventh-century patriarchal *euchologion*, *Codex Coislin gr. 213* (Paris National Library), published by Miguel Arranz, *L'eucologio Constantinopolitano aglia inizi del secolo XI: Hagiasmatarion & archieratikon* (Rome, 1996), 259–294.

[350] See Yiagkos, Κανόνες καὶ λατρεία, 429–434.

[351] Theodore Balsamon was elected patriarch of Antioch but never assumed his office because the Crusaders had installed a Latin patriarch in Antioch. He resided in Constantinople, his birthplace, and became one of the Church's foremost canonists. In a response to the inquiry of Mark, patriarch of Alexandria, concerning certain Latin prisoners and others requesting Holy Communion, Balsamon writes that catechism and a certificate of faith should be required of them before administering the sacrament. The reason for this, he writes, is related to Rome's long years of estrangement from the Church and the West's lack of communion—and because of Rome's departure from the dogmas and customs of the Church. "[Ο]ὐκ ὀφείλει γένος Λατινικὸν ἐκ χειρὸς ἱερατικῆς διὰ τῶν θείων καὶ ἀχράντων μυστηρίων ἁγιάζεσθαι, εἰ μὴ κατάθηται πρότερον ἀπέχεσθαι τῶν Λατινικῶν δογμάτων καὶ συνηθειῶν, καὶ κατὰ κανόνας κατηχηθῇ, καὶ τοῖς ὀρθοδόξοις ἐξισωθῇ." See Balsamon, "Ἐρωτήσεις κανονικαί," 16 in Rallis and Potlis, Σύνταγμα, 4:460.

the antipathies of the populace. Latin liturgical practices, including baptism by affusion or aspersion, offended Orthodox theological and pastoral sensibilities. As the Byzantine Empire began to disintegrate and attempts at union failed, theological positions hardened. By the end of the fifteenth century, Latin converts were received by a *libellus* and chrismation. In rare circumstances, they were rebaptized, but only in response to Latin abuses.

The reception of Latins by chrismation was regularized in 1484 by the holy and great Synod of Constantinople. Declaring Latin baptism valid, the synod decreed that Latin converts were to be catechized properly and received through a *libellus* and a special service of chrismation, which the synod created and disseminated.[352] This service is of special interest and will be discussed below.

During the ensuing two centuries, the Church was obliged to deal with the reception of converts from churches of the Reformation. The mode of their reception was regularized by synodical decisions of the seventeenth and eighteenth centuries.[353] According to these conciliar rulings, Protestant converts from the Lutheran, Calvinist, and Anglican confessions who were already baptized in the name of the Holy Trinity were received by catechism, a *libellus*, and chrismation. Protestant converts from lesser-known groups whose baptism was suspect were rebaptized. This sets the precedent for converts from many groups today (some of Pentecostal origin) about which we know very little.

Discussion of the Greek approach would be incomplete without reference to the mode of receiving Nestorians, non-Chalcedonians, and other Eastern Christians. The Penthekte Synod decreed that Nestorians and non-Chalcedonians are to be received through catechism and a *libellus* only.

The ruling of the Penthekte was clear but was not always applied. Theodore Balsamon, writing in the twelfth century, gives an ambiguous response. In answer to the question of Mark, Patriarch of Alexandria, regarding whether Nestorians, Armenians, and Jacobites were to be received by baptism or by chrismation, Balsamon quotes canon 95 of Trullo verbatim.

---

[352] For the service promulgated by the synod, see Ioannis Karmiris, *Τὰ δογματικὰ καὶ συμβολικὰ μνημεῖα τῆς Ὀρθοδόξου Καθολικῆς Ἐκκλησίας* (Athens, 1953), 987–989. As noted earlier, in later centuries the Russian Church issued its own services for the reception of Latins, Protestants, Nestorians, and non-Chalcedonians.

[353] Ibid., 1015–1019. From 1718 onward, the Russian Church followed the Greek practice and received Protestant converts by chrismation.

CHAPTER FIVE: RECEIVING CONVERTS INTO CHURCH 153

Canon 95 ends with a description of the method by which Nestorians and non-Chalcedonians are to be received—namely, again, by catechism and a *libellus*. However, immediately after citing the canon, Balsamon adds a cryptic concluding sentence: "Therefore, according to the summary of this canon, on one hand the heretics (οἱ μὲν τῶν αἱρεσιωτῶν) are sanctified by baptism, while on the other hand, the others (οἱ δὲ) are perfected only by the holy myrrh."[354]

Was the response of Balsamon purposely equivocal, reflecting new developments in the reception process of these Christians? Later sources of the fourteenth century seem to indicate that in the Greek Church, converts from among the Armenians, other Monophysites, and Nestorians were being received by chrismation.[355] This stricter standard resulted from sociopolitical rather than theological factors. The Russian Church, on the other hand, never digressed from the ruling of the Penthekte Synod. Up to the present time, it receives Nestorians and Monophysites by a *libellus* only.

An important note should be added here. Throughout its history, the Orthodox Church has managed its affairs with prudence and love toward all. But as Metropolitan Kallistos Ware notes, "When leniency seemed to endanger the well-being of the Orthodox flock, exposing them to infiltration and encouraging them to indifferentism and apostasy, then the Church authorities resorted to strictness."[356] The turmoil triggered by the Crusades and the failed attempts at union, for example, generated deep-seated resentments. Later, during the Turkish rule, the determined efforts at proselytism by Latin as well as Protestant missionaries further exacerbated the problem and made dialogue and rapprochement between the churches more difficult, if not impossible.

The state of affairs in the Greek Church changed dramatically in 1755 during a time of strong antipapal and anti-Western feelings, when Cyril V was patriarch of Constantinople. On his own initiative, despite the objections of the Patriarchal Synod, Cyril issued a decree titled *Definition of the Holy Church of Christ Defending the Holy Baptism Given from God, and Spitting upon the Baptisms of the Heretics Which Are Otherwise Administered*, by which he ordered the rebaptism of all heterodox converts with-

---

[354] Balsamon, Ἐρωτήσεις κανονικαί, 32 in Rallis and Potlis, Σύνταγμα 4:473–474.
[355] See Karmiris, Τὰ δογματικά, 1009–1013; Yiagkos, Κανόνες καὶ λατρεία, page#.
[356] Timothy Ware, *Eustratios Argenti: A Study of the Greek Church under Turkish Rule* (Oxford 1964), 85.

out distinction. A year later, in 1756, Cyril's decree was sanctioned by the patriarchs of the East, and it held sway throughout the greater part of the nineteenth century, despite the serious objections of many. (I will say more about the *Definition* in reference to the baptism controversy it provoked and the effects it had on the Greek approach, owing especially to the writings of St. Nikodemos the Hagiorite.[357])

More important, although the *Definition* of Cyril V has never been officially rescinded, the Patriarchate of Constantinople in 1888 reverted to its earlier practices, approved and promulgated by synodical decrees, and established as a general rule that converts should not be rebaptized indiscriminately.[358] In 1903 the Church of Greece guardedly permitted reception by chrismation, and thirty years later, in 1932, it approved a liturgical service of reception by chrismation authored by Archbishop Chrysostom Papadopoulos, similar to that of the Synod of 1484.[359]

The decision of 1888 of the Patriarchate of Constantinople constitutes today the official Greek approach, observed by all the "Greek" Churches, albeit with local variations. Nonetheless, there are within the Greek Church monastic communities and theologians who cling to the strict rigorist positions exemplified in the *Pedalion* (*Πηδάλιον*, or *Rudder*). More will be said about the Greek approach later. My attention now turns to the third mode of reception used by some of the Orthodox Churches in America.

THE CONFLATIONS APPROACH

Erickson uses the term *conflations* to describe the third approach to receiving converts into the Church. "In North America one may find not only the 'Russian' practice and the 'Greek' practice," he writes, "but also some *conflations* of the two, in which the logic behind each is obscured."[360] Fr.

---

[357] While the defenders of rigorism prevailed for well over a century, their ideas never gained wide or permanent approval. In 1875, for example, Joachim II, patriarch of Constantinople, and the Holy Synod, in response to an inquiry by the Church of Greece, noted the diversity of practice among the Churches and left it to the conscience of each local Church to decide the manner of reception, whether by ἀκρίβεια or by οἰκονομία.

[358] M. G. Theotokas, *Νομολογία τοῦ Οἰκουμενικοῦ Πατριαρχείου* (Constantinople, 1897); cited in Ware, *Eustratios Argenti*, 106. Theotokas tells of similar decisions the patriarchate made in 1879 and 1880. See Dragas, "Manner of Reception," 246–248.

[359] Karmiris, *Τὰ δογματικά*, 985–986, 991–992. See also Peter L'Huillier, "Reception of Roman Catholics," 81.

[360] Erickson, "Reception of Non-Orthodox," 10.

CHAPTER FIVE: RECEIVING CONVERTS INTO CHURCH 155

Erickson cites two examples of this approach, one from the *Priest's Guide of the Antiochian Orthodox Christian Archdiocese* and the other from the 1989 "Service for the Reception of Converts" of the Orthodox Church in America (OCA).

The Antiochian *Priest's Guide* specifies that Trinitarian Christians are to be received by instruction, an affirmation of the Orthodox faith, and chrismation.[361] The directives, however, make no distinction between converts and specify no particular service of chrismation. Presumably, all converts are to be received in like manner, regardless of the ecclesial status of their former confessions. In all probability, the Antiochian clergy would have recourse to one liturgical source for the service of reception: Isabel Florence Hapgood's translation of the *Service Book of the Holy Orthodox-Catholic Apostolic Church*, mentioned earlier.[362] But as Erickson points out, the service of reception in Hapgood reflects the Russian practice, intended for Protestant converts.[363]

Late in 1998, however, the Antiochian Archdiocese issued a "Service for the Chrismation of Converts into the Orthodox Faith," compiled for the Department of Liturgics and Translations by Fr. Edward Hughes, a priest of the archdiocese. In a brief introduction, the compiler states that the basic form and text of the service are based on the Barberini Codex and the service of the Synod of 1484.[364] He also states that the service accords with the provisions of the Penthekte Synod and with the policy of the Patriarchate of Antioch, which has required chrismation for all converts who have had a Trinitarian baptism.

This service is, in fact, a conflation, incorporating elements from the Russian services, the Barberini Codex, and the received rite of baptism. The booklet containing the service includes three helpful introductory pieces. The first concerns the candidate, listing the prerequisites for reception,

---

[361] It is interesting that in 1933, the Patriarchate of Antioch required that all heterodox converts be received by baptism.
[362] Erickson, "Reception of Non-Orthodox," 10.
[363] In fact, however, the rubrics of the service in Hapgood mention Roman Catholics/Latins, Armenians, Lutherans, and Reformed Christians (see note 342). An interesting note regarding Hapgood's service book is that for many years it enjoyed a special status among the Orthodox clergy in America: it was one of the very few English translations of the divine services in circulation and was used widely by the clergy of all the jurisdictions.
[364] Unfortunately, however, the dates of the codex and the synod are misstated.

which include a verification of his or her Trinitarian baptism with water, a proper period of catechesis, a confession of sins, and a profession of faith. The second concerns the period of instruction, which should be from six months to a year in length. Several resources for instruction are also listed. The third piece is especially useful. It is a list of more than fifty Protestant denominations that "traditionally affirm the dogma of the Holy Trinity and baptize in the name of the Father and of the Son and of the Holy Spirit."

The 1989 OCA service, according to Fr. Erickson, is beset with problems. "The structure and prayers of the OCA service are basically those of the post-baptismal rite as these would be employed in the Russian practice for the reception of unconfirmed Catholic and mainstream Protestant converts. The resulting service is highly ambiguous."[365] Such a service, however, for the Russian practice would not be suitable for confirmed Catholics, Eastern Catholics, or for Uniates, Nestorians, and non-Chalcedonians.

Fr. Erickson makes a further important point regarding this service and similar ones that are structured on the received postbaptismal rites of anointing with minor modifications in language to suit the occasion. He questions, correctly, the use of prayers and other elements of the formal catechumenate in the rite of reception, since by their nature they are intended for the unbaptized, not for converts with a valid Trinitarian baptism.[366] Though, as shall be seen, conversion rites generally are structured on the rites of the catechumenate, they do not and should not replicate the oaths and prayers.

The Baptism Controversy in the Eighteenth Century

PATRIARCH CYRIL V AND ST. NIKODEMOS

The Greek approach has been influenced especially by the controversial *Definition* that Cyril V, patriarch of Constantinople, issued in 1755[367] and by the writings of St. Nikodemos the Hagiorite.[368] The contentious spirit of the *Definition*, reflecting Cyril's opposition to heretics, especially Latins, is evident in the full title of his decree: *A Definition of the Holy Church of*

---

[365] Erickson, "The Reception of Non-Orthodox," 12–13.
[366] Ibid., 12–13n20.
[367] See Karmiris, *Τὰ δογματικά*, 982–984.
[368] See Metallinos, *I Confess One Baptism*, 24–34.

Christ Defending the Holy Baptism Given from God, and Spitting upon the Baptisms of the Heretics Which Are Otherwise Administered (Ὅρος τῆς ἁγίας τοῦ Χριστοῦ Ἐκκλησίας, συσταίνων μὲν τὸ θεόθεν δοθὲν ἅγιον βάπτισμα, καταπτύων δὲ τε ἄλλως γενόμενα τῶν αἱρετικῶν βαπτίσματα).[369]

Cyril V scorned all heterodox baptisms as "worthless and horrid" (ἀπόβλητα καὶ ἀποτρόπαια), and using other harsh language, he called for the rebaptism of all converts without distinction. The *Definition* states, in part,

> We know only one, our own, Holy, Catholic, and Apostolic Church, and acknowledge only her sacraments ... The [sacraments] ... performed by the heretics are the inventions of corrupt men, and knowing them to be strange (ἀλλόκοτα) and alien (ἀλλότρια) to the whole of the apostolic Tradition, we reject them by common decision. Those coming to us, we receive them as impious (ἀνίερους) and unbaptized ... The [sacraments of the heretics] supply no sanctification to those who receive them ... And those unbaptized baptized (ἀβαπτίστως βαπτιζομένους) who come to the Orthodox faith from [heretical groups] we receive as having been unbaptized, and we baptize them securely (ἀκινδύνως) in accordance with the apostolic and synodical canons.[370]

From this brief excerpt it is not difficult to see that the *Definition* constituted a departure from time-honored practices sanctioned by synodical decisions; this is why Cyril's opponents disavowed him and his initiatives, accusing him of innovation and personal ambition.[371] Cyril V, however, would not be dissuaded. One year later, in 1756, the *Definition* was approved in synod, bearing the signatures of Cyril V; Matthew, patriarch of Alexandria; and Parthenios, patriarch of Jerusalem.

The *Definition* also was endorsed by Eustratios Argenti, the leading theologian of the eighteenth century, who probably had a hand in composing it.[372] Like Cyril V, Eustratios Argenti was a strong advocate of Cyprianic ecclesiology. In addition to the ecclesiological factor, his argument against

---

[369] For the text of the *Definition*, see Karmiris, *Τὰ δογματικά*, 989–991. In the tradition of the East, "to spit" (καταπτύω) upon someone or something is a mark of utter contempt and abhorrence. For an English translation of the *Definition*, see Dragas, "Manner of Reception," 243–245.

[370] Karmiris, *Τὰ δογματικά*, 990–991.

[371] Cyril V may have been motivated more by personal ambition than by theological argumentation in his stand against the heterodox, currying favor among the mercantile classes of Constantinople, which was staunchly anti-Latin. See Yiagkos, *Κανόνες καὶ λατρεία*, 434–436.

[372] For more on Eustratios Argenti and on the turbulent years and events that lead to Cyril's

the Latins was based chiefly on the defective form of Latin baptism—baptism by affusion (ἐπίχυσις) or aspersion (ῥαντισμός),[373] instead of the standard practice, baptism by immersion (either total or partial). He accused both the Latin church and the Protestants of introducing novel liturgical forms. By omitting immersion, he claimed, they destroyed the essential theological and symbolic presuppositions of the baptismal rite: death, burial, resurrection. For Argenti, a baptism not performed by immersion (save in cases of emergency) could not under any conditions be theologically justified, even economically.[374]

While the *Definition* was strongly defended by its supporters, it did not gain universal acceptance. Many of Cyril's successors to the patriarchal throne, for example, were reserved about it and made no real effort to enforce it. Nonetheless, it survived in theory as the official position of the patriarchate through the better part of the nineteenth century. This owed especially to the strong anti-Latin feelings of the populace[375] and to the vigorous defense of the practice of rebaptism by Eustratios Argenti and St. Nikodemos the Hagiorite (1749–1809).[376]

THE ROLE OF THE PEDALION

St. Nikodemos, who would become the chief advocate of rebaptism, agreed with Cyril V and Argenti on the need for correct liturgical forms and carried this argument against the Latins further.[377] He was a resolute opponent of the Roman church, even though he did not hesitate to borrow from,

---

Definition, see Ware, *Eustratios Argenti*, 65–78. See also John Erickson, "On the Cusp of Modernity: The Canonical Hermeneutic of St. Nikodemos the Hagiorite (1748–1809)," *St. Vladimir's Theological Quarterly* 42, no. 1 (1998): 45–66.

[373] Baptism by aspersion (ῥαντισμός) was especially disapproved of and condemned.

[374] Ware, *Eustratios Argenti*, 95.

[375] See Karmiris, *Τὰ δογματικά*, 984–985.

[376] On St. Nikodemos, see, for instance, Theokletos Dionysiatou, Ἅγιος Νικόδημος ὁ Ἁγιορείτης (Athens, 1959); Constantine Cavarnos, *St. Nicodemos the Hagiorite* (Belmont, MA, 1974); George Bebis, "Introduction to Nikodemos of the Holy Mountain," *Nicodemos of the Holy Mountain: A Handbook of Spiritual Counsel* (New York, 1989); Constantine Karaisarides, *Ο Νικόδημος ο Αγιορείτης και το λειτουργικό του έργο* (Athens, 1998); Erickson, "On the Cusp of Modernity," 45–66.

[377] As Yiagkos points out, it is significant that Cyril V was not a supporter of the Kollyvades, the monastic movement with which St. Nikodemos was involved and that sought to defend the "traditional" spirit of Orthodox liturgy and life, especially against the more progressive forces within the Church. See Yiagkos, *Κανόνες και λατρεία*, 436–438.

CHAPTER FIVE: RECEIVING CONVERTS INTO CHURCH 159

adapt, and publish works of Roman Catholic writers. He was a revered ascetic and a learned man with serious scholarly interests. His most influential work is the *Pedalion*, or the *Rudder*,[378] a collection of the canons promulgated by the holy synods, ecumenical as well as local, and by individual fathers, which Nikodemos compiled, in collaboration with his friend and fellow ascetic Agapios the hieromonk.[379]

In addition to the canons, the *Pedalion* contains two subsections written by St. Nikodemos: an "interpretation" (ἑρμηνεία), which is a long paraphrase of the canon in Modern Greek, and, where applicable, a "harmony or concord" (συμφωνία), in which he indicates the relation of a canon to other similar ones in the collection. More important, the *Pedalion* contains extensive commentaries by St. Nikodemos in which he quotes Byzantine canonists and develops, among other things, his ecclesiology and sacramental theology. The *Pedalion* has exerted considerable influence on Church life from the time of its publication in 1800, forty-five years after the *Definition* was promulgated by Cyril V. In fact, as some have noted, the publication of the *Pedalion* marked an important turning point in Greek theological thought.[380]

Two sources played a key role in St. Nikodemos's thinking: the collection of eighty-five canons attributed to the holy Apostles (the so-called Apostolic Canons) and the local Synod of Carthage convened by St. Cyprian in 256.[381] St. Nikodemos assigned great value and significance to these two sources, far more than they had ever enjoyed in previous generations. They shaped his views on the Church and on the sacraments. St. Nikodemos believed that the local or regional Synod of Carthage held under the leadership of St. Cyprian in 256 preceded all other synods in point of time and

---

[378] Ἀγαπίου Ἱερομονάχου καὶ Νικοδήμου Μονάχου, *Πηδάλιον τῆς νοητῆς νηός* (reprint: Athens 1957). For the English translation, see Agapios and Nikodemos, *The Rudder (Pedalion) of the Metaphorical Ship*, trans. D. Cummings (Chicago, 1957).

[379] For more on the *Pedalion* (*Πηδάλιον*), see Theodore Yiagkos, "Τὸ Πηδάλιον σὲ σχέση μὲ παλαιότερες νομοκανονικὲς συλλογές," in Yiagkos, *Κανόνες καὶ λατρεία*, 165–196. See also Vlassios Pheidas, "The *Pedalion* or *Rudder* and Ecclesiastical Consciousness: Current Status and Future Prospects," in *Legacy of Achievement*, ed. G. D. Dragas (Metropolis of Boston, 2009), 719–729.

[380] See Yiagkos, *Κανόνες καὶ λατρεία*, 166; Erickson, "Formation of Orthodox Christian Identity," 309.

[381] Erickson, "Formation of Orthodox Identity," 307–311. There were three regional or local synods held in Carthage between 255 and 256. I refer to the third of these synods.

deserved special attention and consideration.³⁸² Centuries earlier, Byzantine canonists like Zonaras and Balsamon had also believed that the Synod of Carthage was the most ancient, but unlike St. Nikodemos, they did not assign to it the same importance. They considered the actions of the synod concerning the treatment of heretics and schismatics exclusively an African approach with no universal appeal or significance (ὅτι ἀρχῆθεν οὐ παρὰ πᾶσιν ἦν ἐνεργῶν ὁ κανῶν), a reality that is sadly missed by the rigorists.³⁸³

For St. Nikodemos, however, the conciliar letter or the canon that the synod of Carthage issued contained the fundamental and unambiguous truth about the Church and the sacraments. This canon reads, in part, as follows: "We declare that no one can be baptized outside the catholic Church, there being but one baptism, and this being existent only in the catholic Church ... There being but one baptism, and there being but one Holy Spirit, there is also but one Church, founded by Christ our Lord upon ... oneness and unity."³⁸⁴

Essentially, the synod upheld St. Cyprian's belief that outside the limits of the canonical Church there is no grace. The practical result of such an exclusive ecclesiology is to place absolute limits on the action of the Holy Spirit. Thus, where the Holy Spirit is not, valid sacraments do not exist, and salvation is not possible. This limiting concept of grace and Church constitutes the essence of Cyprianic ecclesiology, which St. Nikodemos endorsed. He believed that it constituted the undeniable authoritative standard, or norm. "Heretics and schismatics," he wrote, "are neither priests, being in fact rather sacrilegists; neither clean nor pure, being in fact impure and unclean; neither holy, as not having any Holy Spirit, so neither have they any baptism."³⁸⁵ Hence, he concluded, "The truth of the divine Scripture and right reason prove incontestably that all heretics ought to be baptized."³⁸⁶ This narrow view, it needs to be stressed, is what has led to the rigorist position that all converts should be rebaptized.

---

³⁸² The Synod of 256 was the third over which St. Cyprian presided. The first was convened in 255 and the second and third in 256. The subject of all three synods was rebaptism. The third synod issued a conciliar canonical letter through which it decreed that the baptism of all heretical groups is null and void. See Πηδάλιον, 366–371; *Rudder*, 483–488.

³⁸³ See the comments of Zonaras and Balsamon on the Synod of Carthage: Rallis and Potlis, Σύνταγμα, 2:6, 19.

³⁸⁴ Πηδάλιον, 368–369; *Rudder*, 485–486.

³⁸⁵ Πηδάλιον, 369; *Rudder*, 487.

³⁸⁶ Πηδάλιον, 371; *Rudder*, 488.

CHAPTER FIVE: RECEIVING CONVERTS INTO CHURCH

At this point, a parenthesis is in order. The use of such harsh language by churchmen is difficult to justify. One could argue that such rhetoric is used by some writers as a literary device to alert and caution the faithful of the dangers of heresy, which distort the true faith and undermine the unity of the church. One can also find strong, albeit more controlled, language in some hymns of feasts commemorating Church Fathers who supplied the Church with authoritative explanations of the apostolic faith and tradition, while waging theological battle against heretical teachings.[387] One must admit, however, that vituperative utterances by some churchmen have not always been motivated by high purposes. Today, few people—especially those who live in multicultural, multiethnic, and multireligious societies—take kindly to such language. It is clearly counterproductive and widens, rather than narrows, the divide between people and communities.

For St. Nikodemos, as for St. Cyprian, the canonical and charismatic boundaries of the Church coincide. Outside the Church, there is only darkness and impiety. Hence, any deviation from canonical exactness through the use of *oikonomia* can be construed only as a concession, which changes nothing of and recognizes nothing in any heterodox group. The ecclesiology and sacramental theology of St. Nikodemos were also shaped by the eighty-five so-called Apostolic Canons, which he believed were genuinely apostolic, issued by the twelve apostles through St. Clement of Rome.[388] In fact, however, the eighty-five canons form part of the *Ordinances of the Holy Apostles through Clement*, a document written in the second half of the fourth century, known generally as the *Apostolic Constitutions*, the product of an anonymous compiler from Antioch. The document is a church order—belonging to the genre of early Christian literature that professed to offer authentic apostolic directions in canonical, liturgical, and ethical matters.

---

[387] Such pointed language is evident in the Scriptures, as well, cautioning the faithful against the allure of false teachers (see, for example, 2 Pet. 2:1–22).

[388] In the prolegomena of the *Pedalion*, St. Nikodemos writes the following: "Various councils (σύνοδοι), or rather to say conventions (συνελεύσεις), of the holy Apostles, according to some, were held as follows. The first one in the year 33 or 34 after the birth of Christ, with regard to the selection of an Apostle to take the place of Judas the traitor ... These things being stated, at which one of these conventions did the divine Apostles issue through Clement the present 85 canons of theirs? Regarding this point antiquity has left us no exact information stochastically. Nevertheless, one might say that they ordained them at the said largest and notable convention, when they were about to separate from each other and to be scattered for the preaching of the Gospel" (*Πηδάλιον*, κβ–κγ; *Rudder*, lviii–lx).

The Apostolic Canons were appended to book 8 of the *Apostolic Constitutions*. The canons were endorsed by the Penthekte Synod, thus securing their recognition by the Church. St. Nikodemos regarded them as the "original models and basic foundations" of all the canonical regulations and the very embodiment of the *exactness* (ἀκρίβεια) of the Church's faith and praxis as laid down by the holy Apostles.

Inasmuch as these eighty-five canons constituted for St. Nikodemos the standard of all ecclesial law, any deviation from the norm they established could be justified only for reasons of expediency through the exercise of *oikonomia*. The Church, he said, was governed by two principles: by exactness and by *oikonomia* and condescension (συγκατάβασις). "With these two," he wrote, "the stewards of the Spirit promote the salvation of souls, at times with the one and at times with the other kind."[389]

Since *oikonomia* constitutes a suspension of exactness, it has a limited effect and cannot abrogate exactness. Thus when the particular need or purpose for which *oikonomia* was exercised has been served, the Church, St. Nikodemos believed, is obliged to return to the established norm: "the need of economy having passed away, exactness and the Apostolic Canons must have their place" (τῆς οἰκονομίας παρελθούσης, ἡ ἀκρίβεια καὶ οἱ Ἀποστολικοὶ κανόνες πρέπει να ἔχουν τὸν τόπον τούς).[390] Especially pertinent to this discussion are canons 46, 47, and 68 of the *Ordinances of the Holy Apostles*, which categorically reject all sacraments performed outside the canonical Church. Canon 46, for example, says: "We order any Bishop or Presbyter that has accepted any heretics' baptism or sacrifice, to be deposed; for what consonance (συμφώνησις) has Christ with Beliar? Or what part has the believer with an infidel (ἄπιστος)?"[391]

With the Synod of Carthage and the *Apostolic Canons* as his unshakable foundation, St. Nikodemos contended that the Orthodox Church is the sole steward of grace and the only administrator of valid sacraments. Hence the sacraments of heretics and schismatics are entirely unauthentic. Again, outside the boundaries of the canonical Church, he argued there is no grace—only undifferentiated darkness. Therefore according to him, since the heterodox do not possess true sacraments, all converts without

---

[389] *Πηδάλιον*, 51; *Rudder*, 70.
[390] *Πηδάλιον*, 57; *Rudder*, 74.
[391] *Πηδάλιον*, 51; *Rudder*, 68. See also canons 49 and 50.

distinction must be rebaptized.³⁹² However, the strong position St. Nikodemos took against all heterodox was problematic. It contradicted the decisions of earlier ecumenical and local synods that permitted the reception of certain converts by means other than baptism, recognizing, at least tacitly, the validity of baptism in some communities outside the Church's canonical borders. But such a conclusion was unacceptable for those who held a rigorist position.

To justify his position and reconcile it with the decisions of earlier synods, St. Nikodemos claimed that these synods had acted out of necessity for reasons of expediency, to gain as painlessly as possible a particular objective through the exercise of *oikonomia* and condescension.³⁹³ In this regard, St. Nikodemos saw *oikonomia* as a tool, a clever method of governance by which the Church consents to relax canonical exactness for a given time in order to manage a difficult situation so as to gain a greater good without compromising authenticity.³⁹⁴

The issue of *oikonomia* will be raised again a bit later. Here, however, a few more words on the state of the Church in the eighteenth century will be helpful for understanding the strong anti-Latin feelings that over time

---

³⁹² *Πηδάλιον*, 55–58; *Rudder*, 68–76.

³⁹³ "Δύο είδη κυβερνήσεως και διορθώσεως φυλάττονται εις την του Χριστού Εκκλησίαν. Το εν είδος ονομάζεται *Ακρίβεια*, το δε άλλο ονομάζεται *Οικονομία* και *Συγκατάβασις*, με τα οποία κυβερνούσι την σωτηρίαν των ψυχών οι του πνεύματος οικονόμοι" (*Πηδάλιον*, 53; *Rudder*, 70).

³⁹⁴ In a recent important article, based in part on hitherto unpublished material, Theodoros Yiagkos has argued that St. Nikodemos originally supported the application of sacramental economy regarding the reception of heretical clergy because of his interpretation of canon 68 of the *Ordinances of the Holy Apostles* and other conciliar decisions. Yiagkos claims, further, that St. Nikodemos altered his position in order to conform to the wishes of Dorotheos Voulismas, appointed by the synod of the Ecumenical Patriarchate to review and examine critically (πρὸς ἀνάκρισιν) the copy of the manuscript of the *Pedalion* submitted to the patriarchate in the summer of 1791 to secure its approval for publication. Voulismas was an ardent supporter of the Synod of 1775. See Theodoros Yiagkos, "Ερμηνευτικός σχολιασμός στον 68ο αποστολικό κανόνα από τους συγγραφείς του Πηδαλίου και τον Χριστοφόρο Προδρομίτη," in *Επιστημονική επετηρίδα Θεολογικής Σχολής, Τμήμα Ποιμαντικής και Κοινωνικής Θεολογίας* 13 (Thessaloniki, 2008), 69–93. The conclusions of Yiagkos deserve further consideration and investigation. For more on Dorotheos Voulismas (d. 1818), a prominent eighteenth-century churchman about whom little is known and little has been written, see Nikolaos Zacharopoulos, *Δωρόθεος Βουλησμάς: Ἐπὶ τῇ βάσει τῶν ἀνεκδότων αὐτοῦ ἐπιστόλων* (Thessaloniki, 1969). On Voulismas's reading of the *Pedalion*, see especially 100–105.

permeated the Orthodox populace as a result of papal policies. The following excerpt from Eustratios Argenti's *Manual Concerning Baptism* is but one example of the prevailing sentiments of the times:

So far as they are able, the Papists persecute and make war upon the Orthodox. Without any fresh cause or open justification they have seized churches ... which the Orthodox in their poverty had founded with great trouble and expense; they have seized the Holy Places in Jerusalem; resorting sometimes to direct attacks and sometime to deceit, they have utterly destroyed three of the Patriarchal Thrones; they have compelled the Orthodox in Hungary and Poland to subscribe to Popery; and what further harm could they have done to the Orthodox, which they have not done.[395]

SOCIOPOLITICAL AND RELIGIOUS REALITIES

The position held by Cyril V, Argenti, and others that all converts without distinction should be rebaptized was not new. As has been mentioned, cases of rebaptism occurred sporadically from the schism of 1054 until the matter was regularized by the Synod of 1484.[396] And even after 1484, isolated instances of rebaptism occurred, usually in reaction to Roman clerics who rebaptized Orthodox converts or in response to Latin innovations. These centered on baptism by aspersion or infusion, which was considered a defective liturgical form incapable of embodying symbolically the spiritual realities of Christian baptism.[397] But despite the occasional and isolated instances to the contrary, from 1484 to 1755 the official policy of the Church was to receive Latin and later also Protestant converts[398] through a threefold process that involved instruction, a *libellus*, and chrismation.

---

[395] Quoted in Ware, *Eustratios Argenti*, 78–79. For similar sentiments focused on the nullity of Latin baptism, see St. Nikodemos's comments on canon 46 and 47 of the *Ordinances of the Holy Apostles*: "We declare that the baptism of the Latins is one which falsely is called baptism (ψευδώνυμον βάπτισμα), and for this reason it is not acceptable or recognizable either on the grounds of rigorism (ἀκρίβεια) or on grounds of economy (οἰκονομία) ... That the Latins are heretics there is no need of our producing any proof ... As a result of their having been cut off from the Orthodox Church, they no longer have within them the grace of the Holy Spirit ... It is certainly poor economy when it does not serve to convert the Latins and forces us to transgress the rigorism [or exactness] of the sacred canons and to accept the pseudo-baptism of heretics" (*Πηδάλιον*, 55–56; *Rudder*, 72–74). Compare with his comments on canon 95 of the Penthekte Synod (*Πηδάλιον*, 305; *Rudder*, 402).

[396] For more on the postschism period and the fluctuating practices of reception, see L'Huillier, "Reception of Roman Catholics," 76–79; Dragas, "Manner of Reception," 236–237.

[397] Karmiris, *Τὰ δογματικά*, 979–987.

[398] Ibid., 1015–1019.

CHAPTER FIVE: RECEIVING CONVERTS INTO CHURCH

Beginning in the seventeenth century, a series of events placed new strains on relations between the Orthodox and the Latins. As if the bitter oppression of the Ottomans were not enough, as Timothy Ware (now Metropolitan Kallistos of Diokleia) has shown,[399] the Roman church and the actions of some Western powers and the merchant classes infuriated the Orthodox populace, the former by escalating its proselytizing efforts through various Uniate movements[400] and the latter by interfering in the socioeconomic affairs of the Orthodox populace.

As a result of these activities, an acrimonious sociopolitical and religious climate emerged. In response to these developments, the Russian Church at the Synod of Moscow in 1620 ordered the rebaptism of all converts from the West. However, nearly fifty years later, in 1667, another synod was convened in Moscow that reversed this decision and aligned the Russian practice with the Greek. At the Synod of 1667, the reception of Latin converts by chrismation was reaffirmed and ratified by all the Eastern patriarchates.

Five years later, in 1672, another synod was convened in Jerusalem, for the purpose of confronting and combating Protestant and Latin influences in the Church. Dositheos, patriarch of Jerusalem (1641–1707), presided at this synod and was the principle author of its decrees and confession. Dositheos's *Confession of Faith*, approved by the synod, was received and

---

[399] See Ware, *Eustratios Argenti*, especially 1–64, 161–169.
[400] In 1564 the Society of Jesus (the Jesuits, founded in 1534 and approved in 1540) began a proselytizing campaign to convert the Orthodox populace in Ukraine, a large segment of which was absorbed by the Roman Catholic Kingdom of Lithuania and Poland. In 1596 a synod of pro-Roman Orthodox bishops at Brest-Litovsk proclaimed union with Rome. Thus was born in Polish Ukraine a "Uniate" church, whose members were known as Greek Catholics or Catholics of the Eastern Rite. The synod's action ignited a fierce conflict; the efforts at proselytism, however, continued unabated. Eastern Rite Catholic communities were founded among Ukrainians, Ruthenians, and Hungarians (1596), Yugoslavs (1611), Carpathian Ruthenians (1646), Slovaks (1646), Romanians (1701), Melkites (1724), Bulgars (1860), and Greeks (1860). The Uniate movement caused great harm and poisoned relations between Rome and the Orthodox East, and its effects are felt up to the present. It was not only poorly conceived but also badly executed. In the words of Timothy (now Metropolitan Kallistos) Ware, "The tale of the Uniate movement in Poland makes sorrowful reading: the Jesuits began by using deceit, and ended up by resorting to violence. Doubtless they were sincere men who genuinely desired the unity of Christendom, but the tactics they employed were better calculated to widen the breach than to close it." Timothy Ware, *The Orthodox Church*, 1st ed. (New York, 1978), 105. For a brief description and history of the Greek Catholics, see Ronald Roberson, *The Eastern Christian Churches: A Brief Survey*, 6th ed. (Rome, 1999), 161–188; and the pertinent pages in Ware, *The Orthodox Church*, rev. ed. (New York, 1997) under the title Greek Catholics in the Index..

acclaimed by all the Orthodox as a true expression of the faith. For purposes of this discussion, the Synod of 1672 upheld previous conciliar decisions and did not require the rebaptism of Latin and Protestant converts, as indicated by definition 15 of Dositheos's *Confession of Faith*.[401]

THE LEGACY OF CYRIL V AND THE PEDALION

From this brief review of the historical data, it is clear that Cyril's *Definition*, in effect, abrogated earlier synodical decisions, undid centuries of nuanced liturgical practice, and disrupted the hitherto more or less uniform practices of reception observed by the autocephalous Orthodox Churches.

The more serious problem, however, was not the *Definition* per se; its stipulations were never strictly enforced. But the *Definition* provided the impetus for the emergence of a radically narrow concept of the limits of the Church[402] that St. Nikodemos promoted through the *Pedalion*, the influence of which on Greek ecclesial circles cannot be discounted or minimized. Through St. Nikodemos, the ecclesiology and sacramental theology of St. Cyprian of Carthage resurfaced in the East with newfound vigor, even though, as Fr. Georges Florovsky correctly observed, its practical conclusions were neither accepted nor supported by the consciousness of the Church.[403] With Cyril V and the *Pedalion*, the nuanced approach to heterodox communities and the more inclusive spirit that marked the Byzantine and post-Byzantine periods began to wane, giving way to a more rigid and negative attitude toward other Christians, to a narrow, functional understanding of *oikonomia*, and to an ecclesiology that is patently exclusive, condescending, and triumphalist.

It is not hard to see how troublesome historical circumstances, difficult sociocultural situations, and lingering deep-seated antipathies (warrant-

---

[401] On the Synod of 1672 and the *Confession* of Dositheos, see Karmiris, Τὰ δογματικά, 694–733, 734–773. Dositheos's brief statement on heterodox baptism leaves no doubt that it aligns with earlier conciliar statements. It reads, "Οἱ γὰρ αἱρετικοί, οὓς τὴν αἵρεσιν ἀποσεισαμένους καὶ προστεθέντας τῇ καθολικῇ ἐκκλησίᾳ, δέχεται ἡ Ἐκκλησία, καίτοι ἐλλιπῆ ἐσχηκότες τὴν πίστιν, τέλειον ἔλαβον τὸ βάπτισμα ὅθεν τελείαν ὕστερον τὴν πίστιν κεκτημένοι, οὐκ ἀναβατίζονται" (758).

[402] For a discussion of the limits of the Church and *oikonomia* in modern Orthodox thought, see Emmanuel Clapsis, "The Boundaries of the Church: An Orthodox Debate," *Greek Orthodox Theological Review* 35, no. 2 (1990): 113–127; also in the volume of Clapsis's collected articles, *Orthodoxy in Conversation: Orthodox Ecumenical Engagements* (Geneva, 2000), 114–126.

[403] Florovsky, "Limits of the Church," 118.

ed or unwarranted) can exert a strong negative influence on theological thought and cause the Church, or certain circles within the Church, to become more insular, less irenic, and less willing to enter into a dialogue of love with other Christians and other faiths—characteristic of the patristic tradition and of the Byzantine and post-Byzantine periods. The dangers of a too-narrow understanding of the boundaries of the Church were sounded long ago by Fr. Georges Florovsky, who made the following insightful observation:

> St. Cyprian was right; the sacraments are accomplished only in the Church. But this *in*, he defined hastily and too narrowly. Must we not come rather to the opposite conclusion? *Where the sacraments are accomplished there is the Church*. St. Cyprian started from the silent supposition that *the canonical and charismatic limits of the Church invariably coincide*. And it is this unproven identification that has not been confirmed by the communal consciousness. As a mystical organism, as the sacramental Body of Christ, the Church cannot be adequately described in canonical terms or categories alone. It is impossible to state or discern the true limits of the Church simply by canonical signs or marks … In her sacramental, mysterious being the Church surpasses canonical measurements. For that reason a canonical cleavage does not immediately signify mystical impoverishment and desolation. All that Cyprian said about the unity of the Church and the sacraments can be and must be accepted. But it is not necessary with him to draw the final boundary around the body of the Church by canonical points alone.[404]

St. Nikodemos and the Principle of 'Oikonomia'

OIKONOMIA: CANONICAL STRATAGEM OR JUDICIOUS PASTORAL JUDGMENT?

When reading the commentaries of St. Nikodemos on the reception of Latin converts, one gets the impression that *oikonomia* is less a judicious pastoral judgment and action—a manifestation of the boundless, self-giving love of God within the complexities and trials of human existence and ecclesial life in this fallen and imperfect world—and more a canonical device or stratagem. In his writings, *oikonomia* appears as a tactic by which the Church seeks to moderate a problematic situation, navigating through it

---
[404] Ibid., 119.

with the least possible pain in order to achieve an external end. Offering an explanation for why the Second and Penthekte Ecumenical Synods chose to accept certain converts without rebaptism, he writes,

> One might rightly wonder why the holy Second Ecumenical Council in its 7th canon, but still more so why the Sixth Ecumenical in its 95th canon, failed to disapprove the baptism of all heretics, in accordance with the Apostolic Canons and St. Cyprian's Synod ... The two Ecumenical Councils employed economy ... Because in the times especially of the Second Council the Arians and Macedonians were at the height of their influence, and were not only very numerous but also very powerful ... Hence, for one thing, in order to attract them to Orthodoxy and correct them the easier, and, for another thing, in order to avoid the risk of infuriating them still more against the Church and the Christians and aggravating the evil, those divine Fathers thus managed the matter economically—and condescended to accept their baptism ... In close proximity to the ground of economy there stood also a second reason why they did so. The fact is that those heretics whose baptism they accepted also rigorously observed (ἐφύλαττον ἀπαράλακτον) the kind and the matter of baptism of the Orthodox and were baptized in accordance with the form of the Catholic Church.[405]

In this passage and others like it, St. Nikodemos calls attention to the role liturgical forms play in the application of *oikonomia*. In fact, correct form, especially in baptism, was always an important consideration in dealing with heterodox groups. But as this text indicates, what matters most in the application of *oikonomia* is the welfare of the Church, even if liturgical forms have to be overlooked. *Oikonomia* is a tactical accommodation meant to uphold and preserve the well-being of the Church as it accomplishes what is required in a given circumstance.[406]

In the passage that follows, St. Nikodemos uses the same reasoning to justify the Church's practice of receiving Latin converts by chrismation and not by rebaptism, as he believed the exactness of the canons demanded. He argues that the Church had no recourse but to relax exactness because of the great power and influence of the papacy. But now, he claims, the reason for which *oikonomia* was applied no longer exists. God has set a "guardian" over the flock to protect it from its enemies. Hence, he believed, now is the

---

[405] *Πηδάλιον*, 53; *Rudder*, 70. See also the commentaries on canon 7 of the Second Ecumenical Synod and on canon 95 of the Penthekte, *Pedalion*, 164–165, 220; *Rudder*, 305, 402.
[406] See Erickson, "On the Cusp of Modernity," 64.

appropriate time for the Church to return to exactness, because *oikonomia* constitutes the exception and not the rule. It is enacted for a specific reason, purpose, and time. Its power is limited; "it is not perpetual and indefinite."

> So those preceding us also employed economy and accepted the baptism of the Latins ... because the Papacy or Popery was then in its prime and had all the forces and powers of the kings of Europe in its hands, while on the other hand, our own kingdom was breathing its last gasps ... Hence it would have become necessary, if that economy had not been employed, for the Pope to rouse the Latin races against the Eastern, take them prisoners, kill them, and inflict countless barbarities upon them ... But now that they are no longer able to inflict such woes upon us, as a result of the fact that divine Providence has lent us such a guardian ... what need is there any longer of economy? For there is a limit to economy, and it is not perpetual and indefinite.[407]

Of course, St. Nikodemos was not the first among his contemporaries to use the economic argument to justify the reception of converts without rebaptism. But he was the most influential of those who did so. The *Pedalion* secured an ongoing acceptance of this line of thought, especially among Greek ecclesial and theological circles, as evidenced, for example, by the writings on holy baptism of Konstantinos Oikonomos of the Oikonomoi, an eminent clergyman and theologian of the nineteenth century.[408]

At this point, it bears repeating that canon 7 of the Second Ecumenical Synod and canon 95 of the Penthekte, in reality, constitute ἀκρίβεια or exactness and instruct ecclesial policy on the reception of converts.[409] The un-

---

[407] *Πηδάλιον*, 56; *Rudder*, 73. The God-sent guardians he refers to are the Turks. What irony! While such sentiments may surprise today's readers, they were widespread and deeply felt among the Orthodox populace, as evidenced by Paul of Aleppo, nephew of the archdeacon to the patriarch of Antioch. In the 1650s, while traveling in Ukraine, he wrote the following entry in his diary: "God perpetuate the Empire of the Turks! For they take their impost and enter into no account of religion, be their subjects Christians or Nazarenes, Jews or Samaritans; whereas the accursed Poles [Roman Catholics], not content with taking taxes and tithes from their Christian [Orthodox] subjects, subjected them to the enemies of Christ, the Jews, who did not allow them to build churches or leave them any educated priests" (quoted in Ware, *The Orthodox Church*, 1st ed., 105).

[408] For more on Konstantinos Oikonomos, see Lewis J. Patsavos, "Konstantinos Oikonomos of the Oikonomoi," in *Post-Byzantine Ecclesiastical Personalities*, ed. N. M. Vaporis (Brookline, MA, 1978), 69–85; Athanasios Geromihalos, Ο Κωνσταντινος Οικονομος ο εξ Οικονομων και η εποχη του (Thessaloniki, 1964).

[409] See Hieronymos Kotsonis, *Προβλήματα τῆς ἐκκλησιαστικῆς οἰκονομίας* (Athens, 1957), 186–190.

yielding rigorist position on rebaptism is, in fact, a deviation from the norm and therefore an act of *oikonomia*. As Archbishop Hieronymos Kotsonis observes, *oikonomia* constitutes a departure from the canonical norm. This departure can be either more lenient (ἐπὶ τὸ ἐπιεικέστερον) or stricter (ἐπὶ τὸ αὐστηρότερον) than the authoritative standard prescribed by the canons.[410] The rigorist position that requires the rebaptism of all converts without distinction constitutes *oikonomia* as a departure from the norm toward greater strictness.

IS THE ABSOLUTIST POSITION ON THE BOUNDARIES OF THE CHURCH TENABLE?

St. Nikodemos's absolutist position on grace and on the boundaries of the Church raises some serious questions. Are the underlying principles of his ecclesiology consistent with the Greek patristic tradition, which maintained a more nuanced approach, a more open stance toward heterodox communities, discerning what is "of the Church" outside the canonical boundaries of the Church? Does his sacramental theology accord with that of the canonical and liturgical texts of the Byzantine and post-Byzantine periods that distinguished between what is nonexistent and what is defective and reparable? Is the use of *oikonomia* for purposes of expediency, as he maintained, worthy of the Church? Is such an impulse—such a crafty motivation and intention—proper to the Church's ethos and consistent with its moral principles?

Moreover, what exactly is the Church accomplishing through *oikonomia* if, as St. Nikodemos believed, all sacraments performed outside the Church are null and void? Is the Church rendering something that is invalid (ἄκυρον) and nonexistent into something real and valid (ἔγκυρον)? But that would be a form of magic. The Church would be creating something out of nothing, a power that belongs only to God. On these very points, Fr. Florovsky poses two critical questions:

---

[410] Ibid., 86–93. The ordination of a person before he has reached the age prescribed by the canons (for deacon, twenty-five; presbyter, thirty; bishop, thirty-five) constitutes a departure from exactness (ἀκρίβεια) and an act of *oikonomia* on the side leniency (ἐπὶ τὸ ἐπιεικέστερον). The opposite is true in the reception of Nestorians and Monophysites by chrismation. It is an act of *oikonomia* on the side of strictness (ἐπὶ τὸ αὐστηρότερον).

CHAPTER FIVE: RECEIVING CONVERTS INTO CHURCH

If in fact the Church were fully convinced that in the sects and heresies baptism is not accomplished, to what end would she reunite schismatics without baptism? Surely not in order simply to save them by this step from false shame in the open confession that they have not been baptized. Can such a motive be considered honorable, convincing, and of good repute?[411]

If there is only darkness and impoverishment outside the limits of the canonical Church, as the supporters of Cyprianic ecclesiology believe, what is one to make of the conciliar decisions that did not require the rebaptism of all converts? Do the economic justifications of St. Nikodemos and of his heirs provide reasonable and adequate explanations for these decisions?

The conciliar decisions and the liturgical texts of the Church point in a direction that is different from that of the absolutist position of the rigorists. The Church, as the authentic depository of the apostolic *kerygma* and Tradition, has the power to discern between truth and falsehood and to identify with joy what is authentically of itself wherever it is found. The Church can thereby affirm the existence of grace and light, however bright or dim, beyond its own canonical boundaries.[412] And the Orthodox Church accomplishes this without compromising or surrendering its identity as the one, holy, catholic, and apostolic Church.

The Church is not only the vigilant keeper and interpreter of the message of revelation but also its passionate, heroic, and humble witness. The Church is not a walled city, incommunicative from the inside and impenetrable from the outside. It is the evangelical community of love and peace, infinitely compassionate and tolerant, even when scorned and wronged. The Church is the Body of Christ, the extension and fullness of the incarnation that draws the brokenness of the world into a communion of unity and truth.

In contemplating and enacting this lofty calling and mission to the world, the Church must never lose sight of the historical reality of sin. Nikos Nissiotis reminds us that an authentic ecclesiology is mindful of the "curious and unique dialectic between unshaken communion in *essence* and brokenness in *existence* in the whole creation. This is because the *ecclesia* as sacramental communion is absolutely holy ... but all men yet remain sin-

---

[411] Florovsky, "Limits of the Church," 17.
[412] See Thomas Hopko, "Tasks Facing the Orthodox in the 'Reception' Process of BEM," *Greek Orthodox Theological Review* 30, no. 2 (1985): 236.

ful and in broken relationship both in the ecclesial communion and in the world."[413] On this very point, the sobering reflection of Fr. Florovsky is especially instructive:

> The tragedy of Christendom is precisely that the truth of God is still divergently apprehended ... Our Christian pain is a token of recovery, a recovery which is to come from the Lord ... As a member and priest of the Orthodox Church I believe that the Church in which I was baptized and brought up *is* in very truth *the Church*, i.e., the *true* Church and the *only* true Church ... It does not mean that everything in the past or present state of the Orthodox Church is to be equated with the truth of God. Many things are obviously changeable; indeed many things need improvement. The *true* Church is not yet the *perfect* Church. The Church of Christ has to grow and be built up in history. Yet the whole and the full truth has been already given and entrusted to the Church. Revision and re-statement is always possible, sometimes imperative. The whole history of the Ecumenical Councils in the past is evidence of that. The holy Fathers of the Church were engaged in this task. Yet, on the whole, the deposit was faithfully kept and the testimony of faith was gaining accuracy and precision.[414]

Oikonomia, Church, and Sacraments in Contemporary Theological Thought

PREVAILING THEORIES ON OIKONOMIA

The economic explanations that have been put forth from the time of St. Nikodemos to the present, as Fr. Florovsky pointed out, are, in fact, private theological opinions when one considers their general theological premises.

> The "economic" interpretation of the canons might be probable and convincing, but only in the presence of direct and perfectly clear proofs, whereas it is generally supported by indirect data and most often by indirect intentions and conclusions. The "economic" interpretation is not the teaching of the Church. It is only a private

---

[413] Nikos A. Nissiotis, "The Church as a Sacramental Vision and the Challenge of Christian Witness," in *Church, Kingdom, World*, ed. Gennadios Limouris (Geneva, 1986), 109.
[414] Georges Florovsky, "Confessional Loyalty in the Ecumenical Movement," *The Student World* 43, no. 1 (1950): 59-70. This article was republished in *Inter-Communion*, ed. Donald Baillie and John Marsh (New York, 1952): 196-205. The reference is from the latter volume, 202, 203-204.. .

"theological opinion," very late and very controversial, which arose in a period of theological confusion and decadence in a hasty endeavor to dissociate oneself as sharply as possible from Roman theology.[415]

Several theories of *oikonomia* have been put forth, but the Church has yet to decide conclusively and authoritatively on a commonly accepted definition of ecclesiastical economy. In fact, the Church has neither a doctrine of *oikonomia* nor any official canonical or other text that defines it in detail or in fullness. Its meaning and application have been discussed and debated many times over in scholarly works, including those by Amilkas Alivizatos,[416] Archbishop Hieronymos Kotsonis,[417] John Erickson,[418] Metropolitan Vartholomaios Archondonis (now Ecumenical Patriarch Bartholomew),[419] Metropolitan Chrysostom Constantinides,[420] and others. In an interesting and comprehensive article written in 1965, Francis J. Thomson set forth and analyzed the various opinions on *oikonomia* held by Orthodox theologians up to that time.[421]

The lack of agreement on the meaning and purpose of *oikonomia* was highlighted in recent years by the negative response of several theologians to the text on *oikonomia* developed in 1971 by the Inter-Orthodox Preparatory Commission for the Great and Holy Synod, especially as it pertained to questions concerning the ecclesial nature and the sacraments of other Christian communities.[422] Five Greek theologians of the University

---

[415] Florovsky, "Limits of the Church," 20.
[416] Amilkas Alivizatos, Ἡ οἰκονομία κατὰ τὸ κανονικὸν δίκαιον τῆς Ὀρθοδόξου Ἐκκλησίας (Athens, 1947).
[417] Hieronymos Kotsonis, Προβλήματα τῆς ἐκκλησιαστικῆς οἰκονομίας, especially 14–28. See also Kotsonis, Η κανονικη αποψις περι επικοιωνιας μετα των ετεροδοξον (Athens, 1957).
[418] John Erickson, "Oikonomia in Byzantine Canon Law," in *Law, Church, and Society: Essays in Honor of Tehan Kuttner*, ed. K. Pennington and R. Somerville (Philadelphia, 1977), 225–236.
[419] Bartholomaios Archondonis, "Το πρόβλημα της οικονομίας σήμερον," *Γρηγόριος Παλαμάς* 65 (1982): 20–36.
[420] Chrysostomos Constantinides, *Η αναγνώριση των μυστηρίων*, especially part 2, devoted to "Ἀκρίβεια, οικονομία και αναγνώριση των μυστηρίων," 85–219.
[421] Francis J. Thomson, "An Examination of the Various Theories of Economy Held within the Orthodox Church, with Special Reference to the Economical Recognition of the Validity of Non-Orthodox Sacraments," *Journal of Theological Studies*, n.s. 16 (1965): 368–420.
[422] The preparatory commission's text on *oikonomia* was developed on the basis of an earlier draft presented in 1969 by the Church of Romania. The commission's text was included in chapter 6 of the report of the Secretariat of the Commission published in 1971: "Πρὸς τὴν Μεγάλην Σύνοδον. Εἰσηγήσεις τῆς Διορθοδόξου Προπαρασκευαστικῆς Ἐπιτροπῆς

of Athens were among those who criticized this important text for what they believed would be its unintended destructive and divisive consequences.[423] The document was, of course, defended by others, including the metropolitan of Axome and later archbishop of Thyateira and Great Britain, Methodios Fouyias,[424] and the metropolitan of Ephesus Chrysostom Constantinides.

The draft statement on *oikonomia*, prepared by the Church of Romania, was to be discussed and approved by the preparatory commission and then circulated among the Churches for review, refinement, and final acceptance at the level of an inter-Orthodox preparatory conference.[425] Because of the negative reaction it caused, the topic of *oikonomia* was considered too controversial and was subsequently removed from the commission's agenda by consensus and replaced with other more pressing canonical concerns related to the diaspora, autonomy, autocephaly, and the diptychs.[426]

Unfortunately, the Churches have done little in the ensuing years to address this important and sensitive issue in a substantive way. While the concept of *oikonomia* may defy a detailed description and an absolute definition, it is nonetheless something which has been lived and experienced by the Church from ancient times.[427] Until an authoritative definition is developed and agreed upon, it behooves the local Churches to apply its principles with theological precision as well as pastoral discernment and forbearance in the tradition of the Church Fathers.

ἐπὶ τῶν ἓξ θεμάτων τοῦ πρώτου σταδίου (κεφ. στ.): Ἡ οἰκονομία ἐν τῇ Ὀρθοδόξῳ Ἐκκλησίᾳ" (Chambesy, 1971), 50–65. Regarding the use of *oikonomia* in general and the reaction to the commission's text in particular, see, for example, Emmanuel Clapsis, "The Boundaries of the Church: An Orthodox Debate," in his book, *Orthodoxy in Conversation: Orthodox Ecumenical Engagements* (Geneva, 2000), especially 120–124.

[423] The five professors highly critical of the commission's text are Panagiotis Bratsiotis, Panagiotis Trembelas, Konstantinos Mouratidis, Andreas Theodorou, and Nikolaos Bratsiotis. They submitted their strong objections in a memorandum to the Holy Synod of the Church of Greece, dated June 5, 1972. See Constantinides, *Η αναγνώριση των μυστηρίων*, 103–104.

[424] Methodios Fouyias, "Περὶ ἐκκλησιαστικῆς οἰκονομίας: Ἀπαντήσεις εἰς τοὺς καθηγητὰς τῆς θεολογίας," in *Ἐκκλησιαστικὸς Φάρος* 56–58 (1974–1976), with an English summary and a bibliography. See also the response of Panayiotis Trembelas, "Καὶ πάλιν περὶ οἰκονομίας: Πρὸς τὸν Σεβασμιώτατον Μητροπολίτην Ἀξώμης," in *Ὀρθόδοξος Τύπος* (April 15, **YEAR**): 1–74.

[425] For a brief description of the events surrounding the draft statement on *oikonomia*, see the long footnote in Constantinides, *Η αναγνώριση των μυστηρίων*, 101–107.

[426] See Vartholomeos Archondonis, "'Η οἰκονομία ἐν τῇ Ὀρθοδόξῳ Ἐκκλησίᾳ," in *Ἐπίσκεψις* 3 (March 1972): 13–14.

[427] Ibid.

LOOKING BEYOND PAST CONTROVERSIES

A counterweight to Cyprianic ecclesiology is the theory put forth by St. Augustine, who maintained that under certain conditions, the sacraments of some schismatics and heretics are valid but inefficacious, valid but irregular.[428] For St. Augustine, this distinction was crucial. Metropolitan Kallistos Ware describes the Augustinian position succinctly as follows: "Whereas Cyprian denied heretics both the *ius* and the *potestas* to perform the sacraments, Augustine denied the first, but not necessarily the second ... [A] sacrament performed by heretics or schismatics, while irregular and illegitimate, is nonetheless technically valid provided certain specified conditions are fulfilled."[429]

The sacramental theology of St. Augustine, according to Fr. Florovsky, has not been creatively appropriated by the Orthodox East. He urged Orthodox theologians to "express and explain the traditional canonical practices of the Church in relation to heretics and schismatics on the basis of those general premises which have been established by Augustine."[430] In fact, according to Metropolitan Kallistos, since the eighteenth century a number of Russian theologians have inclined toward the Augustinian approach, while the Greeks have inclined toward the Cyprianic view.[431]

While the traditional approach of the Orthodox Church, as Archbishop Peter L'Huillier has pointed out, is not identical to either the Cyprianic or the Augustinian concept, neither of them has been rejected, and in fact, both have adherents today.[432] One may, however, conclude with some assurance, in accordance with the historical data, that Orthodox theological thought throughout the Byzantine and post-Byzantine periods, as well as in more recent times, has been more moderate and conciliatory than the Cyprianic position is. Orthodox theologians today are more accepting of the view that some non-Orthodox communities are still in some sense members of the Church.

Thanks to the pioneering efforts and initiatives of the Ecumenical Patriarchate in the cause of Christian unity from the earliest days of the twentieth century to the present, Orthodox theological thought has moved well

---

[428] See L'Huillier, "Reception of Roman Catholics," 75.
[429] Ware, *Eustratios Argenti*, 81–82.
[430] Florovsky, "Limits of the Church," 22.
[431] Ware, *Eustratios Argenti*, 82
[432] L'Huillier, "Reception of Roman Catholics," 76.

beyond the insular, inimical, and defensive attitudes that were prevalent during and after the baptism controversy of the eighteenth century. Thanks also to its liberation from the constraints of scholasticism and to its renewed interest in and the development of the thought of the Fathers and the Church's authentic tradition embedded in her sacramental, doctrinal, and pastoral activity, contemporary Orthodox theology is more inclined and more open to deeper and subtler experiences and intuitions as they relate to the Church's own internal development and to its distinct role and mission to the world.

While holding firmly to the belief that the Church can be only one, and that this one true Church is the Orthodox Church, we cannot deny completely the ecclesial nature of other Christian communities. As Metropolitan John Zizioulas says, "It is certainly not easy to exclude from the realm and the operation of the Holy Spirit so many Christians who do not belong to the Orthodox Church. There are saints outside the Orthodox Church."[433] Leontios of Jerusalem, a sixth-century theologian, made a similar observation in his treatise *Against the Monophysites: Testimonies of the Saints and Aporiae*. He wrote,

> It is often possible to observe gifts of miracles among orthodox and heterodox persons alike, not on account of orthodoxy alone ... but on account of the particular individual's natural simplicity and humility and even more, innocence of soul, or on account of his gentle and sympathetic disposition and, to put it simply, his greater personal fitness for so great a gift over the others who share his faith. If the capacity for miracle-working really is present in anyone on account of his opinion alone, then everyone who took the same doctrinal stance must always have miracles in the same way. To tell the truth, though, teachers of the faith often aren't miracle-workers; it is those they have taught who perform signs.[434]

What is valid in a heterodox community is that which remains with them as their portion of the inner core of the Church. The sacraments of some heterodox are valid only because they have kept the inner core of the

---

[433] John D. Zizioulas, "Orthodox Ecclesiology and the Ecumenical Movement," in *Sourozh* 21 (1985): 22.

[434] Leontius of Jerusalem, *Against the Monophysites: Testimonies of the Saints and Aporiae*, ed. and trans. Patrick T. R. Gray (Oxford, 2006), 157; Leontius of Jerusalem, "Τοῦ σόφου κυρ. Λεοντίου Ἱεροσολυμίτου, Ἀπορίαι," in *PG* 86, part 2, 1896–1897. I am grateful to Prof. Christos Arabatzis for bringing this text to my attention.

faith, whereby they are held together in a certain unity with the one true Church, which is both the center of operation of the Holy Spirit and the milieu in which salvation is attained.

Contemporary Orthodox theologians, as Fr. Emmanuel Clapsis observes, "seem to agree that, while the one, holy, catholic, and apostolic Church is the Orthodox Church, this does not mean that other Christian churches and communions are void of ecclesiological significance to the extent that in their lives, church structures and aspects of the catholic faith have been preserved."[435] In our dealings with other Christians, we Orthodox would do well to remember the cautionary words of our Lord to his disciples, who in zeal forbade a man outside of their circle from casting out demons in Jesus' name: "Do not forbid him; for he that is not against you is for you" (Luke 9:50).[436] As Metropolitan Kallistos has correctly observed, "We know where the Church is but we cannot be sure where the Church is not." And he adds, "There is only one Church, but there are many different ways of being related to this one Church, and many different ways of being separated from it. Some non-Orthodox are very close indeed to Orthodoxy, others less so; some are friendly to the Orthodox Church, others indifferent or hostile."[437]

Are All Heresies the Same?

WHAT CONSTITUTES HERESY?

What constitutes heresy? Who is a heretic, and who is a schismatic? While there is a tendency to label as heretical most, if not all, non-Orthodox communities outside the canonical limits of the Orthodox Church, the patristic, canonical, and liturgical tradition is far more nuanced and precise.

Although there were strong opinions even in Christian antiquity about the way converts were to be received, the consensus was to distinguish between heretics and schismatics. The heterodox were categorized into groups based on their closeness to or distance from the Orthodox faith. The manner of their reception was assigned accordingly. In his famous *Let-*

---

[435] Clapsis, *Orthodoxy in Conversation*, 120.
[436] Cf. Matt. 7:15–23. The Lord challenges the arrogant assurances of salvation based only on right words or marvelous deeds that are empty of love and true righteousness.
[437] Ware, *The Orthodox Church*, rev. ed., 308.

ter to Amphilochios on the Canons, St. Basil the Great writes that the local Churches at various times and places used different ways to receive heretics and schismatics.[438] In response to Amphilochios's inquiries, St. Basil states that in the tradition of the "ancients," three groups exist outside the canonical boundaries of the Church, namely, heretics, schismatics, and dissidents, which he defines as follows.[439]

Heretics, according to St. Basil, are those groups that claim to be Christian but, in fact, are not because their understanding of the Triune God is radically different, highly deficient, unrecognizable, and irreconcilable with the Church's faith. The baptism of these groups is clearly null and void and has no substance because they are not Christian. Hence, converts from such groups are to be received as pagans and nonbelievers through the entire rite of baptism.

St. Basil describes *schismatics* as those Christians who are separated from the Church for holding positions and opinions dissimilar to those of the Church but that, nonetheless, are resolvable and reparable: "schisms [are] those at variance with one another for certain ecclesiastical reasons and questions that admit to remedy."[440] Thus, in keeping with "ancient" tradition, St. Basil held the opinion that the baptism of schismatics is acceptable "on the ground that they were still of the Church" (ὡς ἔτι ἐκ τῆς ἐκκλησίας ὄντων).[441] Though separated from the Church by defects that are curable, schismatics should be treated as having vestiges, or marks, of the Church.

Dissidents, by contrast, are those who form rival and illicit communities (παρασυναγωγαί) in opposition to legitimate ecclesial authority. Dissident congregations and assemblies, St. Basil says, are "brought into being by insubordinate presbyters or bishops and by uninstructed laymen."[442] Their separation is caused by insubordination, not doctrinal differences.

---

[438] St. Basil the Great, *Letter to Amphilochios on the Canons*, in *Saint Basil Letters*, Loeb Classical Library, trans. Roy J. Deferrari (Cambridge, MA, 1962), 3:4–47.

[439] Ibid., 3:8–10: "For the ancients decided to accept that baptism which in no wise deviates from the faith. Accordingly they employed the names: heresies, schisms, and illegal congregations. / Ἐκεῖνο γὰρ ἔκριναν οἱ παλαιοὶ δέχεσθαι βάπτισμα, τὸ μὴ δὲν τῆς πίστεως παρεκβαῖνον. Ὅθεν, τὰς μὲν αἱρέσεις ὠνόμασαν, τὰ δὲ σχίσματα, τὰς δὲ παρασυναγωγάς."

[440] Ibid., 11.

[441] Ibid., 12–13.

[442] Ibid., 11.

CHAPTER FIVE: RECEIVING CONVERTS INTO CHURCH

According to these descriptions provided by St. Basil, heretics, properly speaking, are those whose doctrines are alien and dissimilar to the faith of the Church. In time, however, most if not all heterodox came to be called heretics by extension. We would do well in our times to use the label *heretic* with greater precision.

THE CANONICAL TRADITION

For St. Nikodemos and the supporters of Cyprianic ecclesiology, the reception of converts by means other than baptism is clearly an exception to the rule, accomplished through the exercise of *oikonomia*.

Yet the two key canons related to the reception of converts—canon 7 of the Second Ecumenical Synod and canon 95 of the Penthekte Synod—do not use any economic language. The same is true of canon 7 of the Synod of Laodicea (c. 345) and of the decrees made by the synods of 1484, 1667, and 1672; it is also true of the interpretations of the Byzantine canonists. The language of *oikonomia* for the reception of converts was introduced in later times and used by St. Nikodemos in the *Pedalion*.

As Archbishop Peter L'Huillier has observed correctly, the normative procedure for the reception of heterodox converts was established by canon 7 of the Second Ecumenical Synod and not by the Synod of Carthage or the *Apostolic Canons*, as St. Nikodemos and the followers of Cyprianic ecclesiology claim.[443] The approach adopted by the Fathers of the Second Ecumenical Synod, as canon 7 indicates, was, in fact, already an established custom and tradition: "Those heretics who come over to orthodoxy and the society of those who are saved we receive according to the prescribed rite and custom" (Τοὺς προστιθεμένους τῇ ὀρθοδοξίᾳ καὶ τῇ μερίδι τῶν σῳζομένων ἀπὸ αἱρετικῶν δεχόμεθα κατὰ τὴν ὑποταγμένην ἀκολουθίαν καὶ συνήθειαν).[444]

Several decades earlier, the local Synod of Laodicea had already decreed through its seventh canon that certain heretics were admitted to communion through a process that included a recantation of errors, catechism, and chrismation.[445] For the Fathers of the Second Ecumenical Synod, the proximity to or distance from the Orthodox faith constituted the basic and per-

---

[443] See Peter L'Huillier, *The Church of the Ancient Councils: The Disciplinary Work of the First Four Ecumenical Councils* (Crestwood, NY, 1996), 131–135.

[444] Ibid. 131; emphasis mine. See also Πηδάλιον, 163; *Rudder*, 217.

[445] See Πηδάλιον, 422–423; *Rudder*, 554.

manent criterion—the norm—that determined the status of a heterodox group and the mode of reception. Canon 7 of the Second Ecumenical Synod lists the heretical groups of that period, divides them into two categories, and provides for two modes of reception. Accordingly, converts belonging to one of the communities in the first category (Arians, Macedonians, Sabbatians, Novatians, Quartodecimens, and Apollinarians) are to be received by a *libellus* and chrismation. Those in the second category (Eunomians, Montanists, Sabellians, and other heretics) are to be received by baptism.

The other key canon, the ninety-fifth of the Penthekte Synod, repeats canon 7 almost word for word but is different in two ways. First, the names of several new heretical communities were added to the list of heretics, reflecting the sad reality of new divisions. And second, the canon introduced a third mode of reception—namely, by *libellus* only.[446]

Thus, the three distinct modes of reception prescribed by canon 95 of the Penthekte Synod became the norm.[447] From that time on, heterodox converts have been received by and reconciled to the Church in one of three ways:

1. By the full process of initiation—this includes catechism, baptism, and chrismation.

2. By chrismation—this includes catechism, the formal renunciation of errors, and a *libellus*, and anointing with chrism.

3. By a *libellus*—this includes catechism, followed by a formal recantation of errors and profession of faith.

In the first of these three categories, canon 95 lists the old heresies from canon 7 of the Second Synod (Eunomians, Montanists, and Sabellians), along with several new ones: the Paulianists, Manicheans, Valentinians, Marcionists, and "other such heresies." In the second category, those to be received through chrismation, canon 95 includes the same groups mentioned in canon 7. In the new, third category, those to be received by a certificate only, canon 95 lists two communities: the Nestorians and the

---

[446] It is interesting that the three categories reflect different theological positions. Heretics in the strict sense, those who are received by baptism, include various Gnostic and other such sects. Their understanding of God (theology) is highly deficient. The communities in the second category have a flawed understanding of the Holy Trinity. Those in the third category have a faulty Christology. See Klentos, "Rebaptizing Converts," 224–225.

[447] See Kotsonis, *Προβλήματα*, 186–190; Karmiris, "Ways of Accepting Non-Orthodox," 44–46.

Monophysites, whose heretical teachings were condemned by the Third and Fourth Ecumenical Synods, respectively. The canon also mentions the leaders of these heresies, Nestorios, Eutyches, Dioscoros, and Severos, whose teachings must be rejected.

It is interesting that the three distinct modes of reception prescribed by the Penthekte Synod were already in use in the sixth century in the Church of Constantinople. This is confirmed by the epistle that Timothy, a presbyter of the holy great Church of Constantinople, addressed to John the presbyter and *skeuophylax* of the Chalkopatreia Basilica, in which he writes, "We find three arrangements (or orders) for those who draw near to God's holy, catholic, and apostolic Church. The first arrangement is for those who are in need of holy baptism; the second for those who are not baptized but are anointed with holy myrrh; and the third for those who are neither baptized nor anointed, but who only anathematize their own and every other heresy."[448]

THE LITURGICAL TRADITION

The liturgy is often a better barometer by which to judge ecclesial life and practice than are the canons, or as John Klentos puts it, "Canons dictate abstract principles while liturgical texts testify to actual practice."[449]

The oldest extant *euchologion* of the Byzantine or Constantinopolitan Rite, the Barberini Codex, is such a text, witnessing to the actual practice of the Church based on canon 95 of the Penthekte Synod. The Barberini Codex contains a section devoted to the reception of converts titled "The Way You Are to Receive Converts from Heresies into God's Holy, Catholic and Apostolic Church" (Ὅπως χρὴ δέχεσθαι τοὺς ἀπὸ αἱρέσεων μετερχομένους ἐν τῇ ἁγίᾳ τοῦ Θεοῦ καθολικῇ καὶ ἀποστολικῇ ἐκκλησίᾳ).[450] The section begins with a service for the reception of converts by chrismation. The service is preceded by a rubric that identifies the groups that are received in this man-

---

[448] Timothy the Presbyter, "Περὶ τῶν προσερχόμενον τῇ ἁγίᾳ Ἐκκλησίᾳ," in *PG* 86, 13: "Τρεῖς τάξεις εὑρίσκομεν τῶν προσερχομένων τῇ ἁγίᾳ τοῦ Θεοῦ καθολικῇ καὶ ἀποστολικῇ Ἐκκλησίᾳ, θεοφιλέστατε συλλειτουργὲ Ἰωάννη, καὶ πάντων ἐμοὶ προσφιλέστατε. Καὶ πρώτη μὲν τάξις ἐστὶ τῶν δεομένων τοῦ ἁγίου βαπτίσματος. Δευτέρα δὲ, τῶν μὴ βαπτιζομένων, χριομένων δὲ τῷ μύρῳ τῷ ἁγίῳ. Καὶ τρίτη τῶν μήτε βαπτιζομένων, μήτε χριομένων, ἀλλὰ μόνον ἀναθεματιζόντων τὴν ἰδίαν καὶ πᾶσαν ἄλλην αἵρεσιν." A description of the various heresies in each of the three categories. A briefer, summary version of the Epistle is also included (*PG* 86, 69–73).
[449] Klentos, "Rebaptizing Converts," 223.
[450] Parenti and Velkovska, *L'eucologio Barberini*, 152–158.

ner, based on canon 95 of the Penthekte Synod. Another rubric indicates that the service of reception is conducted in front of the baptismal font (ἴστησι δὲ ἕκαστον αὐτῶν ὁ ἱερεὺς ἔμπροσθεν τῆς ἁγίας κολυμβήθρας). Next, the Barberini Codex contains another brief rubric, based on canon 95, regarding the reception of Nestorians and "Eutychianists," who are admitted to communion by a *libellus*. The section concludes with the text of a long *libellus* for converts from Gnostic groups, who must undergo the complete rites of initiation. The rites of reception in the Barberini Codex are contained in later manuscripts, including the important eleventh-century patriarchal *euchologion* Codex Coislin (gr. 213).[451]

The service of reception by chrismation in the Barberini Codex is of particular interest to this discussion. It contains several interesting and instructive features. First, it demonstrates that the process of reception envisioned by the canons and enacted liturgically is structured or modeled after the catechumenate. Like catechumens, converts are required to undergo a process of resocialization that includes instruction in the fundamentals of the faith and the liturgy, worship twice daily (morning and evening), and fasting for ten or fifteen days prior to the day of reception. Following chrismation, the converts continue the fast for another seven days by refraining from eating meat. They are further instructed to wash on the eighth day as neophytes are required to do after baptism. The process of reception is completed by admittance to the Eucharist.

As with the catechumenate, the period of preparation concludes with a rite of renunciation and adherence. The convert publicly renounces the heresiarch and the false teachings of his or her former community and all other heretical teachings. Following the recantations, the convert professes the Orthodox faith. Also as with the catechumenate, each convert is accompanied by a sponsor who speaks on his or her behalf. Should the candidate "not know how to make the responses" at the time of reception, the sponsor does it.

The most revealing feature of the service is that it does not contain any element from the received rites of initiation, except for the standard formula of anointing, "The seal of the gift of the Holy Spirit." This is a crucial point. Converts received by chrismation or by a *libellus* are treated not as pagans

---

[451] Arranz, *L'eucologio Constantinopolitano*, 259–281.

but as Christians who are making the passage from a heretical or schismatic community to the one, holy, catholic, and apostolic Church. This fact is underscored by the prayer that precedes the anointing with chrism:

> O God our Savior, *who desires all people to be saved and to come to the knowledge of the truth* [1 Tim. 2:4], receive your servant (*N*) who has now recovered from error and desires to come to the knowledge of your truth. You have said: *I have other sheep which are not of this fold; them also I must bring, and they will hear my voice; and there will be one flock and one shepherd* [John 10:16]. Guide him in faith to the true knowledge of you, according to the teaching of your holy and glorious Apostles. Deem him worthy of the seal of the divine myron, and the visitation of the Holy Spirit, and the communion of the precious Body and Blood of Christ. Show him to be your perfect servant that he may also be numbered with your flock to the glory and praise of your majesty. For yours is the kingdom....[452]

The convert is then anointed with the holy myron in the same manner as the newly baptized, using, as noted, the standard formula. A second and final prayer follows: "Lord our God, You have deemed to make your servant (*N*) perfect through the Orthodox faith and the seal of the holy myron. Master of all, preserve in him the true faith in you, increase him in righteousness, and adorn him with every gift that is from you. For blessed and glorified...."[453]

The first prayer of the rite is especially significant for two reasons. First, its content makes clear that this anointing does not reiterate the postbaptismal anointing for the making of a Christian. It is, rather, an act of reconciliation. Second, the inclusion of the passage from the Gospel of John (10:16)

---

[452] Parenti and Velkovska, *L'eucologio Barberini*, 153–154. "Ὁ Θεὸς ὁ Σωτὴρ ἡμῶν, ὁ βουλόμενος πάντας ἀνθρώπους σωθῆναι καὶ εἰς ἐπίγνωσιν ἀληθείας ἐλθεῖν, πρόσδεξαι τὸν δοῦλόν σου τὸν δεῖνα τὸν μόλις ἀνανήψαντα ἐκ τῆς πλάνης καὶ ἐπιποθήσαντα εἰς τὴν ἐπίγνωσιν ἐλθεῖν τῆς σῆς ἀληθείας. Σὺ γὰρ εἶπας, καὶ ἄλλα πρόβατα ἔχω ἃ οὐκ ἔστιν ἐκ τῆς αὐλῆς ταύτης. Κἀκεῖνα δεῖ με διαγαγεῖν καὶ τῆς φωνῆς μου ἀκούσωσιν καὶ γενήσεται μία ποίμνη, εἷς ποιμήν. Ποίμανον αὐτὸν ἐν τῇ δόξῃ τῆς ἀληθοῦς εἰς σὲ ἐπιγνώσεως κατὰ τὴν ἔκθεσιν τῶν ἁγίων σου καὶ ἐνδόξων ἀποστόλων, καὶ καταξίωσον αὐτὸν τῆς σφραγῖδος τοῦ θείου μύρου καὶ τῆς τοῦ ἁγίου Πνεύματος ἐπιφοιτήσεως καὶ τῆς μεταλήψεως τοῦ τιμίου σώματος καὶ αἵματος τοῦ Χριστοῦ, καὶ ἀνάδειξον αὐτὸν τέλειον δοῦλόν σου, ἵνα τῇ ποίμνῃ σου συναριθμηθῇ καὶ αὐτὸς εἰς δόξαν καὶ ἔπαινον τῆς μεγαλωσύνης σου. Ὅτι σοῦ ἐστιν ἡ βασιλεία καὶ...."

[453] Ibid., 154–155. "Κύριε ὁ Θεὸς ἡμῶν, ὁ καταξιώσας τέλειον ἀναδεῖξαι τὸν δοῦλόν σου τὸν δεῖνα διὰ τῆς εἰς σὲ ὀρθοδόξου πίστεως καὶ τῆς σφραγῖδος τοῦ Μύρου τοῦ ἁγίου, σύ, Δέσποτα τῶν ἁπάντων, τὴν εἰς σὲ ἀληθῆ πίστιν ἐν αὐτῷ διατήρησον, αὔξων αὐτὸν ἐν δικαιοσύνῃ, καὶ πᾶσιν τοῖς παρὰ σοῦ χαρίσμασιν κατακοσμῶν. Ὅτι εὐλόγηται καὶ δεδόξασται τὸ πάντιμον...."

is especially intriguing. It acknowledges that the Church recognizes the existence of communities outside its own canonical boundaries that hold within them signs or traces of the Church. Christ, the Good Shepherd, has claim over the members of these communities who love and worship him. In his goodness, he guides them to the fullness of truth, bringing them into the one true fold and the unity of faith.

Every element of this ancient conversion rite is well-conceived. It is brief yet comprehensive and, above all, theologically and liturgically correct. It serves as an ideal model. For reasons unknown, it fell into disuse. Other rites, as I have shown, have taken its place, among which is the rite promulgated by the Synod of 1484. It is interesting that the Barberini rite has survived in part in the conversion rite currently used by the Greek Orthodox Archdiocese of America (about which more in a moment).

THE SYNOD OF 1484 AND ITS SERVICE OF RECEPTION

I cannot conclude this review of the liturgical tradition without a word on the Synod of 1484, which established the procedure for the reception of Latin converts: "Latin converts coming to the Orthodox Church are to be received by anointing with myron only, presenting the *libellus* of faith and renouncing the dogmas and customs of the Latins [that are] alien to [our] faith."[454]

The synod issued a special service of reception to be used by all four patriarchates of the East. This service, different from the rite of reception in the Barberini Codex in both length and content, is conducted near the holy doors of the sanctuary and consists of several parts, beginning with introductory prayers, including the Trisagion Prayers and Psalm 50 (51).[455] A series of six questions and responses follows. Through the responses, the convert repudiates Latin errors in dogma and custom, including the *filioque*, the use of *azymes*, and the decree of the failed prounion Council of Florence.[456] The convert then promises to remain steadfast in the Orthodox

---

[454] Karmiris, Τὰ δογματικά, 982.
[455] The entire service is in Karmiris, Τὰ δογματικά, 987–989. An English translation of the service has been provided in Dragas, "Manner of Reception."
[456] There is good reason for citing the prounion Council of Florence held in 1438–1439, at a time when the empire faced the immediate threat of Turkish conquest. In Florence, the Greek delegation succumbed to pressure and signed the decree of union, accepting the major Latin doctrinal positions on the *filioque*, the *azyma*, purgatory, and papal primacy. Met-

CHAPTER FIVE: RECEIVING CONVERTS INTO CHURCH 185

faith and recites the Nicene-Constantinopolitan Creed. Immediately afterward, the presiding bishop or priest anoints the person with holy myron in the manner of the newly baptized, using the standard formula, "The seal of the gift of the Holy Spirit." The anointing is concluded with a long prayer, which reads, in part, as follows:

> Lord our God, by your unutterable mercy you bent the heavens and sojourned among people, teaching them to profess the true and blameless faith: knowledge of the consubstantial and coeternal Trinity and of the worshipful and all-powerful Spirit, who, according to your own unerring mouth, proceeds and subsists from your Father and God, who is without beginning. The same merciful and compassionate Lord, receive your servant (N) who has turned away from the Latin heresy to the truth of your Gospel and your own unerring mouth, and to the pure theology, faith, and tradition of your holy apostles and teachers of piety. Join and unite him to the true dogmas of your holy, catholic, and apostolic Church, making him worthy of your unending and eternal heavenly Kingdom through the knowledge and avowal of the doctrines of piety. Being compassionate and merciful, overlook the transgressions he has committed in life both knowingly and unknowingly. Let him remain steadfast in the Orthodox faith ... Teach him to execute holiness in fear ... Cleanse his soul of the mist of heresy and every other impiety.[457]

---

ropolitan Mark of Ephesus alone did not sign the decree. His stand was strongly supported by the vast majority of the clergy and the populace. Like the Council of Lyon (1274) before it, the Council of Florence failed, rejected overwhelmingly by the Orthodox populace. The fall of Constantinople in 1453 put an end to the efforts at union. The Synod of 1484, convened as an ecumenical synod, officially rejected the Council of Florence. Karmiris, *Τὰ δογματικά*, 982.

[457] Ibid., 988–989. "Κύριε ὁ Θεὸς ἡμῶν, ὁ κλίνας οὐρανοὺς καὶ τοῖς ἐν γῇ δι' ἄφατον ἔλεος ἐπιδημήσας, καὶ διδάξας τοὺς ἀνθρώπους ὁμολογεῖν τὴν ἀληθινὴν καὶ ἄμεμπτον ὁμολογίαν, τὴν τῆς ὁμοουσίου καὶ συναϊδίου Τριάδος ἐπίγνωσιν, καὶ τὸ προσκυνητὸν καὶ παντοδύναμον Πνεῦμα διὰ τοῦ ἀψευδοῦς σου στόματος ὑποφήνας ἐκπορεύεσθαι τοῦτο καὶ ὑφίστασθαι ἐκ τοῦ ἀνάρχου σου Πατρὸς καὶ Θεοῦ, αὐτός, Δέσποτα, τὸν δοῦλόν σου (δεῖνα), τὸν ἐπιστρέφοντα ἐκ τῆς Λατινικῆς αἱρέσεως πρὸς τὴν ἀλήθειαν τοῦ εὐαγγελίου σου καὶ τὸ ἀψευδοῦς σου στόματος καὶ τὴν τῶν ἁγίων σου Ἀποστόλων καὶ διδασκάλων τῆς εὐσεβείας ἀκραιφνῆ θεολογίαν, ὁμολογίαν τε αὐτῶν καὶ παράδοσιν, πρόσδεξαι, ὡς ἐλεήμων καὶ συμπαθής, συνάπτων αὐτὸν καὶ ἑνῶν τοῖς ἀληθέσι δόγμασι τῆς ἁγίας σου καθολικῆς καὶ ἀποστολικῆς Ἐκκλησίας, καταξιῶν τε αὐτὸν τῆς ἀτελευτήτου καὶ ἀϊδίου τῶν οὐρανῶν βασιλείας, τῇ ἐπιγνώσει καὶ ἀνακηρύξει τῶν τῆς εὐσεβείας δογμάτων. Πάριδε οὖν, ὡς συμπαθὴς καὶ ἐλεήμων, τὰ ἐν γνώσει τε καὶ ἀγνοίᾳ ἐν τῷ βίῳ πλημμεληθέντα αὐτῷ. Στερέωσον αὐτὸν διαμένειν ἐν τῇ ὀρθοδόξῳ πίστει ... [Δ]ίδαξον αὐτὸν ἐπιτελεῖν ἁγιωσύνην ἐν φόβῳ σου ... [Κ]άθαρον αὐτοῦ τὴν ψυχὴν αἱρετικῆς ἀχλύος καὶ πάσης ἄλλης δυσσεβείας."

The service concludes with Psalm 144 (145), the Fervent Litany, and the *apolysis*.

Several features of this brief rite of reception require further comment. Following the disavowal of Latin errors—focused essentially on the *filioque*, the decrees of the Council of Florence, and the *azymes*—and the recitation of the creed, the candidate is immediately anointed with holy chrism. The rite does not contain, as one would expect, a prayer to introduce the purpose of the anointing. Moreover, the prayer that follows the anointing does not contain any reference to the anointing or to the Holy Spirit, except for the reference to the eternal procession of the Spirit from the Father. In fact, the tone of the prayer is penitential. Clearly, this underscores the fact that this service constitutes a rite of reconciliation and not a reiteration of postbaptismal anointing.

It is interesting that, unlike the rite in the Barberini Codex, here there is no mention of catechesis or fasting. The rite, however, includes the text of a *libellus*, which the newly anointed convert presents to the celebrant bearing his or her signature to be recorded or filed in the church registry. In the signed text, the person affirms and confesses the Orthodox faith and submits to the doctrines and canons of the seven ecumenical synods and other local synods espoused by the "Church of the Greeks" (τῶν Γραικῶν). The convert also renounces all the "strange" customs and "profane innovations" of the Latins.

There is, however, one unanswered question. Why did the Synod of 1484 feel compelled to create a new rite of reception by chrismation specifically for Latin converts, when a conversion rite by chrismation already existed in the *euchologia*? Is it possible that these rites had been neglected over time and had fallen into disuse? Were they deemed inappropriate for Latin converts, and if so, why? It is known from Mark of Ephesus (d. 1445) that the reception of Latins by chrismation was already an established practice, at least by the middle of the fifteenth century.[458]

This long cursory review of the historical, canonical, and liturgical data was necessary to place in perspective the Greek approach to reception procedures. Before I turn to the challenge before the Holy Eparchial Synod of the Greek Orthodox Archdiocese of America as it contemplates changes

---

[458] Ibid., 981.

in reception procedures, the wise counsel of Gennadios Scholarios, patriarch of Constantinople (1453–1456) during a turbulent time of extreme conflict, recalls the open and benevolent spirit of the Orthodox Church toward other Christians—a spirit that would not wane even under pressure from forces within and without the Church. Gennadios's remarks are especially instructive.

To the question posed by the monks of Mt. Sinai regarding the treatment of Latin, Armenian, and other pilgrims and visitors to their monastery, Gennadios wrote the following:

> We say that you should give them [the Armenians and Latins] the antidoron, since they are Christians and have come a long distance on pilgrimage to the Master's tomb. Even though [they are] separated from us on account of some issues of faith and are considered heterodox, as Christians they seek our blessing with faith and piety; and we are obliged to give it to them. The [saying] "Do not give what is holy to the dogs" is meant for unbelievers, that is, for Jews and Saracens and Pagans and Manicheans and others who use Christianity as a pretense, but are not Christian ... Furthermore, listen to the Lord who said, "For he who is not against us is on our side," and "Whosoever comes to Me, I will not cast out." Do not give them only the great mystery of Communion. If however one of them wishes to remain there with you or has gotten ill, let him first deny his ancestral belief, then confess the faith of the catholic Church, and so be deemed worthy of such Communion. This is the custom of the catholic Church of Christians.[459]

---

[459] Ἐπιστολὴ πρὸς Σοφιανὸν καὶ πάντας τοὺς μοναχοὺς τοῦ Σινᾶ. See Theodoros N. Zisis, Γεννάδιος Β' Σχολάριος: Βίος, συγγράμματα, διδασκαλία, Ἀνάλεκτα Βλατάδων 30 (Thessaloniki, 1980), 331–332. For the entire text of the letter, see Karmiris, Τὰ δογματικά, 1013–1014. Gennadios thought of the Armenians and Latins not as heretics in the strict sense of the word but as schismatics, as separated heterodox Christians. "Ἡμεῖς δὲ λέγομεν ἵνα διδῶτε αὐτοῖς [Ἀρμενίοις καὶ Λατίνοις] καὶ τὸ ἀντίδωρον. Χριστιανοὶ γάρ εἰσι, καὶ διὰ τοῦτο ἔρχονται ἐκ τοσούτων διαστημάτων εἰς προσκύνησιν τοῦ Δεσποτικοῦ τάφου. Εἰ γοῦν καὶ ἐσχισμένοι εἰσὶν ἀφ' ἡμῶν διά τινα ζητήματα τῆς πίστεως καὶ εἰσὶν ἑτερόδοξοι, ἀλλ' ὡς χριστιανοὶ μετὰ πίστεως καὶ εὐλαβείας ζητοῦσι τὸν ἁγιασμὸν ἡμῶν, καὶ ἡμεῖς ὀφείλομεν διδόναι. Τὸ γὰρ "μὴ δότε τὰ ἅγια τοῖς κυσί" καὶ τὰ ἑξῆς, περὶ τῶν ἀπίστων νοεῖται, ἤγουν Ἰουδαίων καὶ Σαρακηνῶν καὶ Ἑλλήνων καὶ Μανιχαίων καὶ ἄλλων, οἵτινες προποιοῦνται τὸν Χριστιανισμόν, μὴ ὄντες χριστιανοί ... Ἀκούετε δὲ καὶ τοῦ Κυρίου εἰπόντος, ὅτι "ὁ μὴ ὢν καθ' ἡμῶν, ὑπὲρ ἡμῶν ἐστι" καί, τὸν "ἐρχόμενον πρός με οὐκ ἐκβάλλω ἔξω." Τὸ μέγα μυστήριον τῆς κοινωνίας μόνον μὴ δίδοτε αὐτοῖς. Εἰ δέ τις ἀπ' αὐτῶν βουληθῇ προσμεῖναι αὐτόθι ἢ νοσηθῇ, ἀρνήσεται μὲν πρῶτον τὴν πάτριον δόξαν, ὁμολογήσει δὲ τὴν δόξαν τῆς Καθολικῆς Ἐκκλησίας, ἀξιούντες αὐτὸν τῆς τοιαύτης κοινωνίας. Τοῦτό ἐστιν ἡ συνήθεια τῆς Καθολικῆς τῶν χριστιανῶν Ἐκκλησίας."

The Rite of Reception in the Greek Orthodox Archdiocese

THE PRIEST'S HANDBOOK

His Eminence Archbishop Demetrios and the venerable hierarchs of the Holy Synod of the Archdiocese recently initiated procedures for the long-overdue revision and expansion of *The Priest's Handbook*,[460] which contains, among other things, both directives and a rite for the reception of converts.

The rite of reception in *The Priest's Handbook* is titled "The Service of Receiving Non-Orthodox into the Orthodox Church (Chrismation)."[461] A note at the end of the service indicates that it is "followed by the Ecumenical Patriarchate of Constantinople" and that it was first published in the book by Pavlos Menevisoglou (now metropolitan of Sweden), *The Holy Myrrh in the Eastern Orthodox Church* (Thessaloniki 1972).[462] In fact, this book is the metropolitan's doctoral dissertation published in the series Ἀνάλεκτα Βλατάδων.

The service, as Metropolitan Pavlos states, reflects the prevailing practice of the Ecumenical Patriarchate and follows the broad outlines prescribed by the Synod of Constantinople (1484) for the reception of Roman Catholics.[463] Before discussing the service, it is necessary to focus upon an indispensable component of any liturgical service: rubrics, or directives.

RUBRICS: THE NEED FOR CLARITY AND PRECISION

The first thing that one notices about the service in the *Handbook* is the lack of adequate rubrics. Hidden in the text are three important but imprecisely stated rubrics. The first of these appears halfway through the opening

---

[460] *The Priest's Handbook* (New York, 1987), issued by Archbishop Iakovos as a guide for priests, was meant "to establish uniformity in the celebration of the holy sacraments and other holy services of the Church; assist in establishing greater order and reverence in the holy temple and the parish in general; and [help the priest] fulfill his duties: pastoral, educational, charitable, and social with a priestly conscience and decorum" (57; for the Greek text, see 1).

[461] Ibid., 27–29 (Greek), 85–87 (English).

[462] Ibid., 29 (Greek), 87 (English). Pavlos Menevisoglou, Τὸ ἅγιον μύρον ἐν τῇ Ὀρθοδόξῳ Ἀνατολικῇ Ἐκκλησίᾳ: Ἰδία κατὰ τὰς πηγὰς καὶ τὴν πρᾶξιν τῶν Νεωτέρων χρόνων τοῦ Οἰκουμενικοῦ Πατριαρχείου Ἀνάλεκτα Βλατάδων 14 (Thessaloniki, 1972).

[463] Menevisoglou, Τὸ ἅγιον μύρον, 207; the service itself is found on 208–209.

CHAPTER FIVE: RECEIVING CONVERTS INTO CHURCH

section of the service. A brief reference is made to the candidate's having been previously instructed. Later, another brief rubric describes the application of the holy chrism. Finally, in the note describing the origins of the service, there is a reference on its use. According to this last rubric, the service is to be used "for those occasions when non-Orthodox are accepted into the Orthodox Church with Holy Myrrh (Chrism) only."[464] But we are not told specifically who these non-Orthodox Christians are. Are they Roman Catholics as well as Protestants? And of the many Protestant denominations, are all included or only some? If only some, which ones? And what of Nestorians and Monophysites—is the service intended for them as well?

Further, very little, if anything, is said about the candidate. What prerequisites must he or she fulfill? What documents are required to establish proof of baptism in the name of the Holy Trinity? What of minors—can they be accepted without parental consent? Should the candidate have a sponsor and what would his or her role be? As already noted, the service presupposes that the candidate has been catechized, but for how long? And what should be the nature and content of this instruction? Should the candidate be required to fast, and for how long? While there is no mention of a signed *libellus*, should one be required? And if required, should not the archdiocese provide the appropriate forms? And on the subject of certificates, is the certificate of chrismation currently in circulation adequate? Finally, it would be important to add a directive at the end of the service instructing the priest to enter the appropriate data in the parish baptismal registry book.

The text does not contain any rubrics indicating when, where, and how the service should be conducted. Having the ancient rites of initiation in mind, it seems appropriate to suggest that the service be conducted near the holy doors of the sanctuary just before the start of the Divine Liturgy (on a Sunday or a feast day) in the presence of the assembled congregation. The addition of a new member to the community is an ecclesial event. The rite should not be reduced to a private affair. Following the service, the new Orthodox Christian should be greeted and received by the assembled members of the community, participate with them in the Divine Liturgy, and receive Holy Communion at the appropriate time.

---

[464] *Priest's Handbook*, 29 (Greek) and 87 (English).

The service in *Priest's Handbook* contains a brief rubric, taken almost verbatim from the service of 1484, that describes the manner by which the candidate is anointed with chrism on various parts of the body: "After this the priest anoints with holy Myrrh (Chrism) the candidate's forehead, ears, chin, hands, breast, and knees." One may rightly ask, Why these particular body parts? The forehead seems appropriate, but why the chin? And if we anoint the ears, why not the other sensory organs—eyes, nose, and mouth? More important, how practical are the last two, breast and knees? It is not only a matter of modesty; it is also a practical consideration because of the garments that men and women wear today. Also missing from this rubric is a small but important detail, probably because it is understood. Nevertheless, it would be useful to remind the priest to trace the sign of the Cross on the forehead when applying the holy chrism.

Assessing the Service of Reception in The Priest's Handbook

THE ENARXIS

The service of reception in *The Priest's Handbook* is brief and consists of three parts: the *enarxis*, the anointing, and the *apolysis*. The *enarxis* is exactly the same as the one in the service promulgated by the Synod of 1484. It includes the standard opening doxology by the celebrant ("Blessed is our God"), the prayer "Heavenly King," the Trisagion, the call to worship ("Come let us bow down") and Psalm 50/51. The service book does not indicate, however, who is responsible for reciting these prayers and the psalm. Is it the priest, the reader, or the candidate, or some combination?

The use of Psalm 50/51 is telling. It is the most famous of the penitential psalms and is used frequently in Orthodox worship. It is a prayer for pardon but also for restoration to grace and purity. At the heart of interior restoration is the Holy Spirit—the Comforter, the Spirit of Truth and of adoption, by whom we are called children of God. Everything in the *enarxis* points to the restorative or reconciliatory nature of the office.

THE SECOND PART OF THE SERVICE

The second section of this office, the anointing, follows broadly the outline of the service of 1484 and has two declaratory statements, a profession of faith, the anointing with holy myron, and a prayer after the anointing.

There are, however, some striking differences between the two services. For, example, in the service of 1484, as in every other conversion rite beginning with the text in the Barberini Codex, the candidate is asked by the celebrant if he or she wishes to enter into the Orthodox Church. The service in *The Priest's Handbook* has no such question. Instead, the candidate immediately declares his or her intention without any prompting from the celebrant. Perhaps a more fitting opening would be a brief question addressed to the candidate by the priest. For example, "(N), do you wish to enter into union with the Orthodox Church?"

More important, the service of 1484 contains a series of questions and responses by which the candidate explicitly rejects Latin errors and innovations. However, unlike all other services of conversion that have survived in conciliar documents and liturgical texts, some of which are still in use in one form or another, the service in *The Priest's Handbook* does not contain any specific recantations. The closest the text comes to a recantation—broad as it is—can be found in the first of two declaratory statements the candidate makes: "Today, I, by the grace of God and on my own free will, having received proper instruction, change ($\mu\varepsilon\vartheta\acute{\iota}\sigma\tau\alpha\mu\alpha\iota$) by the seal of the Holy Spirit from the (denomination) to the Orthodox Church and do confess before God and man that I believe...."

The immediate question is this: Should a revised conversion service contain some form of recantation? I would answer in the affirmative but with the stipulation that the form be simple and direct, certainly not polemic or burdened with detailed anathemas. The recantations should also be introduced by a question: "(N), do you wish to renounce heretical teachings and all their wrongs?" A form of recantation would follow, even as simple as the following: "I, (N), having received proper instruction, renounce all false teachings, ancient and modern, and change." The inclusion of even such a brief statement, general as it is, underscores the very reason and purpose for which a conversion takes place. As John Klentos points out, "Religious conversion is a sensitive passage from former belief to newfound conviction. One must lay aside previously held notions and commit to a new understanding of reality and way of living out this new worldview."[465] The renunciation, even in the simplest of forms, is an affirmation of transition, a real, concrete passage from something old to something new.

---

[465] Klentos, "Rebaptizing Converts," 217.

A second point of special interest in the first declaratory statement is the difference in language between the original Greek text and the English translation regarding the transition from one faith community to another. Here semantics play an important role. The original Greek reads: "μεθίσταμαι ... ἀπὸ τῆς ... εἰς τὴν Ἑλληνικὴν Ὀρθόδοξον Ἐκκλησίαν." According to the Greek, the transition is from a church and not from a denomination, as the English translation has it. The distinction between *church* and *denomination* is important for its ecclesiological implications.

WHAT CONSTITUTES PROPER INSTRUCTION?

A third point of interest in the first declaratory statement is the reference to proper instruction. Here, several Byzantine and post-Byzantine conciliar and liturgical texts provide some guidance as to what constitutes proper instruction. Obviously, proper instruction entails exposure to the basic teachings of the Orthodox Church as they relate to theology, liturgy, discipline, and the way of applying the truths of the faith to everyday living. But it also involves addressing specific theological and practical issues that differentiate the Orthodox from each candidate's community of origin.

On this point, the long lists of renunciations in some conciliar and liturgical texts can help the instructor identify the important specific items of instruction that pertain to Roman Catholics,[466] Protestants,[467] and the Oriental Orthodox.[468] It would be helpful if the archdiocese were able to

---

[466] As mentioned earlier, the recantations in the service of 1484 for the reception of Latins include differences that relate to the *filioque*, *azymes*, purgatory, and papal primacy. To this list we could add the more recent Roman Catholic doctrines of the immaculate conception and papal infallibility. One could also raise specific issues that pertain to the sacraments, church governance, and liturgical observances.

[467] The *Book of Needs* (76–78), for example, contains a series of recantations for Lutherans and Reformed Christians that pertain to the *filioque*, apostolic succession, sacred tradition, the number of sacraments, the Eucharistic elements, predestination (for the Reformed), the cult of the saints, icons, and holy relics. Similar recantations from a Russian conversion rite are cited by Karmiris, *Τὰ δογματικά*, 1020–1024.

[468] The traditional *libellus* for the Nestorians centers on rejection of the term *Theotokos* based on the heretical doctrine that in the incarnate Christ there are two different natures and two separate persons, one divine and the other human. Orthodox doctrine holds that the incarnate Christ is a single person, at once God and Man (Θεάνθρωπος). The Monophysite *libellus* centers on renouncing the heretical teaching that in the incarnate Christ there are not two natures, the divine and human, but one only, the divine nature, which completely absorbed the human nature. As noted earlier, according to recent studies, the Monophysite controversy owed mostly to linguistic and terminological differences.

provide parish clergy with adequate instruction material. Perhaps the Holy Eparchial Synod will consider commissioning the preparation of manuals of instruction for each of the major non-Orthodox Christian communities.

THE PROFESSION OF FAITH

The initial declaratory statement of the candidate concludes with the recitation of the Nicene-Constantinopolitan Creed, the summary of the Orthodox faith, as in the service of 1484. A second declaratory statement follows in which the candidate affirms belief in the doctrines promulgated by the seven ecumenical synods, pledges to uphold the traditions of the Church, and vows to honor his or her calling as a faithful member of the Orthodox Church. The statement is an improvisation, based partly on the *libellus* and partly (in spirit, at least) on the celebrant's prayer of the service of 1484. Should the Holy Synod decide to retain the service in its present form, this second declaratory statement should be revisited and rewritten.

THE ANOINTING AND THE CONCLUDING PRAYERS

Immediately following the profession of faith, the priest anoints the candidate with holy myron in the manner described earlier, using the standard formula, "The seal of the gift of the Holy Spirit. Amen." The anointing is concluded with a short prayer by the priest. It is significant that this prayer is borrowed directly, with some minor changes, from the conversion rite in the Barberini Codex, which passed into later patriarchal *euchologia*. This prayer in *The Priest's Handbook* is the same as the second and final prayer in the conversion rite of the Barberini Codex. The service concludes with the Fervent Litany and the standard *apolysis*. Needless to say, it is abundantly clear from its contents that this service does not constitute a reiteration of the postbaptismal anointing but is reconciliatory in nature.

Points to Ponder

RESPECTFUL SUGGESTIONS

With due recognition of the received liturgical texts and customs, I respectfully submit several suggestions that the holy synod may wish to consider.

First, whatever form a revised service of reception may take, it is essential that it be accompanied by clear and complete rubrics. Second, the service in

The Priest's Handbook should be restructured on the lines of the Barberini Codex. Maintain the *enarxis* and the *apolysis* in their received form, but add or change some other features. Begin the second part of the service with a question soliciting a response from the candidate as to his or her intention. To the candidate's initial declaratory statement, add some form of recantation, and rewrite the second declaratory statement.

More important, add a preanointing prayer, which is missing from both the service of 1484 and the service in *The Priest's Handbook*. This is a serious omission. Every important liturgical act is preceded by an appropriate priestly prayer. Take, for example, the baptismal rite. The prebaptismal and postbaptismal anointings alike are preceded by a prayer. Inasmuch as the service in *The Priest's Handbook* already contains the second of the two prayers in the Barberini *euchologion*, it would be most fitting if the first prayer were included, as well. Through its remembrance, request, and intention clauses, the prayer summarizes the entire purpose and process of conversion—reception.

Some may express concern that the prayer from the Barberini Codex is inappropriate for Roman Catholics and perhaps others, inasmuch as it may give the impression that the service constitutes a reiteration of postbaptismal anointing because of the request to "make him (her) worthy of the seal of the divine myron and the visitation of the Holy Spirit." The prayer in the Barberini Codex, however, both in intention and content, is not even remotely similar to the postbaptismal prayer of anointing. Moreover, invoking the presence of the Spirit is a common liturgical occurrence. Worshippers pray, for example, at the beginning of every service, "Heavenly King, Comforter, the Spirit of Truth ... come and abide in us." And at every Divine Liturgy, we ask the Father to send the Holy Spirit upon the assembled people and upon the Gifts. Besides, the sacrament of chrismation is not used only at baptism to impart the gift of the Holy Spirit and to signify his indwelling presence. It serves other purposes as well, including the reception of converts and the reconciliation of returning apostates Orthodox Christians who have lapsed into heresy.[469]

---

[469] For the uses of holy chrism, see Menevisoglou, Τὸ ἅγιον μύρον, 188–227. In addition to its use in the postbaptismal anointing, the reception of converts, and the return of lapsed Orthodox, holy chrism is also used to consecrate the holy Table, *antimensia*, and icons at the consecration of churches, as well as for the anointing of the relics, if they exist, at their

Other suggestions made in the course of the text should be reviewed and, if deemed appropriate, be incorporated into the rubrics. These suggestions include the time and place of the service, the appropriateness of a fast, the manner of anointing, required documentation, and an authoritative list of the non-Orthodox who qualify to be received by chrismation. Some conversion rites require the candidate to confess his or her sins at some point prior to the celebration of the rite. The prayer of forgiveness, however, is omitted. It is incorporated in some form in the rite of reception. Should such a confession be required and why?

ON THE RECEPTION OF ORIENTAL ORTHODOX CHRISTIANS

Full communion with the Oriental Orthodox remains an unfinished task, even though in recent times, through a series of theological dialogues, the Churches have affirmed their fundamental agreement in the understanding of the apostolic faith and tradition.[470] However ambiguous the relations may remain or however different the reception of Oriental Christians may have been in a given historical period, one thing is clear: the standard or normative practice for reception of these Christians was established by the Penthekte Synod and confirmed by the liturgical practice of the Church.

In accordance, therefore, with the decision of the Penthekte Synod, which constitutes exactness, Nestorian and Monophysite Christians should be received by a *libellus* only, having first been properly instructed. However, since 1888 the Ecumenical Patriarchate, using *oikonomia επὶ τὸ αὐστηρότερον*, has been receiving Oriental Orthodox Christians by chrismation.[471] The holy synod may choose to clarify this issue and to prepare, for the use of parish clergy, a properly worded *libellus* to be given to the candidate, recited publicly, and signed by her or him. The issuance of a suggested outline of "proper" instruction or, even better, a manual of instruction would be especially useful.

---

translation, when newly recognized saints are proclaimed officially. In years past, Orthodox kings and emperors also were anointed; this practice, however, was abandoned long ago.

[470] See Thomas FitzGerald and Emmanuel Gratsias, eds., *Restoring the Unity of Faith: The Orthodox–Oriental Theological Dialogue* (Brookline, MA, 2007).

[471] The practice of receiving Nestorians and Monophysites by chrismation predates the decision of 1888. As noted earlier, there is evidence from as early as the eleventh and twelfth centuries that reception by chrismation was used by the patriarchates of the East. See Karmiris, *Τὰ δογματικά*, 1009–1013.

WHICH RITE SHOULD WE USE?

It is my hope that review of the historical, canonical, and liturgical antecedents of the conversion rites will be of some help to the venerable members of the holy synod grappling with the revision of *The Priest's Handbook*, which, of course, requires a decision on an acceptable rite of conversion.

Of the several conversion rites that were given to me to review, reflecting Russian, Antiochian, and Greek practices, I believe the most appropriate one is the suggested modified version of the text in *The Priest's Handbook*, which I have proposed. Compared with the others, it is simpler and free of harsh and accusatory language. In its modified form, it is more traditional and, I believe, appropriate for Roman Catholic as well as for mainline Protestant converts. More important, the text (original or modified) does not contain any elements from the received rites of baptism; this is vital for rites of conversion by which non-Orthodox Christians with valid baptism (by economy or otherwise) are united to the Orthodox Church.

The received rites of baptism are meant for the unbaptized children of Orthodox parents and for non-Christians, for converts from other religions (Judaism, Islam, Hinduism, Buddhism, etc.), for pagans, for sectarians, and for heretics in the strict sense. I have not touched upon converts from other religions here. Some liturgical and other historical texts provide a *libellus* for such occasion, the main purpose of which is to emphasize the chief differences between the two faiths, the non-Christian and the Orthodox. The *libellus* forms part of the process of catechesis. It is an instrument both for recantation and instruction.

Given the opportunity to receive non-Christian adults for baptism, the received baptismal rites should be celebrated as they were intended, at different stages of the process. But this is a matter for another time.

A Proposed Rite of Reception

SERVICE FOR THE RECEPTION OF CONVERTS
into the Orthodox Church by Chrismation

The service is conducted at the conclusion of the Orthros and before the Divine Liturgy, on a Sunday or a feast day, in front of the holy gate of the sanctuary. The candidate, having been carefully examined as to intentions and properly instructed over time in the essentials of the Orthodox faith by the priest, is presented by the sponsor, who attests to the candidate's good character and affirms the earnest desire of the candidate to enter into the Orthodox Church. The candidate, having fasted for one week prior to the service and having been instructed in the rituals that are to take place, holds a lit candle and the booklet containing the service.[472]

****

Turning toward the sponsor, the priest speaks.

Priest: Are you sponsoring this man/woman for entry into the Orthodox Church?

Sponsor: Yes, Father. I have the honor to present (*N*) for entry into our holy Church. I attest to his/her good character and affirm his/her earnest desire to become a member of the Orthodox Church. Furthermore, I pledge, by God's grace, to help him/her grow in the life of Christ within the Church.

The Priest turns toward the holy Table and intones the opening doxology:

Priest: Blessed is our God, always, now and forever, and to the ages of ages.

People: Amen.

---

[472] This proposed service is an expanded version of that found in *The Priest's Handbook*. Its structure is based on the rite promulgated by the Synod of 1484 and on the rite in the Barberini Codex. The rubric on fasting and the two priestly prayers are from the Barberini Codex. This service is intended for the reception of non-Orthodox Christians whose churches and confessions affirm the doctrine of the Holy Trinity and the divinity of Christ and baptize by water in the name of the Father and of the Son and of the Holy Spirit. It is expected that a comprehensive list of these churches and confessions, as determined by the Holy Eparchial Synod of the Greek Orthodox Archdiocese, would be appended to this or any other service approved by the synod.

Priest: Heavenly King, Comforter, the Spirit of Truth, present in all places and filling all things, the treasury of blessings and Giver of life: come and abide in us. Cleanse us from all impurity and save our souls, O Good One.

People: Holy God, Holy Mighty, Holy Immortal, have mercy on us. (3)

Glory to the Father and the Son and the Holy Spirit, now and forever, and to the ages of ages. Amen.

All-holy Trinity, have mercy on us. Lord, forgive our sins. Master, pardon our transgressions. Holy One, visit and heal our infirmities, for the glory of your name.

Glory to the Father and the Son and the Holy Spirit, now and forever, and to the ages of ages. Amen.

Our Father, who art in heaven, hallowed be Thy name. Thy Kingdom come. Thy will be done on earth as it is in heaven. Give us this day our daily bread. And forgive us our trespasses, as we forgive those who trespass against us. And lead us not into temptation, but deliver us from evil.

Priest: For yours is the kingdom, the power, and the glory of the Father and the Son and the Holy Spirit, now and forever, and to the ages of ages.

People: Amen.

Reader: Lord, have mercy. (12)

Come, let us worship God, our King, and bow down before Him. Come, let us worship Christ, our King and God, and bow down before Him. Come, let us worship Christ, truly our King and God, and bow down before Him.

Reader (or Candidate): [Recites Psalm 50 (51).]

Priest (*addressing the candidate*): (*N*), do you wish to unite yourself to the Orthodox Church?

Candidate: Yes, Father, I do with all my heart.

Priest: (*N*), do you renounce previously held erroneous beliefs and all heretical dogmas and teachings, both ancient and modern?

Candidate: Yes, Father, I renounce all false doctrines and erroneous teachings. Today, by the grace of God and of my own free will, having received proper instruction, I wish to be accepted into the Orthodox Church by the seal of the gift of the Holy Spirit.

Priest: (*N*), do you accept the dogmas, teachings, liturgy, canons, discipline, and moral principles of the Orthodox Church?

Candidate: Yes, Father, I do. I worship the Triune God, Father, Son, and Holy Spirit and I confess, agree with, and accept the ecumenical synods and their dogmas and decrees, the holy canons, and all the teachings and traditions of the Orthodox Church.

Priest: (*N*), do you promise, by God's grace, to remain firm in the Orthodox faith and to live your life in accordance with the teachings of the Orthodox Church?

Candidate: Yes, Father. By God's grace, I so solemnly promise.

Priest: Confess now the sacred symbol of our faith.

Candidate: [Recites the Nicene-Constantinopolitan Creed.]

After reciting the creed, the Candidate bows his/her head. The Priest places his hand upon the head of the Candidate and recites the following prayer.

Priest: Let us pray to the Lord.

People: Lord, have mercy.

Priest: O God our Savior, who desires all people to be saved and to come to the knowledge of the truth, receive your servant (*N*) who has now recovered from error and desires to come to the knowledge of your truth. You have said, "I have other sheep that are not of this fold; I must bring them also, and they will heed my voice; and there will be one flock and one shepherd." Guide him (her) in faith to the true knowledge of you, according to the teaching of your holy and glorious apostles. Deem him (her) worthy of the seal of the divine myron, and the visitation of the Holy Spirit, and the communion of the precious Body and Blood of Christ. Show him (her) to be your perfect servant that he (she) also may be numbered with your flock to the glory and praise of your majesty. For yours is the kingdom and the power and the glory, together with your eternal Father and your all-holy, good, and life-giving Spirit, now and forever, and to the ages of ages.

People: Amen.

The Priest then anoints the Candidate with the holy chrism using the standard formula.

Priest: The seal of the gift of the Holy Spirit. Amen.

He traces the sign of the Cross with the holy chrism on the candidate's forehead and anoints the eyelids, ears, nose, and mouth, repeating the standard formula with each application. He then says this prayer.

Priest: Let us pray to the Lord.

People: Lord, have mercy.

Priest: Lord our God, you have deemed to raise your servant (*N*) to perfection through the Orthodox faith and the seal of the holy myron. Master of all, preserve in him/her the true faith in you, increase him/her in righteousness, and adorn him/her with every gift that is from you. For blessed and glorified is your most honored and majestic name, of the Father and the Son and the Holy Spirit, now and forever, and to the ages of ages.

People: Amen.

Priest: (*N*), enter into our community of faith, the holy Orthodox Church and worship our Triune God: Father, Son, and Holy Spirit, now and forever, and to the ages of ages.

New Member: Amen.

Priest: Have mercy on us, O God, according to your steadfast love. We pray You, hear us, and have mercy.

People: Lord have mercy. (3)

Priest: Again we pray for our Archbishop (*N*).

People: Lord have mercy. (3)

Priest: Again we pray for mercy, life, peace, health, salvations, visitation, protection, forgiveness and remission of the sins of the servant of God (*N*), of his/her sponsor (*N*), and of all the people here present who await your great and rich mercy.

People: Lord have mercy. (3)

Priest: For you are a merciful and loving God and to you we give glory, to the Father and the Son and the Holy Spirit, now and forever, and to the ages of ages.

People: Amen.

Reader: *Sings the Apolytikia of Pentecost and of the Patron Saint of the new member of the Church.*

Priest: [*Says the apolysis.*]

The priest offers brief words of welcome to the new member of the Church, after which he or she returns to the pews and awaits the start of the Divine Liturgy. The chanter or reader sings verses of Psalm 144 (145) or the apolytikion of the day, while the priest prepares for the start of the Divine Liturgy. At the appointed time, the new member, escorted by his or her sponsor, comes forward to receive Holy Communion. At the conclusion of the Divine Liturgy, the new member is welcomed appropriately by the members of the congregation.

***

A Certificate Professing the Orthodox Faith (Libellus)

Conforming to the established tradition, I present this written profession of faith to the reverend priest (*N*) of the Church of (*Saint*) in (*City*) on (*Date*), whereby I express my fervent desire to join the holy Orthodox Church. I renounce all false doctrines and erroneous teachings. I confess the Orthodox faith and embrace the dogmas, decrees, and canons of the holy ecumenical synods. I accept all the teachings and traditions of the Orthodox Church and promise to live by them.

(*Signature*)

Printed Name

6

THE LORD'S DAY IN ORTHODOX LITURGICAL PRACTICE AND SPIRITUALITY[473]

Come, all you nations, learn the power of this awesome mystery; for Christ our Savior, the Word who was in the beginning, was crucified for us, and was buried of His own will, and arose from the dead, that He might save all things. Let us worship Him.[474]

The Weekly Celebration of the Paschal Mystery

With an exceptional and extensive repertoire of hymns such as the one in this chapter's epigraph,[475] sung at Vespers and Orthros, and a recurring cycle of eleven Gospel lessons solemnly intoned at the Sunday Orthros,[476] each of which narrates an event related to

---

[473] The present essay is an expanded version of the one published in *Sunday, Sabbath, and the Weekend: Managing Time in a Global Culture*, ed. Edward O'Flaherty and Rodney L. Petersen, with Timothy A. Norton (Grand Rapids, MI; Cambridge, UK, 2010), 67–84.

[474] Third tone *sticheron*, Saturday Vespers.

[475] The large collection of hymns praising, explaining, and interpreting the Paschal mystery is codified essentially in the liturgical book *Oktoechos*, or *Parakletike*, which contains the weekly cycle of feasts structured on a recurring cycle of eight weeks, one for each of the eight tones of Byzantine music. The same and other similar hymns are also contained in the *Pentekostarion*, the liturgical book of the Paschal season, and, in part, the *Triodion*, the liturgical book of Pre-Lent, Great Lent, and Holy Week.

[476] Orthros is the morning service of the Orthodox Church. It is the longest and most elaborate of the several services that compose the daily office (Vespers, Apodeipnon or Compline, Mesonyktikon or midnight service, Orthros, and services of the first, third, sixth, and ninth hours). For more on the daily office, see Robert Taft, *The Liturgy of the Hours in East and West: The Origins of the Divine Office and Its Meaning for Today* (Collegeville, MN,

the resurrection of Christ and his postresurrection appearances and meals, the Orthodox Church marks the weekly celebration of the Paschal mystery: the crucifixion, burial, resurrection, and exaltation of our Lord and Savior Jesus Christ.

In the Orthodox Church, the liturgical day is reckoned from one sunset to the next, a concept borrowed from Judaism that permeated the liturgical life of the Church from its earliest days.[477] Thus the evening, and therefore the service of Vespers, marks the beginning of each liturgical day. Accordingly, the weekly celebration of Christ's resurrection commences with Vespers on Saturday evening and comes to a climax with the service of Orthros and the Divine Liturgy—the rite by which the Orthodox Church celebrates the sacrament of the Eucharist—on Sunday morning. Consequently, Sunday, the first day of the week, is the principal day, the ἀρχή (beginning) of the Christian week because it is the day of the Lord's resurrection, which constitutes the fundamental truth and the absolute fact of the Christian faith (1 Cor. 15:1–28).[478] The hymnographer summarizes the mystery with these words: "Let us believers speak of divine things, of the incomprehensible mystery of your crucifixion and your ineffable resurrection. For today death and Hades have been led captive and the race of mortal man has been clothed with incorruption. Therefore, we cry with joy: Glory to your resurrection, O Christ."[479]

The Paschal mystery is also at the center of the Eucharistic *anamnesis* in both Divine Liturgies of the Byzantine rite. The Divine Liturgy of St. Basil the Great, for example, contains these words:

1986), 13–91, 273–291. See also Ioannis Fountoulis, Ἡ Ἀκολουθία τοῦ Ὄρθρου (Thessaloniki, 1966); Fountoulis, Μοναχικὸς Ὄρθρος (Thessaloniki, 1978).

[477] Under the influence of the Roman–Byzantine practice, the start of the day at midnight also entered into the life of the Church. Both concepts, the Jewish and the Roman–Byzantine, coexist in the Orthodox Church, though the Hebraic tradition is the more dominant. A striking example that points to the coexistence of these two practices can be detected in the Church's fasting rule. While the liturgical day begins at sunset, the prescribed fast for a particular day or in preparation for Holy Communion usually starts at some point before or at midnight. For more on Jewish and Greco-Roman calendars and Christian feasts, see Ioannis Fountoulis, Τελετουργικὰ θέματα (Athens, 2007), 3:197–206.

[478] "Now after the Sabbath, toward the dawn of the first day of the week, Mary Magdalene and the other Mary went to see the sepulcher." (Matt. 28:1; cf. Mark 16:1–2; Luke 24:1; John 20:1).

[479] Third tone resurrection *kathisma*, Sunday Orthros.

Do this in remembrance of me. For as often as you eat this Bread and drink this Cup, you proclaim my death, and you confess my resurrection. Therefore, Master, we also, remembering his saving Passion and life-giving Cross, his three-day burial and resurrection from the dead, his ascension into heaven, and enthronement at your right hand, God and Father, and his glorious and awesome second coming [and] offering to you these gifts from your own gifts, at all times and in all places we praise you, we bless you, we give thanks to you, and we pray to you, Lord our God.[480]

The Components and Ethos of the Byzantine Liturgical Rite

As a result of unity of life with the risen and glorified Christ, the Church is oriented toward the eschaton, toward the end times, from which it draws its essential identity and self-understanding. The vision of God's Kingdom both orders and fuels the Church's life and ministry, its existence in and *diakonia* (service) to the world. And this vision of the Kingdom is attained and experienced chiefly through liturgical celebration. Thus any insight into the faith and practice of the Orthodox Church is not possible without an adequate knowledge and a proper understanding of Orthodox worship and liturgy.[481]

Worship, as I have noted elsewhere, is a fundamental and indispensable activity of the Church. Through its worship, or liturgy, the Church finds its fullest expression and realization.[482] The liturgy is the place where Orthodox Christians meet the self-giving of God, who draws us unto himself. It is the environment in which we meet our own human lives in unforeseen and unexpected forms. It is the milieu in which we touch eternity and experience a reality that both transcends us and transforms us.

The liturgy is the Church's faith in motion. It is the unique setting in which it celebrates formative events and remembers the revealed truths about God, creation, and humanity. "In the true Orthodox tradition," as Metropolitan Kallistos Ware notes, "there is no divorce between theology and worship, between private meditation and public prayer. All genuine worship, while embracing the emotions, must also be reflective, intelligent,

---

[480] *The Divine Liturgy of Our Father among the Saints Basil the Great* (Brookline, MA, 1988), 29.
[481] See Mother Mary and Kallistos Ware, *The Festal Menaion* (London, 1969; South Canaan, PA, 1990), 65–66.
[482] Alkiviadis C. Calivas, *Aspects of Orthodox Worship* (Brookline, MA, 2003), 1–3.

CHAPTER SIX: THE LORD'S DAY IN LITURGICAL PRACTICE   205

and essentially theological ... And at the same time all genuine theology must be a living theology—not an abstract exercise of the reasoning powers, but a vision of God's Kingdom."[483] Through prayer and dogma, the Church invites us to continually discover, experience, and realize our true and eternal mode of being, to become that which God has intended us to be.

The elements and structures of Orthodox worship constitute the venerable liturgical system known as the Byzantine rite,[484] which constitutes the final unification of liturgical practice in the Orthodox Church. The rite takes its name indirectly from Constantinople, the great imperial city that was established in 324 by Constantine the Great, the first Christian emperor, and inaugurated in 330 as the new capital of the Roman Empire. Constantinople, named after its founder, was built on the small port city of Byzantion or Byzantium, an ancient Greek colony founded in the seventh century BC by Byzas of Megara, located strategically on the Bosporus, the strait between Europe and Asia Minor.

As the primary see of the Christian East, Constantinople developed into a renowned liturgical center. Its rite represents the intermingling of parochial and monastic practices and the reception, assimilation, synthesis, and development of the rich liturgical traditions of Eastern Christianity that were directly inherited from the praxis and the experiences of the apostolic and postapostolic Church. Like all classical liturgical rites, the Byzantine rite comprises several basic components and certain characteristic theological and ritual attributes that can be summarized best by the words of St. Germanos of Constantinople (ca. 730) in his commentary on the Divine Liturgy: "The church is an earthly heaven, in which the supernatural God dwells and walks about."[485] In and through the liturgy, God is present to his people, taking them unto himself, unveiling his divine love, beauty, and holiness.

Each component of the liturgy has but one purpose: to bring us to the threshold of another world, to an encounter with the living the God. Through each of its expressions—setting, word, sound, symbol, ritual, and

---

[483] *Festal Menaion*, 66.
[484] For an excellent concise account of the development of the Byzantine rite, see Robert Taft, *The Byzantine Rite: A Short History* (Collegeville, MN, 1992). Also see Calivas, *Aspects of Orthodox Worship*, 54–62, 63–101.
[485] Paul Meyendorff, *St. Germanus of Constantinople on the Divine Liturgy* (Crestwood, NY, 1984), 57.

interpretation—the liturgy seeks to grace the worshipper with the presence of the inexpressible beauty, the searing truth, the boundless love, the indescribable joy, and the deathless life of the Triune God.

The Festal Calendar, Sunday, and the Resurrection of Christ

One of the essential components of the Byzantine rite is its comprehensive calendar of feasts and fasts.[486] The festal calendar is composed of an annual cycle of fixed and movable feasts and a weekly cycle of feasts that succinctly but ingeniously summarizes the annual festal cycle.[487] Both cycles, the annual and the weekly, center on the Paschal mystery, which is at the heart of Orthodox worship.

Annually, on the first Sunday after the first full moon of the spring equinox (customarily following the Jewish Passover), when the solemnities of

---

[486] In addition to the calendar, the Byzantine rite has a wide range of liturgical services, including three Eucharistic liturgies, sacramental rites, burial rites, and a variety of other occasional services and ceremonials. It also has a daily office composed of seven prayer hours with eight services, the chief of which are Vespers and Orthros. In addition, it has a system of biblical readings. Moreover, it contains a variety of ritual symbols, an array of processions, and distinctive gestures that include forms of blessing and bodily prayer postures. It also features highly developed and distinctive forms of the liturgical arts—namely, architecture, iconography, hymnography, music, implements, and textiles (vestments, cloths, and veils).

[487] The weekly festal cycle begins on Sunday, with the celebration of Christ's victory over death and corruption. Monday, the second day, is dedicated to the angels. On Tuesday the Church honors St. John the forerunner, prophet, and baptist and through him all the prophets. Thursday is dedicated to the holy Apostles and to St. Nicholas, who stands as the model of all hierarchs, the successors to the Apostles and teachers of the faith. On Saturday the Church commemorates the martyrs, the ascetics, and all who have fallen asleep in the hope of the resurrection. On Wednesday and Friday the Church brings into special focus the combined mystery of the Cross and the person of the Virgin Mary, the Theotokos. Wednesday and Friday are also fast days, when we contemplate the awful darkness of the fallen world expressed in the betrayal of Judas (Wednesday) and the crucifixion (Friday). The liturgical year, with its succession of feasts and fasts, commemorates events in the life of our Lord, his mother the Theotokos, St. John the Baptist, the Holy Apostles, and the myriads of saints, whose sanctity is but a shining ray of the holiness of Christ. In accordance with ancient custom, the liturgical year begins in September and ends in August. Its feasts are divided into two categories, the movable and the fixed. The movable feasts are related to the celebration of Pascha, a period of nineteen weeks that begins with the pre-Lenten season and ends with the Sunday of All Saints, the week after Pentecost. The fixed feasts, like Christmas and Theophany and the feasts of the saints, occur on the same date each year. Christmas and Theophany, for example, are celebrated annually on December 25 and January 6, respectively, while the feast of St. Catherine is celebrated on November 25 annually.

CHAPTER SIX: THE LORD'S DAY IN LITURGICAL PRACTICE 207

Great and Holy Week have been completed, the Church celebrates gloriously and joyously "the chosen and holy day, the feast of feasts and the festival of festivals,"[488] the resurrection of our Lord, God, and Savior Jesus Christ. As the annual commemoration of the resurrection is celebrated on a Sunday in the spring of each year, so the weekly commemoration of the resurrection also occurs on the first day of the week, Sunday. By the end of the first century, the Christian community had bestowed on Sunday its own distinct and special title naming it Κυριακὴ ἡμέρα, the Lord's Day.[489]

The observance of the Lord's Day as consecrated to the service of God is a Christian institution, the unique Christian festival. It is "the day the Lord has made" (Ps. 117/118:24)—the day, that is, on which God acted decisively to liberate the world from the tyranny of sin, death, and corruption by raising Jesus from the dead. The resurrection confirmed the authenticity of Christ's remarkable earthly life, vindicated the truth of his unique and compelling teachings, sealed his extraordinary works, and revealed the transformative power of his redemptive life-creating death.[490]

The resurrection of Christ constitutes the most radical and decisive deliverance of humankind. When Christ rose from the dead, he raised the whole race of Adam (1 Cor. 15:20–22). In and through the risen and exalted Christ, God receives all flesh.[491] Christ has become the Land of the Living[492] for those on either side of death who believe in his name (John 20:31). The

---

[488] *Heirmos*, eighth ode of the Paschal canon.
[489] The name also passed into the Latin language, *dominica*. By the third century it had become the ordinary name for Sunday in the Latin West. The Romance languages have also retained the name: *domenica, domingo, dimanche*.
[490] On the theological implications of Christ's resurrection, see Alkiviadis C. Calivas, *Great Week and Pascha in the Greek Orthodox Church* (Brookline, MA, 1992), 89–97.
[491] See Christos Yannaras, *Elements of Faith* (Edinburgh, 1995), 114–118.
[492] The term *land of the living* (ἡ χώρα τῶν ζώντων) is borrowed from the inscription on the fourteenth-century mosaic icon of Jesus Christ in the church (*katholikon*) of the fourth-century Monastery of Chora in Constantinople, now the Kariye (Chora) Museum. The Greek word *chora* (χώρα) means land, country, or countryside. The monastery was established outside the city walls built by the Emperor Constantine; it was called Chora because it lay outside the city. The monastery was destroyed and restored several times. The last restoration was undertaken by the scholar and humanitarian Theodore Metochites in 1312. The phrase *land of the living* is also found in several Psalms (26/27:13, 51/52:5, 114/116:9, 141/142:5). It is also found in Isaiah 38:11, Jeremiah 11:19, and Job 28:13. For example, Psalm 26/27:13 reads, "I believe that I shall see the goodness of the Lord in *the land of the living*." The same phrase in the Septuagint reads ἐν γῇ ζώντων. The word γῆ means land or earth. Ezekiel 26:20 has a similar phrase, ἐπὶ γῆς ζωῆς, which is translated "in the land of the living."

resurrection from the dead is more than a future promise and event; it is more than a condition or state of being. It is, first and last, a person, Jesus Christ, who said, "I am the resurrection and the life" (John 11:25). This wondrous mystery is recounted and explained succinctly in the *anaphora* of the Divine Liturgy of St. Basil. It bears repeating for its eloquence and theological depth.

> And when the fullness of time had come, you spoke to us through your Son himself, through whom you created the ages. He, being the splendor of your glory and the image of your being, upholding all things by the word of his power, thought it not robbery to be equal with you, God and Father. But, being God before all ages, He appeared on earth and lived with humankind. Becoming incarnate from a holy Virgin, He emptied himself, taking the form of a servant, conforming to the body of our lowliness, that He might change us in the likeness of the image of his glory. For, since through man sin came into the world and through sin death, it pleased your only-begotten Son, who is in your bosom, God and Father, born of a woman, the holy Theotokos and ever-virgin Mary; born under the law, to condemn sin in his flesh, so that those who died in Adam may be brought to life in him, your Christ. He lived in this world, and gave us precepts for salvation. Releasing us from the delusions of idolatry, he guided us to the sure knowledge of you, the true God and Father. He acquired us for himself, as his chosen people, a royal priesthood, a holy nation. Having cleansed us by water and sanctified us with the Holy Spirit, He gave himself as ransom unto death in which we were held captive, sold under sin. Descending into Hades through the Cross, that he might fill all things with Himself, he loosed the bonds of death. He rose on the third day, having opened a path for all flesh to the resurrection from the dead, since it was not possible that the Author of life would be dominated by corruption. So He became the first-fruits of those who have fallen asleep, the first-born of the dead, that He might be himself the first in all things.[493]

Human beings may share in and experience the resurrection of Christ in two ways. Christ's resurrection is the source of the continual mystical and spiritual regeneration of our dead souls, and it is the cause of our resurrection from the dead on the Last Day. Thus for Christians, Sunday, the day of Christ's resurrection, is always the special and unique day that sheds light upon the rest of the week inasmuch as it contains the "deeper messages about the history and meaning of our own personal lives."[494]

---

[493] *Divine Liturgy of Saint Basil the Great*, 26–28.
[494] William C. McCready, "The Role of Sunday in American Society: Has It Changed?," in Searle, *Sunday Morning*, 118.

At every liturgical synaxis, and especially at every Eucharistic assembly on Sunday, the faithful are reminded of their baptismal pledge and empowered to pursue their high calling: to renounce daily the false values of the fallen world and to follow the risen and glorified Lord Jesus Christ, by thinking and doing, through grace, all those things that are true, honorable, just, pure, good, noble, natural, and sinless (Phil. 4:8).

The resurrection of Christ also made possible the miracle of the Church. The profound experience of the risen and glorified Lord enabled the Apostles to evangelize the world. That same unshakable belief in the resurrection empowers the Church in every age and place to proclaim and affirm with earnestness of purpose and steadfastness of faith God's plan for the cosmos, the ultimate theosis or divinization of humankind and the transformation of the created order.[495]

The Privileged Position of Sunday, the Lord's Day

The primacy of the Lord's Day, to which the New Testament alludes (Acts 20:7–12; 1 Cor. 16:2; Rev. 1:10), is affirmed by the liturgical praxis of the early Church. For example, the *Didache* (14),[496] which some scholars believe is a composite document that developed in stages beginning as early as AD 50–70, includes this significant reference: "And on the Lord's Day, after you have come together, break bread and offer the Eucharist, having first confessed your offenses, so that your sacrifice may be pure."

Another important witness to the significance of Sunday for the Christian community is St. Justin the Martyr. Writing around AD 150, he notes:

> On the day named after the sun, all who live in city or countryside assemble in one place. The memoirs of the apostles or the writings of the prophets are read ... The president addresses us and exhorts us ... Then we stand and pray ... When we have finished praying, bread,

---

[495] For a lucid explanation of the doctrine of theosis, see Norman Russell, *Fellow Workers with God: Orthodox Thinking on Theosis* (Crestwood, NY, 2009). See also Georgios Mantzarides, *The Deification of Man: St. Gregory Palamas and the Orthodox Tradition* (Crestwood, NY, 1984).

[496] See Kurt Niederwinner, *The Didache: A Commentary* (Minneapolis, 1998); Frank Hawkins, "The Didache," in *The Study of the Liturgy*, ed. Cheslyn Jones, Geoffrey Wainwright, Edward Yarnold, and Paul Bradshaw (New York, 1992), 84–86. Recent views favor a later date for the *Didache*, the middle or late second century, but based on elements from an earlier period.

wine, and water are brought up ... The president then prays and gives thanks ... and the people give their assent with an "Amen." Next, the gifts over which the thanksgiving has been spoken are distributed and everyone shares in them ... It is on Sunday that we assemble, because Sunday is the first day: the day on which God transformed darkness and matter and created the world, and the day on which Jesus Christ our Savior rose from the dead.[497]

Written two centuries later, St. Basil the Great's treatise *On the Holy Spirit* emphasizes the significance of tradition, the doctrinal implications, and the spiritual value of the Lord's Day:

> Concerning the teachings of the Church, whether publicly proclaimed (*kerygma*) or reserved to members of the household of faith (*dogmas*), we have received some from written sources, while others have been given to us secretly, through apostolic tradition. Both sources have equal force in true religion. No one would deny either source—no one, at any rate, who is even slightly familiar with the ordinances of the Church. If we attacked unwritten customs, claiming them to be of little importance, we would fatally mutilate the Gospel, no matter what our intentions—or rather, we would reduce the Gospel teaching to bare words ... We all stand for prayer on Sunday, but not everyone knows why. We stand for prayer on the day of the Resurrection to remind ourselves of the grace we have been given; not only because we have been raised with Christ and are obliged to seek the things that are above, but also because Sunday seems to be an image of the age to come ... This day foreshadows the state which is to follow the present age: a day without sunset, nightfall, or successor, an age which does not grow old or come to an end. It is therefore necessary for the Church to teach her newborn children to stand for prayer on this day, so that they will always be reminded of eternal life, and not neglect preparations for their journey.[498]

From these and other sources it is clear that Sunday, the Lord's Day, has always had a privileged position in the life of the Church as a special time for worship and celebration.[499]

---

[497] Justin the Martyr, *First Apology*, 67.
[498] St. Basil, *On the Holy Spirit* (Crestwood, NY, 1980), 98, 100–101.
[499] See Jean Danielou, *The Bible and the Liturgy* (Notre Dame, 1956), 242–261.

Sunday: The Time for Worship

Anyone even remotely familiar with the Orthodox Church cannot help but notice that worship in general, the Sunday celebration of the Divine Liturgy in particular, remains at the very heart of the Church's life.[500] Whatever the level of knowledge or the intensity of faith Orthodox Christians may bring to the Divine Liturgy, it is their chief liturgical experience, their window onto the spiritual world, and the means by which the new life in Christ acquired through baptism is continuously nourished and advanced. Through the Eucharist, the Church calls its faithful people to share in the life of Christ, have communion with the Holy Spirit, enjoy a foretaste of the things to come, and enter into fellowship with one another as "fellow citizens of the saints and members of the household of God" (Eph. 2:19).

By setting forth the Church's living and authentic tradition, the sacred rites of the Church communicate to people the meaning and purpose of life and help them see, understand, interpret, and internalize both the tragedy of the human condition in its fallen state and the limitless expanse and potential of the new life in Christ offered freely to all. Worship shapes the vision, the knowing, and the relationships of Orthodox people; it constitutes the Church's critical educative, formative, restorative, and transformative agent and environment.

Every Sunday, the Church gathers to realize this eschatological fullness through the celebration of the Eucharist by which the Kingdom—the hope and salvation of the world—are revealed in time. At the Eucharist, as Fr. Boris Bobrinskoy says, "the Holy Spirit actualizes the plenary and unique presence of Christ in his multiple dimensions: the creative Logos, the Jesus of history, the Christ of glory, the Lord of the Parousia and of the judgment."[501] The Eucharist recapitulates the Christ event by which the comprehensive renovation and glorious transfiguration of the world have already begun. Through word, symbol, ritual action, and sacrament, the faithful experience the fullness of Christ's presence and the fulfillment of his promise that "where two or three are gathered in my name, there am I in the midst of them" (Matt. 18:20).

---

[500] See Robert Taft, "Sunday in the Eastern Tradition," in Searle, *Sunday Morning*, 49–74; Nikodemos Skrettas, "Η Κυριακή," in *Τὸ Χριστιανικὸν ἑορτολόγιον*, Σειρά ποιμαντική βιβλιοθήκη 15 (Athens, 2007), 265–321.

[501] Boris Bobrinskoy, *The Mystery of the Trinity* (Crestwood, NY, 1999), 169.

The Eucharist is at the center of Orthodox worship; it is the source and summit of the Church's life.[502] It is constitutive of the very existence of the Church and the condition of its growth. At the Eucharist, the Church is continuously changed from a human community into the Body of Christ, the temple of the Holy Spirit, and the holy people of God. Hence, it is inconceivable to the Orthodox mind that under normal circumstances, an observance of the Lord's Day is possible without the celebration of the Divine Liturgy.

Sunday: The Day of the Spirit

It is no coincidence that both the resurrection of Christ and the giving of the Holy Spirit took place on a Sunday; it is part of the divine plan of salvation. According to the Gospel of John, the risen Lord gave the Spirit to his Apostles on Sunday, the very evening of the day of the resurrection (John 20:19–23). The Book of Acts (2:1–4) records that Pentecost, the principal event marking the descent and outpouring of the Holy Spirit, also occurred on a Sunday, fifty days after the resurrection of Christ. H. B. Porter notes that "the powers which the Spirit bestows on the Church are in fact exhibited and set forth in a special way on Sunday."[503] Orthodox Christians experience this fact especially in and through the celebration of the Divine Liturgy.

The *epiclesis* in the *anaphora* of both Eucharistic liturgies reminds us that every Divine Liturgy constitutes a continuous Pentecost, a renewal and a confirmation of the constant coming of the Holy Spirit to the Church and its members. The *epiclesis* in the Divine Liturgy of St. John Chrysostom, for example, reads, "Once again we offer to you this spiritual worship without the shedding of blood, and we ask, pray, and entreat you, send down Your Holy Spirit upon us and upon these gifts here presented."[504]

---

[502] See Alexander Schmemann, *The Eucharist: Sacrament of the Kingdom* (Crestwood, NY, 1988). See also the series of articles in *Το μυστύριο της Θείας Ευχαριστίας*, Σειρά Ποιμαντική Βιβλιοθήκη 4 (Athens, 2004); Nikodemos Skrettas, *Η Θεία Ευχαριστία και τα προνόμια της Κυριακής κατά τη διδασκαλία των Κολλυβάδων* (Thessaloniki, 2008)..Hugh Wybrew, *The Orthodox Liturgy: The Development of the Eucharistic Liturgy in the Byzantine Rite* (Crestwood, NY, 1990).

[503] Harry Boone Porter, *The Day of Light: The Biblical and Liturgical Meaning of Sunday* (Greenwich, CT, 1960), 44. The feast of Pentecost is celebrated fifty days after Pascha. It is the second-oldest of the major annual feasts of the Church. See Theodoros Koumarianos, "Οι εορτες της Αναλήψεως και της Πεντηκοστης," *Τὸ Χριστιανικὸν ἑορτολόγιον*, 211–235.

[504] *The Divine Liturgy of St. John Chrysostom* (Brookline, MA, 1985), 22. The epiclesis in

Through the whole action of the Divine Liturgy—from the gathering of the people, to the hearing and explication of God's Word, the transfer of the holy Gifts, the exchange of the kiss of peace, the creed, the offering, consecration, and communion of the Eucharistic elements, and the departure in peace to attend to the affairs of everyday life—the Holy Spirit acts to communicate to the faithful the gift of Christ's presence and thereby the gifts of the future age and Kingdom: forgiveness, purification, sanctification, *koinonia*, incorruptibility, and eternal life.

At the Divine Liturgy, Orthodox Christians come to experience and celebrate the inrush of eternal life into our perishable, mortal existence, accomplished through the presence of the Holy Spirit, who vivifies the Church and perfects each member. Everything in the Church is by the Holy Spirit, as a hymn of Pentecost suggests: "The Holy Spirit provides all things; He pours forth prophecy and perfects the priesthood. He taught wisdom to the illiterate and showed forth the fishermen as theologians. He holds together the whole institution of the Church. Wherefore, O Comforter, one in essence and throne with the Father and the Son, glory to you."[505]

Church, Eucharist, Sunday, and the Eighth Day

In the theological, liturgical, and canonical tradition of the Orthodox Church, it is clear that Church, the Eucharist, Sunday, and the eighth day are integrally related and inherently bound. Worship, witnessing, structures, and above all the sacraments constitute the face and the voice of the Church. The Eucharist in particular, in the words of Metropolitan John Zizioulas, is "an event constitutive of the Church, enabling the Church to be."[506]

And the Eucharist, through which the gifts of the future age are communicated to believers, is the principal activity of the faith community every single Sunday of the year. So strong is the relationship between the Eucharist and Sunday that the canons deal strictly with those who deliberately scorn the Sunday synaxis. Canon 80 of the Penthekte Ecumenical Synod of 691–692, for example, says the following:

---

the Liturgy of St. Basil is similar: "We pray to you and call upon you, O Holy of Holies, that by the favor of your goodness, your Holy Spirit may come upon us and upon the gifts here presented." *Divine Liturgy of Saint Basil the Great*, 30.

[505] Sticheron of Vespers of the Feast of Pentecost.

[506] John D. Zizioulas, *Being as Communion: Studies in Personhood and the Church* (Crestwood, NY, 1985), 21.

> If any bishop, or presbyter, or deacon, or anyone else on the list of the clergy, or any layman, without any grave necessity or any particular difficulty compelling him to be absent from his own church for a very long time, fails to attend church on Sundays for three consecutive weeks, while living in the city, if he be a cleric let him be deposed from office; but if he be a layman, let him be removed from Communion.[507]

Attendance at and participation in the Divine Liturgy is an essential requirement of the Christian life not in fulfillment of a vague religious obligation but for "the inestimable privilege of glorifying God."[508] St. Maximos the Confessor says that we come to the Eucharist to

> partake of the grace of the Holy Spirit which is always present there ... This grace transforms and changes each person who is found there and in fact remolds him in proportion to what is more divine in him and leads him to what is revealed through the mysteries which are celebrated, even if he does not himself feel this because he is still among those who are "children" in Christ, unable to see either the depths of the realities or the grace operating in it.[509]

Through the Divine Liturgy we remember and celebrate in joy and thanksgiving the whole mystery of the divine economy, God's household plan for the salvation of the world—from creation to the incarnation, the Passion, resurrection, glorification, and the Parousia of the Son and Word of God—which is recounted in the *anaphora* of both Divine Liturgies.[510] The whole drama of the economy is brought to climax with the *anamnesis* of the Paschal mystery:

> Remembering, therefore, the saving command ["Do this..."], and all that came to pass for our sake, the cross, the tomb, the resurrection on the third day, the ascension into heaven, the enthronement at the right of the Father, and the second glorious coming, offering to You these gifts from Your own gifts, at all times and in all places, we praise You, we bless You, we give thanks to You, and we pray to You, Lord our God.[511]

---

[507] See Πηδάλιον (Athens, 1957), 290; *Rudder* (Chicago, 1957), 384. The *Pedalion* (Πηδάλιον, "Rudder") is an annotated collection of the holy canons compiled by Agapios and Nikodemos of the Holy Mountain. It was first published in 1800. An English translation of the 1908 edition was published by D. Cummings in 1957.
[508] Taft, "Sunday in the Eastern Tradition," 52.
[509] St. Maximos the Confessor, *Mystagogy* 24, in *Maximus Confessor: Selected Writings*, trans. George C. Berthold, Classics of Western Spirituality (New York, 1985), 206–207.
[510] See the *anaphora* in the Divine Liturgies of St. Basil the Great and St. John Chrysostom.
[511] The *anaphora* in *Divine Liturgy of St. John Chrysostom*, 21–22.

The Eucharist is the messianic banquet, the meal of the Kingdom, the marriage supper of the Lamb, to which God's people are called to attend and share (Rev. 19:9). It is, as Fr. Alexander Schmemann notes, the sacrament of the coming of the risen and reigning Lord and of our meeting and communion with him at his heavenly table.[512] We affirm this truth when we sing the Cherubic Hymn at the Divine Liturgy: "We who mystically represent the Cherubim sing the thrice holy hymn to the life-giving Trinity. Let us now set aside all the cares of life *that we may receive the King of all invisibly escorted by the angelic hosts.*"[513]

At the Eucharist we meet the Triune God and enter into his "eternal present." We experience the past, present, and future of the history of salvation as one reality. By the power of the Holy Spirit, we, and through us the whole of the created order, intersect eternity and are given a foretaste of the glory that is to be (Rom. 8:18–24). The realities of the Kingdom break through to reveal the Church as the gift of the eighth day, which is the successor of this earthly time with its activities of birth and decay that is destined to pass away.[514] The resurrection of Christ is the beginning of the new creation. And Sunday, the day *par excellence* of the Eucharist, is not only the first day of the week on which Christ was raised from the dead but also the eighth day, the image of the future age, the day without end, which will have neither evening nor succession.

For the early Christians, the number eight signified completion and fulfillment. The Fathers applied the idea to Sunday—at once the first and the eighth day—because it is consecrated by the resurrection of Christ, the very promise of eternal life. The seven-day week is seen as a symbol of recurring time of the present world. The eighth day, on the other hand, is the figure of the future life, the life that follows the sensible world, which is enclosed in the hebdomad (ἑβδομάς). Sunday reveals the new life at the end of the ages, the unending day of the Kingdom, "when God will wipe away every tear ... when death shall be no more, when mourning, crying, and pain shall be no more, when night shall be no more, when there will be no need of light, or lamp, or sun ... for the glory of God will be the light and the lamp will be the Lamb" (Rev. 21:4, 23, 22:5).[515]

---

[512] Schmemann, *Eucharist*, 43.
[513] *Divine Liturgy of Saint John Chrysostom*, 12–14.
[514] For more on the use and meaning of the eighth day in the Scriptures and the Fathers, see Jean Danielou, *The Bible and the Liturgy*, 262–286.
[515] See Roger T. Beckwith and Wilfrid Stott, *This Is the Day* (London, 1978), 117–124.

Sunday and the Eucharist represent the summit of the Christian life. On Sunday at the Eucharist the community gathers to remember, celebrate, and partake of the mystery of salvation, the source of spiritual joy on our journey toward the eternal Kingdom of God, the gates of which have already been opened through baptism. The realities of the eighth day are made manifest to those who come with faith to the altar and table of the Lord.

Sunday: The Day of Light for the People of the Light

Sunday is also the day of light. It is dedicated not to the celestial sun but to the "Sun of Righteousness" (Mal. 4:2), Christ, who is the Light of the world (John 8:12). "By claiming the First Day as their own," writes H. B. Porter, "Christians declare themselves as children of the Father of lights and fellow-heirs with Jesus Christ, a people whom he has delivered from the darkness."[516]

In the Scriptures and the tradition of the Church, light—uncreated and wholly other from every kind of material light—is a primary symbol or image of the Triune God both in his essence and his energies.[517] St. John the Apostle and Evangelist assures us that "God is light and in him is no darkness at all" (1 John 1:5). St. Paul tells us that God, whom no man has ever seen or can see and who alone has immortality, dwells in unapproachable light (1 Tim. 6:16). In the Scriptures, God's glory or presence is likened to a brilliant fiery light.[518] The Psalmist sings, "The Lord reigns; let the earth be glad! Clouds and thick darkness are round about him; righteousness and justice are the foundation of his throne. Fire goes before him, and burns up his adversaries round about. His lightings lighten the world" (Ps. 96/97:1–4). Or as St. John writes in his Gospel, "In him [Christ] was life, and the life was the light of men. The light shines in the darkness, and the darkness has not overcome it" (John 1:4–5). Prayers of the Church also speak of God in terms of light, as in, for example, the prayer of the mid-first hour: "Eternal

---

[516] Porter, *Day of Light*, 33.
[517] According to the teaching of the Greek Fathers, the transcendent God remains transcendent, unknowable, and unapproachable in his essence, as he also communicates himself to the world through his uncreated energies, or divine powers and unoriginate works. For the distinction between essence and energy in God, see *Gregory Palamas: The Triads*, trans. Nicholas Gendle, Classics of Western Spirituality (New York, 1983), 93–111.
[518] See, for example, the description of the event of the transfiguration of Christ in Matt. 17:1–8; Mark 9:2–8; Luke 9:28–36; and of Pentecost in Acts 2:1–4.

God and Lord, the light without beginning and everlasting, Creator of the universe, fountain of mercy, sea of goodness, and inscrutable abyss of love, shine upon us the light of your countenance."[519]

In the book of Genesis, the creative activity of God on the first day begins with the creation of light: "In the beginning God created the heavens and the earth ... And God said, "Let there be light;" and there was light. And God saw that the light was good ... And there was evening and there was morning, one day" (1:1–5). Light is also associated with the new creation, the beginning of another way of being and doing pioneered by Christ: "You are a chosen race, a royal priesthood, a holy nation, God's people, that you may declare the wonderful deeds of him who called you out of darkness into his marvelous light. Once you were no people but now you are God's people; once you had not received mercy but now you have received mercy" (1 Pet. 2:9–10).

Light is also related to the new life in Christ. In his letter to the Ephesians, St. Paul declares, "Once you were darkness, but now you are light in the Lord; walk as children of light for the fruit of light is found in all that is good and right and true" (Eph. 5:8–9). And the Lord himself said of his followers, "You are the light of the world ... Let your light so shine before men, that they may see your good works and give glory to your Father who is in heaven" (Matt. 5:14, 16).

The motif of light runs through many of the hymns of the divine services of the Church, as well, appearing, for example, in the ancient evening hymn of Vespers, "O joyful light of the holy glory of the immortal Father, heavenly, holy, blessed—Jesus Christ" (Φῶς ἱλαρὸν ἁγίας δόξης)[520] and the "Hymns of Light" in the eight tones for the daily Lenten Orthros service.[521] On the feast of Pentecost, we sing, "The Father is Light; the Word is Light; and the Holy Spirit is Light, who was sent to the Apostles in the form of fiery tongues; and thus through Him all creation is illumined and guided to worship the Holy Trinity."[522]

---

[519] Prayer of the mid-third hour, attributed to St. Basil the Great. See Ὡρολόγιον τὸ Μέγα (Athens, 1973), 80.
[520] For the full text of the hymn see, for example, *Festal Menaion*, 83.
[521] See *The Lenten Triodion*, trans. Mother Mary and Kallistos Ware (London, 1978), 662–667.
[522] Exapostilarion hymn of Pentecost. See *The Pentecostarion* (Boston, MA, 1990), 416.

The hymn that often concludes the rites of Holy Communion at the Divine Liturgy declares, "We have seen the true light; we have received the heavenly Spirit; we have found the true faith, worshipping the undivided Trinity, which has saved us."[523]

Sunday Is Everything:

THE DAY OF SANCTIFICATION, REST, AND GODLY ACTION

For Orthodox people, as Robert Taft observes, Sunday is everything, just as it was in the early Church.[524] Sunday was and continues to be, above all, a day for holy synaxis, a day for the celebration of the Divine Liturgy, in and through which the risen and reigning Lord is present to his people that he may grant to them his divine perfections, holiness (ἁγιότης), incorruptibility ἀφθαρσία), and immortality (ἀθανασία).

The idea of the sacredness and splendor of the Lord's Day is so ingrained in the Orthodox conscience that no one attends the divine services dressed shabbily or casually. However deep or shallow one's inner awareness and sensitivities may be, everyone knows intuitively that one comes before God as "a new creation" (2 Cor. 5:17), clothed in appropriate dignified apparel. "Church clothes," even if plain and simple, are perceived as an extension of one's baptismal garment, the garment that signifies the newness of life in Christ.[525] The Church is a Eucharistic community because it is first a baptismal community, God's own people called out of darkness into his marvelous light (1 Pet. 2:9–10).

Sunday, as the weekly Pascha—the perpetual first day of the new creation and the unending eighth day of the Kingdom—is a day of rejoicing. Hence, no one is permitted to fast or to kneel in sorrow or in penance. Moreover, since the Eucharist unites the members of the Church both to Christ and to one another, the Eucharistic assembly becomes the image of

---

[523] See, for example, *Divine Liturgy of St. John Chrysostom*, 32.
[524] Taft, "Sunday in the Eastern Tradition," 51. Also see Skrettas, "Κυριακή," 269.
[525] Immediately after one is baptized and chrismated, he or she is clothed with a baptismal garment. The act of clothing is accompanied by an affirmation ("The servant of God is clothed with the garment of righteousness in the name of the Father and of the Son and of the Holy Spirit. Amen") and a hymn ("Most merciful Christ our God, bestow upon me a robe of light, you who array yourself in light as with a garment"). See, for example, *Sacraments and Services, Book 1* (Northridge, CA, 1993), 29–30.

CHAPTER SIX: THE LORD'S DAY IN LITURGICAL PRACTICE

the new humanity gathered around the risen Lord, empowered, nourished, and perfected by his love and mercy. Thus Sunday, simultaneously first and eighth and which is differentiated from all the other days of week by the celebration of the Eucharist, reminds us that the Church is the eschatological community of God, a community that experiences the new life in Christ and witnesses to the presence of God's Kingdom in history.

Salvation comes through a community, the Church. Thus Christian existence is inherently corporate. This corporality is mirrored at every liturgical service, most especially at the Divine Liturgy. Sunday, then, in addition to other things, is also a day for community feastings and family gatherings. It is the preeminent day for ordinations, baptisms, and marriages,[526] all of which are fundamentally ecclesial events, inasmuch as all sacraments belong to the Church and are intrinsic to its life of grace.

Some say that "the Sabbath of the Old Testament began as a day of rest and became a day of worship, whereas the Sunday of the New Testament began as a day of worship and, in the history of the Church, became a day of worship and rest."[527] As we know, Sunday was declared a day of rest—at least for segments of the populace—in 321 by Constantine, the first Christian emperor. Long before him, however, Christians were known to observe the day with special solemnity. The emperor's edict served only to enhance the festival by facilitating divine worship and providing more amply for the restful activity of godly service. Although the temptation exists, Christians must be careful not to confuse rest with idleness, inactivity, and purposeless leisure.[528]

While rest is an element of the Lord's Day, it is not the essential one, as some would have us believe. After all, during the first three centuries of the Church's life, Sunday was an ordinary workday. What gives Sunday its privileged status is the gathering of people for the celebration of the Eucharist. Sunday is the Church's preeminent day of worship, the day on which the faith community gathers to celebrate the Kingdom of God already given as the very pledge of salvation. For a Christian who is in touch with the wellsprings of the faith, Sunday is, above all else, a day for corporate worship, for Christian fellowship, and for godly service through works of love.

---

[526] See, for example, Porter, *Day of Light*, 65–77.
[527] Thomas K. Carroll and Thomas Halton, *Liturgical Practice in the Fathers* (Wilmington, DE, 1988), 18.
[528] See Skrettas, "Κυριακή," 268–276.

The Name 'Lord's Day'

A small but compelling sign of the early Church's efforts to reshape the fabric of human life in accordance with the truths and the values of the Gospel comprised the names the Church chose to designate the days of the week. For the growing number of pagan converts, these names, rooted in the Church's Judaic past, constituted a dramatic shift in the way time was conceived and lived.

The week, with its seven-day cycle by which time was measured, gradually gained currency among the people of the ancient world. It was customary in ancient cultures to assign the names of their planet-gods to each day of the week. In fact, in the prevailing civil calendar, the days of the week in English are the Teutonic (Germanic) equivalents of the ancient Roman planetary names.[529]

In contrast, the early Christians adopted a different system. They embraced the Jewish tradition and assigned numerical names to the days of the week based on the creation narrative in the book of Genesis.[530] By adopting these names, the Church proclaimed its belief and trust in the sovereignty of the Triune God. Time, space, human life, and the entire cosmos are not under the control and influence of the false planet-gods but under the rule of the Triune God, the Author of life and the Lord of history, "the Creator of heaven and earth, and of all things visible and invisible."[531]

The tradition of the early Church lives in the native languages of the people in whose lands Orthodox Christianity prospered and flourished. The ecclesial as well as the civil calendars in most of these lands use numerical names for some days of the week and proper names for other days, replicating the Jewish names.[532] In Greek, for example, Monday, the second

---

[529] The ancient Roman planetary names are *sun, moon, Mars, Mercury, Jupiter, Venus,* and *Saturn*. See David Ewing Duncan, *Calendar: Humanity's Epic Struggle to Determine a True and Accurate Year* (New York 1998), 45–46.

[530] See Josef A. Jungmann, *The Early Liturgy* (Notre Dame, 1959), 23.

[531] The phrase is from the first article of the Nicene-Constantinopolitan Creed, the official symbol of faith of the Orthodox Church, and it refers to God the Father, the Almighty.

[532] The ancient pagan names have been retained for the days of the week in the Romanian language, as in other Romance languages. Saturday, however, is called *Sambata* (Sabbath), and Sunday is called *Duminica*, the Lord's Day. In the Albanian language, the days of the week bear pagan names.

day of the week, is called the second day (Δευτέρα).[533] It is followed by the third, fourth, and fifth days (Τρίτη, Τετάρτη, Πέμπτη). The seventh day is called the Sabbath day (Σάββατον), and the sixth day is called by its numerical equivalent or, more traditionally, the Day of Preparation (Παρασκευή).

The first day of the week (ἡ πρώτη or ἡ μία τῶν Σαββάτων; Mark 16:2), is known by its distinctly Christian name, the Lord's Day (ἡ ἡμέρα τῆς Κυριακῆς), a name that comes from the Book of Revelation: "I was in the Spirit on the Lord's day, and I heard behind me a loud voice" (1:10). This day is the day on which Christ the Lord, ὁ Κύριος, rose from the dead and appeared to his disciples. While nearly all Orthodox people call Sunday the Lord's Day, the Russian Orthodox and other Slavic people constitute an exception. They call Sunday Resurrection Day (*Voskresen'e*; Ἀναστάσιμος ἡμέρα), a name known and used by Christians as early as the fourth century.[534]

Christian Identity: A Reality Check

I have set before the reader an ideal understanding of the Lord's Day in the hope that it may help to heighten awareness of its significance as a special day that shapes the personal, familial, and communal life of a Christian. It would be wrong, however, to assume that every Orthodox Christian experiences Sunday with the knowledge and the passion described here. Such an assumption fails to take into account the degrees of knowledge, the levels of spiritual awareness, and the inevitable fluctuations people experience in pursuit of their Christian vocation. That said, it is important to note that a correlation exists between the Lord's Day and Christian identity. The way one thinks of and spends the Lord's Day says much about the depth and breadth of one's Orthodox Christian identity.

The danger facing the Church and its members today is not so much the swings people experience in their spiritual pursuits but the blurring or the loss of the Orthodox vision of life, the loss or the absence of the sense of God, of his loving and transforming presence in the affairs of everyday life. As God ceases to be relevant in the lives of people, the need for worship diminishes and fades away. Occasional church attendance leads to casual

---

[533] In the Russian language Monday is known as the First Day after the Resurrection and Tuesday as the Second Day after the Resurrection, and so forth.
[534] See Jungmann, *Early Liturgy*, 21.

membership, which can "lead to a movement away from the Church, not so much in a sense of renunciation or joining another body, but in the sense that Orthodox Christianity no longer is a prime definer of one's identity."[535]

Fr. Georges Florovsky was correct to state unequivocally that "the Church is ultimately real precisely as a worshipping community, a community or congregation of worshipping members-persons. She grows in her fullness in the process of worship."[536] Precisely because the Church is primarily a worshipping community, regular church attendance is crucial for the maintenance of a vibrant and living faith that upholds and nurtures Christian identity. As Mark Searle puts it, "the identity of the Church and of the individual Christian is tied to the weekly assembly. Scripturally, theologically, and liturgically, there can be no Christians without Church, no Church without assembly."[537]

The Sunday assembly is so decisive and vital to the Church and its members that an ancient third-century church order, *The Didascalia of the Twelve Apostles*, considers intentional absence from the assembly a cause for great concern because it constitutes a dismemberment of Christ's Body, the Church. Absence from the assembly deprives Christ and, by extension, his Church of a member.

> When you are teaching, command and exhort the people to be faithful to the assembly of the church. Let them not fail to attend, but let them gather faithfully together. Let no one deprive the Church by staying away; if they do, they deprive the body of Christ of one of its members! For you must not only think only of others but of yourself as well, when you hear the words that our Lord spoke: "Who does not gather with me, scatters" (Matt. 12:30). Since you are the members of Christ, you must not scatter yourselves outside the Church by failing to assemble there. For we have Christ for our Head, as He Himself promised and announced, so that "you have become sharers with us" (2 Pet. 1:4). Do not, then, make light of your own selves, do not deprive our Savior of his members, do not rend, do not scatter his Body.[538]

---

[535] See "Report to His Eminence Archbishop Iakovos—Commission: Archdiocesan Theological Agenda," in *Greek Orthodox Theological Review* 34, no. 3 (1989): 301.

[536] Georges Florovsky, "Worship and Everyday Life: An Eastern Orthodox View," in *Studia Liturgica* 2, no. 4 (1963): 272.

[537] Mark Searle, "The Shape of the Future: A Liturgist's Vision" in *Sunday Morning*, 139.

[538] *The Didascalia of the Twelve Apostles*, 13. See Lucien Deiss, *Springtime of the Liturgy*, trans. Matthew J. O'Connell (Collegeville, MN, 1979), 176–177.

At the Eucharistic assembly we appropriate the saving grace of God and share in the life and the faith of the ecclesial community. There we learn and relearn, affirm and reaffirm who we are as persons and as community. There we are transformed to become servants of redemption, trained to recognize justice and injustice. There we hear the words of life and apprehend salvation. There is the place of our deification.

Sadly, some choose to forfeit the gift and to go away (John 6:67). Others, however, remain steadfast and confess, as Simon Peter did, "Lord, to whom shall we go? You have the words of eternal life; and we have believed, and have come to know, that you are the Holy One of God" (John 6:68).

Recovering the Unique Mystical Quality of the Lord's Day

For those who have fallen under the sway of the secular culture of our times, Sunday has become less a day of worship and more a day for relaxation and private time—a day for sleeping in, for catching up on household chores, for the pursuit of hobbies and personal care, or for any number of recreational activities.[539] On top of this, Sunday has developed into a favored day for playing various team sports, claiming especially the attention of school-age children and their parents. In addition, the creation of the "three-day weekend" has made it easier for people to "get away" for brief holidays, making Sunday worship less attractive. On the other hand, the abolition of the so-called blue laws has turned Sunday into another workday for many people and into a shopping day for others. Thus for large segments of the population, Sunday has become neither a day for worship nor a day for rest, at least in the traditional Christian sense.

From the Christian perspective, rest is more than leisure; it is more than the suspension of workplace demands and more than an escape from the burdens and routines of daily life. To be true and edifying, rest must include more than self-indulging activities, more than fun and merriment. It must embrace opportunities for godly service and provide time for quiet reflection and for replenishment and perfection of one's energies—physical, intellectual, emotional, and spiritual. Such an inclusive and energizing rest is especially formed, informed, and vivified by personal prayer and communal worship.

Recreational activities, while they may lend themselves to casual and in-

---

[539] See McCready, "The Role of Sunday," 104–110.

frequent church attendance, are not the root cause of the problem. They are, after all, necessary ingredients of an authentic human life. Infrequent church attendance owes largely to the lack of motivation that springs from flawed priorities. When Sunday is reduced to a "day off," it is robbed of its unique mystical quality. When we abandon the Eucharistic assembly for leisure time and recreation, we forgo the regenerative powers that flow out of the liturgical assembly. The liturgy is, after all, the gateway to heaven, a place of mystery, flooded by the presence of God. It is where we develop and nurture our intimate union with Christ and with his mystical body, the Church. The liturgy is the place in which God works to change the very core of our being, making us by grace what he is by nature.

At the heart of the Gospel is the truth of God's solidarity with his creatures, of the presence of his rule, his gentle mercy, and his tender love. We have been made for worship. Our hearts, as St. Augustine observed, remain restless until they rest in the presence of God. The yearning for the wholly Other is deeply embedded in the human soul. It cannot be eradicated. Therefore, one either learns to come before the true God in prayer and solemn feast or deludes oneself with the worship of idols, the forms of which are many in this fallen and wounded world.

7

THE SUNDAY LUCAN PERICOPES IN THE BYZANTINE LECTIONARY
A GUIDE FOR SEMINARIANS AND HOMILISTS[540]

Introduction

Even a casual acquaintance with the liturgy of the Orthodox Church reveals clearly that the Bible lives in the Church. Or as Fr. Theodore Stylianopoulos aptly puts it, "The centrality of Christ's saving work, prophesied in the Old Testament and revealed in the New, means that the gospel message is proclaimed not only in the scriptures, but also properly speaking, in all aspects of the church's life which are intrinsically evangelical—her identity, worship, sacraments, mission, creed, theology, and practice."[541]

Of the fifty Gospel pericopes assigned to the Sunday Divine Liturgy in the *Evangelion*,[542] the liturgical Gospel book of the Orthodox Church,

---

[540] This essay was first published in *Studies in Orthodox Hermeneutics: A Festschrift in Honor of Theodore G. Stylianopoulos*, ed. Eugen Pentiuc, John Fotopoulos, and Bruce Beck (Brookline, MA 2016), 365-383 with the following remarks: It is a special privilege to contribute to this celebratory volume honoring a highly respected and admired colleague whose friendship I cherish deeply. A man of great personal integrity, theological acumen, and genuine piety, Fr. Theodore has tiuched the minds and hearts of countless people through his exemplary Christian life, insightful writings, and effective teaching and pastoral ministries. His exceptional contributions to the theological endeavor are worthy of every praise and expressions of gratitude.

[541] Theodore G. Stylianopoulos, "Gospel," in *The Encyclopedia of Eastern Orthodox Christianity*, vol. I, John A. McGukin, ed. (Oxford, 2011), 278.

[542] To this number we must add another six pericopes that belong to the festal calendar. They are read annually on the Sundays before and after the feasts of the Elevation of the Cross, Christmas, and Theophany.

the fifteen of the Gospel of St. Luke are of special interest because of the peculiar rubrics associated with them; rubrics that bewilder and confuse fledgling seminarians and homilists. This essay is written with the needs of these individuals in mind. However, before I address the Sunday Lucan lessons, a few introductory remarks on the Byzantine lectionary system would be helpful.

The Byzantine Lectionary System

The Byzantine or Constantinopolitan Rite is the common inheritance of all the Orthodox Churches from at least the twelfth century.[543] One of the essential components of the rite is its lectionary or organized system of lections (ἀναγνώσματα) from the Old and New Testaments for reading at sacred services.[544] The practice of reading, interpreting, and explaining Scripture lessons at Eucharistic liturgies and other sacred services dates from the earliest days of the Church. St. Paul, for example, alludes to the practice (Colossians 4:16; cf. Revelation 1:1–3) and St. Justin the Martyr writing in the middle of the second century attests to it:

> On the day named after the sun, all who live in the city or countryside assemble. The memoirs of the apostles or the writings of the prophets are read for as long as time allows. When the lector has finished, the

---

[543] For a concise history of the Byzantine Rite see Robert F. Taft, *The Byzantine Rite: a Short History* (Collegeville, MN: 1992); and Panagiotis Trembelas, Λειτουργικοὶ Τύποι Αἰγύπτου καὶ Ἀνατολῆς (Athens 1961), 323–369.

[544] On the use of Holy Scripture in the Orthodox Church and the history of the lectionary, see the several informative articles in Ἱερουργεῖν τὸ Εὐαγγέλιον:Ἡ Ἁγία Γραφὴ στὴν Ὀρθόδοξη Λατρεία, vol. 10 in the series Σειρὰ Ποιμαντικὴ Βιβλιοθήκη (Athens 2004); and the studies of Vasileios Exarchos, Τὸ παρ' ἡμῖν ἰσχύον σύστημα βιβλικῶν ἀναγνωσμάτων (Athens 1935); Daniel Galadza, "The Jerusalem Lectionary and the Byzantine Rite," in *Rites and Rituals of the Christian East*, Bert Groen, Daniel Galadza, Nina Glibetic, and Gabriel Radle, eds. (Leuven-Paris-Walpole, MA 2014),181–200; David M. Petras, "The Gospel Lectionary of the Byzantine Church," in *St. Vladimir's Theological Quarterly (SVTQ)*, 41, 2 & 3 (1997), 113–140; W. Jardine Grisbrooke, "Word and Liturgy: the Eastern Orthodox Tradition," in *Studia Liturgica*, 16:3–4 (1986/1987), 13–30; Ioannis Fountoulis, «Ὁ Ἀπόστολος Παῦλος στὴ θεία λατρεία,» in his Τελετουργικὰ Θέματα, vol. 2 (Athens 2006), 25–40; and Ἑρμηνεία Εὐαγγελίων τῶν Κυριακῶν, vol.1 and 2, Ioannis Fountoulis, ed. (Thessaloniki 1972 and 1973); Georges Barrois, *Scripture Readings in Orthodox Worship* (Crestwood, NY 1977); Thomas Hopko, "The Bible in the Orthodox Church," 66–99; Demetrios Constantelos, "The Holy Scriptures in Orthodox Worship," in *The Greek Orthodox Theological Review*, 12:1 (1966), 7–83; and A Monk of the Eastern Church, *The Year of Grace of the Lord* (Crestwood, NY 1980); For an extensive bibliography on the subject see Taft, *The Byzantine Rite*, 49–51 (note 17).

president addresses us and exhorts us to imitate the splendid things we have heard.[545]

The Byzantine lectionary evolved in stages through the gradual merging and adaptation of the lectionary systems of two great liturgical centers of the Greek East, Jerusalem and Constantinople. While the Byzantine system was heavily influenced by the ancient Jerusalem lectionary, Constantinople gave it its final form. The Patriarchate of Constantinople was not only the recipient but also a source of liturgical practice and, more important, its chief arbiter and transmitter.

Beginning with the eighth century, the Byzantine lectionary system was codified in three separate liturgical books:[546] the *Evangelion* (Εὐαγγέλιον), *Apostolos* (Ἀπόστολος),[547] and *Prophetologion* (Προφητολόγιον).[548] Of three books,[549] the *Evangelion* is the object of special honor. It is venerated as the

---

[545] Justin the Martyr, *First Apology*, 67.
[546] See Elena Velkovska, "Byzantine Liturgical Books" in A. J. Chupungco, editor, *Handbook For Liturgical Studies* (Collegeville, MN 1997), 225–227; *The Festal Menaion* (South Canaan, PA 1990),535-543; and Ioannis M. Fountoulis, Τελετουργικὰ Θέματα, vol. 3 (Athens 2007), 8–25. On the *Typikon* and the *Euchologion* see Alkiviadis Calivas, *Aspects of Orthodox Worship* (Brookline, MA 2003), 63–124.
[547] The *Apostolos* (also known as *Praxapostolos*) contains pericopes from the Book of Acts, the fourteen Epistles of St. Paul, and the seven universal epistles. The *Apostolos* also includes the antiphons and introits of major feasts, as well as prokeimena, alleluiaria, and communion hymns, all of which are executed by the reader or chanter.
[548] The Old Testament lessons, based on the Greek Septuagint, were codified in the *Anagnostikon*, which in recent times is called *Prophetologion*. The *Anagnostikon* was last printed in 1595. From then its contents were incorporated into the *Triodion, Pentecostarion*, and *Menaia*. Recently, through the efforts of the Church of Greece the Hellenic Biblical Society has published a version of the *Prophetologion* in the original Greek Septuagint with a Modern Greek translation. See Προφητολόγιον: Τὰ Λειτουργικὰ Ἀναγνώσματα ἀπὸ τὴν Παλαιὰν Διαθήκην (Athens 2008 and 2009). Fr. Ephrem Lash and Bishop Demetri Khoury have compiled and edited a version of the *Prophetologion* in English and have made their work available online: www.anastasis.org.uk/prophetologion and www.antiochian.org/content/bishop-demetri
[549] Some add a fourth book, the *Psalter*, which contains the one hundred and fifty Psalms attributed to David and the Nine Odes, eight of which are from the Old Testament and one, the Ninth, from the New Testament which is comprised of the Magnificat (the Song of the Mary) and the Benedictus (the Prayer of Zacharias, the father of St. John the Baptist). Technically, however, the *Psalter* is not part of the lectionary system. Rather, it is the primary prayer book of the Church. The Psalms and Nine Odes form the superstructure around which the services of the daily office have been fashioned. Psalms are also used in the Eucharistic liturgies and other divine services. For more on the *Psalter* see the *Psalter of*

icon of Christ *par excellence*. It is kissed, carried in processions, placed on the holy Table, and reverenced with other honorific acts.

The Byzantine lectionary is based on four cycles—Sunday, Saturday, weekday, and festal—each of which is complete in itself but also dependent on the others. Of the four, the Sunday system of readings was developed first, followed closely by the cycle of Saturday, which in the East is regarded a liturgical day from at least the fourth century, if not earlier. The weekday series of readings was the last to emerge and came about as a result of the daily celebration of the Divine Liturgy, especially in monasteries.[550] The festal cycle is both old and new. It is open-ended, in continuous evolution, as new feasts—local or universal in nature—are added to the calendar. The lessons in the festal cycle are essentially a *lectio electa*—chosen for their appropriateness to the feast.

In the course of a given liturgical year, the length of which is determined by the date of Pascha, the Byzantine lectionary presents the New Testament almost in its entirety through the prescribed pericopes (περικοπαί) in the *Apostolos* and *Evangelion*. Significantly, the book of Revelation is not part of the lectionary system. Nonetheless, the faithful are encouraged to read and study it.[551] The Old Testament is read only during certain seasons and on a restricted number of feast days and only from a select number of books.[552]

With few exceptions, the present system of readings for Sundays, Saturdays, weekdays, and feast days was established in Constantinople well before the tenth century, as confirmed by the tenth-century *Typikon of the Great Church*,[553] which doubtlessly reflects earlier established practices, as

---

St. David, the Prophet King together with the Nine Odes (Boston 1974); and J.A. Lamb, *The Psalms in Christian Worship* (London 1962).

[550] By the late Middle Ages the Eucharist was celebrated daily in many monastic communities, even though daily communion is not practiced. Most monks commune weekly. Emperor Constantine IX (1042–1055) provided special subsidies for the daily celebration of the Eucharist at Hagia Sophia. Previously, it was celebrated only on Sundays, Saturdays, and feast days. The tenth-century Typikon of the Great Church does not give daily readings. See Petras, *Gospel Lectionary*, 123.

[551] See, for example, the chapter, "Grace and Judgment in the Book of Revelation," in Theodore G. Stylianopoulos, Encouraged by the Scriptures: Essays on Scripture, Interpretation, and Life (Brookline, MA 2011), 179–199.

[552] See Grisbrooke, "Word and Liturgy," 17–22; and Barrois, Scripture Readings, 18–19 and 70.

[553] The Typikon of the Great Church is one of the principal sources for the liturgy of Constantinople. It has been preserved in two manuscripts, Patmos 266 (end of ninth

happens with most, if not all, extant liturgical sources.[554]

According to Ioannis Fountoulis, the Sunday system of readings had received its basic form by the end of the fifth century.[555] From the writings of St. John Chrysostom (347–407) and others we learn that before the seventh century the Eucharistic liturgies of Constantinople had three readings, one from the Old Testament and two from the New Testament.[556] By the time of St. Germanos of Constantinople (+733), however, the Old Testament lection had already disappeared from the Eucharistic liturgies and from most other sacramental rites of the Byzantine Rite.[557] The readings were now limited to two, one from the *Apostolos* and the other from *Evangelion*.

Both the *Evangelion* and *Apostolos* contain two large collections of lessons totaling several hundred pericopes from the New Testament. The first, and by far the largest collection, is based on the movable cycle of feasts centered on Pascha. In earlier times, this collection was referred to as the *synaxarion*,[558] indicating the lessons in the *Apostolos* and *Evangelion* to be read at the Divine Liturgy during the liturgical year. It contains a set of prescribed readings for 333 of the 365/6 days of the year. The thirty-two missing days are Wednesday and Friday of Cheesefare week and the five

---

century) and Hagios Stavros 40 (ca 950). A critical edition of the latter has been published in two volumes by Juan Mateos, Le Typicon de la Grande Eglise, in the series Orientalia Christiana Anelecta, 165 (Rome 1962) and 166 (Rome 1963). Volume I contains the fixed feasts and volume II, the mobile feasts.

[554] For example, the incipit (ἀρχοτελεῖα) of the Saturday and Sunday Epistle and Gospel lessons, starting with Monday after Pentecost to the Sunday of Meatfare, are listed in Mateos, Le Typicon II, 140–167.

[555] Ioannis Fountoulis, «Σύστημα τῶν ἁγιογραφικῶν ἀναγνωσμάτων στὴν Ὀρθόδοξη λατρεία: πλεονεκτήματα, μειονεκτήματα, δυνατότητες βελτιώσεως,» in Ἱερουργεῖν τὸ Εὐαγγέλιον, 73.

[556] See, F. E. Brightman, *Eastern Liturgies* (Piscataway, NJ 2004—a facsimile reprint of the original edition titled, *Liturgies Eastern and Western*, volume 1, *Eastern Liturgies*, Oxford 1896), 527, 531.

[557] See Paul Meyendorff, *St. Germanus of Constantinople on the Divine Liturgy* (Crestwood, NY 1984), 20, 78–81. See also, Juan Mateos, *La Celebration de la Parole dans la Liturgie Byzantine* (Rome 1971), 131. The ancient Divine Liturgies of St. Iakovos (James) the Brother of the Lord (Antiochian–Jerusalem rite) and St. Mark the Apostle (Alexandrian rite) contain three and four readings respectively.

[558] See Gabriel Bertoniere, *The Sundays of Lent in the Triodion: the Sundays without a Commemoration* in the series *Orientalia Christiana Analecta*, 253 (Rome 1997), 200. The term synaxarion has several uses. It denotes a liturgical calendar designating the pericopes to be read at the Divine Liturgy. It is also used for a collection of brief hagiographical texts. In current usage, it refers mainly to the brief account of an event or life of a saint found in the Menaia, Triodion, and Pentecostarion after the kontakion.

weekdays of the six weeks of the Lenten period, on which the Divine Liturgy is not celebrated.

The second collection in both books is based on the fixed feasts, the *menologion*, which starts on September 1, the beginning of the civil and ecclesiastical year in Byzantium. The *menologion* also contains a set of two pericopes, one from the *Apostolos* and the other from the *Evangelion* for the Divine Liturgy of a given feast. Some feasts also have a Gospel lesson assigned to the Orthros. Other feasts also have three Old Testament readings assigned to the vespers.[559]

In addition to these two large collections, the *Evangelion* contains two other smaller sets. The first is comprised of the eleven Morning (Ἑωθινά) Gospel lessons assigned to the Sunday Orthros, each of which narrates an event related to the resurrection of Christ and his post-resurrection appearances and meals. These pericopes are read in rotation in a recurring cycle of eleven weeks.[560] The second consists of Gospel lessons assigned to sacramental rites and other services.

The Synaxarion Collection

The *Evangelion* begins with the Gospel of John on the Sunday of Pascha. The Gospel of John is read continuously, with few exceptions, every day up to and including the Sunday of Pentecost. During the same fifty-day period, the lessons of the *Apostolos* are from the Book of Acts. Professor Fountoulis suggests that the pairing of the Gospel of John with Acts during the Paschal season is an ancient tradition.[561]

---

[559] The vigils of Christmas and Theophany have seven and thirteen Old Testament lessons respectively, while the Paschal vigil has fifteen. In current practice only three of the assigned readings are read. On the use of the Old Testament see Eugen Pentiuc, *The Old Testament in Eastern Orthodox Tradition* (New York 2014). See also Miltiadis Konstantinou, «Ἡ χρήση καὶ ἡ ἑρμηνεία τῆς Παλαιᾶς Διαθήκης ἐν Χριστῷ καὶ εἰς τὴν Ἐκκλησίαν,» in *Ἱερουργεῖν τὸ Εὐαγγέλιον*, 93–116.

[560] For the history of the Eleven Morning Gospels see Panayiotis Skaltsis, *Λειτουργικὲς Μελέτες*, II (Thessaloniki 2009), 275–293. The recurring cycle of readings commences annually on the Sunday of All Saints and ends on the fifth Sunday of Lent the following year. During the Paschal season, from the Sunday of Thomas to the Sunday of Pentecost, the pericopes are not read in their regular sequence but are assigned to specific Sundays and feasts of the season.

[561] Fountoulis, «Σύστημα ἁγιογραφικῶν ἀναγνωσμάτων,» 73.

CHAPTER SEVEN: THE SUNDAY LUCAN PERICOPES

In fact, the pairing of the two lessons—Epistle and Gospel—is not accidental. Though it is not always immediately apparent, the Epistle lesson is meant to complement and reinforce the message of the Gospel pericope. This important detail should not be lost on the homilist who strives to explain the Scriptures and apply their teachings to everyday life.

From Monday after Pentecost the readings in the *Apostolos* are organized in five periods covering a span of thirty-five weeks, that is, from the day after Pentecost in one year to Palm Sunday of the following year. The sequence of readings begins with the Epistles of St. Paul.[562] They are followed by the universal epistles in their biblical order. Significantly however, the Saturday and Sunday pericopes in the *Apostolos* are taken exclusively from the Epistles of St. Paul, beginning with the Epistle to the Romans which is given special prominence. As a result, Sunday worshippers rarely, if ever, hear lessons from any of the seven universal epistles.

The Gospel lessons, on the other hand, are organized in four periods, starting with the Gospel of John, as noted initially. Lessons from the Gospel of Matthew follow and cover a period of seventeen weeks (or less) depending on the early or late date of Pascha from one year to the next.[563] The Matthean pericopes start on the day after Pentecost and end on the Friday after the Elevation of the Cross in mid-September.

The pericopes from the Gospel of Luke begin on the Monday immediately following the Sunday after the Elevation of the Cross and end at the beginning of the Triodion. More on the period of Luke will follow.

The Gospel of Mark is associated with Great Lent and is read on the Saturdays and Sundays of the Lenten period, except for the first Sunday. The Gospel of Mark (chapters 1—7) is also read on the weekdays from the twelfth to the sixteenth week of Matthew and on the weekdays from thirteenth to the seventeenth week of Luke (chapters 8—14). As with the other Gospels, the "missing" passages in the continuous reading—*lectio continua*—of Mark are found in the services of Holy Week, Pascha, and the menologion.

---

[562] The Epistle to Philemon is not included in the synaxarion section but is read on the occasion of the saint's feast day, November 22.
[563] The seventeenth Sunday of Matthew, for example, is never read in sequence, only if Pascha falls on March 22 (Julian calendar). Sometimes it is read before the beginning of the Triodion if there is an insufficient number of Sundays to cover the gap between the fifteenth Sunday of Luke which ends the Lucan cycle and the sixteenth Sunday of Luke which begins the Triodion.

Interestingly as suggested by Daniel Galadza, the ancient Jerusalem lectionary had a reverse order.[564] The Gospel of Luke, at least in part, was assigned to the Lenten season and Mark to the period now held by Luke. Gabriele Bertoniere has shown that the Gospel of Luke left a mark on the hymnic material of the Triodion, especially for the second, fourth, and fifth Sundays of Lent.[565] Hymnic and other data, though limited, indicate that the ancient Jerusalem lectionary assigned the parables of the Prodigal Son, the Good Samaritan, and the Rich Man and Lazaros to these three Sundays.[566]

The Gospel of Luke in the 'Evangelion'

In the received lectionary the Gospel of Luke is associated with the New Year, which by decree of the Roman Emperor Octavius Augustus (ca. 30 BC–AD 14) began on September 23. However, by the end of the fifth century (ca. 461) for practical reasons, the beginning of the New Year was transferred to September 1. The Orthodox Church to the present day celebrates the beginning of the New Year on September 1. Professor Fountoulis suggests that the Gospel of Luke was chosen for this period because of the four Gospels it alone provides us with a narrative account of the very beginnings of the earthly life of Jesus, starting with the accounts of the birth of John the Baptist and the Annunciation of Mary which herald the coming of the Messiah.[567]

The lectionary assigns seventeen Sunday lections to the Gospel of St. Luke.[568] The last two, the sixteenth and the seventeenth do not belong to the Lucan cycle as such but to the season of the Triodion which commences with the three week pre-Lenten season (Ἀπόκρεω) with its four Sundays. The first two of these Sundays are known traditionally as the *Sunday of the Publican and the Pharisee* and the *Sunday of the Prodigal Son* respectively,

---

[564] See Galadza, "The Jerusalem Lectionary and the Byzantine Rite," 192–193.
[565] See Bertoniere, *Sundays of Lent*.
[566] See Petras, *Gospel Lectionary*, 127–131 and Fountoulis, Ἑρμηνεία Εὐαγγελίων τῶν Κυριακῶν, 15.
[567] Fountoulis, Ἑρμηνεία Εὐαγγελίων τῶν Κυριακῶν, 12.
[568] See Theodoros Koumarianos, «Τὰ ἁγιογραφικὰ ἀναγνώσματα τῶν Κυριακῶν τῆς περιόδου Ματθαίου καὶ Λουκᾶ,» in Ἱερουργεῖν τὸ Εὐαγγέλιον, 237–259; and Ioannis M. Fountoulis, editor, Ἑρμηνεία Εὐαγγελίων τῶν Κυριακῶν, 1 (Thessaloniki 1972).

named after the two parables unique to the Gospel of Luke that are read at the Divine Liturgy on these two Sundays.

As with the other Gospels in the *Evangelion*, the entire Gospel of Luke is read annually through the pericopes in the synaxarion and menologion. The Lucan weekday cycle begins on Monday immediately following the Sunday after the Elevation of the Cross with the pericope, Luke 3:19–21.[569] The course reading of Luke continues to the end of the eleventh week, after which only on Saturdays and Sundays. From the twelfth week, as mentioned earlier, the weekday readings are from the Gospel of Mark. Interestingly, while Sunday is considered the first day of the week, in the *Evangelion* the numbering of the week begins with Monday and ends with Sunday.

The Sunday pericopes of Luke begin on the Sunday following the Sunday after the Elevation of the Cross. Since the feast of the Elevation (or Exaltation) of the Precious and Life-giving Cross is celebrated annually on September 14, the Sunday after the Elevation of the Cross occurs on September 15 at the earliest and September 21 at the latest. Hence, the First Sunday of Luke falls on September 22 at the earliest and September 28 at the latest.

The Sunday Pericopes of Luke

Of the fifteen Sunday pericopes in the Lucan period the material of seven are unique to the third Gospel and eight have parallel readings in Matthew and Mark.

The lesson for Sunday of the first week is from chapter 5:1–11 (cf. Matthew 4:18–22; Mark 1:16–20), which tells the story of the calling of the first disciples. The lesson for the second Sunday (6:31–36; cf. Matthew 5:38–48) contains Jesus' teaching on love for one's enemies. The third Sunday, Luke 7:11–16, narrates the miracle of the raising of the widow's son at Nain, an event unique to Luke. Two parables, that of the Sower (8:5–15; cf. Matthew 13:1–23; Mark 4:1–20) and of the rich man and Lazaros (16:19–31) are assigned to the fourth and fifth Sundays respectively, the

---

[569] Luke 1:1—3:28 are recorded in the *menologion* for the feasts of the: Nativity of St. John the Baptist (June 24) and the Annunciation of Mary (March 25); the Nativity (December 25), Circumcision (January 1), Theophany (January 6), and Meeting of our Lord (February 2).

latter parable being unique to Luke. The sixth Sunday tells the story of the healing of the Gerasene demoniac (8:26–39; cf. Matthew 8:28–34; Mark 5:1–20) and the seventh the healing of a woman with the flow of blood and the raising of Jairus' daughter (8:41–56; cf. Matthew 9:18–26; Mark 5:21–43). This is followed by two parables also unique to Luke, that of the Good Samaritan (10:25–37) on the eighth Sunday and that of the Rich Fool (12:16–21) on the ninth Sunday. The tenth Sunday tells the story of the healing of the crippled woman on the Sabbath and the ire it provoked in the ruler of the synagogue (13:10–17).[570] On the eleventh Sunday we read the Parable of the Great Banquet (14:16–24; cf. Matthew 22:1–14) and on the twelfth Sunday the story of the healing of the ten lepers (17:12–19), which is unique to Luke.[571] The thirteenth Sunday tells the story of the rich young man searching for eternal life (18:18–27; cf. Matt. 19:16–26; Mark 10:17–23), while the fourteenth Sunday provides another healing story, that of the blind beggar of Jericho (18:35–43; cf. Mark 10:46–52). The fifteenth Sunday tells another story unique to Luke, the conversion of Zacchaeus the tax collector (19:1–10).

Six of the Sunday Lucan pericopes recount miracles, five parables, two life-changing encounters, and two are didactic in the narrow sense, since, in one way or another, every pericope contains didactic material. Clearly, miracle stories and parables are given special prominence in both the Matthean and Lucan Sunday pericopes. The same is true for the Sunday pericopes in the periods of John and Mark. Moreover, of the fifteen Sunday Lucan pericopes, four have parallel readings in the Matthean Sunday cycle;[572] and two Sundays in the Matthean cycle have parallel readings in the period of Mark.[573]

In the tenth-century *Typikon of the Great Church*, the thirty-two (or thirty-three) Saturdays and Sundays that comprise the Matthean and Lucan periods are numbered consecutively together with the incipit (ἀρχοτε-

---

[570] A similar event is recorded in Matthew (12:9–14) and Mark (3:1–6).
[571] Matthew (8:2–4) and Mark (1:40–45) record the cleansing of a single leper.
[572] The parallel readings are: first Luke with second Matthew (4:18–23), the calling of the first disciples; sixth Luke with fifth Matthew (8:28–34; 9:1) the healing of the demoniac(s); eleventh Luke with fourteenth Matthew (22:2–14), the great banquet; and thirteenth Luke with twelfth Matthew (19:16–24), the young man in search of eternal life.
[573] Sixth Matthew (9:1–8) with Mark 2:1–12 (Second Sunday of Lent), healing of the paralytic; and tenth Matthew (17:14–23) with Mark 9:17–31 (Fourth Sunday of Lent), healing of a boy with an unclean spirit.

λεῖα) of the Epistle and Gospel readings assigned to each of these days.[574] A similar arrangement is found in other documents. However, in most, if not all, Greek Kanonia,[575] at least from the sixteenth century, if not earlier, the consecutive numbering of weeks is maintained only in the *Apostolos*. Emmanuel Glyzonios, for example, in 1587 published thirty-five Kanonia, one for each day in the five-week period within which the date of Pascha can fall in a given year.[576] In his Kanonia, the succession of readings of the *Apostolos* maintains the continuous numerical order. The four Gospel periods, however, are treated differently. The Sundays in the period of John have proper names reflecting the theme of the Gospel or the feast. The period of the Triodion is left out. The Sundays of Matthew and Luke are each numbered successively from the first to the fifteenth (or seventeenth) Sunday. Thus there is one number for the apostolic reading and another for the Gospel.

The Peculiar Features of the Sunday Lucan Pericopes

The Sunday pericopes of Luke are, in some ways, different from those of the other three periods. Some are sometimes suppressed while others are usually read out of sequence. And annually, the series is interrupted by another series of readings.

When a major feast, such as the Entry of the Theotokos (November 21), falls on a Sunday the Lucan pericope is suppressed in favor of the festal.[577] Of course, this occurs in the other periods as well but not with the same

---

[574] See Mateos, *Le Typicon*, 140–167. This arrangement, for example, is found in the Epistle and Gospel Readings section of the text of the *Divine Liturgy of St. John Chrysostom* published by the Holy Cross Orthodox Press (Brookline, MA 1985).

[575] A kanonion is the briefest form of a digest of the Typikon. It provides for each Sunday of a given year the tone of the week, the Gospel lesson of the Orthros, the Epistle and Gospel lesson for the Divine Liturgy and other pertinent information.

[576] The five week period in the Kanonia of Glyzonios is based on the Julian calendar, which was in force at the time. Hence, the first Kanonion is for March 22, the earliest possible day for Pascha and the final Kanonion is for April 25, the last possible day for Pascha. This five week period superimposed on the new calendar is April 4 to May 8, making up the thirteen day difference in the calendars. Until the calendar issue is resolved, Orthodox Churches celebrate Pascha on the same day, although it is not be the same date. On the date of Pascha see Alkiviadis Calivas, *Challenges and Opportunities: the Church in her Mission to the Word* (Brookline, MA), 125–142.

[577] In 2014 there were two occurrences: the feasts of Sts. Matthew (November 16) and Andrew (November 30).

frequency. For monastic communities and autocephalous churches that observe the monastic *Typikon of St. Savas* this is not a problem because both lessons are read in succession. However, the *Typikon of the Great Church of Christ* promulgated by the Ecumenical Patriarchate of Constantinople in 1888, which determines the liturgical practice of the churches under its jurisdiction or are influenced by it, limits the readings at the Divine Liturgy to only two, one each from the *Apostolos* and the *Evangelion*.

The Lucan Sunday series is also interrupted annually by the Feasts of Christmas and Theophany. Both feasts are preceded and succeeded by a Sunday before and after the feast, each of which has its own Epistle and Gospel lesson.[578]

Another feature in the Lucan series is related to the date of Pascha in a given year. For example, if only one Sunday separates the twelfth Sunday of Luke and the beginning of the Triodion we read the fifteenth of Luke on that Sunday. If there are two Sundays, we read the fifteenth of Luke and the seventeenth of Matthew (The Canaanite Woman: Matthew 15: 21–28) in that order. If there are more than two Sundays, we add, as needed, the fifteenth and the sixteenth of Matthew (Matthew 22: 35–46 and Matthew 25:14–30, respectively). A similar problem is related to the month of December. If December has five Sundays, we read the fourteenth of Luke (Luke 18:35–43) on the first Sunday (December 1, 2, or 3) and the thirteenth of Luke (18:18–27) on the preceding Sunday, the last in November. The reason for this will be explained below.

The more intriguing feature of the Lucan series are the six pericopes which the Typikon assigns to specific Sundays, thereby shifting their order. For example, in 2015 the pericope of the fourth Sunday will be read after the second and the pericope of the thirteenth Sunday after the ninth. In the paragraphs that follow I will explain the reason for this repositioning of the pericopes while providing a brief homiletical commentary for each to further elucidate the matter.

---

[578] These pericopes are: Sunday before Christmas (Hebrews 11:9–10, 32–40; Matthew 1:1–25) and after Christmas (Galatians 1:11–19; Matthew 2:13–23); Sunday before Theophany (2 Timothy 4:5–8; Mark 1:1–8) and after Theophany (Ephesians 4:7–13; Matthew 4:12–17).

The Six Mobile Lucan Sundays

The Fourth Sunday of Luke is the first of the pericopes assigned to a specific Sunday: the Sunday of the Holy Fathers of the Seventh Ecumenical Synod (787), which was originally celebrated on a fixed day, October 11,[579] and later assigned to the Sunday that falls between the eleventh and the seventeenth of October. In the Lucan sequence, the fourth Sunday, which recounts the Parable of the Sower and the Seed (Luke 8:5–15; cf. Matthew 13:3–23; Mark 4:2–20), usually falls close to the day of the feast. It was therefore assigned to it, especially because the parable, among other things, speaks to the ministry of the episcopate in particular and to the task of the clergy in general to proclaim the Gospel.

When his disciples questioned Jesus on the meaning of the Parable of the Sower, he revealed to them that they are recipients of the unique grace of knowing: "to you has been given to know the mysteries of the Kingdom of God; but for others they are in parables" (Luke 8:10). This saying was deemed applicable to the Fathers of the Church who are graced and inspired by the Holy Spirit to delve into the mysteries of the faith and to teach them to others (cf. 2 Timothy 2:2). The task of the episcopate, and by extension the presbyterate, is to sow the seed of faith in the hearts of people; and the seed they sow "is the word of God" (8:11), which has the power to transform lives. While all Orthodox Christians who share in the life of the Church are responsible to receive, know, live, and defend the Orthodox faith, the authority of the teaching ministry is vested primarily in the episcopate gathered in synod, and especially in ecumenical synod.

The parable also poses a challenge to the clergy who may become disillusioned with the seeming weak results of their labors and lament their perceived ineffectiveness. The world around them may scorn, ignore, or reject the message of salvation. But despite the apparent failures, distractions, and obstacles to belief—the disastrous results of the initial seeding in the parable—the harvest will be incredibly rich. The center of attention is not the sower but the seed, the word of God. While the word receives mixed reception, the will of God will not be thwarted. In every generation faith-

---

[579] See Juan Mateos, *Le Typicon*, I. 66. The Epistle and Gospel lessons assigned to the feast in this Typikon are Hebrews 13:7–16 and Matthew 5:14–18. There is no mention of transposing the feast to the nearest Sunday.

ful people will hear and accept the message of God's salvation and yield fruit, each equal to his ability: "thirtyfold and sixtyfold and a hundredfold" (Mark 4:8). Ultimately God will prevail and bring his promises to fruition. The task of the clergy, as servants of redemption, is to sow the seed with determination, courage, humble confidence, and joy.

The parable also challenges everyone who hears it, clergy and laity alike. All are asked to weigh carefully and honestly their willingness to receive and hold the word of God in their heart. The word of God, as with the seed, is distributed widely and richly but it produces fruit analogous to the soil (i.e., heart) that receives it. Hearing the word is easy but keeping it is difficult. Through his teachings and life Christ revealed the ultimate truths and meanings of life. He does not judge; he asks for faith. And faith is to accept and embody that which is revealed. The response becomes the judgment.

The Fifth Sunday of Luke recounts the Parable of the Rich Man and Lazaros (Luke 16:19–31), which the Typikon assigns to the Sunday that falls between October 30 and November 5. Why? In the late fifth century Europe experienced a cataclysmic event, a devastating eruption of Mt. Vesuvius, the catastrophic results of which were felt as far away as Constantinople. So profound was the experience of the volcanic dust that swept over the region that the event was remembered annually in Constantinople with a stational Divine Liturgy on November 6.[580] Eventually, the remembrance was transferred to the Sunday nearest to but before November 6. The Gospel lesson originally assigned to the commemoration—the parable of the rich man and Lazaros—was retained. This also explains why the readings suddenly jump to chapter sixteen, only to return back to the earlier chapters of the Gospel the next Sunday.

The parable was selected for this commemoration to raise the peoples' awareness of the fragility and unpredictability of life and the sudden reversal of fortunes that natural disasters, manmade calamities, and unexpected physical illnesses can bring to persons, families, and whole societies. Such misfortunes often lead to social upheavals and great personal tragedies. In the wake of such adversities, many, like Lazaros, find themselves helpless, standing humbly by the gate of the rich, desiring to be fed with the few morsels that fall from their table (16:21).

---

[580] See Mateos, *Le Typicon*, I, 90–92.

At first glance, the parable appears to be a judgment on wealth. The kingdom of God, however, is gained neither by wealth nor by poverty but by a humble and contrite heart that trusts in the ultimate goodness and power of God. The contrast is not between the rich and the poor but between the truly pious and the impious. The truly pious—both rich and poor—recognize and act on the plight of those whom the world neglects and despises: the suffering poor, the outcasts and dispossessed, and the sick. The impious are the self-absorbed—whether privileged or deprived—who will not produce the deeds of loving kindness that would indicate repentance from their self-centered callous way of life.[581] The fault of the rich man was not his wealth but his indifference to the commandments of God and the plight of his neighbor. The parable poses an urgent question: When the intruder death comes, in what condition will it find us? After death all deficiencies are irrevocable (16:26).

The parable makes it clear that when faith is deficient or lacking or when indifference, greed, or immorality abound, even the presence of a most wondrous event—a resurrection from the dead—will not move cold, calculating, narcissistic, and misguided hearts. "If they do not hear Moses and the prophets, neither will they be persuaded though one rise from the dead" (16:31).

A detail worthy of special attention is that the rich man of the parable is nameless. The poor man, however, is named *Lazaros*, which means "God is my help." By giving the poor man a name, Jesus clothes him with dignity and honor. The rich self-absorbed man, on the other hand, remains nameless, robbed of every mark of distinction, even the most basic, a name. We are all called to become a Lazaros, which is to say, persons who respond, even if imperfectly, to the continual activity of God in human affairs and are empowered by grace to meet the unexpected and abrupt changes in the circumstances of life with patience, courage, faith, and hope in the knowledge that God has provided something better for us (Hebrews 11:40).

The Tenth and Eleventh Sundays of Luke are always assigned to the first half of the month of December, including the two Sundays before the Nativity of Christ, during which Abraham, the Forefathers, and the Prophets of the Old Testament are commemorated as the Church prepares to cele-

---

[581] For a vivid portrayal of the ungodly see Wisdom of Solomon 2:1–24.

brate the feast of Christmas. The earliest day for the reading of the Tenth Sunday is December 4, followed by the Eleventh Sunday on December 11 and the Sunday before Christmas on December 18. The latest day for the tenth Sunday is December 10, followed by the Eleventh on December 17 and the Sunday before Christmas on December 24. The Tenth and Eleventh Sundays of Luke are always read in sequence.

The pericopes of these two Sundays are meant to serve as an introduction to Christmas. Their relationship to the feast, however, is not immediately apparent. The pericope of the Tenth Sunday (Luke 13: 10–17) narrates the healing of the crippled woman. The only apparent connection to the feast of Christmas is the reference to Abraham (13:16) and by extension to the patriarchs and prophets of the Old Testament who prophesied the advent of the Messiah. The pericope affords the homilist the opportunity to speak on the importance of the Old Testament in Orthodox worship, theology, and spirituality; highlight the patristic use of typology to interpret the Old Testament in the light of Christ; and remind people that Abraham is the father of all who imitate his faith (Romans 4:1–25). On another level, the healing of the crippled woman and every other healing miracle is connected to and reveals the mystery of the incarnation. When the Word became flesh, God graced human nature with intrinsic dignity and supreme value. In Christ the whole creation was fashioned anew. His miracles are the sign of God's kingdom already present in our midst. The story also allows the homilist to speak on the role of women in sacred history (13:16) and the Church and especially of the role of Mary the Theotokos.

The pericope of eleventh Sunday, which recounts the Parable of the Great Banquet (14:16–24), is assigned to the Sunday of the Forefathers (τῶν Προπατόρων). The parable emphasizes the universality of the Gospel and the joys of God's salvation in Christ. The Banquet stands as an image of God's kingdom to which all people are invited that they may share in the gifts and graces of God through a receptive, glad, and trusting heart. The unresponsive, self-absorbed, and self-assured people who are careless with the things of God forfeit their standing, "have me excused." But the will of God will not be thwarted by human irresponsibility. The shocking paradox is that the Banquet chamber will not remain empty; it will be filled by presumed sinners and outcasts (14:21–24); by those who heed God's call, repent, and do his will.

CHAPTER SEVEN: THE SUNDAY LUCAN PERICOPES   241

In the present age, between the two comings of Christ, the Divine Liturgy is for us the messianic banquet, the meal of the kingdom, the time and place in which the heavenly joins and mingles with the earthly. Weekly, we are invited to participate in this feast that we may encounter the Triune God who is present to his people to share his life with them—purifying, enlightening, perfecting, and deifying all who are careful with the things of God.

The Twelfth Sunday of Luke, which recounts the miracle of The Healing of the Ten Lepers (Luke 17:12–19), one of whom was a Samaritan, who alone returned to thank Jesus. This lesson is always read on the Sunday following the Sunday after Theophany, which is to say on January 14 at the earliest and January 20 at the latest. Through the healed Samaritan, a despised heretic and foreigner, the pericope serves to emphasize that salvation, wrought by God through the incarnation, passion, resurrection, and glorification of his only-begotten Son, is for all people. In Christ "there is neither Greek nor Jew, circumcised nor uncircumcised, barbarian, Scythian, slave nor free, Christ is all in all" (Colossians 3:11). The Samaritan understood this fully. In Christ he found more than healing; he found God's salvation and so he returned to him joyfully to give thanks.

The story highlights the virtue of gratitude—thanksgiving, εὐχαριστία. St. Paul exhorts us to "give thanks in all circumstances; for this is the will of God in Christ Jesus for you" (1 Thessalonians 5:18). Every Orthodox Christian by virtue of his faithful participation at the Divine Liturgy—the Eucharist—is gradually transformed by grace into a *Eucharistic person*, one who is able in everything to give thanks to God for blessings seen and unseen.

The Fifteenth Sunday of Luke recounts the story of Zacchaeus (Luke 19:1–10), which marks a turning point in the Gospel of Luke. From Jericho where Zacchaeus lived, Jesus and his disciples will go up to Jerusalem where the passion story will unfold. The story of Zacchaeus also marks a turning point in the liturgical year. The preceding joyful season of Christmas, Theophany, and the Meeting of the Lord will give way to the season of repentance. The conversion of Zacchaeus announces the Gospel of forgiveness and salvation: "The Son of Man came to seek and to save the lost" (Luke 19:10). The story of Zacchaeus—the story of a life-changing encounter—concludes the period of Luke. It brings us to the threshold of the Lenten season. As noted previously, the remaining two Lucan Sundays, the sixteenth and the seventeenth belong to the season of the Triodion.

A concluding remark: It is difficult to know precisely when, how, and by whom the Byzantine lectionary system was devised. We do know that the system was never discussed or approved by an Ecumenical Synod. Hence it is both proper and right for the Church in her collective wisdom to initiate a review of the Lectionary and to revise it accordingly to meet the needs and concerns of the Church in twenty-first century. Not only the times but the limitations within the inherited system require that we study it prayerfully, critique it reverently, and revise prudently what needs revision. [582]

---

[582] See Petras, Gospel Lectionary, 136-140, and Fountoulis, «Σύστημα ἁγιογραφικῶν ἀναγνωσμάτων,» 67–78. In 1960 the First Pan-Orthodox Conference on the Great and Holy Synod placed on the agenda of items for study and resolution the use of the Bible in worship and more specifically, the redistribution of the biblical pericopes and the wider use of the Old Testament in worship. See Ἡ Πρώτη Πανορθόδοξος Διάσκεψις: Κείμενα—Πρακτικά (Constantinople 1962), 117, 129.

8

LITURGY AND LANGUAGE[583]

Introduction

Several years ago, I was invited to deliver a brief paper on the theme, "Orthodox worship in the Diaspora: the Case of America," at a conference sponsored by the Theological School of the Aristotle University of Thessaloniki to commemorate the life and work of the late eminent scholar and professor of Liturgics, Ioannis M. Fountoulis.[584] In my report I noted the difficulty Orthodox people in America experience when celebrating and praying the Divine Liturgy together because of the absence of one official English translation of the service shared in common by all the churches. Indeed, within and among the several Orthodox churches there exist multiple translations. During the question and answer period that followed, a learned clergyman intervened and said, "The solution to your language problem in America is very simple. Stop using English. Keep to the original Greek."

Of course, the proposed solution is no solution for, at least, two reasons. It does not take into account the realities of parish life in America and it contradicts the very purpose for which the liturgy exists. In the first instance, most American born generations neither speak nor understand well

---

[583] It is a distinct honor to contribute to this celebratory volume honoring Archbishop Demetrios, the eminent biblical scholar, insightful theologian, gifted teacher, and wise hierarch–a cultured man of diverse gifts, astonishing intelligence, integrity and gentle strength, an exemplar of Christian virtue, an esteemed and valued colleague who has honored me with his friendship and love.

[584] As part of the proceedings, the faculty presented a festschrift in two volumes honoring the late Professor: *Γηθοσυνον Σεβασμα: Αντιδωρον τιμης και μνημης εις τον μακαριστον καθηγητην της Λειτουργικης Ιωαννην Μ. Φουντουλην (+2007)*, Panayiotis I. Skaltsis and Nikodemos A. Skrettas, eds., vol. I & II (Thessaloniki, 2013).

enough the mother tongue of their forebears, let alone the original Biblical and liturgical Greek. This poses a problem because the primary purpose of worship is to draw people into the mystery of salvation, into a joyful encounter with the Triune God.

In his first letter to the Corinthians St. Paul cautioned that liturgical speech or sound without intelligibility contributes little or nothing toward building up the Church and edifying the people's faith (1Cor. 14:6-11). When words, symbols and ritual actions—the building blocks of the liturgy—make little or no sense, the educative, formative, evocative, restorative, and transformative powers of the liturgy are crippled. Hence, to fulfill its purpose authentic worship must be reasonable and intelligible.

Some will claim that this is not absolute and will point by way of example to the experience of the emissaries of Prince Vladimir of Kiev, as recorded in the *Russian Primary Chronicle* (ca 987). On their visit to Constantinople, the emissaries participated in the liturgy at the cathedral church of Hagia Sophia. They described their experience with these glowing words: "And the Greeks led us to the edifice where they worship their God, and we knew not whether we were in heaven or on earth ...We only know that God dwells there among men, and that their service is fairer than the ceremonies of other nations. For, we cannot forget that beauty."

True enough! The setting of the liturgy (the splendor of the church, the icons, the chants, the ceremonials) has the power to impress the mind, inspire the soul, and touch the heart. However at some point, worshippers, according to the desire and ability of each, will want more; they will seek understanding. Before Sts. Cyril and Methodios set out to evangelize the Slavs, they devised an alphabet for them and translated the Scriptures and the liturgical texts so that they could hear, believe, and celebrate joyfully in their native tongue the mighty deeds of God (Acts 2:6. Cf. Acts 8:26-40).

Language manifests identity and affiliation. It links persons to a particular people or community. This is why most parishes of the Greek Orthodox Archdiocese of America (henceforth as GOA) have established Greek schools to teach the young, even if only rudimentarily, the language of their forebears and imbue them with the ideals of their ethnic and cultural heritage which, parenthetically, has been infused with the spirit of Orthodox Christianity.

But language is also a basic communicative tool, a means of conveying and sharing knowledge, information, ideas, and feelings through the use of sounds, signs, and gestures. Language by nature is both personal and interpersonal. It generates not only self awareness but an awareness of the other who also speaks and listens. Language creates dialogue and implies action.

Words and actions are basic elements of the Church's sacred rituals. Through these rites the Triune God is present to his people and the people come before him humbly in prayer and solemn feast. The liturgy is the meeting ground of heaven and earth; it is the place where people meet the self-giving of God (Matt. 18:20) and offer him due worship and praise. For this reason liturgical prayer must be intelligible, dignified, and appropriate for public recitation.

The spiritual life of the parish community and its individual members is centered chiefly on the weekly celebration of the Divine Liturgy, with its two essential foci: the ambo and the Table, which is to say, the proclamation of God's Word and the Eucharist. Through the Divine Liturgy we share truly in the reality of the Christ-event in a symbolic, iconic, and sacramental manner. Word and sacrament continuously nourish, renew, and advance the new life in Christ acquired through baptism and chrismation. But the power of the sacraments is not magical. It remains active and is perfected only when it is interiorized; when it becomes a state of being and a way of life "by hearing with faith" (Gal. 3:2; Cf. Rom. 10:17).

Liturgical Language in the Greek Orthodox Archdiocese of America

For the better part of the twentieth century the use of English in the liturgical services of most, if not all, Orthodox Churches in America was limited and in some circles frowned upon.[585] As a result, people with little

---

[585] Article II of the Constitution or Charter of the Archdiocese granted by the Ecumenical Patriarchate on January 1, 1931 and in effect until 1977, states that "the language of the Archdiocese is the Greek language." In fact, the founding Charter issued on August 11, 1922 states that the Archdiocese was established "for the benefit of Christians who dwell here, belong to the Holy Orthodox Eastern Church, and have as their liturgical language, either exclusively or principally, the Greek language, which the Holy Gospels and other books of the New Testament were written in" (article1). The two subsequent Charters issued on November 29, 1977 and January 18, 2003 do not mention a liturgical language and are more inclusive regarding membership in the Archdiocese. For these and other documents, see Paul G. Manolis, *The History of the Greek Church in America: in Acts and Documents*,

or no knowledge of Greek did not have direct or full access to the riches of the Orthodox liturgy and were therefore largely deprived of its formative and transformative powers.

Catechetical instruction, however, in most places was conducted in English and a few translations of liturgical texts were available to those who sought them for personal edification or to follow the divine services with a book in hand.[586]

ARCHBISHOP MICHAEL'S PIONEERING EFFORTS

Archbishop Michael (+1958) was the first to officially introduce limited use of English in the Divine Liturgy, allowing for the reading of the Scripture lessons in both Greek and English and for the recitation of the Creed and the Lord's Prayer in both languages.[587] He also endorsed and promoted preaching in both languages, a practice already in place at parishes served by bilingual clergy. In addition, he took action to make available a bilingual text of the Divine Liturgy that carried the imprimatur of the Archdiocese.

In June 1950 he directed Holy Cross Orthodox Press (henceforth as HCOP) to reproduce the third edition of the bilingual text of the Divine Liturgy published by the Faith Press in London.[588] He wrote the following introductory statement, which appears in the inside cover of the book.

---

vol. I, II, and III (Berkley, CA, 2003). See also, *Charters of the Greek Orthodox Archdiocese of America* (New York, 2003). For a brief history of the Charters, see Lewis J. Patsavos, "History of the Charters," in *History of the Greek Orthodox Church in America*, Miltiades B. Efthimiou and George A. Christopoulos, eds. (New York, 1984), 67-92.

[586] An early English translation of the sacred services for liturgical use was published by Isabel Florence Hapgood (1851-1928), the American ecumenist, writer and translator especially of Russian and French texts: *Service Book of the Holy Orthodox Catholic Apostolic Church* (New York, 1906 and 1922). The earliest English translation of major parts of the Euchologion was produced by John Glen King, *The Rites and Ceremonies of the Greek Church in Russia: Containing an account of its doctrine, worship, and discipline* (London, 1772, and reproduced in 1970 by AMS Press of New York).

[587] The same ruling was affirmed by the 17th Clergy-Laity Congress held in Denver, CO in 1964 and approved by the Ecumenical Patriarchate. See the introductory letter of Archbishop Iakovos (Protocol Number 148)), dated October 9, 1970 in *DECISIONS of the 20th Clergy-Laity Congress of the Greek Orthodox Archdiocese of North and South America* (New York, 1970). A summary note (L21EC0012) referring to the decision of the 17th Congress, says that prayers may also be read in Greek and English at marriages, baptisms, and funerals.

[588] *The Divine Liturgy of St. John Chrysostom—The Greek text with a rendering in English* (Brookline, MA 1950). The publisher is listed as, The Greek Orthodox Theological Institute Press, the forerunner of HCOP. Holy Cross Orthodox School of Theology was founded in 1937 and was known also as The Greek Orthodox Theological Institute of Holy Cross.

It is stated that the present publication is a photocopy reprint of the one used in the Greek Orthodox Church of St. Sophia in London.[589] It is produced with special permission given to the Greek Archdiocese of America. It will be used in all the holy churches of the Archdiocese as the only publication that bears its imprimatur. All Greek Orthodox are urged to have the text in hand and follow the Divine Liturgy from it. Most especially the young people are exhorted to do this, since it is primarily for them that the Archdiocese proceeded to produce the present edition. We hope wholeheartedly that with the help of this publication the Divine Liturgy will be understood by all for the spiritual benefit of all.

From the Archbishop's Keynote Address at the Clergy-Laity Congress held in St. Louis, MO on November 30, 1950 we learn that the press had produced 30,000 copies for distribution to the parishes. Each copy was to be sold for one dollar.[590] To my knowledge, this small, pocket size book was not reproduced again by the Archdiocese.

ARCHBISHOP IAKOVOS AND THE NEW REALITIES

Although English was used sparingly in the services through the 1960's and early 1970's, the need for increased use of English and the preparation of English translations of the sacred services was widely recognized. To fill this need, some enterprising individuals began to produce and publish English translations of the sacred services often with the encouragement of Archbishop Iakovos, even though official authorization of their work was withheld.[591]

---

[589] As a young priest, Archbishop Michael served at the Cathedral of St. Sophia in London, while pursuing graduate studies in England. On the life and work of Archbishop Michael see Makarios Niakaros, *Ο Αρχιεπισκοπος Αμερικης Μιχαηλ Κωνσταντινιδης: Η συμβολη του στην Εκκλησια, στην θεολογια, και στον διαλογο με τον συγχρονο κοσμο* (Thessaloniki, 2017).

[590] For the address of Archbishop Michael see *Encyclicals and Documents of the Greek Orthodox Archdiocese of North and South America*, Demetrios J. Constantelos, ed. (Patriarchal Institute for Patristic Studies: Thessaloniki, 1976), 505.

[591] Among the several bilingual texts that were produced and widely distributed are those of Fr. George Mastrantonis, *The Divine Liturgy of St. John Chrysostom of the Eastern Orthodox Church* (St. Louis, MO 1966); Fr. George Papadeas, *The Divine Liturgy of St. John Chrysostom* (New York 1968 and Daytona FL. 1981); and *The Divine Liturgy & The Sunday Gospels* published in 1968 by Ecumenical Publications and dedicated to the 1968 Clergy-Laity Congress. Also important were the two bilingual editions of the Mikron Euchologion published by Frs. N. Michael Vaporis and Evagoras Constantinidis. Also valuable was the bilingual edition of the services of Holy Week and Pascha compiled and published by Fr. George Papadeas, followed later by those of Frs. N. Michael Vaporis and Leonidas Contos of the Narthex Press.

In his Keynote Address, "Toward the Decade 1970-1980," delivered at the Clergy-Laity Congress in New York (June 28-July 4, 1970), Archbishop Iakovos spoke boldly about the challenges confronting the Church at the dawn of a new decade. One such concern, he noted, was the need for liturgical reform and conscientious religious living in a bilingual Archdiocese, which at the time encompassed North and South America, an Archdiocese whose people spoke not only Greek but also English, Spanish, French, and Portuguese.[592] He commented on the concerns of the American-born generations and the need to cultivate among the people a conscientious Orthodox Christian way of life. He also recognized the need for adequate English translations of the divine services and recommended to the Congress the draft translation of the Divine Liturgy of St. John Chrysostom (henceforth as CHR), which Fr. Nicon D. Patrinacos had prepared at his direction. (Fr. Patrinacos published his translation in 1974 without the official authorization of the Archdiocese).[593] At the Congress the Archbishop also announced the appointment of a Liturgical Commission under the chairmanship of Bishop Timotheos. The Commission was charged to study various liturgical matters and prepare an official translation of the Divine Liturgy and other services based on the work of Fr. Patrinacos.[594]

The same Congress created both history and turmoil when the delegates adopted the following resolution of the Liturgical Committee:

> At the outset it should be clearly understood that nothing in this report is to be interpreted as a repudiation or denial of the Greek language in the ecclesiastical services performed in the Greek Orthodox Archdiocese of North and South America. Officially, since the Clergy-Laity Congress held in Denver (1964) there is authorization for only the most limited use of languages other than Greek in ecclesiastical services. The Committee in its deliberations, however, ascertained that languages other than Greek are in fact being used in various parishes throughout the Archdiocesan Districts to meet

---

[592] I am grateful to Fr. Joachim Cotsonis, Librarian of Hellenic College/Holy, for providing me with a copy of this address and other pertinent material on file in the archives of the Library.

[593] Nicon D. Patrinacos, *The Orthodox Liturgy: The Greek text with a completely new translation followed by notes on the text, the Sunday Gospel and Apostolic readings* (Garwood, NJ 1974).

[594] See *Encyclicals and Documents*, 758-763. Commission members included Frs. Nicon Patrinacos, Stanley Harakas, Alkiviadis Calivas, and Dr. George Bebis. Periodically, the Commission was brought to strength by new appointments.

specific local situations. The committee determined that the use of languages other than Greek has occurred because of the needs of the communicants and the need to make Greek Orthodoxy relevant to 20th Century man. Therefore, the committee respectfully reports as follows: WHEREAS, language is an indispensable tool for the teaching and understanding and practice of the faith; WHEREAS, the people of this Archdiocese speak a number of languages: Greek, English, Spanish, French, or Portuguese; WHEREAS, we conceive it important and in the Orthodox tradition that the teaching, liturgy and mysteries of the Church be transmitted to the people in their own vernacular language; BE IT RESOLVED that this Congress recommends that the Archdiocese permit the use of the vernacular language as needed in church services in accordance with the judgment of the parish priest in consultation with his bishop. BE IT FURTHER RESOLVED that in those instances of need for further consultation the matter shall be referred to the Archbishop.[595]

For the delegates the proposed resolution was both reasonable and realistic. For others, however, it became a bone of contention and sparked a clash of cultural attitudes. It was met with fierce opposition and caused a crisis in many parishes, due primarily to the misrepresentation and mischaracterization of the facts by the two Greek daily newspapers in New York that claimed the Greek language was being abolished from the Church.[596]

To allay fears, Archbishop Iakovos issued an encyclical on September 21, 1970 stating: "The Holy Synod of the Ecumenical Patriarchate...found the furor which was created unfounded, but in order...to satisfy those who in good faith had expressed their concern, determined that it would be appropriate to emphasize the first two articles of the Constitution, which was granted in 1931...By calling to mind the second article of the Constitution, it is emphasized that the language of the Greek Orthodox Archdiocese of North and South America is Greek. In this regard, however, the Holy Synod, having in mind the bilingual character of the constituency, and the decision regarding language, taken at the 17th biennial Clergy-Laity Congress, Denver, Colorado, 1964, directs the Archdiocese, in special circumstances, ac-

---

[595] See *DECISIONS*, 55-56. Copies of this bilingual text are kept in the archives of the Archdiocese and the Library at Hellenic College/Holy Cross.

[596] In 1965 the US Congress passed new immigration laws. As a result, thousands of Greek immigrants began to pour into the country and populate many of the urban parishes, often injecting new life in them. For the new immigrants, the parish became the life-line for their ethnic and cultural identity.

cording to its best judgment, and where it feels the need exists, to permit the partial use of English in the Divine Liturgy as well as in the sacraments."[597]

Two years later, in 1972, in his Keynote Address at the 21st Biennial Clergy-Laity Congress, titled "Speak the Truth in Love," Archbishop Iakovos returned to the language issue saying, "How essential truth and love are to our ecclesiastical life you know well. For a proper appreciation of both, you need only recall the deplorable aftermath to our last Congress... Because what really happened two years ago in New York...was that certain persons did violence to truth and love as expressions of Greek Orthodoxy, at the very time when its influence was on the rise. It was not the language of the Greeks that was threatened in that Congress, but the language of God: the language of truth and love," (2-3).[598]

Despite the fears of some, the GOA remains bilingual to this day, even as the use of English has increased through the years in response to local needs.

A SECOND AUTHORIZED TRANSLATION

When the Divine Liturgy book authorized by Archbishop Michael was no longer in circulation, new translations by well-intentioned clergy began to fill the void. However, none of these texts were officially authorized by the Archdiocese. For more than two decades the GOA was without an official text. This was corrected in 1976 when the translation of the aforementioned Liturgical Commission was published with the approval of the Archdiocese: "Authorized for devotional and liturgical use by worshippers within the Greek Orthodox Archdiocese of the Americas."[599]

The Commission viewed its text as "a collective endeavor [that] includes a number of varying attitudes and techniques of interpreting the original Greek and of expressing it by modern linguistic media into the English language."[600] The new text included only the most basic rubrics for the priest

---

[597] See *Encyclicals and Documents*, 756-757.
[598] Copies of the Keynote Address are on file at the Archdiocese and the Library of Hellenic College/Holy Cross.
[599] The imprimatur was issued by Archbishop Iakovos. See *The Orthodox Liturgy: The Greek text of the Ecumenical Patriarchate with a translation into English by the Liturgical Commission of the Greek Orthodox Archdiocese of North and South America, authorized to be used within the Greek Orthodox Church of the Americas* (Garwood, NJ, 1976), 3. Henceforth noted as *The Orthodox Liturgy (LC)*.
[600] Ibid. 5

given that it was prepared mainly for use by the people. The foundational draft from which the Commission drew inspiration and developed its translation was the text prepared and published in 1974 by Fr. Patrinacos.[601] From what I know, the 1976 text of the Commission was not reprinted.

Multiple English Translations

According to one account, by the nineteen-nineties there were over forty translations of the divine services circulating within the Orthodox churches in America, the literary quality and accuracy of which were uneven. Some were the work of individuals while others the product of committees. Only a few bore an official imprimatur.[602] One or more of these many translations found their way into the sanctuaries and pews of parish churches throughout the United States.

By the 1980s most of the Orthodox churches in America had adopted at least one official English translation of the Divine Liturgy which the clergy were expected to use according to the rules set forth by each jurisdiction. The GOA constituted an exception, in the sense that two of its official texts (1950 and 1976) were no longer in print. This was remedied only recently with the publication of a new bilingual text approved by Archbishop Demetrios and the Holy Eparchial Synod of the GOA. The translation was produced by a special translation committee appointed by Archbishop Demetrios. An important predecessor to the new translation was produced by the faculty of Holy Cross.

---

[601] The members of the Commission who saw the work completed as regards both to theological concepts and linguistic rendering were Frs. Nicon Patrinacos, Robert Stephanopoulos, Anthony Coniaris, George Nicozisin, Alkiviadis Calivas, and Dr. George Bebis. Advice and constructive suggestions were received from Fr. Stanley Harakas, Fr. Theodore Stylianopoulos, Dr. Constantine Trypanis, and Dr. Deno Geannacoplos. See, *The Orthodox Liturgy (LC)*, 6-7.

[602] See for example, *The Divine Liturgy according to St. John Chrysostom with appendices* (New York, 1967), approved by the Great Council of Bishops of the Russian Orthodox Greek Catholic Church of America (now known as the Orthodox Church in America); *Service Book of the Holy Eastern Orthodox Catholic and Apostolic Church according to the use of the Antiochian Orthodox Christian Archdiocese of New York and All North America* (1971) and *The Liturgikon: The Book of divine services for the priest and deacon* (New York, 1989) authorized by the Antiochian Archdiocese; *Holy Liturgy for Orthodox Christians* (Romanian Episcopate—Detroit, MI 1975); and *The Divine Liturgy of St. John Chrysostom* (Serbian Orthodox Church, 1990).

THE HOLY CROSS FACULTY TRANSLATION

In the spring of 1982 the faculty of Holy Cross dedicated several of its monthly faculty colloquia to the study of English translations of CHR then in circulation. As result of this study, the faculty decided to create a new English translation based on contemporary biblical, liturgical, historical, and patristic scholarship. The faculty consulted several existing texts but used the 1976 translation of the Liturgical Commission as its foundational working document, given that faculty members had served on the Commission.

The project began with a new translation of the Nicene-Constantinopolitan Creed. Work on the entire text of CHR followed. The aim of the translators was to produce a translation that would be faithful to the meaning of the original Greek but read and sound as an original English text.[603] Needless to say, the faculty received the blessings of Archbishop Iakovos to proceed with the project.

Although an official set of principles was not developed, the translators drew lessons from the work of other Orthodox theologians and litterateurs and the efforts of Roman Catholics who were translating liturgical texts following the Second Vatican Council.[604] Essentially, the faculty sought to preserve faithfully the meaning but not necessarily the form of the original Greek text with its complex syntax and sentence structure. The goal was to produce an accurate, clear, and elegant text in contemporary American English, one that could stir the heart and illumine the mind; a text that could become a living prayer for both the clergy and the people.[605] Of course, the success or failure of the endeavor would be measured and judged by others. The translators offered their text "as a working translation with the prayer

---

[603] See *The Divine Liturgy of Saint John Chrysostom: a new translation by members of the faculty of Hellenic College/Holy Cross Greek Orthodox School of Theology* (Brookline, MA 1985), xi.

[604] For a brief account of the translation of Roman Catholic liturgical texts, see Kevin .D. Magas, "Issues in Eucharistic Praying: Translating the Roman Canon," in *Worship*, 89:6 (November 2015), 482-505. For a discussion on the difficulties a translator of liturgical texts faces with many examples, see Robert Taft, "On Translating Liturgically," in *Logos: A Journal of Eastern Christian Studies*. 39:2-4 (1998), 155-184. (The entire volume is dedicated to liturgical translation).

[605] According to Archbishop Iakovos the task of the translator is to "render the true meaning, theology, or generally the spiritual ideal of the original text even in a more analytical manner; then the translator becomes a contributor toward spiritual rebirth," in T*oward the Decade 1970-1980*, 10.

CHAPTER EIGHT: LITURGY AND LANGUAGE   253

and hope that its use in [the] churches will result in further improvements and refinements so that in the very near future we will share one English translation as we now do the same Greek text."[606]

Translating liturgical texts is both a task and an art. It is a search for meanings and context; an act of interpreting and conveying meanings with accuracy and clarity.[607] As Fr. Robert Taft puts it, "One translates not words but meaning...A so-called literal translation is not a translation at all, but a distortion of the recipient language to conform to the donor language."[608] Yet, words matter. Meanings have to be transmitted accurately and appropriately with words that are accessible, comprehensible, and dignified according to the requirements of the recipient language, which in our case is American English.

Not all faculty members saw the project to completion but all participated in its development through their valuable advice and constructive suggestions, including Archbishop Demetrios, then Bishop of Vresthena and Professor of Biblical Studies and Christian Origins at Holy Cross.[609] A working draft was widely distributed for field testing, review, and comments.[610] The final text was published in 1985 in a bilingual edition in several forms by HCOP,[611] anticipating the official approval of the Holy Eparchial Synod of the Archdiocese.[612]

The faculty translation, as it came to be known, gained wide acceptance and circulation, even though it had not received the imprimatur of the

---

[606] *Divine Liturgy—faculty translation*, xi.
[607] See Ephrem Lash, "Translating Liturgy," in *Logos*, 39:2-4 (1998), 191-195.
[608] Taft, "On Translating Liturgically," 167.
[609] *Divine Liturgy—faculty translation*, xi-xii. "The principal translators were: Fathers Alkiviadis Calivas, Theodore Stylianopoulos, N. Michael Vaporis, Thomas FitzGerald, and Peter Chamberas. Offering important contributions were: Fr. George Papademetriou and Dr. Athan Anagnostopoulos. Assisting at various times were Bishop Demetrios Trakatellis, Dr. George Bebis, Professor Ioanna Clarke, Fr. Stanley Harakas, Dr. Lewis Patsavos, Fr. John Travis, and Dr. Penelope Tzougros."
[610] In addition to the hierarchs of the GOA, the text was reviewed by Bishop Kallistos Ware of Diokleia who provided valuable suggestions. It was also sent to several other theologians, litterateurs, and priests. For the list of reviewers, see *Divine Liturgy–faculty translation*, xii.
[611] A priest's bilingual edition was produced together with a bilingual pew edition. The latter includes an introduction to the Divine Liturgy (history and theological meaning), a set of thanksgiving prayers for Holy Communion, the Epistle and Gospel Lessons of the Sunday lectionary, memorial services for the dead, and the eight Sunday resurrectional apolytikia.
[612] *Divine Liturgy–faculty translation*, xi.

Archdiocese.[613] An endorsement of the text came in 1989 in the form of a recommendation from Archbishop Iakovos who wrote the prologue to the third edition. He makes the following statement: "This prologue is not a prologue to the Divine Liturgy per se, but a prologue to its third edition. And it is a prologue which I write with a feeling of many thanks to the Faculty of our Hellenic College/Holy Cross Greek Orthodox School of Theology whose faith, industry, and unselfishness produced this superb translation ... I write this prologue to the present edition for yet another reason, perhaps more important reason. Since this third edition is addressed to you my beloved co-celebrants, the Bishops and Priests of our Archdiocese. I have no doubt that this volume will be acquired and used by all people as well as by other Orthodox clergymen, theologians, and students of the Divine Liturgy..."[614]

THE TRANSLATION OF THE SCOBA LITURGICAL COMMISSION

In July 1991 representatives of Holy Cross, St. Vladimir's Seminary, and the Antiochian Archdiocese met in New York City to discuss the production of a common translation of CHR. It was agreed that the Holy Cross translation would be used as the foundational draft. It was further agreed that the project would be placed under the authority and supervision of the Standing Conference of Canonical Orthodox Bishops in America (SCOBA), the forerunner of today's Assembly of Canonical Orthodox Bishops of the United States of America.[615]

On October 29, 1991 Archbishop Iakovos, the chairman of SCOBA together with the Executive Committee appointed a special twelve member Liturgical Commission to undertake the task.[616] Over the course of three years the committee studied the texts in use by the various jurisdictions,

---

[613] Conceivably, the Synod was reluctant to grant an imprimatur because the translation left out parts of CHR that had fallen into disuse in parish usage.

[614] *Divine Liturgy–faculty translation* (third edition), ix.

[615] I am grateful to Ms. Nikie Calles, Director of Archives of the GOA, for providing me with copies of several documents from the SCOBA Liturgical Commission files (143-LC) and other useful material in the archives of the Archdiocese.

[616] Committee members included: the Rt. Rev. Basil Essey, Frs. Leonidas Contos, Alexander Golitzin, Edward Hughes, James Jorgenson, Michel Najim, Jack Sparks, Theodore Stylianopoulos, N. Michael Vaporis, and Alkiviadis Calivas, Dr. Paul Meyendorff, and Mr. Charles Ajalat, Esq., who acted as the coordinator. At different times others joined the Commission and offered their expertise.

reflected upon the original Greek, consulted the received Slavonic, Rumanian, and Arabic texts, and drew on biblical, patristic, and liturgical sources for its work. The objective of the committee was to produce a translation that would reflect contemporary English and word order characterized by accuracy of expression and clarity.

The Commission circulated a draft to a large group of hierarchs, priests, musicians, and scholars for review and suggestions, some of which were negative primarily because the text was in contemporary English. The Commission completed its work in the summer of 1994 and submitted the final text to the secretariat of SCOBA. The text included three sets of limited rubrics reflecting Greek, Slavonic, and Arabic usages.

Sadly however, the text was set aside and then forgotten due to the disturbance that followed the Conference of Canonical Orthodox Bishops convened at the Antiochian Village in Ligonier, PA on November 30-Decemeber 2, 1994.[617]

The translation remains hidden in the files of SCOBA and of the members of the Commission. Hopefully, the Assembly of Canonical Orthodox Bishops of the United States of America, of which Archbishop Demetrios is chairman, will recover this valuable text and direct its Committee on the Liturgy to study it carefully while consulting more recent translations. An organically united Orthodox Church in America, as I have noted elsewhere, will be obliged at some point to authorize the publication of its own official texts of the divine services adapted to the requirements and realities of our time, culture, and society and based on sound theological reflection and liturgical scholarship.[618] The day will come when all Orthodox Christians in America will share a common English translation of the sacred services as a concrete manifestation of their unity.

NARTHEX PRESS EDITIONS

In 1994 Narthex Press of Northridge, CA under the supervision of Fr. Spencer Kezios began producing a series of bilingual service books. In 1996 Narthex Press published The Liturgikon, an abbreviated bilingual version of the Greek Ιερατικον. *The Liturgikon*, its companion edition, *The Divine Liturgy*,

---

[617] On the Conference, see *A New Era Begins: Proceedings of the 1994 Conference of Orthodox Bishops in Ligonier, PA*, George Bedrin and Philip Tamoush, eds. (Ligonier, PA 1994).
[618] See Alkiviadis C. Calivas, *Aspects of Orthodox Worship* (Brookline, MA, 2003), 115.

and several other books of Narthex Press became popular among the clergy of the GOA and beyond. Fr. Leonidas Contos was the principal translator of the Divine Liturgies and sacraments published by Narthex Press.

Archbishop Demetrios and the New Translation of the Greek Orthodox Archdiocese

A BRIEF HISTORY

Prompted by Archbishop Demetrios, the Holy Eparchial Synod of the GOA "for reasons of uniformity in worship throughout the Holy Archdiocese,"[619] embarked on an ambitious program: the creation of a new authorized translation of the divine services starting with CHR. Initially, the project began with the preparation of a new translation of the Nicene-Constantinopolitan Creed by the Holy Eparchial Synod. The translation was finalized and distributed to the parishes in 2004 bearing the imprimatur of the Synod.[620]

Subsequently, Archbishop Demetrios appointed a committee to develop a complete Greek language text of CHR with extensive rubrics. The committee was chaired by Metropolitan Methodios of Boston.[621] The Greek text "was developed [by] studying various Greek editions of the Liturgy and the scholarship on the manuscripts, in order to create a coherent Greek language text for use in America. This text was approved by the Ecumenical Patriarchate in 2011 and became the basis for the translation of [the] new English text."[622]

Afterward, Archbishop Demetrios, in concert with the Holy Eparchial Synod, established a special committee to produce the new authorized translation of CHR. This committee also functioned under the chairmanship of Metropolitan Methodios. The names of the members of the committee, however, have not been made public.

---

[619] See "Message from His Eminence Archbishop Demetrios," in *The Liturgy of St. John Chrysostom: Priest Edition* (Brookline, MA 2015), viii. Henceforth noted as *CHR: Priest Edition*.

[620] See the four-page laminated folder produced by the Archdiocese, with the Creed and the Lord's Prayer in Greek and English.

[621] Committee members included Fr. Philip Zymaris, Fr. Alkiviadis Calivas, and Archdeacon Panteleimon Papadopoulos. Not all recommendations of the committee were adopted in the final text.

[622] See *CHR: Priest Edition*, x.

The Committee's draft was reviewed by the Archbishop, the members of the Eparchial Synod, and a group of select clergy of the Archdiocese.[623] The final version, containing the original Greek text and the new English translation with rubrics and notes, was submitted to the Ecumenical Patriarchate for approval. In a letter to Archbishop Demetrios dated October 30, 2014, His All Holiness Patriarch Bartholomew conveyed the joy and blessings of the Mother Church, saying in part, "the labor-intensive and most careful and studious translation...by the special committee of the Holy Eparchial Synod...was thoroughly examined and studied after having been submitted to our Ecumenical Patriarchate. It was judged by our Modesty and the Holy and Sacred Synod as complete and well done from every aspect, rending fully and authentically in [English] the original Greek text."[624]

The copyright for the new bilingual text was obtained in 2015. It was published and distributed by HCOP in early 2016. The first edition with its "considerable number of liturgical rubrics,"[625] was published exclusively for the clergy, as indicated by the sub-title, *Priest Edition*. A bilingual pew edition followed shortly thereafter.

THE NEW TRANSLATION: ITS PURPOSE AND GOALS

According to Archbishop Demetrios, the new translation "builds upon the strengths of earlier translations and remedies certain deficiencies existing in them." Its goal, according to the Archbishop, is to nurture and enrich the minds and souls of worshippers, both priests and laypeople. In a message addressed to the clergy he writes, "As you offer up words of praise and supplications through this new translation, you will cultivate and enrich the minds and souls of the believers, leading them into the deeper meaning of the awesome and bloodless Sacrifice of the Eucharist. You will lead them from prayer to communion with God, in the knowledge that through the receiving of the Lord's Body and Blood we are united with Him."[626]

Expanding on the Archbishop's words, the translators note that the objective of the new text is to "bring more coherence to the liturgical life of the parishes of [the] Archdiocese. For decades well-meaning clergy and pub-

---

[623] Ibid. x
[624] Ibid. vi-vii.
[625] Ibid. viii.
[626] Ibid. viii.

lishers have published their own translations of liturgical texts and hymns, filling an important need of our parishes. While often excellent work, the variety made joint celebrations of the Liturgy very challenging...In addition most of the publications did not offer rubrics for the celebrants. This too created confusion...For these reasons, the Eparchial Synod appointed a committee...to develop a new translation and text with rubrics for celebrants for the Archdiocese of America."[627]

The translation committee informs the reader that its work "included in-depth comparisons with existing translations."[628] Although these texts are not identified, I believe the Holy Cross faculty translation was probably the foundational working draft of the committee because the similarities between the two texts are striking. The differences are equally noticeable. Let me mention a few: revisions in syntax and word order; instances of literal equivalency;[629] a liking for Latin-root words,[630] and a preference for the older, more common translation of the Greek word ανθρωπος and its cognates that are scattered throughout the liturgical books.[631]

There are also some inconsistencies in the new text. For example, the term αναιμακτος θυσια is sometimes translated as "bloodless sacrifice(s)" and other times as "a sacrifice without the shedding of blood," the latter was used first in the faculty text. The τρισαγιος υμνος is rendered as Trisagion Hymn and as thrice-holy hymn. The word θυσιαστηριον is consistently translated as "Altar of sacrifice," which seems to be redundant since an altar is the place on which a sacrifice is offered. While most previous translations retain uniformity in the structure of petitions in the same litany, as in the original Greek, the new "Litany of Completion" does not; and inexplicably, a connective "and" has been inserted before the last petition in the series. In addition, the use of unfamiliar or difficult words, like impassibly and

---

[627] Ibid. x.
[628] Ibid. x.
[629] Compare, for example, the Prayer of the Third Antiphon in the two texts.
[630] For example, celestial and terrestrial over heavenly and earthly, carnal over sinful or worldly, remission of sins over forgiveness of sins, impassibly and immutably over without change or alteration.
[631] The faculty translation sought to use gender-inclusive language when translating the word ανθρωπος (human being) and its cognates: "For You are a loving God" over "For You, O God, love mankind," "for us" instead of "for us men," "you have created man and woman in Your image and likeness" in place of "You have created man in your image..." The search for a more adequate translation of ανθρωπος and its cognates continues.

immutably, tends to obstruct rather than aid understanding.⁶³²

The translators tell us that their text "is not the final word," that it "will need to be reviewed, refreshed, edited, and emended in new editions." This openness is praiseworthy and encouraging but also challenging especially because some textual and rubrical issues remain unresolved and await further scrutiny.⁶³³

Of course, only time will tell how effective the new text will be in achieving its stated goal to create uniformity of practice and bring "both reader and hearer into new depths of meaning."⁶³⁴ The first will be easier to measure and achieve, the latter more difficult but doable. For now, we express gratitude to the anonymous translators for their good work and applaud them for their admirable efforts.⁶³⁵

---

⁶³² See the Prayer of the Cherubic Hymn, *CHR: Priest Edition*, 35. Impassibly and immutably are used for the Greek ατρεπτως και αναλλοιωτος. In the hymn, "Only begotten Son," however, we find "without change" for ατρεπτως. *CHR: Priest Edition,* 9. Significantly, in the same hymn «εις ων της Αγιας Τριαδος» is rendered, "being one with the Holy Trinity" rather than the usual "being one of the Holy Trinity."

⁶³³ For a discussion on some of these unresolved issues, see Calivas, *Aspects of Orthodox Worship*, 193-226. Taft, "Translating Liturgically," and his multi-volume study *A History of the Liturgy of St. John Chrysostom.*

⁶³⁴ *CHR: Priest Edition*, x.

⁶³⁵ It has come to my attention that the translators have already prepared additional materials that are now under review.